Y0-DOI-326

Ordo Templi Orientis

Contents

Chapter 1

Ordo Templi Orientis

Ordo Templi Orientis (**O.T.O.**) ('Order of the Temple of the East' or 'Order of Oriental Templars') is an international fraternal and religious organization founded at the beginning of the 20th century. English author and occultist Aleister Crowley has become the best-known member of the order.

Originally it was intended to be modelled after and associated with European Freemasonry,[1] such as Masonic Templar organizations, but under the leadership of Aleister Crowley, O.T.O. was reorganized around the Law of Thelema as its central religious principle. This Law—expressed as "Do what thou wilt shall be the whole of the Law"[2] and "Love is the law, love under will"[3]—was promulgated in 1904 with the writing of *The Book of the Law*.

Similar to many secret societies, O.T.O. membership is based on an initiatory system with a series of degree ceremonies that use ritual drama to establish fraternal bonds and impart spiritual and philosophical teachings.

O.T.O. also includes the *Ecclesia Gnostica Catholica* (EGC) or Gnostic Catholic Church, which is the ecclesiastical arm of the Order. Its central rite, which is public, is called Liber XV, or the Gnostic Mass.

1.1 History

1.1.1 Origins

The early history of O.T.O. is difficult to trace reliably. It originated in Germany or Austria between 1895 and 1906.[4] Its apparent founder was Carl Kellner (probably with the German spelling Karl),[4] a wealthy Austrian industrialist, in 1895 (although nothing verifiable is known of the Order until 1904).[5]

Theodor Reuss (1855–1923) collaborated with Kellner in creating O.T.O., and succeeded him as head of O.T.O. after Kellner's death. Under Reuss, charters were given to occult brotherhoods in France, Denmark, Switzerland, the U.S.A. and Austria. There were nine degrees, of which the first six were Masonic.[5]

In 1902, Reuss, along with Franz Hartmann and Henry Klein, purchased the right to perform the Rite of Memphis and Mizraim of Freemasonry, the authority of which was confirmed in 1904 and again in 1905. Although these rites are considered to be irregular, they, along with the Swedenborg Rite formed the core of the newly established Order.[6]

1.1.2 O.T.O. and Aleister Crowley

Reuss met Aleister Crowley and in 1910 admitted him to the first three degrees of O.T.O. Only two years later, Crowley was placed in charge of Great Britain and Ireland, and was advanced to the X° (tenth degree). The appointment included the opening of the British section of O.T.O., which was called the *Mysteria Mystica Maxima* or the M∴M∴M∴.[5] Crowley then went to Berlin to obtain instructional manuscripts and the title of *Supreme and Holy King of Ireland, Iona and all the Britains within the Sanctuary of the Gnosis*.[5] Within the year, Crowley had written the Manifesto of the M∴M∴M∴

which described its basic ten-degree system with Kellner's three degree *Academia Masonica* forming the seventh, eighth and ninth degrees.

In 1913, Crowley composed the Gnostic Mass while in Moscow, which he described as being the Order's "central ceremony of its public and private celebration".[7] In 1914, soon after World War I broke out, he moved to the United States of America. It was around this time that Crowley decided to integrate Thelema into the O.T.O. system, and in 1915 prepared revised rituals for use in the M∴M∴M∴.

In 1917, Reuss wrote a *Synopsis of Degrees* of O.T.O. in which the third degree was listed as "Craft of Masonry" and listed the initiations involved as "Entered Apprentice, Fellow Craft, Master Mason" and elaborated on this with "Full instruction in Craft Masonry, including the Catechism of the first three degrees, and an explanation of all the various Masonic systems". The same document shows that the fourth degree of O.T.O. is also known as the Holy Royal Arch of Enoch. It was summarized by Reuss as the Degree of "Scotch Masonry," equivalent to "Scotch Mason, Knight of St. Andrew, Royal Arch", and he described it as "Full instruction in the Scottish degrees of Ancient and Accepted Masonry".[8]

In 1919, Crowley attempted to work this Masonic-based O.T.O. in Detroit, Michigan. The result was that he was rebuffed by the Council of the Scottish rite on the basis that O.T.O. rituals were too similar to orthodox Masonry. He described this in a 1930 letter to Arnold Krumm-Heller:

> However, when it came to the considerations of the practical details of the rituals to be worked, the general Council of the Scottish Rite could not see its way to tolerate them, on the ground that the symbolism in some places touched too nearly that of the orthodox Masonry of the Lodges.[9]

Crowley subsequently rewrote the initiation rituals of the first three degrees, and in doing so removed most of those rituals' ties to Masonry. He did not, however, rewrite the fourth degree ritual, which remains in its form and structure related to the various Royal Arch rituals of Masonry.

Crowley wrote that Theodore Reuss suffered a stroke in the spring of 1920. In correspondence with one of Reuss's officers, Crowley expressed doubts about Reuss's competence to remain in office. Relations between Reuss and Crowley began to deteriorate, and the two exchanged angry letters in November 1921. Crowley informed Reuss that he was availing himself of Reuss's abdication from office and proclaiming himself Outer Head of the Order. Reuss died on October 28, 1923 without designating a successor, though Crowley claimed in later correspondence that Reuss had designated him. Crowley biographer Lawrence Sutin, among others, casts doubt on this claim, although there is no evidence for or against it, and no other candidate stepped forward to refute Crowley by offering proof of succession. In 1925, during a tumultuous Conference of Grand Masters, Crowley was officially elected as Outer Head of the Order (or O.H.O.) by the remaining administrative heads of O.T.O.[10]

During WWII, the European branches of O.T.O. were either destroyed or driven underground. By the end of the war, the only surviving O.T.O. body was Agapé Lodge in California, although there were various initiates in different countries. Very few initiations were being performed. At this time, Karl Germer, who had been Crowley's representative in Germany, migrated to the USA after being released from Nazi confinement. On March 14, 1942, Crowley appointed him as his successor as Outer Head of the Order,[11] and Germer filled the office after the death of Crowley in 1947.

1.1.3   O.T.O. after Aleister Crowley

After Crowley's death Germer attempted to keep O.T.O. running, with questionable success. Crowley had granted a charter to run an O.T.O. Camp in England to Gerald Gardner, and Germer acknowledged Gardner as the O.T.O.'s main representative in Europe. The two men met in 1948 in New York to discuss plans, but Gardner's continuing ill health led to Germer replacing him with Frederic Mellinger in 1951. Also in 1951 Germer granted a charter to run an O.T.O. Camp in England to Kenneth Grant, who had briefly served as Crowley's secretary during the 1940s. Grant was to be expelled and his charter revoked in 1955 however, and from that time onwards the O.T.O.'s representative in the U.K. was a IX° member, Noel Fitzgerald.[12]

Germer died in 1962 without naming a successor. It was not until 1969 that Grady McMurtry invoked emergency authorization from Crowley and became the Frater Superior of O.T.O. McMurtry did not claim the title of Outer Head of the Order, stating in 1974 that "There is at present no Outer Head of the Order for Aleister Crowley's Ordo Templi

Orientis. The Outer Head of the Order is an international office (see p. 201, The Blue Equinox) and Aleister Crowley's Ordo Templi Orientis is not at this time established organizationally to fulfill the requirements of its Constitution in this respect."[13] He began performing initiations in 1970. O.T.O. was incorporated under the laws of the State of California on March 26, 1979. The corporation attained federal tax exemption as a religious entity under IRS Code 501(c)3 in 1982. Grady McMurtry died in 1985, having successfully saved O.T.O. from possible extinction.

McMurtry requested that members of the Sovereign Sanctuary of the Gnosis (i.e. the members of the Ninth Degree) elect the next Caliph, which they did in 1985. William Breeze was elected,[14] taking the name *Hymenaeus Beta*. In the Fall 1995 issue of *The Magical Link*, he is designated "Hymenaeus Beta X°"; in the Fall 1997 issue of *The Magical Link*, he is designated "Hymenaeus Beta XI°"; by May 2005, he is designated "O.H.O. Hymenaeus Beta XII°" on the O.T.O. website.[15]

In 1996, Sabazius X° was appointed as National Grand Master General (G.M.G.) for the U.S. Grand Lodge. In 2005, Frater Hyperion X° was appointed the National G.M.G. of the newly formed UK Grand Lodge. Frater Shiva X° was appointed the G.M.G. of Australia Grand Lodge in 2006.

1.2 Philosophy of O.T.O.

O.T.O. was described by Crowley as the "first of the great Old Æon orders to accept The Book of the Law". O.T.O. originally borrowed ritual material from irregular Masonic organizations,[8] and although some related symbolism and language remains in use, the context has changed to Thelema and its tenets.

> The Order offers esoteric instruction through dramatic ritual, guidance in a system of illuminated ethics, and fellowship among aspirants to the Great Work of realizing the divine in the human.[16]

O.T.O. has two core areas of ritual activity: initiation into the Mysteries, and the celebration of Liber XV, the Gnostic Mass. In addition, the Order organizes lectures, classes, social events, theatrical productions and artistic exhibitions, publishes books and journals, and provides instruction in Hermetic science, yoga, and magick.

Crowley wrote in his *Confessions*:

> ... the O.T.O. is in possession of one supreme secret. The whole of its system [is] directed towards communicating to its members, by progressively plain hints, this all-important instruction.

Of the first set of initiations, he wrote:

> ... the main objects of the instruction [are] two. It [is] firstly necessary to explain the universe and the relations of human life therewith.
> Secondly, to instruct every man [and woman] how best to adapt his [or her] life to the cosmos and to develop his faculties to the utmost advantage. I accordingly constructed a series of rituals, Minerval, Man, Magician, Master-Magician, Perfect Magician and Perfect Initiate, which should illustrate the course of human life in its largest philosophical aspect.

The initiation rituals after the V° (fifth degree) are such that:

> the candidate is instructed in the value of discretion, loyalty, independence, truthfulness, courage, self-control, indifference to circumstance, impartiality, scepticism, and other virtues, and at the same time assisted him to discover for himself the nature of [the supreme] secret, the proper object of its employment and the best means for insuring success for its use[17]:701

Of the entire system of O.T.O., Crowley wrote in *Confessions*:

It offers a rational basis for universal brotherhood and for universal religion. It puts forward a scientific statement which is a summary of all that is at present known about the universe by means of a simple, yet sublime symbolism, artistically arranged. It also enables each man to discover for himself his personal destiny, indicates the moral and intellectual qualities which he requires in order to fulfil it freely, and finally puts in his hands an unimaginably powerful weapon which he may use to develop in himself every faculty which he may need in his work.[17]:703

1.3   Initiation and teachings

Membership in O.T.O. is based upon a system of initiation ceremonies (or *degrees*) which use ritual drama to establish fraternal bonds between members as well as impart spiritual and philosophical teachings.

The degrees also serve an organizational function, in that certain degrees must be attained before taking on various forms of service in the Order (e.g. taking the degree of K.E.W. is a requirement for ordination as a priest or priestess in *Ecclesia Gnostica Catholica*).

There are thirteen numbered degrees and twelve un-numbered degrees which are divided into three grades or "triads"—the Hermit, the Lover, and the Man of Earth.

Admittance to each degree of O.T.O. involves an initiation and the swearing of an oath which O.T.O claims is similar to those used in Freemasonry.[18][19]

Advancement through the Man of Earth triad requires sponsorship from ranking members. Advancement into the degree of the Knight of the East and West and beyond requires one to be invited by ranking members.

The ultimate goal of initiation in O.T.O. is "to instruct the individual by allegory and symbol in the profound mysteries of Nature, and thereby to assist each to discover his or her own true Identity".[18]

The entire system is as follows:

- **The Man of Earth Triad**
    - 0°—Minerval
    - I°—Man & Brother
    - II°—Magician
    - III°—Master Magician
    - IV°—Perfect Magician & Companion of the Holy Royal Arch of Enoch
    - P.I.—Perfect Initiate, or Prince of Jerusalem

- **Outside all Triads**
    - Knight of the East & West

- **The Lover Triad**
    - V°—
        - Sovereign Prince Rose-Croix, and Knight of the Pelican & Eagle
        - Knight of the Red Eagle, and Member of the Senate of Knight Hermetic Philosophers
    - VI°—
        - Illustrious Knight (Templar) of the Order of Kadosch, and Companion of the Holy Graal
        - Grand Inquisitor Commander, and Member of the Grand Tribunal
        - Prince of the Royal Secret
    - VII°—

- Theoreticus, and Very Illustrious Sovereign Grand Inspector General
- Magus of Light, and Bishop of *Ecclesia Gnostica Catholica*
- Grandmaster of Light, and Inspector of Rites & Degrees

- **The Hermit Triad**
  - VIII°—
    - Perfect Pontiff of the Illuminati
    - Epopt of the Illuminati
  - IX°—Initiate of the Sanctuary of the Gnosis
  - X°—Rex Summus Sanctissimus
  - XI°—Initiate of the Eleventh Degree (This degree is technical, and has no relation to the general plan of the Order)
  - XII°—Frater Superior, and Outer Head of the Order

1.4 Structure

The governing bodies of O.T.O. include:

1. **International Headquarters**
   - Presided over by the **Outer Head of the Order** XII° (O.H.O.—also known as Frater Superior)
   - **Supreme Council**
   - **Revolutionaries**

2. The **Sovereign Sanctuary of the Gnosis** of the IX°

3. The **Secret Areopagus of the Illuminati** of the VIII°

4. The **Grand Tribunal** of the VI°

5. The National **Grand Lodge**
   - Presided over by the **National Grand Master** X°
   - **Executive Council**

6. The **Supreme Grand Council**

7. The **Electoral College**

1.4.1 International

1. The **International Headquarters** is the body that governs O.T.O. worldwide. As a ruling body, it is known as the International **Supreme Council**, which consists of the **Outer Head of the Order** (O.H.O.—also known as Frater Superior), the Secretary General, and the Treasurer General.

2. The **Sovereign Sanctuary of the Gnosis** consists of members who have reached the IX°. Their prime duty is to study and to practice the theurgy and thaumaturgy of the degree, consisting of the Supreme Secret of the Order. However, as a ruling body, they have the authority to

   - ratify and overturn the rulings of the Areopagus
   - act as representatives of the O.H.O. and National Grand Masters when need arises

- fill the office of Revolutionary

- vote within the Secret Areopagus

- have some powers over the installation and removal of the O.H.O. and National Grand Masters

3. The **Secret Areopagus of the Illuminati** is a philosophical Governing Body composed of those who have reached the VIII°. It has the authority to reverse the decisions of the Grand Tribunal.

4. The **Grand Tribunal** is composed of members of the degree of Grand Inquisitor Commander (a sub-degree of the VI°). Their primary duty is to hear and arbitrate disputes and complaints not resolved at the level of Chapters and Lodges.

1.4.2   National

1. At the national level, the highest body is the **Grand Lodge**, which is ruled by the **National Grand Master**. Within the Grand Lodge is an **Executive Council**, which consists of the Board of Directors, who are the National Grand Master, the Grand Secretary General, and the Grand Treasurer General.

2. The **Supreme Grand Council** consists of members of the VII° appointed by the National Grand Master X°. They are charged with:

- the government of the whole of the Lovers Triad

- Hearing and deciding appeals of the decisions of the Electoral College

- Hearing reports of the Sovereign Grand Inspectors General VII° as to the affairs of the Initiate members of the Lovers Triad

3. The **Electoral College** consists of eleven members of the V° and is the first of the governing bodies. Its primary duty is to oversee the affairs of the Man of Earth Triad.

O.T.O. has a federally recognized tax-exempt status in the USA under IRS section 501c(3). It also has California charitable corporation status.

Current Grand Lodges

The **US Grand Lodge** is the governing body of O.T.O. in the United States of America. The U.S. National Grand Master is Frater Sabazius X°, who was appointed in 1996.

According to its website, the Mission Statement of U.S.G.L. is as follows:

> Ordo Templi Orientis U.S.A. is the U.S. Grand Lodge (National Section) of Ordo Templi Orientis, a hierarchical, religious membership organization. Our mission is to effect and promote the doctrines and practices of the philosophical and religious system known as Thelema, with particular emphasis on cultivating the ideals of individual liberty, self-discipline, self-knowledge, and universal brotherhood. To this end, we conduct sacramental and initiatory rites, offer guidance and instruction to our members, organize social events, and engage in educational and community service activities at locations throughout the United States.[20]

As of Feb 28, 2014 US Grand Lodge had 1,508 members in 62 local bodies.[21]

The **UK Grand Lodge** is the governing body of O.T.O. in the United Kingdom. The UK National Grand Master is Frater Hyperion X°, who was appointed in 2005 (93 years after the last Grand Master for the UK, Aleister Crowley, was elevated to that office).

The **Australian Grand Lodge** is the governing body of O.T.O. in Australia and its territories, chartered in April 2006. The A.G.L. National Grand Master is Frater Shiva X°.

The **Croatian Grand Lodge** is the governing body of O.T.O. in Croatia and its territories, chartered in May 2014. The C.G.L. National Grand Master is Frater Abrasax X°.

The **Italian Grand Lodge** is the governing body of O.T.O. in Italy and its territories, chartered in May 2014. The I.G.L. National Grand Master is Frater Phanes X°.

1.4.3 The Gnostic Catholic Church

Main article: Ecclesia Gnostica Catholica

The *Ecclesia Gnostica Catholica*, or Gnostic Catholic Church, is the ecclesiastical arm of O.T.O. Its central activity is the celebration of Liber XV, The Gnostic Mass. In recent years, other rites have been written and approved for use within the church. These include Baptism, Confirmation (into the Laity), and Ordination (for Deacons, Priests & Priestesses, and Bishops), and Last Rites. There are also several "unofficial" rituals that are celebrated within the context of E.G.C., including Weddings, Visitation and Administration of the Virtues to the Sick, Exorcism, and Rites for Life and Greater Feasts.

1.4.4 O.T.O. bodies

At the Man of Earth level, there are three levels of Local Body, which are Camps, Oases, and Lodges.

1. **Camps** tend to be the smallest and are not required to perform initiations. They are encouraged to celebrate the Gnostic Mass.

2. **Oases** must be capable of initiating through the III° and are required to perform the Gnostic Mass six times yearly.

3. **Lodges** are expected to celebrate the Gnostic Mass on a regular basis, work towards establishing a permanent temple, and have the ability to initiate through IV°/P.I.

4. **Chapters of Rose Croix** are bodies established by members of the Lover Grade. A Chapter is headed by a Most Wise Sovereign. They are generally charged with arranging social activities, such as plays, banquets, and dances. They also work to promote harmony among the members by tact and friendliness.

5. **Guilds** are groups recognized by O.T.O. International designed to promote a profession, trade, science or craft. Subject to approval by the Areopagus, they make their own regulations and coordinate their own efforts. There are currently three Guilds: the Psychology Guild, the Translators' Guild, and the Information Technology Guild.

6. The term **Sanctuary** is sometimes used to indicate a group of initiates organized for E.G.C. activities. This designation currently reflects no formal chartering process or official standing within the Order.

1.5 Questions of legitimacy

Several competing factions have claimed to be legitimate heirs to Aleister Crowley. Both before and after McMurtry revived O.T.O. in California, others came forward with various claims of succession.

Although Karl Germer expelled Kenneth Grant from O.T.O. in 1955, Grant went on to claim himself Outer Head of Ordo Templi Orientis in a series of influential books.[22] His organization has recently changed its name to the Typhonian Order and no longer claims to represent O.T.O.

Hermann Metzger, another claimant, had been initiated into O.T.O. under Germer in Germany in the 1950s, and headed the Swiss branch of the Order. After Germer's death he attempted to proclaim himself head of O.T.O. However, his claims were ignored by everyone outside of his country and he never pressed the issue. He died in 1990.

Marcelo Ramos Motta (1931–1987), a third claimant, was never initiated into O.T.O. at all,[23] but claimed on the basis that Germer's wife, Sasha, told him that Karl's last words stated that Motta was "the follower." He sued for ownership of Crowley's copyrights, which were denied to him by the U.S. District Court in Maine. Motta died in 1987, although various small groups calling themselves Society O.T.O. (S.O.T.O.) continue to exist and claim authority from him.

1.5.1   Court cases

O.T.O. as revived by McMurtry has won two court cases regarding its legitimacy as the continuation of the O.T.O. of Aleister Crowley:

- 1976: the Superior Court in Calaveras County, California recognizes Grady McMurtry as the authorized representative of O.T.O.

- 1985: in the 9th Federal District Court in San Francisco, McMurtry is found to be the legitimate head of O.T.O. within the United States, and that O.T.O. under McMurtry is the continuation of the O.T.O. of Aleister Crowley, and the exclusive owner of the names, trademarks, copyrights and other assets of O.T.O. This decision is appealed to the 9th Circuit Court of Appeals and upheld. The Supreme Court declined to hear a final appeal. After the case, the US O.T.O. purchased the Crowley copyrights from the official receiver, even though the US court decision declared that they were the rightful owners.

The following case is also significant in the Order's history, though it does not have as much bearing on the issue of legitimacy:

- 2002: The United Kingdom High Court, in Ordo Templi Orientis v. John Symonds, Anthony Naylor and Mandrake Press, finds that O.T.O. as revived by McMurtry is the sole owner of the copyrights for all of the works of Aleister Crowley. In its particulars of claim, O.T.O. had pled two mutually exclusive routes to ownership of the copyrights:

    - (a) through Crowley's will as the named beneficiary O.T.O., a route to title that had been affirmed in U.S. Federal Court but had never been tested under English law, and

    - (b) the "bankruptcy route", on which theory O.T.O. acquired title to the copyrights from 1991 from the UK Crown Official Receiver in Bankruptcy.

    The Chancery Master agreed that these two routes were largely mutually exclusive; if Crowley's copyrights were not an asset in his undischarged bankruptcy, then O.T.O. bought nothing, and could only claim through the will, under which the copyrights would have to pass; but if the rights were an asset in bankruptcy, then Crowley had lacked any power to make O.T.O. a bequest of them in his will. The court examined the bankruptcy aspect first, finding that O.T.O. acquired good title.

The copyrights were thus Crown property between 1935 and 1991, making dozens of books—even many of O.T.O.'s own editions—unauthorized. Had the "will route" been tried, it would have given O.T.O. an opportunity to gain recognition in UK court as the legitimate continuation of Crowley's O.T.O., since that is a precondition to being found the rightful beneficiary of his will. Thus, the issue of the organization's legitimacy did arise at trial, since it was pled into court, but it was not ruled upon. While there is no way to know whether, had it been tested, it would have been confirmed or denied, O.T.O. made thorough legal preparations for this aspect of their case as detailed in their "Particulars of Claim". However it would be misleading to cite this case as affirming the organization's historical legitimacy, since that issue went untried.

In Australia in 2005, O.T.O. began a defamation case against the site GaiaGuys for material put up on their website that directly accused O.T.O., particularly in Australia, of participating in acts of child abuse and sacrifice. The court found in favour of O.T.O.[24]

1.6   Criticisms

In February 2006, a long-time high-ranking member and occult author, T. Allen Greenfield, called for the resignation of upper management and stepped down from all managerial duties in protest. He went on to write a detailed analysis of "the failure of the O.T.O." and the "culture of fear" which he says currently exists within O.T.O. which is included as the last chapter and Epilogue of his book *The Roots of Modern Magick*.[25] Although he is no longer a member of O.T.O. he continues to be a critic of the current Frater Superior of the Order, Hymenaeus Beta.[26][27]

1.7 See also

1.8 Notes

[1] Sabazius X° and AMT IX°. History of Ordo Templi Orientis. Retrieved June 13, 2006.

[2] Crowley, Aleister. *Liber AL vel Legis*, I:40

[3] Crowley, Aleister. *Liber AL vel Legis*, I:57

[4] Nicholas Goodrick-Clarke, The Occult Roots of Nazism, p. 61. Goodrick-Clarke touches this topic as he gives some general remarks on the occultism of that time.

[5] King, Francis. *The Magical World of Aleister Crowley*, pp. 78–81

[6] Chaos Out of Order/Decline and revival: the rebirth of the Rite Footnotes 40–42,

[7] Crowley, Aleister (1929) *The Confessions of Aleister Crowley* ch. 73. Mandrake Press

[8] King, Francis (1973). *The Secret Rituals of the O.T.O.* Samuel Weiser, Inc. ISBN 0-87728-144-0

[9] Starr, Martin. *Aleister Crowley: Freemason!*. Retrieved June 17, 2006.

[10] Kaczynski (2002), p.332

[11] Kenneth Grant and the Typhonian Ordo Templi Orientis, by P.R. Koenig

[12] Orpheus, Rodney (2009). "Gerald Gardner & Ordo Templi Orientis". *Pentacle Magazine* (30). pp. 14–18. ISSN 1753-898X.

[13] Koenig, Peter. *All we want is a 'Caliph'*, The Ordo Templi Orientis Phenomenon. Retrieved February 13, 2008

[14] Koenig, Peter. *Minutes of the Special Ninth Degree Caliphate Election*, The Ordo Templi Orientis Phenomenon. Retrieved February 13, 2008

[15] US Grand Lodge, OTO: OTO News, May 2, 2005 entry. Retrieved February 13, 2008

[16] O.T.O. *About OTO*.

[17] Crowley, Aleister. The Confessions of Aleister Crowley, ch. 72.

[18] O.T.O. *Initiation*.

[19] Free Encyclopedia of Thelema (2005). *Oath*. Retrieved November 17, 2005.

[20] O.T.O. US Grand Lodge Program Synopsis and Mission Statement.

[21] *usgl_annual_report_IVxxi.pdf* (PDF), retrieved 2014-06-04

[22] Grant, Kenneth. *Aleister Crowley & the Hidden God* Muller 1973

[23] There seem to be many statements to the contrary. For instance, the Maine District Court http://www.parareligion.ch/dplanet/html/maine.htm the court stated, under Findings of Fact, "Motta was initiated into the OTO by Germer in California in 1955 or 1956. Tr. at 39-40." Motta by his own published account claims his O.T.O. membership was conferred personally by Karl Germer. Motta, M. (1987) 'O.T.O. News', in: Crowley, A., Motta M. (ed). (1987) Thelemic Magick Unexpurgated Commented Part I, being The Oriflamme VI(5). Rio de Janeiro: Society Ordo Templi Orientis in Brasil, pp. 293-295. A further account (at various places on his website) by researcher P.R. Koenig states, "While it cannot (yet) be definitely proved that Motta was a member of the Order, neither can it be disproved." http://www.parareligion.ch/dplanet/html/s4.htm Various websites by his followers claim he was, for instance http://angg.twu.net/members.ozemail.com.au/~{}realoto/nclr12.html and http://www.castletower.org/or5c.html which also cites the Maine Court.

[24] Boswell, Alex. Pro bono effort muzzles religion slur in *Lawyers Weekly*, 6 December 2006

[25] Greenfield, T. Allen. *The Roots of Modern Magick: 1700 thru 2000*, pp. 182–195. ISBN 1-4116-8978-X

[26] Greenfield, T. Allen (2006). *A Statement Regarding the Ordo Templi Orientis*

[27] Koenig, Peter. "Minutes of the Special Ninth Degree Caliphate Election". *The Ordo Templi Orientis Phenomenon*. Retrieved March 10, 2012.

1.9   References

- Crowley, Aleister (1979). *The Confessions of Aleister Crowley*. London; Boston : Routledge & Kegan Paul.

- del Campo, Gerald. (1994). *New Aeon Magick: Thelema Without Tears*. St. Paul, Minnesota : Llewellyn Publications.

- Evans, Dave (2007). *Aleister Crowley and the 20th Century Synthesis of Magick*. Hidden Press, Second Revised Edition. ISBN 978-0-9555237-2-4

- Hymenaeus Beta (ed.) (1990) *The Equinox: Vol.III, No.10*. York Beach Samuel Weiser ISBN 978-0-87728-719-3

- Kaczynski, Richard. (2002). *Perdurabo, The Life of Aleister Crowley*. New Falcon Publications ISBN 1-56184-170-6

- King, Francis (1973). *The Secret Rituals of the O.T.O.* Samuel Weiser, Inc. ISBN 0-87728-144-0

- King, Francis (1978). *The Magical World of Aleister Crowley*. Coward, McCann & Geoghegan. ISBN 0-698-10884-1

1.10   External links

- International Headquarters, O.T.O.

- US Grand Lodge, O.T.O.

- Survey of O.T.O. History, with an Emphasis on Marin County, CA

- The Invisible Basilica of Sabazius X°

- Graph of O.T.O. membership 1988–2005

- A Statement Regarding the Ordo Templi Orientis by Allen H. Greenfield

- The Ordo Templi Orientis Phenomenon

- The Ordo Templi Orientis is an academic history of the O.T.O. by Christian Giudice, published in The Occult World, ed. by Christopher Partridge (Routledge, 2014)

Chapter 2

William Breeze

William Breeze (born August 12, 1955) is an American musician and occultist, a member of the band Coil, and the current international leader of Ordo Templi Orientis. Under the name **Hymenaeus Beta** he is a leading editor of the occult works of English author Aleister Crowley, the founder of the philosophy and religion of Thelema.

2.1 Musical activity

Breeze is a musician who plays electric viola, mandolin, guitar, bass and electronics. In the early years of his career he worked with poet-percussionist and Velvet Underground cofounder Angus MacLise. Footage of Breeze performing alongside Maclise was shown at the exhibition *Dreamweapon: The Art and Life of Angus MacLise (1938 – 1979)* from May 10–29, 2011 curated by Johan Kugelberg and Will Swofford Cameron.[1]

Breeze has played with Psychic TV and appears on the recordings *Thee Fractured Garden* (1995), *Cold Blue Torch* (1995), *Trip Reset* (1996) and *Spatial Memory* (1996) and is mostly credited as playing viola and viola synthesizer.[2] He was a member of Coil from 1997 through 2004, playing electric viola. He is currently a member of the band Current 93.

2.2 Occult activities

Breeze has been involved in the occult since the 1970s. He was involved in the publishing of Aleister Crowley's *Magical and Philosophical Commentaries on The Book of the Law* (edited by John Symonds and Kenneth Grant; 93 Publishing, 1974) and was a student of Marcelo Ramos Motta, who described him as "an ex-Probationer who failed to keep his Oath and perform his Task and was cut contact with as a result."[3] In 1978, Breeze was initiated into the Minerval degree of Ordo Templi Orientis. During the next few years, he advanced through the *Man of Earth* degrees of O.T.O., taking his IV° & P.I. at Tahuti Lodge in New York City in January 1985.

Following the death of *Caliph* Hymenaeus Alpha (Grady McMurtry), Breeze was elected as Frater Superior of Ordo Templi Orientis in a special election by all the active IX° members of O.T.O.[4] He assumed the name *Hymenaeus Beta*.

2.2.1 Editorial work

Breeze is known in the occult community (under his pseudonym Hymenaeus Beta) as the editor of several of the works of Aleister Crowley.[5]

Some of the works he has edited include:

- *The Equinox, Volume III, Number 10*, Weiser Books.

- *The Equinox of the Gods*, New Falcon Publications.

- *The Heart of the Master & Other Papers*, Thelema Media.

- *The Law is for All*, Thelema Media.

- *Magick: Liber ABA: Book 4*. Weiser Books.

- *The General Principles of Astrology*. Weiser Books. ISBN 0-87728-908-5

- *Diary of a Drug Fiend*. Red Wheel/Weiser.

- *Freedom is a Two-Edged Sword*, co-edited with Marjorie Cameron, authored by Jack Parsons, 1989, New Falcon Publications

2.3 See also

- Lon Milo DuQuette

- Richard Kaczynski

- Rodney Orpheus

- Lionel Snell

- James Wasserman

2.4 Notes

[1] "Angus MacLise | DREAMWEAPON : Boo-Hooray". *boo-hooray.com*. Retrieved March 10, 2012.

[2] "William Breeze Discography at Discogs". Retrieved 2009-08-14.

[3] Motta, Marcelo (1981). *The Equinox, vol. V no. 4*. Nashville: Thelema Publishing Co.

[4] Koenig, Peter. "Minutes of the Special Ninth Degree Caliphate Election". *The Ordo Templi Orientis Phenomenon*. Retrieved March 10, 2012.

[5] Koenig, Peter. "Minutes of the Special Ninth Degree Caliphate Election". *The Ordo Templi Orientis Phenomenon*. Retrieved March 10, 2012.

2.5 External links

- William Breeze at AllMusic

- William Breeze discography at Discogs

Chapter 3

Marjorie Cameron

Marjorie Cameron Parsons Kimmel (April 23, 1922 – June 24, 1995), known simply as "Cameron," was an artist, poet, actress, occultist, and wife of rocket pioneer and occultist Jack Parsons. After serving in the U.S. Navy during the Second World War, Cameron settled in Pasadena, California, and met Parsons, who believed her to be the "Elemental woman"—an earthly incarnation of the Thelemite goddess Babalon—that he and Scientology founder L. Ron Hubbard had invoked in the early stages of a series of sex magick rituals called the Babalon Working. She is now regarded as a countercultural icon and key figure in the development of postwar Los Angeles art.

3.1 Biography

3.1.1 Early life: 1922–1945

Cameron was born in Belle Plaine, Iowa, on April 23, 1922.[1] Her father, the railway worker Hill Leslie Cameron, was the adopted child of a Scots-Irish family, while her mother, Carrie Cameron (*née* Ridenour) was of Dutch ancestry.[2] She was their first child, followed by three further siblings: James (b. 1923), Mary (b. 1927), and Robert (b. 1929).[3] They lived on the wealthier north side of town, although life was nevertheless hard due to the Great Depression.[4] Attending Whittier Elementary School and then Belle Plaine High School, where she did well at art, English, and drama but failing algebra, Latin, and civic lessons, she also joined the athletics, glee club, and chorus.[5] She enjoyed going to the cinema, and had sexual relationships with various men; falling pregnant, her mother performed an illegal home abortion.[6] In 1940 the Cameron family relocated to Davenport in order for Hill to work at the Rock Islands Arsenal munitions factory. Cameron completed her final year of high school education at Davenport High School, there having romantic relations with both a man and a woman.[7] Leaving school, she worked as a display artist in a local department store.[7]

Following U.S. entry into the Second World War, in February 1943 she signed up for the Women Accepted for Volunteer Emergency Service, a part of the U.S. Navy. Initially sent to a training camp at Iowa State Teachers College in Cedar Falls, she was then posted to Washington D.C., where she served as a cartographer for the Joint Chief of Staff, in the course of his duties meeting U.K. Prime Minister Winston Churchill in May 1943.[8] She was reassigned to the Naval Photographic Unit in Anacostia, where she worked as wardrobe mistress for propaganda documentaries, in the course of which she met various Hollywood stars.[9] When her brother James returned to the U.S. injured from service overseas, she went AWOL and returned to Iowa to see him, a result of which she was court martialed and confined to barracks for the rest of the war.[10] For reasons unknown to her, she received an honorable discharge from the military in 1945, traveling to Pasadena, California, where her family had relocated, with both her father and brothers securing work at the Jet Propulsion Laboratory there.[11]

3.1.2 Jack Parsons: 1946–1952

In Pasadena, Cameron ran into a former colleague, who invited her to visit the large American Craftsman-style house where he was currently lodging, 1003 Orange Grove Avenue, also known as "The Parsonage." The house was so-called because its lease was owned by Jack Parsons, a rocket scientist who had been a founding member of the JPL who was also a devout follower of the new religious movement founded by English occultist Aleister Crowley in 1904, Thelema. Parsons was the head of the Agape Lodge, a branch of the Thelemite Ordo Templi Orientis (OTO).[12] Unbeknownst to Cameron, Parsons had just finished a series of rituals utilizing Enochian magic with his friend and lodger L. Ron Hubbard, all with the intent of attracting an "Elemental" woman to be his lover. Upon encountering Cameron, with her striking red hair and blue eyes, he considered her to be the individual whom he had invoked.[13] After they met at the Parsonage on 18 January 1946, they were instantly attracted to each other, and spent the next two weeks in Parsons' bedroom together. Although Cameron was unaware of it, Parsons saw this as a form of sex magic that constituted part of the Babalon Working, a rite to invoke the birth of Thelemite goddess Babalon onto Earth in human form.[14]

Cameron briefly traveled to New York City to see a friend, there discovering that she was pregnant, and again decided to terminate the pregnancy.[15] Parsons meanwhile had founded a company with Hubbard and his girlfriend Sara Northrup, Allied Enterprises, into which he invested his life savings. It nevertheless became apparent that Hubbard was a confidence trickster, who tried to flee with Parsons' money, resulting in the break-up of their friendship.[16] Returning to Pasadena, Cameron consoled Parsons, painting a picture of Sara with her legs severed below the knee.[17] Parsons decided to sell 1003, which was then demolished, and the couple instead moved to Manhattan Beach. It was there, on 19 October 1946, that he and Cameron married at San Juan Capistrano courthouse in Orange County, in a service witnessed by his best friend Edward Forman.[18] Having an aversion to all religion, Cameron initially took no interest in Parsons' Thelemite beliefs and occult practices, although he maintained that she had an important destiny, giving her the magical name of "Candida", often shortened to "Candy", which became her nickname.[19]

Cameron decided to travel to Paris, France, with the intention of studying art at the Académie de la Grande Chaumière, hoping that they would admit her with a letter of recommendation from Pasadena's Art Centre School. She also hoped to use the trip to visit England and meet with Crowley, to explain to him Parsons' Babalon Working. Traveling via New York aboard the *SS America*, upon arrival she learned that Crowley had died, and that she was unable to join the college. She found post-war Paris "extreme and bleak", although befriended Juliette Greco before spending three weeks in Switzerland and then returning home.[20] When Cameron developed catalepsy, Parsons suggested that she read Sylvan Muldoon's books on astral projection, also encouraging her to read James Frazer's *The Golden Bough*, Heinrich Zimmer's *The King and the Corpse*, and Joseph Campbell's *The Hero with a Thousand Faces*.[21] Although she still did not accept Thelema, she began to be increasingly interested in the occult, and in particular the use of the tarot.[21]

Parsons and Cameron felt that their relationship was breaking up, and contemplated divorce.[22] She decided to spend some time away, traveling to the artistic commune at San Miguel de Allende, there befriending the artist Renate Druks. Parsons meanwhile moved into a house known as the "Concrete Castle" on Redondo Beach, having a brief relationship with an Irishwoman named Gladis Gohan before Cameron returned.[23] Parsons and Cameron moved to the coach house at 1071 South Orange Grove, while he began work at the Bermite Powder Company, where be began constructing explosives for the film industry.[24] They began holding parties once more that were attended largely by bohemians and members of the beat generation, with Cameron attending the jazz clubs of Central Avenue with her friend, the sculptor Julie Macdonald.[25] Earning some of her own money, Cameron produced some illustrations for fashion magazines, also selling some of her paintings, with a number being purchased by her friend, the artist Jirayr Zorthian.[26] Parsons and Cameron had decided to travel to Mexico for a few months.[27] On the day before they planned to leave, June 17, 1952, he received a rush order of explosives for a film set, and he begun work on it at his house.[28] In the midst of this project, an explosion destroyed the building during which Parsons was fatally wounded, and upon being rushed to the Huntington Memorial Hospital by emergency services was declared dead.[29] Cameron did not want to see the body, instead retreating to San Miguel in Mexico, asking her friend George Frey to oversee the cremation.[30]

3.1.3 Mental instability: 1952–

In Mexico, Cameron began performing blood rituals in which she cut her own wrist, in the hope of communicating with Parsons' spirit. As part of these rituals, she claimed to have received a new magical identity, Hilarion.[31] When she learned that an unidentified flying object had been seen over Washington D.C.'s Capitol Building she considered it a response to

Parsons' death.[31] After two months, she returned to California, where she attempted suicide.[32] Increasingly interested in occultism, she read through her husband's papers, coming to understand the purpose of his Babalon Working and furthermore believing that the spirit of Babalon had been incarnated into herself.[33] She came to believe that Parsons had been murdered by the police or anti-zionists, and continued her attempts at astral projection to commune with him.[34] Her mental stability was deteriorating, and she became convinced that a nuclear test on Eniwetok Atoll would result in the destruction of the California coast.[35] Though unproven, there is evidence that she was institutionalized in a psychiatric ward during this period, before having a brief affair with African-American jazz player Leroy Booth, a relationship that would have been illegal at the time.[36]

3.1.4   Emergence in the Southern California Beat Culture

After Jack's death, Cameron retreated to Lamb Canyon near Beaumont, California where she lived without water or electricity. She embarked on a series of magical workings in an attempt to make contact with her deceased husband. She also established a relationship with Jane Wolfe, another devotee of Aleister Crowley, and Wolfe ultimately became her mentor. She produced a series of illustrations for a book of poetry Jack had written for her before his death "Songs for the Witch Woman". After several years, Cameron eventually moved back to Los Angeles where she lived in Venice Beach and Topanga Canyon. The Beat Culture was prevalent in both places, and she met the artists Wallace Berman and George Herms.[4] She became a friend and artistic inspiration to both men. Her artwork appeared in the first issue of Berman's literary and artistic journal Semina in 1955 and Berman's photograph of Cameron appeared on the cover of the same 1955 issue. [5] Cameron's image "Peyote Vision" was included in a solo exhibit of Berman's at the Ferus Gallery in 1957 and was cited as the reason for the gallery being temporarily closed by the LAPD Vice Squad. [6] Berman was arrested, stood trial, convicted of displaying lewd and obscene materials, and fined $150. It was the last public gallery show for both Berman and Cameron.

3.2   Filmography

Paul Mathison and the actor Samson DeBrier introduced Cameron to film maker Kenneth Anger, who cast her in a leading role opposite Anais Nin in his film *Inauguration of the Pleasure Dome* (1954), a depiction of an occult initiation rite as envisioned by Aleister Crowley. With red hair and heavy eye makeup, Cameron played both Kali and the Scarlet Woman wrapped in a red Spanish shawl. Cameron collaborated with filmmaker Curtis Harrington to commemorate her output as a visual artist in *The Wormwood Star* (1955), a short film recording the art and atmosphere of her candlelit studio. Most of the paintings and drawings documented in this film were later lost or destroyed. She also co-starred alongside Dennis Hopper as the Water Witch in Harrington's feature film *Night Tide* (1961). In 1969 she appeared in an unreleased short film shot in New Mexico, *Thumbsuck*, by artist John Chamberlain.

3.3   Later Years and Death

Cameron spent several years in the late 1960s in Velarde, New Mexico. She returned to Los Angeles and eventually resided in a small bungalow in West Hollywood, CA. She continued her writing and artwork based on her mystical visions and dreams. She was an ardent student of astrology and incorporated her astrological impressions into a major body of work "Pluto Transiting the Twelfth House" (1978-1986). She became an adept practitioner of T'ai Chi Ch'uan, and remained a strong presence in the life of her daughter Crystal and her grandchildren. In 1989 Cameron co-edited with O.T.O. leader Hymenaeus Beta an edition of the occult writings of Parsons. Also that year, Cameron's artworks were surveyed in an exhibition, titled The Pearl of Reprisal, at the Los Angeles Municipal Art Gallery curated by Edward Leffingwell. [7] Cameron died of cancer at the VA West Los Angeles Medical Center in 1995.

3.4 Artistic Legacy

Cameron is regarded as a key figure within postwar Los Angeles art and counterculture. Her mystical life and art, which often depicts images of an otherworldly nature drawn from the Elemental Kingdom and the astral plane, are the subject of "Cameron: Songs for the Witch Woman," a retrospective at the Museum of Contemporary Art, Los Angeles (MOCA).[37] Her work has also appeared in group exhibitions at the Whitney Museum of American Art, the Getty Museum, the Centre Pompidou, Martin-Gropius Bau in Berlin, and other museums around the world.

3.4.1 Footnotes

[1] Kaczynski 2010, p. 538; Kansa 2011, p. 9.

[2] Kaczynski 2010, p. 538; Kansa 2011, pp. 9–11.

[3] Kansa 2011, pp. 11–12.

[4] Kansa 2011, pp. 12, 15.

[5] Kansa 2011, pp. 13–14.

[6] Kansa 2011, p. 17.

[7] Kansa 2011, p. 18.

[8] Kaczynski 2010, p. 538; Kansa 2011, pp. 18–22.

[9] Kansa 2011, pp. 22–23.

[10] Kaczynski 2010, p. 538; Kansa 2011, p. 24.

[11] Kaczynski 2010, p. 538; Kansa 2011, p. 27.

[12] Kansa 2011, pp. 28–29.

[13] Pendle 2005, pp. 259–260; Kansa 2011, pp. 35–37.

[14] Pendle 2005, pp. 263–264; Kansa 2011, p. 29.

[15] Kansa 2011, pp. 37–38.

[16] Pendle 2005, pp. 267–269; Kansa 2011, pp. 38–39.

[17] Kansa 2011, p. 39.

[18] Pendle 2005, pp. 275, 277; Kansa 2011, p. 39.

[19] Kansa 2011, pp. 39–41.

[20] Kansa 2011, pp. 43–45.

[21] Kansa 2011, pp. 48–49.

[22] Kansa 2011, p. 48.

[23] Pendle 2005, p. 288; Kansa 2011, pp. 51–53.

[24] Pendle 2005, pp. 294, 297; Kansa 2011, p. 57.

[25] Pendle 2005, pp. 294–295; Kansa 2011, pp. 57–63.

[26] Kansa 2011, p. 61.

[27] Pendle 2005, pp. 296–297; Kansa 2011, p. 64.

[28] Pendle 2005, p. 299; Kansa 2011, p. 65.

[29] Pendle 2005, pp. 1–6; Kansa 2011, pp. 65–66.

[30] Kansa 2011, pp. 67–68.

[31] Kansa 2011, p. 74.

[32] Kansa 2011, pp. 74–75.

[33] Kansa 2011, pp. 75–77.

[34] Kansa 2011, pp. 77–79.

[35] Kansa 2011, p. 79.

[36] Kansa 2011, pp. 80–81.

[37] ""MOCA Presents "Cameron: Songs for the Witch Woman"". Retrieved 2 August 2014.

3.4.2 Sources

- Carter, John (2004). *Sex and Rockets: The Occult World of Jack Parsons* (new edition). Port Townsend: Feral House. ISBN 978-0922915972.

- Kaczynski, Richard (2010). *Perdurabo: The Life of Aleister Crowley* (second edition). Berkeley, California: North Atlantic Books. ISBN 978-0-312-25243-4.

- Kansa, Spencer (2011). *Wormwood Star: The Magickal Life of Marjorie Cameron*. Oxford: Mandrake. ISBN 978-1-906958-08-4.

- Parsons, John Whiteside (2008). *Three Essays on Freedom*. York Beach, Maine: Teitan Press.

- Pendle, George (2005). *Strange Angel: The Otherworldly Life of Rocket Scientist John Whiteside Parsons*. Weidenfeld & Nicolson. ISBN 978-0753820650.

- Starr, Martin P. (2003). *The Unknown God: W.T. Smith and the Thelemites*. Bollingbrook, Illinois: Teitan Press. ISBN 0-933429-07-X.

3.5 External links

- The Wormwood Star (1955), a short film portrait of Cameron by Curtis Harrington.
- Cameron-Parsons Foundation
- Marjorie Cameron at the Internet Movie Database

Frontispiece

Crowley was Parsons' guru.

Chapter 4

William C. Conway

William C. Conway (May 15, 1865 – 1969) was the leader of a mystical sect in the Latter Day Saint movement that combined the teachings of Joseph Smith with Druidry and some of the ideas of Aleister Crowley and the Ordo Templi Orientis.

A native of Redondo Beach, California, Conway was a member of The Church of Jesus Christ of Latter-day Saints (LDS Church) and held the office of high priest in the Melchizedek priesthood and bishop in the Aaronic priesthood. Conway was also a member of the Ordo Templi Orientis (O.T.O.), and was initiated into the XI° order of the O.T.O. on January 1, 1945 by Franklin Thomas or perhaps at some earlier date by Victor Neuburg.[1][2] In the O.T.O., Conway was referred to as **Tau Lucifer II**.[1]

In the early 1950s, Conway began to claim that he had possession of the Urim and Thummim and the seer stone that Joseph Smith used to translate the Book of Mormon. He generally accepted the teachings of Mormonism, but began to teach that the LDS Church had been incorrect to abandon the practice of plural marriage, which Smith had taught. Conway also believed in the major tenets of Druidry—particularly reincarnation—and sought to incorporate them into Mormonism.[1]

In 1955, a Zapotec tribe of the Yucatan Peninsula in Mexico declared Conway to be a prophet and the mouthpiece of Jesus Christ. Conway began claiming that he was the reincarnation of Moroni, a prophet in the *Book of Mormon*, and that a reincarnated Joseph Smith, "Our Druid Brother", had visited him.[3] In 1958, Conway published an open letter wherein he set out a number of his beliefs. He taught that menstrual blood was corrupt and that menstruation could be eliminated through righteousness.[4] He also taught that through priesthood alchemy, common metals could be transmutated into gold and that a Book of Mormon prophet named Mulek had blessed Los Angeles to be a holy gathering place. Conway taught that the "One Mighty and Strong" prophesied of in Mormon scripture was a nineteenth-century "young white Indian" from Yucatan named Eachta Eachta Na.[4]

Conway established a church which he called the **Perfected Church of Jesus Christ of Immaculate Latter-day Saints**,[4] which he sometimes referred to as the **Restored Apostolic Church of Jesus Christ of Immaculate Latter-day Saints**.

Conway's partner was a Zapotec woman who gave birth to twins in 1956; Conway declared that she had conceived by means of an "immaculate conception".[1] Conway died at the age of 104.[2]

4.1 Notes

[1] Peter-R. König, "Per Aftera ad Astra: Anal Intercourse and the O.T.O.", *"Das OTO-Phänomen* (1994, Arbeitsgemeinschaft für Religions und Weltanschauungsfragen, ISBN 978-3-927890-14-5).

[2] Massimo Introvigne, "The Devil Makers: Contemporary Evangelical Fundamentalist Anti-Mormonism", *Dialogue: A Journal of Mormon Thought* **27**(1):154 (Spring 1994) at p. 165–166 fn. 32.

[3] "Occultic Infiltration", *Salt Lake City Messenger*, no. 80, Nov. 1991.

[4] J. Gordon Melton (1996, 5th ed.). *Encyclopedia of American Religions* (Detroit, Mich.: Gale) p. 570.

4.2 References

- Kate B. Cater (1969). *Denominations that Base their Beliefs on the Teachings of Joseph Smith, the Mormon Prophet* (Salt Lake City, Utah: Daughters of Utah Pioneers)

- Russell R. Rich (1967, 2d ed.). *Those Who Would be Leaders: Offshoots of Mormonism* (Provo, Utah: Brigham Young University)

- Steven L. Shields (1990, 4th ed.). *Divergent Paths of the Restoration* (Independence, Mo.: Herald House) ISBN 0-942284-13-5

- Jerald and Sandra Tanner (1988). *The Lucifer–God Doctrine* (Salt Lake City, Utah: Utah Lighthouse Ministry)

Chapter 5

Aleister Crowley

Aleister Crowley (/ˈkroʊli/; born **Edward Alexander Crowley**; 12 October 1875 – 1 December 1947) was an English occultist, ceremonial magician, poet, painter, novelist, and mountaineer. He founded the religion and philosophy of Thelema, identifying himself as the prophet entrusted with guiding humanity into the Æon of Horus in the early 20th century.

Born to a wealthy Plymouth Brethren family in Royal Leamington Spa, Warwickshire, Crowley rejected this fundamentalist Christian faith to pursue an interest in Western esotericism. He was educated at the University of Cambridge, where he focused his attentions on mountaineering and poetry, resulting in several publications. Some biographers allege that here he was recruited into a British intelligence agency, further suggesting that he remained a spy throughout his life. In 1898 he joined the esoteric Hermetic Order of the Golden Dawn, where he was trained in ceremonial magic by Samuel Liddell MacGregor Mathers and Allan Bennett. Moving to Boleskine House by Loch Ness in Scotland, he went mountaineering in Mexico with Oscar Eckenstein, before studying Hindu and Buddhist practices in India. He married Rose Edith Kelly and in 1904 they honeymooned in Cairo, Egypt, where Crowley claimed to have been contacted by a supernatural entity named Aiwass, who provided him with *The Book of the Law*, a sacred text that served as the basis for Thelema. Announcing the start of the Æon of Horus, *The Book* declared that its followers should adhere to the code of "Do what thou wilt" and seek to align themselves with their Will through the practice of magick.

After an unsuccessful attempt to climb Kanchenjunga and a visit to India and China, Crowley returned to Britain, where he attracted attention as a prolific author of poetry, novels, and occult literature. In 1907, he and George Cecil Jones co-founded a Thelemite order, the A∴A∴, through which they propagated the religion. After spending time in Algeria, in 1912 he was initiated into another esoteric order, the German-based Ordo Templi Orientis (OTO), rising to become the leader of its British branch, which he reformulated in accordance with his Thelemite beliefs. Through the OTO, Thelemite groups were established in Britain, Australia, and North America. Crowley spent the First World War in the United States, where he took up painting and campaigned for the German war effort against Britain, later revealing that he had infiltrated the pro-German movement to assist the British intelligence services. In 1920 he established the Abbey of Thelema, a religious commune in Cefalù, Sicily where he lived with various followers. His libertine lifestyle led to denunciations in the British press, and the Italian government evicted him in 1923. He divided the following two decades between France, Germany, and England, and continued to promote Thelema until his death.

Crowley gained widespread notoriety during his lifetime, being a recreational drug experimenter, bisexual and an individualist social critic. As a result, he was denounced in the popular press as "the wickedest man in the world" and erroneously labelled a Satanist. Crowley has remained a highly influential figure over Western esotericism and the counter-culture, and continues to be considered a prophet in Thelema. In 2002, a BBC poll ranked him as the seventy-third greatest Briton of all time.

5.1 Early life

5.1.1 Youth: 1875–94

Crowley was born as Edward Alexander Crowley at 30 Clarendon Square in Royal Leamington Spa, Warwickshire, on 12 October 1875.[2] His father, Edward Crowley (1834–87), was trained as an engineer, but his share in a lucrative family brewing business, Crowley's Alton Ales, had allowed him to retire before his son was born.[3] His mother, Emily Bertha Bishop (1848–1917), came from a Devonshire-Somerset family and had a strained relationship with her son; she described him as "the Beast", a name that he revelled in.[4] The couple had been married at London's Kensington Registry Office in November 1874,[5] and were evangelical Christians. Crowley's father had been born a Quaker, but had converted to the Exclusive Brethren, a faction of a Christian fundamentalist group known as the Plymouth Brethren, with Emily joining him upon marriage. Crowley's father was particularly devout, spending his time as a travelling preacher for the sect and reading a chapter from the Bible to his wife and son after breakfast every day.[6] Following the death of their baby daughter in 1880, in 1881 the Crowleys moved to Redhill, Surrey.[7] At the age of 8, Crowley was sent to H.T. Habershon's evangelical Christian boarding school in Hastings, and then to Ebor preparatory school in Cambridge, run by the Reverend Henry d'Arcy Champney, whom Crowley considered a sadist.[8]

In March 1887, when Crowley was 11, his father died of tongue cancer. Crowley described this as a turning point in his life,[9] and he always maintained an admiration of his father, describing him as "his hero and his friend".[10] Inheriting a third of his father's wealth, he began misbehaving at school and was harshly punished by Champney; Crowley's family removed him from the school when he developed albuminuria.[11] He then attended Malvern College and Tonbridge School, both of which he despised and left after a few terms.[12] He became increasingly sceptical regarding Christianity, pointing out inconsistencies in the Bible to his religious teachers,[13] and went against the Christian morality of his upbringing by smoking, masturbating, and having sex with prostitutes from whom he contracted gonorrhea.[14] Sent to live with a Brethren tutor in Eastbourne, he undertook chemistry courses at Eastbourne College. Crowley developed interests in chess, poetry, and mountain climbing, and in 1894 climbed Beachy Head before visiting the Alps and joining the Scottish Mountaineering Club. The following year he returned to the Bernese Alps, climbing the Eiger, Trift, Jungfrau, Mönch, and Wetterhorn.[15]

5.1.2 Cambridge University: 1895–98

Having adopted the name of Aleister over Edward, in October 1895 Crowley began a three-year course at Trinity College, Cambridge, where he was entered for the Moral Science Tripos studying philosophy. With approval from his personal tutor, he changed to English literature, which was not then part of the curriculum offered.[16] Crowley spent much of his time at university engaged in his pastimes, becoming president of the chess club and practising the game for two hours a day; he briefly considered a professional career as a chess player.[17] Crowley also embraced his love of literature and poetry, particularly the works of Richard Francis Burton and Percy Bysshe Shelley.[18] Many of his own poems appeared in student publications such as *The Granta*, *Cambridge Magazine*, and *Cantab*.[19] He continued his mountaineering, going on holiday to the Alps to climb every year from 1894 to 1898, often with his friend Oscar Eckenstein, and in 1897 he made the first ascent of the Mönch without a guide. These feats led to his recognition in the Alpine mountaineering community.[20]

For many years I had loathed being called Alick, partly because of the unpleasant sound and sight of the word, partly because it was the name by which my mother called me. Edward did not seem to suit me and the diminutives Ted or Ned were even less appropriate. Alexander was too long and Sandy suggested tow hair and freckles. I had read in some book or other that the most favourable name for becoming famous was one consisting of a dactyl followed by a spondee, as at the end of a hexameter: like *Jeremy Taylor*. Aleister Crowley fulfilled these conditions and Aleister is the Gaelic form of Alexander. To adopt it would satisfy my romantic ideals.

Aleister Crowley, on his name change.[21]

Crowley later claimed to have had his first significant mystical experience while on holiday in Stockholm in December 1896.[22] Several biographers, including Lawrence Sutin, Richard Kaczynski, and Tobias Churton, believed that this was the result of Crowley's first same-sex sexual experience, which enabled him to recognise his bisexuality.[23] At Cambridge, Crowley maintained a vigorous sex life, largely with female prostitutes, from one of whom he caught syphilis, but eventually he took part in same-sex activities, despite their illegality.[24] In October 1897, Crowley met Herbert Charles Pollitt, president of the Cambridge University Footlights Dramatic Club, and the two entered into a relationship. They broke apart because Pollitt did not share Crowley's increasing interest in Western esotericism, a breakup that Crowley would regret for many years to come.[25]

In 1897, Crowley travelled to St Petersburg in Russia, later claiming that he was trying to learn Russian as he was considering a future diplomatic career there.[26] Biographers Richard Spence and Tobias Churton suggested that Crowley had done so as an intelligence agent under the employ of the British secret service, speculating that he had been enlisted while at Cambridge.[27]

In October 1897, a brief illness triggered considerations of mortality and "the futility of all human endeavour", and Crowley abandoned all thoughts of a diplomatic career in favour of pursuing an interest in the occult.[28] In March 1898, he obtained A.E. Waite's *The Book of Black Magic and of Pacts* (1898), and then Karl von Eckartshausen's *The Cloud Upon the Sanctuary* (1896), furthering his occult interests.[29] In 1898 Crowley privately published 100 copies of his poem *Aceldama: A Place to Bury Strangers In*, but it was not a particular success.[30] That same year he published a string of other poems, including *White Stains*, a Decadent collection of erotic poetry that was printed abroad lest its publication be prohibited by the British authorities.[31] In July 1898, he left Cambridge, not having taken any degree at all despite a "first class" showing in his 1897 exams and consistent "second class honours" results before that.[32]

5.1.3   The Golden Dawn: 1898–99

In August 1898, Crowley was in Zermatt, Switzerland, where he met the chemist Julian L. Baker, and the two began discussing their common interest in alchemy.[33] Back in London, Baker introduced Crowley to George Cecil Jones, a member of the occult society known as the Hermetic Order of the Golden Dawn, which had been founded in 1888.[34] Crowley was initiated into the Outer Order of the Golden Dawn on 18 November 1898 by the group's leader, Samuel Liddell MacGregor Mathers. The ceremony took place at the Isis-Urania Temple in London's Mark Masons Hall, where Crowley accepted his motto and magical name of "Frater Perdurabo", literally meaning "Brother Vigor"[35] in Latin, although often explained to mean figuratively as "Brother I shall endure to the end".[36] Biographers Richard Spence and Tobias Churton have suggested that Crowley joined the Order under the command of the British secret services to monitor the activities of Mathers, who was known to be a Carlist.[37]

Crowley moved into his own luxury flat at 67–69 Chancery Lane and soon invited a senior Golden Dawn member, Allan Bennett, to live with him as his personal magical tutor. Bennett taught Crowley more about ceremonial magic and the ritual use of drugs, and together they performed the rituals of the *Goetia*,[38] until Bennett left for South Asia to study Buddhism.[39] In November 1899, Crowley purchased Boleskine House in Foyers on the shore of Loch Ness in Scotland. He developed a love of Scottish culture, describing himself as the "Laird of Boleskine", and took to wearing traditional highland dress, even during visits to London.[40] He continued writing poetry, publishing *Jezebel and Other Tragic Poems*, *Tales of Archais*, *Songs of the Spirit*, *Appeal to the American Republic*, and *Jephthah* in 1898–99; most gained mixed reviews from literary critics, although *Jephthah* was considered a particular critical success.[41]

Crowley soon progressed through the grades of the Golden Dawn, and was ready to enter the group's inner Second Order.[42] He was unpopular in the group; his bisexuality and libertine lifestyle had gained him a bad reputation, and he developed feuds with members like W.B. Yeats.[43] When the Golden Dawn's London lodge refused to initiate Crowley into the Second Order, he visited Mathers in Paris, who personally upgraded him.[44] A schism had developed between Mathers and the London members of the Golden Dawn, who were unhappy with his autocratic rule.[45] Acting under Mathers' orders, Crowley – with the help of his mistress and fellow initiate Elaine Simpson – attempted to seize the Vault of Rosenkreutz, a temple space at 36 Blythe Road in West Kensington, from the London lodge members. When the case was taken to court, the judge ruled in favour of the London lodge, as they had paid for the space's rent, leaving both Crowley and Mathers isolated from the group.[46] Spence suggested that the entire scenario was part of an intelligence operation to undermine Mathers' authority.[47]

5.1.4   Mexico, India, Paris, and marriage: 1900–03

In 1900, Crowley travelled to Mexico via the United States, settling in Mexico City and taking a local woman as his mistress. Developing a love of the country, he continued experimenting with ceremonial magic, working with John Dee's Enochian invocations. He later claimed to have been initiated into Freemasonry while in the city, and spending time writing, he wrote a play based on Richard Wagner's *Tannhäuser* as well as a series of poems, published as *Oracles* (1905).

Eckenstein joined him later that year, and together they climbed several mountains, including Iztaccihuatl, Popocatepetl, and Colima, the latter of which they had to abandon owing to a volcanic eruption.[48] Spence has suggested that the purpose of the trip might have been to explore Mexican oil prospects for British intelligence.[49] Leaving Mexico, Crowley headed to San Francisco before sailing for Hawaii aboard the *Nippon Maru*. On the ship he had a brief affair with a married woman named Mary Alice Rogers; claiming to have fallen in love with her, he wrote a series of poems about the romance, published as *Alice: An Adultery* (1903).[50]

Briefly stopping at Japan and Hong Kong, Crowley reached Ceylon, where he met with Allan Bennett, who was there studying Shaivism. The pair spent some time in Kandy before Bennett decided to become a Buddhist monk in the Theravada tradition, travelling to Burma to do so.[51] Crowley decided to tour India, devoting himself to the Hindu practice of *raja yoga*, from which he claimed to have achieved the spiritual state of *dhyana*. He spent much of this time studying at the Meenakshi Amman Temple in Madura, and also wrote poetry which was published as *The Sword of Song* (1904). He contracted malaria, and had to recuperate from the disease in Calcutta and Rangoon.[52] In 1902, he was joined in India by Eckenstein and several other mountaineers: Guy Knowles, H. Pfannl, V. Wesseley, and Jules Jacot-Guillarmod. Together the Eckenstein-Crowley expedition attempted K2, which had never been climbed. On the journey, Crowley was afflicted with influenza, malaria, and snow blindness, and other expedition members were also struck with illness. They reached an altitude of 20,000 feet (6,100 m) before turning back.[53]

Arriving in Paris in November 1902, he associated largely with the painter Gerald Festus Kelly, and through him became a fixture of the Parisian arts scene, authoring a series of poems on the work of an acquaintance, the sculptor Auguste Rodin, published as *Rodin in Rime* (1907).[54] One of those frequenting this milieu was W. Somerset Maugham, who after briefly meeting Crowley later used him as a model for the character of Oliver Haddo in his novel *The Magician* (1908).[55] Returning to Boleskine in April 1903, in August Crowley wed Gerald's sister Rose Edith Kelly in a "marriage of convenience" to prevent her entering an arranged marriage; the marriage appalled the Kelly family and damaged his friendship with Gerald. Heading on a honeymoon to Paris, Cairo, and then Ceylon, Crowley fell in love with Rose and worked to prove his affections. While on his honeymoon, he wrote her a series of love poems, published as *Rosa Mundi and other Love Songs* (1906), as well as authoring the religious satire *Why Jesus Wept* (1904).[56]

5.2 Developing Thelema

5.2.1 Egypt and *The Book of the Law*: 1904

Had! The manifestation of Nuit.
The unveiling of the company of heaven.
Every man and woman is a star.
Every number is infinite; there is no difference.
Help me, o warrior lord of Thebes, in my unveiling before the Children of men!

The opening lines of *The Book of the Law*.

In February 1904, Crowley and Rose arrived in Cairo. Claiming to be a prince and princess, they rented an apartment in which Crowley set up a temple room and began invoking ancient Egyptian deities, also studying Islamic mysticism and Arabic.[57] According to Crowley's later account, Rose regularly became delirious and informed him "they are waiting for you". On 18 March, she explained that "they" were the god Horus, and on 20 March proclaimed that "the Equinox of the Gods has come". She led him to a nearby museum, where she showed him a seventh-century BCE mortuary stele known as the Stele of Ankh-ef-en-Khonsu; Crowley thought it important that the exhibit's number was 666, the number of the beast in Christian belief, and in later years termed the artefact the "Stele of Revealing".[58]

According to Crowley's own later claims, on 8 April he heard a disembodied voice that claimed to be that of Aiwass, an entity who was the messenger of Horus, or Hoor-Paar-Kraat. Crowley said that he wrote down everything the voice told him over the course of the next three days, and titled it *Liber AL vel Legis* or *The Book of the Law*.[59] The book proclaimed that humanity was entering a new Aeon, and that Crowley would serve as its prophet. It stated that a supreme moral law was to be introduced in this Aeon, "Do what thou wilt shall be the whole of the law", and that people should learn to live in tune with their Will. This book, and the philosophy that it espoused, became the cornerstone of Crowley's religion, Thelema.[60] Crowley claimed that at the time he had been unsure what to do with *The Book of the Law*. Often resenting it, he said that he ignored the instructions which the text commanded him to perform, which included taking the Stele of Revealing from the museum, fortifying his own island, and translating the book into all the world's languages. According to his account, he instead sent typescripts of the work to several occultists he knew, putting the manuscript itself away and ignoring it.[61]

5.2.2   Kangchenjunga and China: 1905–06

Returning to Boleskine, Crowley came to believe that Mathers had begun using magic against him, and the relationship between the two broke down.[62] On 28 July 1905, Rose gave birth to Crowley's first child, a daughter named Lilith, with Crowley authoring the pornographic *Snowdrops From a Curate's Garden* to entertain his recuperating wife.[63] He also founded a publishing company through which to publish his poetry, naming it the Society for the Propagation of Religious Truth in parody of the Society for Promoting Christian Knowledge. Among its first publications were Crowley's *Collected Works*, edited by Ivor Back.[64] His poetry often received strong reviews (either positive or negative), but never sold well. In an attempt to gain more publicity, he issued a reward of £100 for the best essay on his work. The winner of this was J.F.C. Fuller, a British Army officer and military historian, whose essay, *The Star in the West* (1907), heralded Crowley's poetry as some of the greatest ever written.[65]

Crowley decided to climb Kangchenjunga in the Himalayas of Nepal, widely recognised as the world's most treacherous mountain. Assembling a team consisting of Jacot-Guillarmod, Charles Adolphe Reymond, Alexis Pache, and Alcesti C. Rigo de Righi, the expedition was marred by much argument between Crowley and the others, who felt that he was reckless. They eventually mutinied against Crowley's control, with the other climbers heading back down the mountain as nightfall approached despite Crowley's warnings that it was too dangerous. Subsequently, Pache and several porters were killed in an accident, something for which Crowley was widely blamed by the mountaineering community.[66]

Spending time in Moharbhanj, where he took part in big game hunting and wrote the homoerotic work *The Scented Garden*, Crowley met up with Rose and Lilith in Calcutta before being forced to leave India after shooting dead a native man who tried to mug him.[67] Briefly visiting Bennett in Burma, Crowley and his family decided to tour Southern China, hiring porters and a nanny for the purpose.[68] Spence has suggested that this was part of Crowley's job as an intelligence agent, in order to report on the region's opium trade.[69] Crowley smoked opium throughout the journey, which took the family from Tengyueh through to Yungchang, Tali, Yunnanfu, and then Hanoi. On the way he spent much time on spiritual and magical work, reciting invocations from the *Goetia* on a daily basis.[70]

While Rose and Lilith returned to Europe, Crowley headed to Shanghai to meet old friend Elaine Simpson, who was fascinated by *The Book of the Law*; together they performed rituals in an attempt to contact Aiwass. Crowley then sailed to Japan and Canada, before continuing to New York City, where he unsuccessfully solicited support for a second expedition up Kangchenjunga.[71] Upon arrival in Britain, Crowley learned that his daughter Lilith had died of typhoid in Rangoon, something he later blamed on Rose's increasing alcoholism. Under emotional distress, his health began to suffer, and he underwent a series of surgical operations.[72] He began short-lived romances with actress Vera "Lola" Stepp and author Ada Leverson,[73] while Rose gave birth to Crowley's second daughter, Lola Zaza, in February 1907.[74]

5.2.3   The A∴A∴ and the Holy Books of Thelema: 1907–09

With his old mentor George Cecil Jones, Crowley continued performing the Abramelin rituals at the Ashdown Park Hotel in Coulsdon, Surrey. Crowley claimed that in doing so he attained *samadhi*, or union with Godhead, thereby marking a turning point in his life.[75] Making heavy use of hashish during these rituals, he wrote an essay on "The Psychology of Hashish" (1909) in which he championed the drug as an aid to mysticism.[76] He also claimed to have been contacted once again by Aiwass in late October and November 1907, adding that Aiwass dictated two further texts to him, "Liber VII" and "Liber Cordis Cincti Serpente", both of which were later classified in the corpus of Holy Books of Thelema.[77] Crowley wrote down more Thelemic Holy Books during the last two months of the year, including "Liber LXVI", "Liber Arcanorum", "Liber Porta Lucis, Sub Figura X", "Liber Tau", "Liber Trigrammaton" and "Liber DCCCXIII vel Ararita", which he again claimed to have received from a preternatural source.[78] Crowley claimed that in June 1909, when the manuscript of *The Book of the Law* was rediscovered at Boleskine, he developed the opinion that Thelema represented objective truth.[79]

Crowley's inheritance was running out.[80] Trying to earn money, he was hired by George Montagu Bennett, the Earl of Tankerville, to help protect him from witchcraft; recognising Bennett's paranoia as being based in his cocaine addiction, Crowley took him on holiday to France and Morocco to recuperate.[81] In 1907, he also began taking in paying students, whom he instructed in occult and magical practice.[82] Victor Neuburg, whom Crowley met in February 1907, became his sexual partner and closest disciple; in 1908 the pair toured northern Spain before heading to Tangier, Morocco.[83] The following year Neuburg stayed at Boleskine, where he and Crowley engaged in sadomasochism.[84] Crowley continued to write prolifically, producing such works of poetry as *Ambergris*, *Clouds Without Water*, and *Konx Om Pax*,[85] as well as his first attempt at an autobiography, *The World's Tragedy*.[86] Recognising the popularity of short horror stories, Crowley wrote his own, some of which were published,[87] and he also published several articles in *Vanity Fair*, a magazine edited by his friend Frank Harris.[88] He also wrote *Liber 777*, a book of magical and Qabalistic correspondences that borrowed from Mathers and Bennett.[89]

Into my loneliness comes --
The sound of a flute in dim groves that haunt the uttermost hills.
Even from the brave river they reach to the edge of the wilderness.
And I behold Pan.

The opening lines of Liber VII (1907), the first of the Holy Books of Thelema to be revealed to Crowley after *The Book of the Law*.[90]

In November 1907, Crowley and Jones decided to found an occult order to act as a successor to the Hermetic Order of the Golden Dawn, being aided in doing so by Fuller. The result was the A∴A∴. The group's headquarters and temple were situated at 124 Victoria Street in central London, and their rites borrowed much from those of the Golden Dawn, but with an added Thelemic basis.[91] Its earliest members included solicitor Richard Noel Warren, artist Austin Osman Spare, Horace Sheridan-Bickers, author George Raffalovich, Francis Henry Everard Joseph Feilding, engineer Herbert Edward Inman, Kenneth Ward, and Charles Stansfeld Jones.[92] In March 1909, Crowley began production of a biannual periodical titled *The Equinox*. He billed this periodical, which was to become the "Official Organ" of the A∴A∴, as "The Review of Scientific Illuminism".[93]

Crowley had become increasingly frustrated with Rose's alcoholism, and in November 1909 he divorced her on the grounds of his own adultery. Lola was entrusted to Rose's care; the couple remained friends and Rose continued to live at Boleskine. Her alcoholism worsened, and as a result she was institutionalised in September 1911.[94]

5.2.4 Algeria and the Rites of Eleusis: 1909–11

In November 1909, Crowley and Neuburg travelled to Algeria, touring the desert from El Arba to Aumale, Bou Saâda, and then Dā'leh Addin, with Crowley reciting the Quran on a daily basis. During the trip he performed rites of Enochian magic, with Neuburg recording the results, later published in *The Equinox* as *The Vision and the Voice*. Following a mountaintop sex magic ritual, Crowley also performed an invocation to the demon Choronzon involving blood sacrifice, considering the results to be a watershed in his magical career.[95] Returning to London in January 1910, Crowley found that Mathers was suing him for publishing Golden Dawn secrets in *The Equinox*; the court found in favour of Crowley. The case was widely reported on in the press, with Crowley gaining wider fame.[96] Crowley enjoyed this, and played up to the sensationalist stereotype of being a Satanist and advocate of human sacrifice, despite being neither.[97]

The publicity attracted new members to the A∴A∴, among them Frank Bennett, James Bayley, Herbert Close, and James Windram.[98] The Australian violinist Leila Waddell soon became Crowley's lover.[99] Deciding to expand his teachings to a wider audience, Crowley developed the Rites of Artemis, a public performance of magic and symbolism featuring A∴A∴ members personifying various deities. It was first performed at the A∴A∴ headquarters, with attendees given a fruit punch containing peyote to enhance their experience. Various members of the press attended, and reported largely positively on it. In October and November 1910, Crowley decided to stage something similar, the Rites of Eleusis, at Caxton Hall, Westminster; this time press reviews were mixed.[100] Crowley came under particular criticism from West de Wend Fenton, editor of *The Looking Glass* newspaper, who called him "one of the most blasphemous and cold-blooded villains of modern times".i[101] Fenton's articles suggested that Crowley and Jones were involved in homosexual activity; Crowley did not mind, but Jones unsuccessfully sued for libel.[102] Fuller broke off his friendship and involvement with Crowley over the scandal,[103] and Crowley and Neuburg returned to Algeria for further magical workings.[104]

The Equinox continued publishing, and various books of literature and poetry were also published under its imprint, like Crowley's *Ambergris*, *The Winged Beetle*, and *The Scented Garden*, as well as Neuburg's *The Triumph of Pan* and Ethel Archer's *The Whirlpool*.[105] In 1911, Crowley and Waddell holidayed in Montigny-sur-Loing, where he wrote prolifically, producing poems, short stories, plays, and 19 works on magic and mysticism, including the two final Holy Books of Thelema.[106] In Paris, he met Mary Desti, who became his next "Scarlet Woman", with the two undertaking magical workings in St. Moritz; Crowley believed that one of the Secret Chiefs, Ab-ul-Diz, was speaking through her.[107] Based on Desti's statements when in trance, Crowley wrote the two-volume *Book 4* (1912–13) and at the time developed the spelling "magick" in reference to the paranormal phenomenon as a means of distinguishing it from the stage magic of illusionists.[108]

5.2.5   Ordo Templi Orientis and the Paris Working: 1912–14

In early 1912, Crowley published *The Book of Lies*, a work of mysticism that biographer Lawrence Sutin described as "his greatest success in merging his talents as poet, scholar, and magus".[109] The German occultist Theodor Reuss later accused him of publishing some of the secrets of his own occult order, the Ordo Templi Orientis (O.T.O.), within *The Book*. Crowley convinced Reuss that the similarities were coincidental, and the two became friends. Reuss appointed Crowley as head of the O.T.O's British branch, the Mysteria Mystica Maxima (MMM), and at a ceremony in Berlin Crowley adopted the magical name of Baphomet and was proclaimed "X° Supreme Rex and Sovereign Grand Master General of Ireland, Iona, and all the Britons".[110] With Reuss' permission, Crowley set about advertising the MMM and re-writing many O.T.O. rituals, which were then based largely on Freemasonry; his incorporation of Thelemite elements proved controversial in the group. Fascinated by the O.T.O's emphasis on sex magic, Crowley devised a magical working based on anal sex and incorporated it into the syllabus for those O.T.O. members who had been initiated into the eleventh degree. [111]

In March 1913 Crowley acted as producer for *The Ragged Ragtime Girls*, a group of female violinists led by Waddell, as they performed at London's Old Tivoli theatre. They subsequently performed in Moscow for six weeks, where Crowley had a sadomasochistic relationship with the Hungarian Anny Ringler.[112] In Moscow, Crowley continued to write plays and poetry, including "Hymn to Pan", and the Gnostic Mass, a Thelemic ritual that became a key part of O.T.O. liturgy.[113] Churton suggested that Crowley had travelled to Moscow on the orders of British intelligence to spy on revolutionary elements in the city.[114] In January 1914 Crowley and Neuburg settled in to an apartment in Paris, where the former was involved in the controversy surrounding Jacob Epstein's new monument to Oscar Wilde.[115] Together Crowley and Neuburg performed the six-week "Paris Working", a period of intense ritual involving strong drug use in which they invoked the gods Mercury and Jupiter. As part of the ritual, the couple performed acts of sex magic together, at times being joined by journalist Walter Duranty. Inspired by the results of the Working, Crowley authored *Liber Agapé*, a treatise on sex magic.[116] Following the Paris Working, Neuburg began to distance himself from Crowley, resulting in an argument in which Crowley cursed him.[117]

5.2.6   United States: 1914–19

By 1914 Crowley was living a hand-to-mouth existence, relying largely on donations and the membership fees from the O.T.O. and A∴A∴.[118] In May he transferred ownership of Boleskine House to the MMM for financial reasons,[119] and in July he went mountaineering in the Swiss Alps. During this time the First World War broke out.[120] After recuperating from a bout of phlebitis, Crowley set sail for the United States aboard the *RMS Lusitania* in October 1914.[121] Arriving in New York City, he moved into a hotel and began earning money writing for the American edition of *Vanity Fair* and undertaking freelance work for the famed astrologer Evangeline Adams.[122] In the city, he continued experimenting with sex magic, through the use of masturbation, female prostitutes, and male clients of a Turkish bathhouse; all of these encounters were documented in his diaries.[123]

Professing to be of Irish ancestry and a supporter of Irish independence from Great Britain, Crowley began to espouse views supporting Germany in their war against Britain. He became involved in New York's pro-German movement, and in January 1915 German spy George Sylvester Viereck employed him as a writer for his propagandist paper, *The Fatherland*, which was dedicated to keeping the US neutral in the conflict.[125] In later years, detractors denounced Crowley as a traitor to Britain for this action.[126] In reality, Crowley was a double agent, working for the British intelligence services to infiltrate and undermine Germany's operation in New York. Many of his articles in *The Fatherland* were hyperbolic, for instance comparing Kaiser Wilhelm II to Jesus Christ; in July 1915 he orchestrated a publicity stunt – reported on by *The New York Times* – in which he declared independence for Ireland in front of the Statue of Liberty; the real intention was to make the German lobby appear ridiculous in the eyes of the American public.[127] It has been argued that he encouraged the German Navy to destroy the *Lusitania*, informing them that it would ensure the US stayed out of the war, while in reality hoping that it would bring the US into the war on Britain's side.[128]

Crowley entered into a relationship with Jeanne Robert Foster, with whom he toured the West Coast. In Vancouver, headquarters of the North American O.T.O., he met with Charles Stansfeld Jones and Wilfred Talbot Smith to discuss the propagation of Thelema on the continent. In Detroit he experimented with anhalonium at Parke-Davis, then visited Seattle, San Francisco, Santa Cruz, Los Angeles, San Diego, Tijuana, and the Grand Canyon, before returning to New York.[129] There he befriended Ananda Coomaraswamy and his wife Alice Richardson; Crowley and Richardson performed sex magic in April 1916, following which she became pregnant and then miscarried.[130] Later that year he took a "magical retirement" to a cabin by Lake Pasquaney owned by Evangeline Adams. There, he made heavy use of drugs and undertook a ritual after which he proclaimed himself "Master Therion". He also wrote several short stories based on J.G. Frazer's *The Golden Bough* and a work of literary criticism, *The Gospel According to Bernard Shaw*.[131]

In December he moved to New Orleans, his favourite US city, before spending February 1917 with evangelical Christian relatives in Titusville, Florida.[132] Returning to New York, he moved in with artist and A∴A∴ member Leon Engers Kennedy, in May learning of his mother's death.[133] After the collapse of *The Fatherland*, Crowley continued his association with Viereck, who appointed him contributing editor of arts journal *The International*. Crowley used it to promote Thelema, but it soon ceased publication.[134] He then moved to the studio apartment of Roddie Minor, who became his partner and Scarlet Woman. Through their rituals, Crowley believed that they were contacted by a preternatural entity named Alamantrah. The relationship soon ended.[135]

In 1918, Crowley went on a magical retreat in the wilderness of Esopus Island on the Hudson River. Here, he began a translation of the *Tao Te Ching*, painted Thelemic slogans on the riverside cliffs, and – he later claimed – experienced what he interpreted as past life memories of being Ge Xuan, Pope Alexander VI, Alessandro Cagliostro, and Eliphas Levi, also painting Thelemic slogans on the riverside cliffs.[136] Back in New York, he moved to Greenwich Village, where he took Leah Hirsig as his lover and next Scarlet Woman.[137] He took up painting as a hobby, exhibiting his work at the Greenwich Village Liberal Club and attracting the attention of the *New York Evening World*.[138] With the financial assistance of sympathetic Freemasons, Crowley revived *The Equinox* with the first issue of volume III, known as "The Blue Equinox".[139] He spent mid-1919 on a climbing holiday in Montauk before returning to London in December.[140]

5.2.7 Abbey of Thelema: 1920–23

Now destitute and back in London, Crowley came under attack from the tabloid *John Bull*, which labelled him traitorous "scum" for his work with the German war effort; several friends aware of his intelligence work urged him to sue, but he decided not to.[141] When he was suffering from asthma, a doctor prescribed him heroin, to which he soon became addicted.[142] In January 1920, he moved to Paris, renting a house in Fontainebleau with Leah Hirsig; they were soon joined in a *ménage à trois* by Ninette Shumway, and also by Leah's newborn daughter Anne "Poupée" Leah.[143] Crowley had ideas of forming a community of Thelemites, which he called the Abbey of Thelema after the Abbaye de Thélème in François Rabelais's satire *Gargantua and Pantagruel*. After consulting the *I Ching*, he chose Cefalù (on Sicily, Italy) as a location, and after arriving there, began renting the old Villa Santa Barbara as his Abbey on 2 April.[144]

Moving to the commune with Hirsig, Shumway, and their children Hansi, Howard, and Poupée, Crowley described the scenario as "perfectly happy ... my idea of heaven."[145] They wore robes, and performed rituals to the sun god Ra at set times during the day, also occasionally performing the Gnostic Mass; the rest of the day they were left to follow their own interests.[146] Undertaking widespread correspondences, Crowley continued to paint, wrote a commentary on *The Book of the Law*, and revised the third part of *Book 4*.[147] He offered a libertine education for the children, allowing them to play all day and witness acts of sex magic.[148] He occasionally travelled to Palermo to visit rent boys and buy supplies, including drugs; his heroin addiction came to dominate his life, and cocaine began to erode his nasal cavity.[149] There was no cleaning rota, and wild dogs and cats wandered throughout the building, which soon became unsanitary.[150] Poupée died in October 1920, and Ninette gave birth to a daughter, Astarte Lulu Panthea, soon afterwards.[151]

New followers continued to arrive at the Abbey to be taught by Crowley. Among them was film star Jane Wolfe, who arrived in July 1920, where she was initiated into the A∴A∴ and became Crowley's secretary.[152] Another was Cecil

Frederick Russell, who often argued with Crowley, disliking the same-sex sexual magic that he was required to perform, and left after a year.[153] More conducive was the Australian Thelemite Frank Bennett, who also spent several months at the Abbey.[154] In February 1922, Crowley returned to Paris for a retreat in an unsuccessful attempt to kick his heroin addiction.[155] He then went to London in search of money, where he published articles in *The English Review* criticising the Dangerous Drugs Act 1920 and wrote a novel, *Diary of a Drug Fiend*, completed in July. On publication, it received mixed reviews; he was lambasted by the *Sunday Express*, which called for its burning and used its influence to prevent further reprints.[156]

Subsequently, a young Thelemite named Raoul Loveday moved to the Abbey with his wife Betty May; while Loveday was devoted to Crowley, May detested him and life at the commune. She later claimed that Loveday was made to drink the blood of a sacrificed cat, and that they were required to cut themselves with razors every time they used the pronoun "I". Raoul drank from a local polluted stream, soon developing a liver infection resulting in his death in February 1923. Returning to London, May told her story to the press.[157] *John Bull* proclaimed Crowley "the wickedest man in the world" and "a man we'd like to hang", and although Crowley deemed many of their accusations against him to be slanderous, he was unable to afford the legal fees to sue them. As a result, *John Bull* continued its attack, with its stories being repeated in newspapers throughout Europe and in North America.[158] The Fascist government of Benito Mussolini learned of Crowley's activities and in April 1923 he was given a deportation notice forcing him to leave Italy; without him, the Abbey closed.[159]

5.3   Later life

5.3.1   Tunisia, Paris, and London: 1923–29

Crowley and Hirsig went to Tunis, where, dogged by continuing poor health, he unsuccessfully tried again to give up heroin,[160] and began writing what he termed his "autohagiography", *The Confessions of Aleister Crowley*.[161] They were joined in Tunis by the Thelemite Norman Mudd, who became Crowley's public relations consultant.[162] Employing a local boy, Mohammad ben Brahim, as his servant, Crowley went with him on a retreat to Nefta, where they performed sex magic together.[163] In January 1924, Crowley travelled to Nice, France, where he met with Frank Harris, underwent a series of nasal operations,[164] and visited the Institute for the Harmonious Development of Man, thinking positively of its founder, George Gurdjieff.[165] Destitute, he took on a wealthy student, Alexander Zu Zolar,[166] before taking on another American follower, Dorothy Olsen. Crowley took Olsen back to Tunisia for a magical retreat in Nefta, where he also wrote *To Man* (1924), a declaration of his own status as a prophet entrusted with bringing Thelema to humanity.[167] After spending the winter in Paris, in early 1925 Crowley and Olsen returned to Tunis, where he wrote *The Heart of the Master* (1938) as an account of a vision he claimed to have experienced while in trance.[168] In March Olsen became pregnant, and Hirsig was called to take care of her; she miscarried, following which Crowley took Olsen back to France. Hirsig later distanced herself from Crowley, who then denounced her.[169]

According to Crowley, Reuss had named him head of the O.T.O. upon his death, but this was challenged by leader of the German O.T.O., Heinrich Tränker. Tränker called the Hohenleuben Conference in Thuringia, Germany, which Crowley attended. There, prominent members like Karl Germer and Martha Küntzel championed Crowley's leadership, but other key figures like Albin Grau, Oskar Hopfer, and Henri Birven backed Tränker by opposing it, resulting in a split in the O.T.O.[170] Moving to Paris, where he broke with Olsen in 1926, Crowley went through a large number of Scarlet Women over the following years, with whom he experimented in sex magic.[171] Throughout, he was dogged by poor health, largely caused by his heroin and cocaine addictions.[172] In 1928, Crowley was introduced to young Englishman Israel Regardie, who embraced Thelema and became Crowley's secretary for the next three years.[173] That year, Crowley also met Gerald Yorke, who began organising Crowley's finances but never became a Thelemite.[174] He also befriended Thomas Driberg; Driberg did not accept Thelema either.[175] It was here that Crowley also published one of his most significant works, *Magick in Theory and Practice*, which received little attention at the time.[176]

In December 1929 Crowley met the Nicaraguan Maria Teresa Sanchez, who became his most significant Scarlet Woman of the period.[177] Crowley was deported from France by the authorities, who disliked his reputation and feared that he was a German agent.[178] So that she could join him in Britain, Crowley married Sanchez in August 1929.[179] Now based in London, Mandrake Press agreed to publish his autobiography in a limited edition six-volume set, also publishing his novel *Moonchild* and book of short stories *The Stratagem*. Mandrake went into liquidation in November 1930, before the entirety of Crowley's *Confessions* could be published.[180] Mandrake's owner P.R. Stephenson meanwhile wrote *The Legend of Aleister Crowley*, an analysis of the media coverage surrounding him.[181]

5.3.2 Berlin and London: 1930–38

In April 1930, Crowley moved to Berlin, where he took Hanni Jaegar as his new Scarlet Woman; the relationship was troubled.[182] In September he went to Lisbon in Portugal to meet the poet Fernando Pessoa. There, he decided to fake his own death, doing so with Pessoa's help at the Boca do Inferno rock formation.[183] He then returned to Berlin, where he reappeared three weeks later at the opening of his art exhibition at the Gallery Neumann-Nierendorf. Crowley's paintings fitted with the fashion for German Expressionism; few of them sold, but the press reports were largely favourable.[184] In August 1931, he took Bertha Busch as his new lover; they had a violent relationship, and often physically assaulted one another.[185] He continued to have affairs with both men and women while in the city,[186] and met with famous people like Aldous Huxley and Alfred Adler.[187] After befriending him, in January 1932 he took the communist Gerald Hamilton as a lodger, through whom he was introduced to many figures within the Berlin far left; it is possible that he was operating as a spy for British intelligence at this time, monitoring the communist movement.[188]

I have been over forty years engaged in the administration of the law in one capacity or another. I thought that I knew of every conceivable form of wickedness. I thought that everything which was vicious and bad had been produced at one time or another before me. I have learnt in this case that we can always learn something more if we live long enough. I have never heard such dreadful, horrible, blasphemous and abominable stuff as that which has been produced by the man (Crowley) who describes himself to you as the greatest living poet.

Justice Swift, in Crowley's libel case.[189][190]

Crowley left Busch and returned to London,[191] where he took Pearl Brooksmith as his new Scarlet Woman.[192] Undergoing further nasal surgery, it was here in 1932 that he was invited to be guest of honour at Foyles' Literary Luncheon, also being invited by Harry Price to speak at the National Laboratory of Psychical Research.[193] In need of money, he launched a series of court cases against people whom he believed had libelled him, some of which proved successful. He gained much publicity for his lawsuit against Constable and Co for publishing Nina Hamnett's *Laughing Torso* (1932) – a book he thought libelled him – but lost the case.[194] The court case added to Crowley's financial problems, and in February 1935 he was declared bankrupt. During the hearing, it was revealed that Crowley had been spending three times his income for several years.[195]

Crowley developed a platonic friendship with Deidre Patricia O'Doherty; she agreed to bear his child, who was born in May 1937. Named Randall Gair, Crowley nicknamed him Aleister Atatürk.[196] Crowley continued to socialise with friends, holding curry parties in which he cooked particularly spicy food for them.[197] In 1936, he published his first book in six years, *The Equinox of the Gods*, which contained a facsimile of *The Book of the Law* and was considered to be volume III, number 3, of *The Equinox* periodical. The work sold well, resulting in a second print run.[198] In 1937 he gave a series of public lectures on yoga in Soho.[199] With the A∴A∴ effectively defunct, Crowley was now living largely off contributions supplied by the O.T.O.'s Agape Lodge in California, led by rocket scientist John Whiteside "Jack" Parsons.[200] Crowley was intrigued by the rise of Nazism in Germany, and influenced by his friend Knüsel believed that Adolf Hitler might convert to Thelema; when the Nazis abolished the German O.T.O. and imprisoned Germer, who fled to the US, Crowley then lambasted Hitler as a black magician.[201]

5.3.3 Second World War and death: 1939–47

When the Second World War broke out, Crowley wrote to the Naval Intelligence Division offering his services, but they declined. He associated with a variety of figures in Britain's intelligence community at the time, including Dennis Wheatley, Roald Dahl, Ian Fleming, and Maxwell Knight,[202] and claimed to have been behind the "V for Victory" sign first used by the BBC; this has never been proven.[203] In 1940, his asthma worsened, and with his German-produced medication unavailable, he returned to using heroin, once again becoming addicted.[204] As the Blitz hit London, Crowley relocated to Torquay, where he was briefly hospitalised with asthma, and entertained himself with visits to the local chess club.[205] Tiring of Torquay, he returned to London, where he was visited by American Thelemite Grady McMurtry, to whom Crowley awarded the title of "Hymenaeus Alpha".[206] He stipulated that though Germer would be his immediate successor, McMurty should succeed Germer as head of the O.T.O. after the latter's death.[207] With O.T.O. initiate Lady Frieda Harris, Crowley developed plans to produce a tarot card set, designed by him and painted by Harris. Accompanying this was a book, published in a limited edition as *The Book of Thoth* by Chiswick Press in 1944.[208] To aid the war effort, he wrote a proclamation on the rights of humanity, *Liber Oz*, and a poem for the liberation of France, *Le Gauloise*.[209] Crowley's final publication during his lifetime was a book of poetry, *Olla: An Anthology of Sixty Years of Song*.[210] Another of his projects, *Aleister Explains Everything*, was posthumously published as *Magick Without Tears*.[211]

In April 1944 Crowley briefly moved to Aston Clinton in Buckinghamshire,[212] where he was visited by the poet Nancy Cunard,[213] before relocating to Hastings in Sussex, where he took up residence at the Netherwood boarding house.[214] He took a young man named Kenneth Grant as his secretary, paying him in magical teaching rather than wages.[215] He was also introduced to John Symonds, whom he appointed to be his literary executor; Symonds thought little of Crowley, later publishing negative biographies of him.[216] Corresponding with the illusionist Arnold Crowther, it was through him that Crowley was introduced to Gerald Gardner, the future founder of Gardnerian Wicca. They became friends, with Crowley authorising Gardner to revive Britain's ailing O.T.O.[217] Another visitor was Eliza Marian Butler, who interviewed Crowley for her book *The Myth of the Magus*.[218] Other friends and family also spent time with him, among them Doherty and Crowley's son Aleister Atatürk.[219] On 1 December 1947, Crowley died at Netherwood of chronic bronchitis aggravated by pleurisy and myocardial degeneration, aged 72.[220] His funeral was held at a Brighton crematorium on 5 December; about a dozen people attended, and Louis Wilkinson read excerpts from the Gnostic Mass, *The Book of the Law*, and "Hymn to Pan". The funeral generated press controversy, and was labelled a Black Mass by the tabloids. Crowley's ashes were sent to Germer in the US, who buried them in his garden in Hampton, New Jersey.[221]

5.4   Beliefs and thought

Main article: Thelema

Crowley's thought was not always cohesive, and was influenced by a variety of sources, ranging from eastern religious movements and practices like Hindu yoga and Buddhism, scientific naturalism, and various currents within Western esotericism, among them ceremonial magic, alchemy, astrology, Rosicrucianism, Kabbalah, and the Tarot.[222] Philosopher John Moore opined that Crowley's thought was rooted in Romanticism and the Decadent movement,[223] an assessment shared by historian Alex Owen, who noted that Crowley adhered to the "modus operandi" of the decadent movement throughout his life.[224]

Crowley believed that the twentieth century marked humanity's entry to the Aeon of Horus, a new era in which humans would take increasing control of their destiny. He believed that this Aeon follows on from the Aeon of Osiris, in which paternalistic religions like Christianity, Islam, and Buddhism dominated the world, and that this in turn had followed the Aeon of Isis, which had been maternalistic and dominated by goddess worship.[225] Thelema revolves around the idea that human beings each have their own True Will that they should discover and pursue, and that this exists in harmony with the Cosmic Will that pervades the universe.[226] The moral code of "Do What Thou Wilt" is believed by Thelemites to be the faith's ethical law, although academic Marco Pasi noted that this was not anarchistic or libertarian in structure, as Crowley saw individuals as part of a wider societal organism.[227]

Crowley believed in the objective existence of magic, which he chose to spell "Magick". In his book *Magick in Theory and Practice*, Crowley defined Magick as "the Science and Art of causing change to occur in conformity with Will".[228] He also told his disciple Karl Germer that "Magick is getting into communication with individuals who exist on a higher plane than ours. Mysticism is the raising of oneself to their level."[229] Crowley saw Magick as a third way between religion and science, giving *The Equinox* the subtitle of "The Method of Science; the Aim of Religion".[230]

Both during his life and after it, Crowley has been widely described as a Satanist, usually by detractors. Crowley stated he did not consider himself a Satanist, nor did he worship Satan, as he did not accept the Christian world view in which Satan was believed to exist.[231] He was also accused of advocating human sacrifice, largely because of a passage in *Book 4* in which he stated that "A male child of perfect innocence and high intelligence is the most satisfactory victim". This was intended as a veiled reference to male masturbation.[232]

5.5 Personal life

Crowley biographer Martin Booth asserted that Crowley was "self-confident, brash, eccentric, egotistic, highly intelligent, arrogant, witty, wealthy, and, when it suited him, cruel".[233] Similarly, Richard Spence noted that Crowley was "capable of immense physical and emotional cruelty".[234] Biographer Lawrence Sutin noted that Crowley exhibited "courage, skill, dauntless energy, and remarkable focus of will" while at the same time showing a "blind arrogance, petty fits of bile, [and] contempt for the abilities of his fellow men".[235] The Thelemite Lon Milo DuQuette noted that Crowley "was by no means perfect" and "often alienated those who loved him dearest."[236]

Crowley enjoyed being outrageous and flouting conventional morality,[237] with John Symonds noting that he "was in revolt against the moral and religious values of his time".[238] Crowley's political thought was subjected to an in-depth study by academic Marco Pasi, who noted that for Crowley, socio-political concerns were subordinate to metaphysical and spiritual ones.[222] Pasi argued that it was difficult to classify Crowley as being either on the political left or right, but he was perhaps best categorised as a "conservative revolutionary" despite not being affiliated with the German-based conservative revolutionary movement.[239] Pasi noted that Crowley sympathised with extreme ideologies like Nazism and Marxism-Leninism, in that they wished to violently overturn society, and hoped that both Nazi Germany and the Soviet Union might adopt Thelema.[240] Crowley described democracy as an "imbecile and nauseating cult of weakness",[241] and commented that *The Book of the Law* proclaimed that "there is the master and there is the slave; the noble and the serf; the 'lone wolf' and the herd".[227] In this attitude he was influenced by the work of Friedrich Nietzsche and by Social Darwinism.[242] Crowley also saw himself as an aristocrat, describing himself as Laird Boleskine; he had contempt for most of the British aristocracy,[243] and once described his socio-political views as "aristocratic communism".[244]

Crowley was bisexual, and exhibited a sexual preference for women.[245] In particular he had an attraction toward "exotic women",[246] and claimed to have fallen in love on multiple occasions; Kaczynski stated that "when he loved, he did so with his whole being, but the passion was typically short-lived".[247] Even in later life, he was able to attract young bohemian women to be his lovers, largely due to his charisma.[248] During same-sex anal intercourse, he usually played the passive role,[249] which Booth believed "appealed to his masochistic side".[250] Crowley argued that gay and bisexual people should not suppress their sexual orientation, commenting that a person "must not be ashamed or afraid of being homosexual if he happens to be so at heart; he must not attempt to violate his own true nature because of public opinion, or medieval morality, or religious prejudice which would wish he were otherwise."[251] On other issues he adopted a more conservative attitude; he opposed abortion on moral grounds, believing that no woman following her True Will would ever desire one.[252]

5.5.1 Views on race and gender

Biographer Lawrence Sutin stated that "blatant bigotry is a persistent minor element in Crowley's writings".[253] Sutin thought Crowley "a spoiled scion of a wealthy Victorian family who embodied many of the worst John Bull racial and social prejudices of his upper-class contemporaries",[254] noting that he "embodied the contradiction that writhed within many Western intellectuals of the time: deeply held racist viewpoints courtesy of their culture, coupled with a fascination with people of colour".[255] Crowley insulted his close Jewish friend Victor Neuburg using anti-Semitic slurs, and he had mixed feelings for Jews as a group. Although he praised their "sublime" poetry and claimed that the "Jewish race" contained "imagination, romance, loyalty, probity and humanity in an exceptional degree", he also thought that centuries of persecution had led some Jews to exhibit "avarice, servility, falseness, cunning and the rest".[256] He was also known to praise various ethnic and cultural groups, for instance he claimed that the Chinese people exhibited a "spiritual superiority" to the English,[257] and praised Muslims for exhibiting "manliness, straightforwardness, subtlety, and self-respect".[258]

Crowley also exhibited a "general misogyny" that Booth believed arose from his bad relationship with his mother.[259] Sutin noted that Crowley "largely accepted the notion, implicitly embodied in Victorian sexology, of women as secondary social beings in terms of intellect and sensibility".[260] Crowley described women as "moral inferiors" who had to be treated with "firmness, kindness and justice".[261]

5.6   Legacy and influence

Crowley has remained an influential figure, both amongst occultists and in popular culture, particularly that of Britain, but also of other parts of the world. In 2002, a BBC poll placed Crowley seventy-third in a list of the 100 Greatest Britons.[262] Richard Cavendish has written of him that "In native talent, penetrating intelligence and determination, Aleister Crowley was the best-equipped magician to emerge since the seventeenth century." [263] Wouter Hanegraaff asserted that Crowley was an extreme representation of "the dark side of the occult",[264] while philosopher John Moore opined that Crowley stood out as a "Modern Master" when compared with other prominent occult figures like George Gurdjieff, P.D. Ouspensky, Rudolf Steiner, or Helena Blavatsky,[265] also describing him as a "living embodiment" of Oswald Spengler's "Faustian Man".[266] Biographer Tobias Churton considered Crowley "a pioneer of consciousness research",[267] and Sutin thought that he had made "distinctly original contributions" to the study of yoga in the West.[268]

Thelema continued to develop and spread following Crowley's death. In 1969, the O.T.O. was reactivated in California under the leadership of Grady Louis McMurtry;[269] in 1985 its right to the title was unsuccessfully challenged in court by a rival group, the Society Ordo Templi Orientis, led by Brazilian Thelemite Marcelo Ramos Motta.[269] Another American Thelemite was the filmmaker Kenneth Anger, who had been influenced by Crowley's writings from a young age.[270][271] In the United Kingdom, Kenneth Grant propagated a tradition known as Typhonian Thelema through his organisation, the Typhonian OTO, later renamed the Typhonian Order.[272] Also in Britain, an occultist known as Amado Crowley claimed to be Crowley's son; these claims have been refuted by academic investigation. Amado argued that Thelema was a false religion created by Crowley to hide his true esoteric teachings, which Amado claimed to be propagating.[273] Crowley's birth date, 12 October, is celebrated as "Crowleymas".[274]

Several Western esoteric traditions other than Thelema were also influenced by Crowley. Gerald Gardner, founder of Gardnerian Wicca, made use of much of Crowley's published material when composing the Gardnerian ritual liturgy,[275] and the Australian witch Rosaleen Norton was also heavily influenced by Crowley's ideas.[276] L. Ron Hubbard, the American founder of Scientology, was involved in Thelema in the early 1940s (with Jack Parsons), and it has been argued that Crowley's ideas influenced some of Hubbard's work.[277] Two prominent figures in religious Satanism, Anton LaVey and Michael Aquino, were also influenced by Crowley's work.[278]

Crowley also had a wider influence in British popular culture. He was included as one of the figures on the cover art of The Beatles' album *Sgt. Pepper's Lonely Hearts Club Band* (1967),[269] and his motto of "Do What Thou Wilt" was inscribed on the vinyl of Led Zeppelin's album *Led Zeppelin III* (1970).[269] Led Zeppelin co-founder Jimmy Page bought Boleskine in 1971, and part of the band's film *The Song Remains the Same* was filmed in the grounds. He sold it in 1992.[279] David Bowie made reference to Crowley in the lyrics of his song "Quicksand" (1971),[269] while Ozzy Osbourne and his lyricist Bob Daisley wrote a song titled "Mr Crowley" (1980).[280]

5.7   Bibliography

Main article: List of works by Aleister Crowley

5.8   References

5.8.1   Footnotes

[1] "Louise Muhler". *SFGate*. San Francisco Chroncile. Retrieved 9 December 2014.

[2] Booth 2000, pp. 4–5; Sutin 2000, p. 15; Kaczynski 2010, p. 14.

[3] Booth 2000, pp. 2–3; Sutin 2000, pp. 31–23; Kaczynski 2010, pp. 4–8; Churton 2011, pp. 14–15.

[4] Booth 2000, p. 3; Sutin 2000, pp. 18–21; Kaczynski 2010, pp. 13–16; Churton 2011, pp. 17–21.

[5] Booth 2000, p. 3; Kaczynski 2010, p. 13–14; Churton 2011, p. 17.

[6] Booth 2000, pp. 3–4, 6, 9–10; Sutin 2000, pp. 17–23; Kaczynski 2010, pp. 11–12, 16.

[7] Booth 2000, pp. 6–7; Kaczynski 2010, p. 16; Churton 2011, p. 24.

[8] Booth 2000, pp. 12–14; Sutin 2000, p. 25–29; Kaczynski 2010, pp. 17–18; Churton 2011, p. 24.

[9] Booth 2000, p. 15; Sutin 2000, pp. 24–25; Kaczynski 2010, p. 19; Churton 2011, pp. 24–25.

[10] Booth 2000, p. 10; Sutin 2000, p. 21.

[11] Sutin 2000, pp. 27–30; Kaczynski 2010, pp. 19, 21–22.

[12] Booth 2000, pp. 32–39; Sutin 2000, pp. 32–33; Kaczynski 2010, p. 27; Churton 2011, pp. 26–27.

[13] Booth 2000, pp. 15–16; Sutin 2000, pp. 25–26; Kaczynski 2010, p. 23.

[14] Booth 2000, pp. 26–27; Sutin 2000, p. 33; Kaczynski 2010, pp. 24,27; Churton 2011, p. 26.

[15] Booth 2000, pp. 39–43; Sutin 2000, pp. 30–32, 34; Kaczynski 2010, pp. 27–30; Churton 2011, pp. 26–27.

[16] Booth 2000, p. 49; Sutin 2000, pp. 34–35; Kaczynski 2010, p. 32; Churton 2011, pp. 27–28.

[17] Booth 2000, pp. 51–52; Sutin 2000, pp. 36–37; Kaczynski 2010, p. 23.

[18] Kaczynski 2010, p. 35.

[19] Booth 2000, pp. 50–51; Kaczynski 2010, pp. 33–35.

[20] Symonds 1997, p. 13; Booth 2000, pp. 53–56; Sutin 2000, pp. 50–52; Kaczynski 2010, p. 35, 42–45, 50–51; Churton 2011, p. 35.

[21] Crowley 1989, p. 139.

[22] Symonds 1997, p. 14; Booth 2000, pp. 56–57; Kaczynski 2010, p. 36; Churton 2011, p. 29.

[23] Sutin 2000, p. 38; Kaczynski 2010, p. 36; Churton 2011, p. 29.

[24] Booth 2000, pp. 59–62; Sutin 2000, p. 43; Churton 2011, pp. 27–28.

[25] Booth 2000, pp. 64–65; Sutin 2000, pp. 41–47; Kaczynski 2010, pp. 37–40, 45; Churton 2011, pp. 33–24.

[26] Spence 2006, pp. 19–20; Sutin 2000, p. 37; Kaczynski 2010, p. 35; Churton 2011, pp. 30–31.

[27] Spence 2006, pp. 19–20; Churton 2011, pp. 30–31.

[28] Booth 2000, pp. 57–58; Sutin 2000, pp. 37–39; Kaczynski 2010, p. 36.

[29] Booth 2000, pp. 58–59; Sutin 2000, p. 41; Kaczynski 2010, pp. 40–42.

[30] Symonds 1997, pp. 14–15; Booth 2000, pp. 72–73; Sutin 2000, pp. 44–45; Kaczynski 2010, pp. 46–47.

[31] Symonds 1997, p. 15; Booth 2000, pp. 74–75; Sutin 2000, pp. 44–45; Kaczynski 2010, pp. 48–50.

[32] Booth 2000, pp. 78–79; Sutin 2000, pp. 35–36.

[33] Booth 2000, pp. 81–82; Sutin 2000, pp. 52–53; Kaczynski 2010, pp. 52–53.

[34] Booth 2000, pp. 82–85; Sutin 2000, pp. 53–54; Kaczynski 2010, pp. 54–55.

[35] "perdurabo - translation - Latin-English Dictionary - Glosbe". *Glosbe*. Retrieved 2015-10-05.

[36] Booth 2000, pp. 85, 93–94; Sutin 2000, pp. 54–55; Kaczynski 2010, pp. 60–61; Churton 2011, p. 35.

[37] Spence 2008, pp. 22–28; Churton 2011, pp. 38–46.

[38] Booth 2000, pp. 98–103; Sutin 2000, pp. 64–66; Kaczynski 2010, pp. 54–55, 62–64, 67–68; Churton 2011, p. 49.

[39] Booth 2000, pp. 103–105; Sutin 2000, pp. 70–71; Kaczynski 2010, pp. 70–71; Churton 2011, p. 55.

[40] Symonds 1997, p. 29; Booth 2000, pp. 107–111; Sutin 2000, pp. 72–73; Kaczynski 2010, pp. 68–69; Churton 2011, p. 52.

[41] Booth 2000, p. 114–115; Sutin 2000, pp. 44–45; Kaczynski 2010, pp. 61, 66, 70.

[42] Booth 2000, pp. 115–116; Sutin 2000, p. 71–72; Kaczynski 2010, p. 64.

[43] Symonds 1997, p. 37; Booth 2000, pp. 115–116; Sutin 2000, pp. 67–69; Kaczynski 2010, pp. 64–67.

[44] Booth 2000, p. 116; Sutin 2000, pp. 73–75; Kaczynski 2010, pp. 70–73; Churton 2011, pp. 53–54.

[45] Booth 2000, p. 118; Sutin 2000, pp. 73–75; Kaczynski 2010, pp. 74–75; Churton 2011, p. 57.

[46] Booth 2000, pp. 118–123; Sutin 2000, pp. 76–79; Kaczynski 2010, pp. 75–80; Churton 2011, pp. 58–60.

[47] Spence 2008, p. 27.

[48] Booth 2000, pp. 127–137; Sutin 2000, pp. 80–86; Kaczynski 2010, pp. 83–90; Churton 2011, pp. 64–70.

[49] Spence 2008, p. 32.

[50] Booth 2000, pp. 137–139; Sutin 2000, pp. 86–90; Kaczynski 2010, pp. 90–93; Churton 2011, pp. 71–75.

[51] Booth 2000, pp. 139–144; Sutin 2000, pp. 90–95; Kaczynski 2010, pp. 93–96; Churton 2011, pp. 76–78.

[52] Booth 2000, pp. 144–147; Sutin 2000, pp. 94–98; Kaczynski 2010, pp. 96–98; Churton 2011, pp. 78–83.

[53] Booth 2000, pp. 148–156; Sutin 2000, pp. 98–104; Kaczynski 2010, pp. 98–108; Churton 2011, p. 83.

[54] Booth 2000, pp. 159–163; Sutin 2000, pp. 104–108; Kaczynski 2010, pp. 109–115; Churton 2011, pp. 84–86.

[55] Booth 2000, pp. 164–167; Sutin 2000, pp. 105–107; Kaczynski 2000, pp. 112–113; Churton 2011, p. 85.

[56] Booth 2000, pp. 171–177; Sutin 2000, pp. 110–116; Kaczynski 2010, pp. 119–124; Churton 2011, pp. 89–90.

[57] Booth 2000, pp. 181–182; Sutin 2000, pp. 118–120; Kaczynski 2010, p. 124; Churton 2011, p. 94.

[58] Booth 2000, pp. 182–183; Sutin 2000, pp. 120–122; Kaczynski 2010, pp. 124–126; Churton 2011, pp. 96–98.

[59] Booth 2000, pp. 184–188; Sutin 2000, pp. 122–125; Kaczynski 2010, pp. 127–129.

[60] Booth 2000, pp. 184–188; Sutin 2000, pp. 125–133.

[61] Booth 2000, p. 188; Sutin 2000, p. 139; Kaczynski 2010, p. 129.

[62] Booth 2000, pp. 189, 194–195; Sutin 2000, pp. 140–141; Kaczynski 2010, p. 130; Churton 2011, p. 108.

[63] Booth 2000, pp. 195–196; Sutin 2000, p. 142; Kaczynski 2010, p. 132; Churton 2011, p. 108.

[64] Booth 2000, p. 190; Sutin 2000, p. 142; Kaczynski 2010, pp. 131–133.

[65] Booth 2000, pp. 241–242; Sutin 2000, pp. 177–179; Kaczynski 2010, pp. 136–137, 139, 168–169.

[66] Booth 2000, pp. 201–215; Sutin 2000, pp. 149–158; Kaczynski 2010, pp. 138–149; Churton 2011, pp. 111–112.

[67] Booth 2000, pp. 217–219; Sutin 2000, pp. 158–162; Kaczynski 2010, pp. 151–152.

[68] Booth 2000, p. 221; Sutin 2000, pp. 162–163; Churton 2011, p. 114.

[69] Spence 2008, pp. 33–35; Churton 2011, p. 115.

[70] Booth 2000, pp. 221–232; Sutin 2000, pp. 164–169; Kaczynski 2010, pp. 153–154; Churton 2011, pp. 115–118.

[71] Booth 2000, pp. 232–235; Sutin 2000, pp. 169–171; Kaczynski 2010, pp. 155–156; Churton 2011, pp. 118–121.

[72] Booth 2000, pp. 235–236, 239; Sutin 2000, pp. 171–172; Kaczynski 2010, pp. 159–160; Churton 2011, p. 121.

[73] Booth 2000, p. 246; Sutin 2000, p. 179; Kaczynski 2010, pp. 159–160, 173–174.

[74] Booth 2000, pp. 236–237; Sutin 2000, pp. 172–173; Kaczynski 2010, pp. 159–160; Churton 2011, p. 125.

[75] Booth 2000, pp. 239–240; Sutin 2000, pp. 173–174; Kaczynski 2010, pp. 157–160.

[76] Booth 2000, pp. 240–241; Sutin 2000, pp. 173, 175–176; Kaczynski 2010, p. 179; Churton 2011, p. 128.

[77] Booth 2000, pp. 251–252; Sutin 2000, p. 181; Kaczynski 2010, p. 172.

[78] Kaczynski 2010, pp. 173–175.

[79] Sutin 2000, pp. 195–196; Kaczynski 2010, pp. 189–190; Churton 2011, pp. 147–148.

[80] Booth 2000, p. 243.

[81] Booth 2000, pp. 249–251; Sutin 2000, p. 180; Churton 2011, pp. 129–136.

[82] Booth 2000, p. 252.

[83] Booth 2000, pp. 255–262; Sutin 2000, pp. 184–187; Kaczynski 2010, pp. 179–180; Churton 2011, pp. 129–130, 142–143.

[84] Booth 2000, pp. 267–268; Sutin 2000, pp. 196–198; Churton 2011, pp. 146–147.

[85] Booth 2000, pp. 244–245; Sutin 2000, pp. 179, 181; Kaczynski 2010, pp. 176, 191–192; Churton 2011, p. 131.

[86] Booth 2000, pp. 246–247; Sutin 2000, pp. 182–183; Churton 2011, p. 141.

[87] Booth 2000, pp. 254–255; Churton 2011, p. 172.

[88] Kaczynski 2010, p. 178.

[89] Booth 2000, pp. 247–248; Sutin 2000, p. 175; Kaczynski 2010, p. 183; Churton 2011, p. 128.

[90] Crowley 1983. p. 32.

[91] Booth 2000, pp. 263–264; Kaczynski 2010, pp. 172–173; Churton 2011, p. 146.

[92] Sutin 2000, p. 207; Kaczynski 2010, pp. 185–189.

[93] Booth 2000, pp. 265–267; Sutin 2000, pp. 192–193; Kaczynski 2010, pp. 183–184; Churton 2011, p. 144.

[94] Booth 2000, pp. 270–272; Sutin 2000, pp. 198–199; Kaczynski 2010, pp. 182–183, 194; Churton 2011, p. 148.

[95] Booth 2000, pp. 274–282; Sutin 2000, pp. 199–204; Kaczynski 2010, pp. 193–203; Churton 2011, pp. 149–152.

[96] Booth 2000, pp. 282–283; Sutin 2000, pp. 205–206; Kaczynski 2010, pp. 205–208; Churton 2011, p. 160.

[97] Booth 2000, pp. 283–284.

[98] Kaczynski 2010, pp. 210–211.

[99] Booth 2000, p. 285; Sutin 2000, pp. 206–207; Kaczynski 2010, pp. 211–213; Churton 2011, p. 160.

[100] Booth 2000, pp. 286–289; Sutin 2000, pp. 209–212; Kaczynski 2010, pp. 217–228; Churton 2011, pp. 161–162.

[101] Booth 2000, p. 289; Sutin 2000, p. 212; Kaczynski 2010, p. 225; Churton 2011, p. 163.

[102] Booth 2000, pp. 291–292; Sutin 2000, pp. 213–215; Kaczynski 2010, pp. 229–234; Churton 2011, p. 164.

[103] Booth 2000, pp. 293–294; Sutin 2000, p. 215; Kaczynski 2010, pp. 234; Churton 2011, p. 164.

[104] Booth 2000, pp. 289–290; Sutin 2000, pp. 213–214; Kaczynski 2010, pp. 229–230; Churton 2011, pp. 163–164.

[105] Sutin 2000, pp. 207–208; Kaczynski 2010, pp. 213–215; Churton 2011, pp. 158.

[106] Booth 2000, p. 297; Kaczynski 2010, pp. 235–237.

[107] Booth 2000, pp. 297–301; Sutin 2000, pp. 217–222; Kaczynski 2010, pp. 239–248; Churton 2011, pp. 165–166.

[108] Booth 2000, p. 301; Sutin 2000, pp. 222–224; Kaczynski 2010, pp. 247–250; Churton 2011, p. 166.

[109] Booth 2000, p. 302; Sutin 2000, pp. 224–225; Kaczynski 2010, p. 251.

[110] Booth 2000, pp. 302–305; Sutin 2000, pp. 225–226; Kaczynski 2010, pp. 251–255.

[111] Booth 2000, p. 306; Sutin 2000, p. 228; Kaczynski 2010, p. 256.

[112] Booth 2000, pp. 308–309; Sutin 2000, pp. 232–234; Kaczynski 2010, pp. 261–265.

[113] Booth 2000, pp. 309–310; Sutin 2000, pp. 234–235; Kaczynski 2010, p. 264.

[114] Churton 2011, pp. 178–182.

[115] Booth 2000, p. 307; Sutin 2000, p. 218; Kaczynski 2010, pp. 266–267.

[116] Booth 2000, pp. 313–316; Sutin 2000, pp. 235–240; Kaczynski 2010, pp. 269–274.

[117] Booth 2000, pp. 317–319; Sutin 2000, pp. 240–241; Kaczynski 2010, pp. 275–276.

[118] Booth 2000, p. 321.

[119] Booth 2000, pp. 321–322; Sutin 2000, p. 240; Kaczynski 2010, p. 277; Churton 2011, p. 186.

[120] Booth 2000, p. 322; Kaczynski 2010, p. 277.

[121] Booth 2000, p. 323; Sutin 2000, p. 241; Kaczynski 2010, p. 278; Churton 2011, pp. 187–189.

[122] Booth 2000, pp. 323–234; Kaczynski 2010, pp. 281–282, 294.

[123] Booth 2000, p. 325; Sutin 2000, pp. 243–244.

[124] Kaczynski 2010, p. 341.

[125] Booth 2000, pp. 326–330; Sutin 2000, pp. 245–247; Kaczynski 2010, pp. 283–284.

[126] Sutin 2000, p. 247; Churton 2011, p. 186.

[127] Sutin 2000, pp. 247–248; Spence 2008, pp. 67–76; Kaczynski 2010, pp. 284–287, 292–292; Churton 2011, pp. 190–193.

[128] Spence 2008, pp. 82–89; Churton 2011, pp. 195–197.

[129] Booth 2000, pp. 330–333; Sutin 2000, pp. 251–255; Kaczynski 2010, pp. 288–291, 295–297; Churton 2011, pp. 198–203.

[130] Booth 2000, p. 333; Sutin 2000, pp. 255–257; Kaczynski 2010, pp. 298–301.

[131] Booth 2000, pp. 333–335; Sutin 2000, pp. 257–261; Kaczynski 2010, pp. 304–209.

[132] Booth 2000, pp. 336–338; Sutin 2000, pp. 261–262; Kaczynski 2010, pp. 309–313.

[133] Booth 2000, p. 338; Sutin 2000, p. 263; Kaczynski 2010, pp. 313–316.

[134] Booth 2000, pp. 339–340; Sutin 2000, pp. 264–266; Kaczynski 2010, p. 320.

[135] Booth 2000, pp. 342–344; Sutin 2000, pp. 264–267; Kaczynski 2010, pp. 320–330.

[136] Booth 2000, pp. 344–345; Sutin 2000, pp. 267–272; Kaczynski 2010, pp. 330–331.

[137] Booth 2000, pp. 346–350; Sutin 2000, pp. 274–276; Kaczynski 2010, pp. 338–343.

[138] Booth 2000, pp. 344–345; Sutin 2000, pp. 274–276; Kaczynski 2010, pp. 340–341.

[139] Booth 2000, p. 351; Sutin 2000, p. 273; Kaczynski 2010, pp. 342–344.

[140] Booth 2000, pp. 351–352; Sutin 2000, p. 277; Kaczynski 2010, p. 347.

[141] Booth 2000, pp. 355–356; Sutin 2000, p. 278; Kaczynski 2010, p. 356; Churton 2011, p. 246.

[142] Booth 2000, p. 357; Sutin 2000, p. 277; Kaczynski 2010, p. 355.

[143] Booth 2000, pp. 356–360; Sutin 2000, pp. 278–279; Kaczynski 2010, pp. 356–358; Churton 2011, p. 246.

[144] Booth 2000, pp. 360–363; Sutin 2000, pp. 279–280; Kaczynski 2010, pp. 358–359; Churton 2011, pp. 246–248.

[145] Booth 2000, p. 365.

[146] Booth 2000, p. 368; Sutin 2000, p. 286; Kaczynski 2010, p. 361.

[147] Booth 2000, pp. 365–366; Sutin 2000, pp. 280–281; Kaczynski 2010, pp. 365, 372.

[148] Booth 2000, p. 367; Kaczynski 2010, p. 359.

[149] Booth 2000, pp. 366, 369–370; Sutin 2000, pp. 281–282; Kaczynski 2010, pp. 361–362; Churton 2011, pp. 251–252.

[150] Booth 2000, p. 368; Sutin 2000, pp. 286–287.

[151] Booth 2000, pp. 372–373; Sutin 2000, p. 285; Kaczynski 2010, pp. 365–366; Churton 2011, p. 252.

[152] Booth 2000, pp. 371–372; Sutin 2000, pp. 286–287; Kaczynski 2010, pp. 362–365, 371–372.

[153] Booth 2000, pp. 373–374; Sutin 2000, pp. 287–288; Kaczynski 2010, pp. 366–368.

[154] Booth 2000, pp. 376–378; Sutin 2000, pp. 293–294; Kaczynski 2010, pp. 373–376; Churton 2011, pp. 255–256.

[155] Booth 2000, p. 379; Sutin 2000, pp. 290–291; Kaczynski 2010, pp. 377–378; Churton 2011, pp. 258–259.

[156] Booth 2000, pp. 380–385; Sutin 2000, pp. 298–301; Kaczynski 2010, pp. 379–380, 384–387; Churton 2011, p. 259.

[157] Booth 2000, pp. 385–394; Sutin 2000, pp. 301–306; Kaczynski 2010, pp. 381–384, 397–392; Churton 2011, pp. 259–261.

[158] Booth 2000, pp. 394–395; Sutin 2000, pp. 307–308; Kaczynski 2010, pp. 392–394; Churton 2011, pp. 261–262.

[159] Booth 2000, pp. 395–396; Sutin 2000, p. 308; Kaczynski 2010, pp. 396–397; Churton 2011, pp. 263–264.

[160] Booth 2000, pp. 399–401; Sutin 2000, p. 310; Kaczynski 2010, p. 397; Churton 2011, p. 270.

[161] Booth 2000, p. 403; Sutin 2000, pp. 310–311; Kaczynski 2010, p. 398.

[162] Booth 2000, pp. 403–406; Sutin 2000, pp. 313–316; Kaczynski 2010, pp. 399–403; Churton 2011, pp. 270–273.

[163] Booth 2000, pp. 405–406; Sutin 2000, pp. 315–316; Kaczynski 2010, pp. 403–405; Churton 2011, pp. 273–274.

[164] Booth 2000, pp. 407–409; Sutin 2000, pp. 316–318; Kaczynski 2010, p. 405; Churton 2011, p. 274.

[165] Sutin 2000, p. 317; Kaczynski 2010, pp. 406–407; Churton 2011, pp. 281–282.

[166] Booth 2000, pp. 410–412; Sutin 2000, p. 319; Churton 2011, p. 287.

[167] Booth 2000, pp. 412–417; Sutin 2000, pp. 319–320; Kaczynski 2010, pp. 413–415; Churton 2011, pp. 287–288.

[168] Booth 2000, p. 418; Sutin 2000, pp. 323; Kaczynski 2010, p. 417; Churton 2011, p. 323.

[169] Booth 2000, pp. 419–420; Sutin 2000, p. 322; Kaczynski 2010, pp. 417–418; Churton 2011, p. 289.

[170] Booth 2000, pp. 423–424; Sutin 2000, pp. 324–328; Kaczynski 2010, pp. 418–419; Churton 2011, pp. 291–292, 332.

[171] Booth 2000, pp. 425–326; Sutin 2000, pp. 332–334; Kaczynski 2010, pp. 426–427, 430–433.

[172] Booth 2000, pp. 429–430.

[173] Booth 2000, p. 426; Sutin 2000, pp. 336–337; Kaczynski 2010, pp. 432–433; Churton 2011, p. 309.

[174] Booth 2000, pp. 427–428; Sutin 2000, pp. 335–335; Kaczynski 2010, pp. 427–429; Churton 2011, p. 299.

[175] Booth 2000, pp. 428–429; Sutin 2000, pp. 331–332; Kaczynski 2010, p. 423; Churton 2011, pp. 296–298; Pasi 2014, pp. 72–76.

[176] Booth 2000, p. 431; Sutin 2000, p. 339; Kaczynski 2010, pp. 428–429, 426; Churton 2011, pp. 308–309.

[177] Booth 2000, pp. 430–431; Sutin 2000, pp. 340–341; Kaczynski 2010, pp. 433–434; Churton 2011, p. 310.

[178] Booth 2000, pp. 432–433; Sutin 2000, p. 341; Kaczynski 2010, p. 438; Churton 2011, pp. 306, 312–314.

[179] Booth 2000, pp. 434–435; Sutin 2000, pp. 342, 345; Kaczynski 2010, p. 440; Churton 2011, p. 318.

[180] Booth 2000, pp. 436–437; Sutin 2000, p. 344; Kaczynski 2010, pp. 440–443; Churton 2011, p. 317.

[181] Booth 2000, pp. 438–439; Sutin 2000, p. 345; Kaczynski 2010, pp. 442, 447; Churton 2011, p. 321.

[182] Booth 2000, p. 439; Sutin 2000, pp. 351–354; Kaczynski 2010, p. 448; Churton 2011, pp. 333, 335.

[183] Booth 2000, p. 440; Sutin 2000, pp. 354–355; Kaczynski 2010, pp. 449–452; Churton 2011, pp. 336–337; Pasi 2014, pp. 95–116.

[184] Booth 2000, pp. 441–442; Sutin 2000, pp. 360–361; Kaczynski 2010, pp. 455–457; Churton 2011, pp. 337, 346–349.

[185] Booth 2000, p. 445; Sutin 2000, p. 360; Kaczynski 2010, p. 450; Churton 2011, p. 345.

[186] Sutin 2000, pp. 355–357.

[187] Sutin 2000, pp. 355; Kaczynski 2010, pp. 448–449; Churton 2011, pp. 335–336, 338–339.

[188] Booth 2000, pp. 445–446; Sutin 2000, p. 361; Kaczynski 2010, p. 457; Churton 2011, p. 349; Pasi 2014, pp. 83–88.

[189] The United Press (13 April 1934). "Confessed Genius Loses Weird Suit". *The Pittsburgh Press*. Retrieved 18 March 2013.

[190] Sutin 2000, p. 372.

[191] Booth 2000, p. 446; Churton 2011, pp. 355–356.

[192] Booth 2000, p. 453; Sutin 2000, pp. 366–367; Kaczynski 2010, pp. 470–471; Churton 2011, pp. 360–361.

[193] Sutin 2000, pp. 363–364; Kaczynski 2010, pp. 463–465; Churton 2011, p. 357.

[194] Booth 2000, pp. 447–453; Sutin 2000, pp. 367–373; Kaczynski 2010, pp. 466, 468, 472–481; Churton 2011, pp. 358–359, 361–362.

[195] Booth 2000, pp. 454–456; Sutin 2000, p. 374; Kaczynski 2010, pp. 483–484; Churton 2011, p. 363.

[196] Booth 2000, pp. 458–460; Sutin 2000, pp. 373–374; Kaczynski 2010, pp. 481, 489, 496; Churton 2011, pp. 362, 370.

[197] Booth 2000, pp. 461; Kaczynski 2010, pp. 489–490.

[198] Booth 2000, p. 467; Sutin 2000, pp. 380–381; Kaczynski 2010, pp. 490–491, 493, 497–499.

[199] Booth 2000, p. 467; Kaczynski 2010, pp. 495–496; Churton 2011, p. 369.

[200] Booth 2000, p. 466; Sutin 2000, p. 375.

[201] Booth 2000, pp. 468–469; Sutin 2000, pp. 375–380; Kaczynski 2010, pp. 384–385; Churton 2011, pp. 365–366.

[202] Booth 2000, pp. 471–472; Kaczynski 2010, pp. 506–507; Churton 2011, pp. 376–378.

[203] Kaczynski 2010, p. 511–512; Churton 2011, pp. 380–383, 392–396.

[204] Booth 2000, p. 476; Kaczynski 2010, p. 508.

[205] Kaczynski 2010, pp. 509–510; Churton 2011, p. 380.

[206] Kaczynski 2010, p. 527; Churton 2011, p. 403.

[207] Booth 2000, pp. 478–479; Kaczynski 2010, pp. 512, 531–532, 547; Churton 2011, pp. 408–409.

[208] Booth 2000, pp. 473–474; Kaczynski 2010, pp. 501, 503–504, 510, 522, 530–521; Churton 2011, pp. 370, 406.

[209] Kaczynski 2010, pp. 517–518, 522; Churton 2011, p. 397.

[210] Booth 2000, pp. 474–475; Kaczynski 2010, pp. 519–520, 542; Churton 2011, p. 410.

[211] Booth 2000, p. 474; Kaczynski 2010, p. 528; Churton 2011, p. 404.

[212] Booth 2000, p. 475; Kaczynski 2010, p. 530; Churton 2011, pp. 403–404.

[213] Churton 2011, pp. 407–408.

[214] Booth 2000, p. 475; Kaczynski 2010, pp. 532–533.

[215] Kaczynski 2010, p. 533–535; Churton 2011, pp. 409, 411.

[216] Booth 2000, p. 481; Kaczynski 2010, p. 540–541; Churton 2011, pp. 413–414.

[217] Kaczynski 2010, p. 542–544.

[218] Kaczynski 2010, p. 536–537; Churton 2011, p. 412.

[219] Kaczynski 2010, p. 544–555; Churton 2011, p. 416.

[220] Booth 2000, p. 483; Sutin 2000, pp. 417–419; Kaczynski 2010, p. 548; Churton 2011, pp. 417–418.

[221] Booth 2000, pp. 484–485; Kaczynski 2010, pp. 549–551; Churton 2011, p. 418.

[222] Pasi 2014, p. 23.

[223] Moore 2009, pp. 19–40.

[224] Owen 2012, p. 37.

[225] DuQuette 2003, pp. 14–21.

[226] DuQuette 2003, p. 12.

[227] Pasi 2014, p. 49.

[228] DuQuette 2003, p. 11.

[229] Churton 2011, p. 417.

[230] Bogdan & Starr 2012, p. 4.

[231] DuQuette 2003, pp. 2–3; Dyrendal 2012, pp. 369–370.

[232] DuQuette 2003, pp. 5–7.

[233] Booth 2000, p. 125.

[234] Spence 2008, p. 10.

[235] Sutin 2000, p. 148.

[236] DuQuette 2003, p. 9.

[237] Moore 2009, p. 33.

[238] Symonds 1997, p. vii.

[239] Pasi 2014, pp. 49–50.

[240] Pasi 2014, pp. 52–53.

[241] Morgan 2011, p. 166.

[242] Sutin 2000, p. 129; Churton 2011, p. 401; Pasi 2014, p. 48.

[243] Booth 2000, p. 109.

[244] Pasi 2014, p. 50.

[245] Booth 2000, p. 67; Spence 2008, p. 19.

[246] Booth 2000, p. 130.

[247] Kaczynski 2010, p. 91.

[248] Booth 2000, p. 350.

[249] Booth 2000, p. 63; Sutin 2000, p. 159.

[250] Booth 2000, p. 63.

[251] Sutin 2000, p. 128.

[252] Sutin 2000, p. 145.

[253] Sutin 2000, pp. 223–224.

[254] Sutin 2000, p. 2.

[255] Sutin 2000, p. 336.

[256] Booth 2000, pp. 268–269.

[257] Booth 2000, p. 137.

[258] Sutin 2000, p. 180.

[259] Booth 2000, p. 61.

[260] Sutin 2000, p. 28.

[261] Sutin 2000, p. 114.

[262] Churton 2011, p. 3.

[263] Cavendish 1977, pp. 167.

[264] Hanegraaff 2012, p. ix.

[265] Moore 2009, p. 5.

[266] Moore 2009, p. 40.

[267] Churton 2011, p. 88.

[268] Sutin 2000, p. 93.

[269] Bogdan & Starr 2012, p. 7.

[270] Landis 1995, pp. 26–34.

[271] Pilkington, Mark (15 May 2007). "Kenneth Anger: celluloid sorcery and psychedelic Satanism". *Bizarre Magazine*. Archived from the original on 5 December 2010. Retrieved 15 November 2010.

[272] Evans 2007, pp. 284–350.

[273] Evans 2007, pp. 229–283.

[274] Liturgical Calendar for Thelemic Gnosticism (unofficial)

[275] Hutton 2012, pp. 285–306.

[276] Richmond 2012, pp. 307–334.

[277] Urban 2012, pp. 335–368.

[278] Dyrendal 2012, pp. 369–394.

[279] "House of the unholy". *The Scotsman*. 23 November 2007. Retrieved 21 July 2015.

[280] Moreman 2003.

5.8.2 Sources

Bogdan, Henrik; Starr, Martin P. (2012). "Introduction". In Bogdan, Henrik; Starr, Martin P. *Aleister Crowley and Western Esotericism*. Oxford and New York: Oxford University Press. pp. 3–14. ISBN 978-0-19-986309-9.

Booth, Martin (2000). *A Magick Life: The Biography of Aleister Crowley*. London: Coronet Books. ISBN 978-0-340-71806-3.

Cavendish, Richard (1978). "Crowley and After". *A History of Magic*. London: Sphere Books. pp. 167–79.

Churton, Tobias (2011). *Aleister Crowley: The Biography*. London: Watkins Books. ISBN 978-1-78028-012-7.

Crowley, Aleister (1989). *The Confessions of Aleister Crowley: An Autohagiography*. London: Arkana. ISBN 978-0-14-019189-9.

DuQuette, Lon Milo (2003). *The Magick of Aleister Crowley: A Handbook of Rituals of Thelema*. San Francisco: Weiser. ISBN 978-1-57863-299-2.

Dyrendal, Asbjørn (2012). "Satan and the Beast: The Influence of Aleister Crowley on Modern Satanism". In Bogdan, Henrik; Starr, Martin P. *Aleister Crowley and Western Esotericism*. Oxford and New York: Oxford University Press. pp. 369–394. ISBN 978-0-19-986309-9.

Evans, Dave (2007). *The History of British Magick After Crowley*. n.p.: Hidden Publishing. ISBN 978-0-9555237-0-0.

Hanegraaff, Wouter J. (2012). "Foreword". In Bogdan, Henrik; Starr, Martin P. *Aleister Crowley and Western Esotericism*. Oxford and New York: Oxford University Press. pp. vii–x. ISBN 978-0-19-986309-9.

Hutton, Ronald (2012). "Crowley and Wicca". In Bogdan, Henrik; Starr, Martin P. *Aleister Crowley and Western Esotericism*. Oxford and New York: Oxford University Press. pp. 285–306. ISBN 978-0-19-986309-9.

Kaczynski, Richard (2010). *Perdurabo: The Life of Aleister Crowley* (2nd ed.). Berkeley, California: North Atlantic Books. ISBN 978-0-312-25243-4.

Landis, Bill (1995). *Anger: The Unauthorised Biography of Kenneth Anger*. New York: HarperCollins. ISBN 978-0-06-016700-4.

Moreman, Christopher M. (2003). "Devil Music and the Great Beast: Ozzy Osbourne, Aleister Crowley, and the Christian Right". *The Journal of Religion and Popular Culture* **3** (1).

Morgan, Mogg (2011). "The Heart of Thelema: Morality, Amorality, and Immorality in Aleister Crowley's Thelemic Cult". *The Pomegranate: The International Journal of Pagan Studies* **13** (2) (London: Equinox).

Moore, John (2009). *Aleister Crowley: A Modern Master*. Oxford: Mandrake. ISBN 978-1-906958-02-2.

Owen, Alex (2012). "The Sorcerer and His Apprentice: Aleister Crowley and the Magical Exploration of Edwardian Subjectivity". In Bogdan, Henrik; Starr, Martin P. *Aleister Crowley and Western Esotericism*. Oxford and New York: Oxford University Press. pp. 15–52. ISBN 978-0-19-986309-9.

Pasi, Marco (2014) [1999]. *Aleister Crowley and the Temptation of Politics*. Ariel Godwin (translator). Durham: Acumen. ISBN 978-1-84465-696-7.

Richmond, Keith (2012). "Through the Witch's Looking Glass: The Magick of Aleister Crowley and the Witchcraft of Rosaleen Norton". In Bogdan, Henrik; Starr, Martin P. *Aleister Crowley and Western Esotericism*. Oxford and New York: Oxford University Press. pp. 307–334. ISBN 978-0-19-986309-9.

Spence, Richard B. (2008). *Secret Agent 666: Aleister Crowley, British Intelligence and the Occult*. Port Townsend, WA: Feral House. ISBN 978-1-932595-33-8.

Sutin, Lawrence (2000). *Do What Thou Wilt: A Life of Aleister Crowley*. New York: St Martin's Press. ISBN 978-0-312-25243-4.

Symonds, John (1997). *The Beast 666: The Life of Aleister Crowley*. London: Pindar Press. ISBN 978-1-899828-21-0.

Tully, Caroline (2010). "Walk Like an Egyptian: Egypt as Authority in Aleister Crowley's Reception of *The Book of the Law*". *The Pomegranate: The International Journal of Pagan Studies* **12** (1) (London: Equinox).

Urban, Hugh B. (2012). "The Occult Roots of Scientology? L. Ron Hubbard, Aleister Crowley, and the Origins of a Controversial New Religion". In Bogdan, Henrik; Starr, Martin P. *Aleister Crowley and Western Esotericism*. Oxford and New York: Oxford University Press. pp. 335–368. ISBN 978-0-19-986309-9.

5.9   External links

- Works by Aleister Crowley at Project Gutenberg

- Works by or about Aleister Crowley at Internet Archive

- Works by Aleister Crowley at LibriVox (public domain audiobooks)

- Aleister Crowley Collection at the Harry Ransom Center at the University of Texas at Austin

- The Libri of Aleister Crowley Many of the writings of Crowley have been published for free online.

- Aleister Crowley Foundation Dedicated to perpetuating the teachings of Aleister Crowley and Thelema.

- Photos of the Abbey of Thelema in Cefalù Aleister Crowley and the Abbey of Thelema in Cefalù.

- *Perdurabo (Where is Aleister Crowley?)* A film on the Abbey of Thelema by Carlos Atanes.

Crowley in Golden Dawn garb

Crowley during the K2 Expedition

Kangchenjunga, as seen from Darjeeling

Crowley in ceremonial garb, 1912

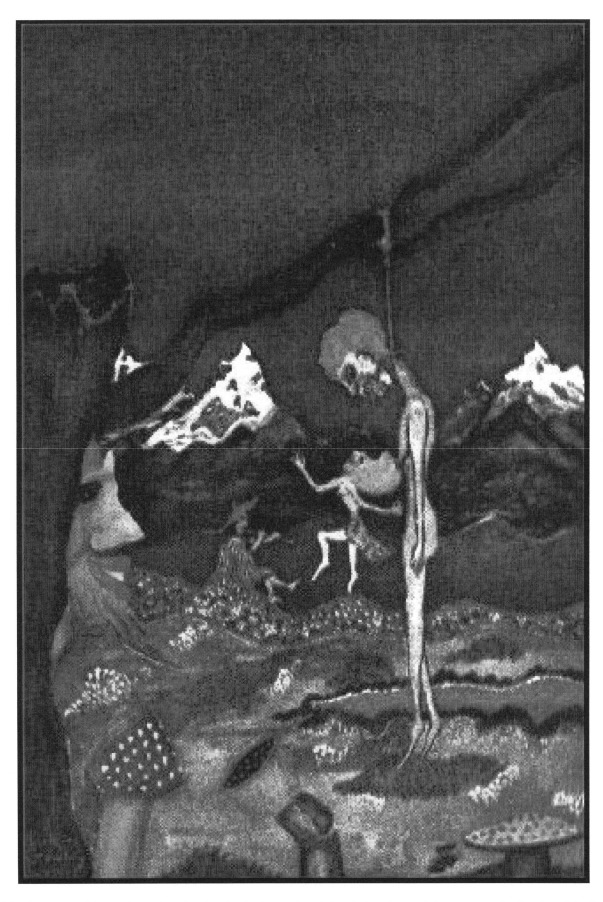

May Morn, *one of Crowley's paintings from his time in the US He explained it thus: "The painting represents the dawning of the day following a witches' celebration as described in* Faust. *The witch is hanged, as she deserves, and the satyr looks out from behind a tree."*[124]

The dilapidated Abbey of Thelema in 2004

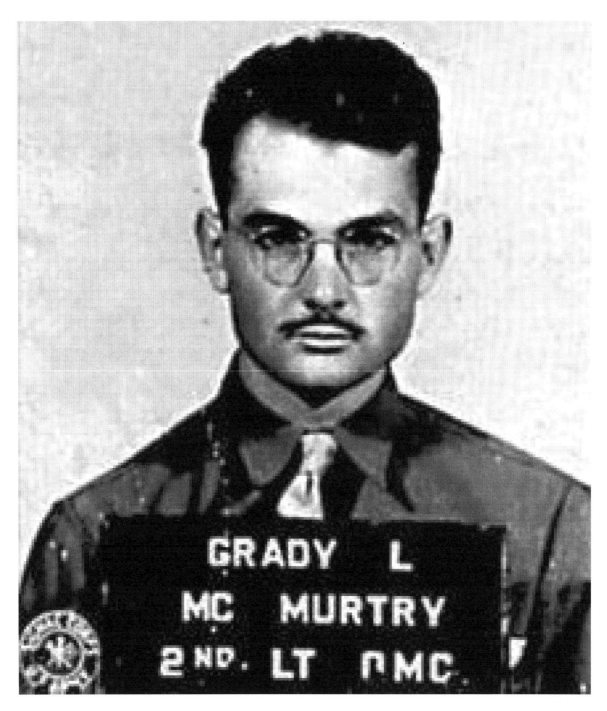

Crowley specified that Grady McMurtry succeed his chosen successor as Head of O.T.O., Karl Germer.

Aleister Crowley's rendition of the Unicursal Hexagram, the symbol of Thelema

Chapter 6

Lon Milo DuQuette

Lon Milo DuQuette, also known as **Rabbi Lamed Ben Clifford**,[1] is an American writer, lecturer, musician, and occultist, best known as an author who applies humor in the field of Western Hermeticism.

6.1 Biography

Born in Long Beach, California and raised in Columbus, Nebraska, he was an aspiring studio musician and recording artist in the 1970s, releasing two singles and an album, *Charley D. and Milo*, on the Epic Records label.[2] He and his partner Charles Dennis Harris (now Charley Packard), opened for Hoyt Axton, Arlo Guthrie and performed with Sammy Davis Jr.[3] In 1972, he quit the music business and for the next 25 years he pursued his interest in mysticism, particularly the work of Aleister Crowley (1875–1947). DuQuette began writing professionally in 1988 and has since published 16 books (translated in 12 languages).[4]

A 2005 gift of a ukelele re-ignited his interest in music. Two self released CD's and a new record contract followed. In 2012, DuQuette released *I'm Baba Lon* on Ninety Three Records, his first studio album in 40 years.[5] On September 3, 2012, Ninety Three released the follow-up, *Baba Lon II*.[6]

He is married to his high school sweetheart, Constance Jean Duquette. They live in Costa Mesa, California and have one son.[7]

6.2 Writings

DuQuette has written several successful books on Western mystical traditions including: Freemasonry, Tarot, Qabalah, ceremonial magic, the Enochian magic of Dr. John Dee, and spirit evocation, Goetia. He is perhaps best known as "an author who injects humor into the serious subjects of magick and the occult." [8] His autobiography, *My Life with the Spirits,* is currently a required text for two classes at DePaul University, Chicago.[9]

Many of DuQuette's books have been dedicated to analyzing and exploring the works of Aleister Crowley (1875–1947), an English occultist, author, poet and philosopher.

DuQuette occasionally appears on radio and television as a guest expert on subjects involving the occult.

He is on the faculty of the Omega Institute for Holistic Studies[10] in Rhinebeck, New York where he teaches *The Western Magical Tradition.*

6.3   Ordo Templi Orientis

Since 1975 DuQuette has been a National and International governing officer of Ordo Templi Orientis, a religious and fraternal organization founded in the early part of the 20th century. Since 1996 he has been O.T.O.'s United States Deputy Grand Master.[11] He is also an Archbishop of Ecclesia Gnostica Catholica, the ecclesiastical arm of O.T.O [12] and the longest living member of the O.T.O after the death of Phyllis Seckler.

6.4   Works

6.4.1   Books

- DuQuette, Lon Milo: & Aleister Crowley, Christopher Hyatt: *Enochian World of Aleister Crowley: Enochian Sex Magick*, New Falcon, 1991.

- DuQuette, Lon Milo: & Christopher Hyatt: *Sex Magic, Tantra & Tarot: The Way of the Secret Lover*, New Falcon, 1991.

- DuQuette, Lon Milo: & Aleister Crowley, Christopher Hyatt: *Aleister Crowley's Illustrated Goetia: Sexual Evocation*, New Falcon, 1992.

- DuQuette, Lon Milo: *Tarot of Ceremonial Magick: A Pictorial Synthesis of Three Great Pillars of Magick: Enochian, Goetia, Astrology*, Weiser Books, 1995.

- DuQuette, Lon Milo: *Angels, Demons & Gods of the New Millennium*, Weiser Books, 1997.

- DuQuette, Lon Milo: *My Life With the Spirits: The Adventures of a Modern Magician*, Weiser Books, 1999.

- DuQuette, Lon Milo: *The Chicken Qabalah of Rabbi Lamed Ben Clifford: Dilettante's Guide to What You Do and Do Not Need to Know to Become a Qabalist*, Weiser Books, 2001.

- DuQuette, Lon Milo: *The Magick of Aleister Crowley: A Handbook of the Rituals of Thelema*, Weiser Books, 2003.

- DuQuette, Lon Milo: *Understanding Aleister Crowley's Thoth Tarot*, Weiser Books, 2003.

- DuQuette, Lon Milo: *The Book Of Ordinary Oracles*, Weiser Books, 2005.

- DuQuette, Lon Milo: *The Key to Solomon's Key: Secrets of Magic and Masonry*, Ccc Publishing, 2006.

- DuQuette, Lon Milo: *Accidental Christ: The Story of Jesus as Told by His Uncle*, Thelema Aura Publishing, 2007.

- DuQuette, Lon Milo: *Enochian Vision Magick*, Weiser Books, 2008.

- DuQuette, Lon Milo: *Low Magick: It's All In Your Head... You Just Have No Idea How Big Your Head Is*, Llewellyn Publications, 2010.

- DuQuette, Lon Milo: *Ask Baba Lon: Answers to Questions of Life & Magick*, New Falcon Publications, 2011.

- DuQuette, Lon Milo & Bratkowsky, James M: "Revolt of the Magicians", Orobas Press, 2011.

- DuQuette, Lon Milo: "Homemade Magick: The Musings and Mischief of a Do-it-yourself Magus" Llewellyn Publications U.S., 2014.

6.4.2   Music

- *Charley D. And Milo—Charley D. Harris and Lon Milo Duquette*, Epic, 1970.

- *I'm Baba Lon*, Ninety Three Records, 2012.

- *Baba Lon II*, Ninety Three Records, 2012.

- *Gentle Heretic*, Ninety Three Records, 2013.

6.4.3   Other media

- *Lon Milo DuQuette's Enochian Magick - The Art of Angelic Evocation*, Hooded Man Productions. 1994.

- *Magical Egypt*, Cydonia, Inc. 2000.

- *Qabalah For the Rest of Us*, Cydonia, Inc. 2002.

- *The Great Work*, Cydonia, Inc. 2008.

- *Lon Milo DuQuette Live and Uncensored—Tarot Kabbalah & Oracles*, Cydonia, Inc. 2005.

- *The Call—Dieter Müh and Lon Milo Duquette*, HaemOccult, 2009.

6.5   See also

- William Breeze

- Richard Kaczynski

- Rodney Orpheus

- Lionel Snell

- James Wasserman

6.6   Notes

[1] "Lon Milo DuQuette: Author of Books On Magick and Mysticism". August 1, 2001. Retrieved 28 March 2012.

[2] Lon Milo DuQuette (January 4, 2011). *Every Little Thing He Does Is Magick*. Interview with Alan Corcoran. www.ocmusicscene. com. Retrieved March 29, 2012.

[3] Berg, Tom (March 7, 2012). "Singer comes back at 63; occult ties help". Orange County Register, p. 1

[4] Beers, Joel (March 8, 2012). "Magickal Mystery Tour". OC Weekly, p. 49

[5] Occult Expert and Author Returns to Musical Roots at the Chance Theater, Associated Press, February 22, 2012

[6] "Lon Milo DuQuette Releases New Song Collection". September 3, 2012. Retrieved 5 October 2012.

[7] DuQuette, Lon Milo (1999-06-01). *My Life With The Spirits: The Adventures of a Modern Magician*. Red Wheel / Weiser. ISBN 1-57863-120-3.

[8] "Lon Milo DuQuette". July 22, 2008. Retrieved 28 March 2012.

[9] Lon Milo DuQuette (April 5, 2010). *America's Occultist: An Interview with Lon Milo DuQuette*. Interview with Star Foster. Patheos. Retrieved March 29, 2012.

[10] "Lon Milo DuQuette - Omega Institute". Retrieved 2010-11-29.

[11] *Agape 1.3* (PDF), retrieved 2010-11-29

[12] Lon Milo DuQuette, *My Life With The Spirits: The Adventures of a Modern Magician* (Red Wheel/Weiser, 1999). ISBN 1-57863-120-3

6.7   References

- Duquette's Writers Net Profile

- PaganNews.com Interview with Lon Milo Duquette

- *Charley D. and Milo* Album

- *I'm Baba Lon* Compact Disc

- *Baba Lon II* Compact Disc

- *Gentle Heretic* Compact Disc

- OC Music Scene Interview

- *Baba Lon II* Release

6.8   External links

- Official website

Chapter 7

Ecclesia Gnostica Catholica

For other Gnostic churches, see Gnostic church (disambiguation).

Ecclesia Gnostica Catholica (**E.G.C.**), or the **Gnostic Catholic Church**, is the ecclesiastical arm of the Ordo Templi Orientis (O.T.O.), an international fraternal initiatory organization devoted to promulgating the Law of Thelema.

Thelema is a philosophical, mystical and religious system elaborated by Aleister Crowley, and based on *The Book of the Law*. The word *Catholic* denotes the universality of doctrine and not a Christian or Roman Catholic belief set.

The chief function of *Ecclesia Gnostica Catholica* is the public and private performance of the Gnostic Mass (*Liber XV*), a eucharistic ritual written by Crowley in 1913. According to William Bernard Crow, Crowley wrote the Gnostic Mass "under the influence of the Liturgy of St. Basil of the Russian Church".[1] Its structure is also influenced by the initiatory rituals of the *Ordo Templi Orientis*.[2] Its most notable separation from similar rites of other churches is a Priestess officiating with a Priest, Deacon, and two Children. In addition to the Eucharist, baptism, confirmation, marriage, and last rites are offered by E.G.C. Marriage is not limited to couples of opposite gender.[3]

About the Gnostic Mass, Crowley wrote in *The Confessions of Aleister Crowley*, "... the Ritual of the Gnostic Catholic Church ... I prepared for the use of the O.T.O., the central ceremony of its public and private celebration, corresponding to the Mass of the Roman Catholic Church."[4] It is the single most commonly performed ritual at O.T.O. bodies, with many locations celebrating the Mass monthly or more frequently. Most O.T.O. bodies make some or all of these celebrations open to interested members of the public, so the Mass is often an individual's first experience of the O.T.O.

Ecclesia Gnostica Catholica has a hierarchical structure of clergy, assisting officers, and laity which parallels the degree structure of the O.T.O. initiatory system. Before 1997, the two systems were more loosely correlated, but since then there have been strict rules concerning minimum O.T.O. degrees required to serve in particular E.G.C. roles.[5]

7.1 Membership

Membership in *Ecclesia Gnostica Catholica* is similar to the Roman Catholic Church, with some important differences. As currently constituted, E.G.C. includes both clergy and laity. Clergy must be initiate members of O.T.O., while laity may affiliate to E.G.C. through baptism and confirmation without undertaking any of the degree initiations of the Order.

Novice clergy are initiate members who participate in the administration of E.G.C. sacraments, although they have not yet taken orders (i.e., been through a ceremony of ordination).

The first ordination in E.G.C. is that of the diaconate. Second Degree initiates of O.T.O. who have been confirmed in E.G.C. can be ordained as Deacons, whose principal duties are to assist the Priesthood.

The sacerdotal ordination admits members to the priesthood. Sacerdotal ordinands must hold at least the K.E.W. degree of O.T.O., a degree only available by invitation. The Priesthood is responsible for administering the sacraments through the Gnostic Mass and other ceremonies as authorized by their supervising Bishops.

The Priesthood is supervised and instructed by the Episcopate, or Bishops. Full initiation to the Seventh Degree of O.T.O. includes episcopal consecration in E.G.C. The Tenth Degree Supreme and Holy King serves as the Primate or chief Bishop for any country in which O.T.O. has organized a Grand Lodge. The Frater (Soror) Superior of O.T.O. is also the Patriarch (Matriarch) of the Church, with ultimate authority over the clergy.

The similarity of the titles of the various E.G.C. offices and ranks reflects some common history with Christian churches. However, E.G.C. does not administer Christian sacraments, and has no Christian ecclesiastical standing.

7.2   Rituals

The principal ritual of *Ecclesia Gnostica Catholica* is the Gnostic Mass, a Eucharistic ceremony written by Aleister Crowley in 1913. Theodor Reuss produced and authorized a German translation in 1918.

The text of the Gnostic Mass makes reference to ceremonies of baptism, confirmation, and marriage. Crowley left some notes towards a baptism ritual, and his *"Liber CVI"* was written for use in a last rites circumstance. The Bishops of the contemporary Church have developed rituals for all of these purposes, as well as infant benedictions, exorcisms, consecration of holy oil, funerals, and home administration of the Eucharist to the sick.[6]

Although some Gnostic Masses are held privately for initiates only, there is nothing 'secret' about E.G.C. rituals as such, and they are commonly open to the public.

7.3   Saints of *Ecclesia Gnostica Catholica*

Main article: Saints of Ecclesia Gnostica Catholica

The Gnostic Saints of *Ecclesia Gnostica Catholica* are a series of historical and mythological figures revered in the religion of Thelema. They are found in the fifth Collect of Liber XV, titled "The Saints".

Two Gnostic Saints have been officially added to the original list. William Blake was so recognized based on a discovered writing by Aleister Crowley which described him as such.[7] Giordano Bruno was more recently added to the list.[8]

7.4   History

The *Ecclesia Gnostica Catholica* descended from a line of French Gnostic revival churches that developed in the 19th century. At that time, these Gnostic churches were essentially Christian in nature. In 1907, Gerard Encausse, Jean Bricaud and Louis-Sophrone Fugairon founded their own, simply called the Gnostic Catholic Church. In 1908, they gave O.T.O. Grand Master Theodor Reuss episcopal consecration and primatial authority in their GCC. Later that year, Reuss incorporated the Gnostic Catholic Church into O.T.O. after the original founders renamed their own church to the Universal Gnostic Church.

The name *"Ecclesia Gnostica Catholica"* was not applied to the church until Crowley wrote the Gnostic Mass in 1913, which Reuss proclaimed to be the church's official rite. This marked the first time an established church was to accept the Law of Thelema as its central doctrine. Reuss then announced a new title for himself: the "Sovereign Patriarch and Primate of the Gnostic Catholic Church".

In 1979, Hymenaeus Alpha X° (Grady McMurtry) separated *Ecclesia Gnostica Catholica* from *Ordo Templi Orientis*, and made it into an independent organization, with himself at the head of both. During this period of separation *Ecclesia Gnostica Catholica* published its own quarterly magazine.[9] However, in 1986, his successor, Hymenaeus Beta, dissolved the separate Gnostic Catholic Church corporation and folded the church back into O.T.O. Since then the Church has expanded greatly, and in recent years several books and articles dealing with the E.G.C. and the Gnostic Mass have been published by its Clergy, most notably by Tau Apiryon & Tau Helena,[10] James Wasserman & Nancy Wasserman,[11] Rodney Orpheus & Cathryn Orchard,[12] and T Polyphilus.[13]

7.5 The Gnostic Creed

A creed is a statement of belief—usually religious belief—or faith. The word derives from the Latin *credo* for "I believe". The creed of Ecclesia Gnostica Catholica—also known as the **Gnostic Creed**—is recited in the Gnostic Mass, during the Ceremony of the Introit.

The text of the Creed is as follows:

> I believe in one secret and ineffable LORD; and in one Star in the Company of Stars of whose fire we are created, and to which we shall return; and in one Father of Life, Mystery of Mystery, in His name CHAOS, the sole vicegerent of the Sun upon the Earth; and in one Air the nourisher of all that breathes.

> And I believe in one Earth, the Mother of us all, and in one Womb wherein all men are begotten, and wherein they shall rest, Mystery of Mystery, in Her name BABALON.

> And I believe in the Serpent and the Lion, Mystery of Mystery, in His name BAPHOMET.

> And I believe in one Gnostic and Catholic Church of Light, Life, Love and Liberty, the Word of whose Law is THELEMA.

> And I believe in the communion of Saints.

> And, forasmuch as meat and drink are transmuted in us daily into spiritual substance, I believe in the Miracle of the Mass.

> And I confess one Baptism of Wisdom whereby we accomplish the Miracle of Incarnation.

> And I confess my life one, individual, and eternal that was, and is, and is to come.

> AUMGN. AUMGN. AUMGN.

7.5.1 Explication of the Creed

The first six articles profess several beliefs by the congregants. The remaining two are confessions. The Creed ends with the Thelemic form of the Pranava, equivalent to the sacred Vedic syllable "Aum" or to the "Amen" of the Judaeo-Christian tradition. On the basic form of the Creed, Tau Apiryon and Helena (1998) write:

> The first 4 clauses are attributed to the four letters of Tetragrammaton YHVH: the Father (Chaos); the Mother (Babalon); the Union of Father and Mother in the Son (Baphomet); and the Daughter, the Bride of the Son (the Church). The two following clauses describe the essential products of the Mass from the perspective of the congregation. The final two clauses are in the form of confession rather than belief and describe parallels between the occurrences in the Mass and the life of the individual.

7.6 See also

- Gnosticism

- Gnosticism in modern times

7.7 Notes

[1] W. B. Crow quoted in T. Apiryon, Introduction to the Gnostic Mass.

[2] King, Francis (1973). *Secret Rituals of the O.T.O.* New York: Samuel Weiser. ISBN 0-87728-144-0

[3] "sabazius_x: Same-Sex Marriage". Retrieved 2009-11-01.

[4] Crowley, Aleister (1929). *The Spirit of Solitude: an autohagiography: subsequently re-Antichristened The Confessions of Aleister Crowley.* London: Mandrake Press.

[5] U.S. Grand Lodge: Membership in E.G.C.

[6] Sabazuis. "Rituals". *The Invisible Basilica.* Retrieved 2011-07-19.

[7] Helena and Tau Apiryon The Gnostic Mass: Annotations and Commentary (footnote). *Ordo Templi Orientis*, 2004.

[8] Sabazius. "From the Grand Master" in Agape, V. 9, No. 1, p. 3. Ordo Templi Orientis, May 1, 2007.

[9] "Ecclesia Gnostica: a bibliographical note". Retrieved 2009-11-25.

[10] T Apiryon; Helena (2001). *Mystery of Mystery: A Primer of Thelemic Ecclesiastical Gnosticism.* Red Flame (2nd ed.). Red Flame. ISBN 0-9712376-1-1.

[11] Wasserman, James; Nancy Wasserman; Aleister Crowley (2010-03-31). *To Perfect This Feast: The Gnostic Mass: Revised Second Edition* (2nd Revised ed.). Sekmet Books. ISBN 0-9718870-3-9.

[12] Huggens, Kim; Sorita d'Este; Emily Carding; Rodney Orpheus; Cathryn Orchard (2009-12-02). *From a Drop of Water - A Collection of Magickal Reflections on The Nature, Creatures, Uses and Symbolism of Water.* Avalonia. ISBN 978-1-905297-34-4.

[13] T Polyphilus. "Vigorous Food & Divine Madness". Retrieved 2011-07-19.

7.8 References

- Crowley, Aleister. Liber XV, The Gnostic Mass.

- Ordo Templi Orientis, U.S. Grand Lodge (2004). Ecclesia Gnostica Catholica. Retrieved January 3, 2005.

- Helena and Tau Apiryon. (1998). *The Creed of the Gnostic Catholic Church: an Examination.* Retrieved Sept. 20, 2004.

- Fr. HydraLVX. *The Gnostic Catholic Creed: Seeds of Self Knowledge*, appearing in *Lion & Serpent: The Official Journal of Sekhet-Maat Lodge* Volume 6, Number 2.

- Thelemapedia (2005). Ecclesia Gnostica Catholica. Retrieved June 9, 2005.

7.9 External links

- Ecclesia Gnostica Catholica homepage

- A Collection of Ecclesia Gnostica Catholica and Gnostic Mass Materials

Chapter 8

Gérard Encausse

Gérard Anaclet Vincent Encausse (July 13, 1865 - 25 October 1916), whose esoteric pseudonym was **Papus**, was the Spanish-born French physician, hypnotist, and popularizer of occultism, who founded the modern Martinist Order.

8.1 Early life

Gerard Encausse was born at Corunna (La Coruña) in Spain on July 13, 1865, of a Spanish mother and a French father, Louis Encausse, a chemist. His family moved to Paris when he was four years old, and he received his education there.

As a young man, Encausse spent a great deal of time at the Bibliothèque Nationale studying the Kabbalah, occult tarot, magic and alchemy, and the writings of Eliphas Lévi. He joined the French Theosophical Society shortly after it was founded by Madame Blavatsky in 1884 - 1885, but he resigned soon after joining because he disliked the Society's emphasis on Eastern occultism.

8.2 Career

8.2.1 Overview

In 1888, he co-founded his own group, the Kabbalistic Order of the Rose-Croix. That same year, he and his friend Lucien Chamuel founded the Librarie du Merveilleux and its monthly revue *L'Initiation*, which remained in publication until 1914.

Encausse was also a member of the Hermetic Brotherhood of Light and the Hermetic Order of the Golden Dawn temple in Paris, as well as Memphis-Misraim and probably other esoteric or paramasonic organizations, as well as being an author of several occult books. Outside of his paramasonic and Martinist activities he was also a spiritual student of the French spiritualist healer, Anthelme Nizier Philippe, "Maître Philippe de Lyon".

Despite his heavy involvement in occultism and occultist groups, Encausse managed to find time to pursue more conventional academic studies at the University of Paris. He received his Doctor of Medicine degree in 1894 upon submitting a dissertation on Philosophical Anatomy. He opened a clinic in the rue Rodin which was quite successful.

Encausse visited Russia three times, in 1901, 1905, and 1906, serving Tsar Nicholas II and Tsarina Alexandra both as physician and occult consultant. In October 1905, he allegedly conjured up the spirit of Alexander III, the Tsar Nicholas's father, who prophesied that the Tsar would meet his downfall at the hands of revolutionaries. Encausse's followers allege that he informed the Tsar that he would be able to magically avert Alexander's prophesy so long as Encausse was alive; Nicholas kept his hold on the throne of Russia until 141 days after Papus's death.

Although Encausse seems to have served the Tsar and Tsarina in what was essentially a shamanic capacity, he was later curiously concerned about their heavy reliance on occultism to assist them in deciding questions of government. During

their later correspondence, he warned them a number of times against the influence of Rasputin.

8.2.2 Involvement and influences

Levi, Tarot, and the Kabbalah

Encausse's early readings in tarot and the lore of the Kabbalah in translation was inspired by the occult writings of Eliphas Lévi, whose translation of the "Nuctemeron of Apollonius of Tyana" printed as a supplement to *Dogme et Rituel de la Haute Magie* (1855), provided Encausse with his *nom de plume*: "Papus" means "physician." [SOURCE NEEDED]

1891 l'Ordre des Supérieurs Inconnus

In 1891, Encausse claimed to have come into the possession of the original papers of Martinez Paschalis, or de Pasqually (c. 1700-1774), and therewith founded an Order of Martinists called l'Ordre des Supérieurs Inconnus. He claimed to have been given authority in the Rite of Saint-Martin by his friend Henri Vicomte de Laage, who claimed that his maternal grandfather had been initiated into the order by Saint-Martin himself, and who had attempted to revive the order in 1887. The Martinist Order was to become a primary focus for Encausse, and continues today as one of his most enduring legacies.

1893-1895 Bishop of l'Église Gnostique de France

In 1893, Encausse was consecrated a bishop of l'Église Gnostique de France by Jules Doinel, who had founded this Church as an attempt to revive the Cathar religion in 1890. In 1895, Doinel abdicated as Primate of the French Gnostic Church, leaving control of the Church to a synod of three of his former bishops, one of whom was Encausse.

1895 - 1888 The Golden Dawn; Kabbalistic Order of the Rose-Croix

In March 1895, Encausse joined the Ahathoor Temple of the Hermetic Order of the Golden Dawn in Paris.

Although Encausse claimed as his "spiritual master" the mysterious magician and healer known as "le Maitre Philippe" (Philippe Nizier), his first actual teacher in the intellectual aspects of occultism was the marquis Joseph Alexandre Saint-Yves d'Alveydre (1842 - 1910). Saint-Yves had inherited the papers of one of the great founders of French occultism, Antoine Fabre d'Olivet (1762 - 1825), and it was probably Saint-Yves who introduced Papus to the marquis Stanislas de Guaita (1861 - 1897).

In 1888, Encausse, Saint-Yves and de Guaita joined with Joséphin Péladan and Oswald Wirth to found the Rosicrucian *Kabbalistic Order of the Rose-Croix*.

1901 Questionable Anti-Zionist writings

In October 1901 Encausse collaborated with Jean Carrère in producing a series of articles in the *Echo de Paris* under the pseudonym *Niet* ("no" in Russian). In the articles Sergei Witte and Pyotr Rachkovsky were attacked, and it was suggested that there was a sinister financial syndicate trying to disrupt the Franco-Russian alliance. Encausse and Carrère predicted that this syndicate was a Jewish conspiracy, and the Anti-Zionist nature of these articles, compounded by Encausse's known connection to the Tsar of Russia, may have contributed to the false allegation that Papus was the author who forged The Protocols of the Elders of Zion.

1908 - 1913 Encausse, Reuss and paramasonry

Encausse never became a consistent (Grand Orient) Freemason. Despite this, he organized what was announced as an "International Masonic Conference" in Paris on June 24, 1908, and at this conference he first met Theodor Reuss, and the two men apparently exchanged patents:

Reuss elevated Encausse as X° of the Ordo Templi Orientis as well as giving him license to establish a "Supreme Grand Council General of the Unified Rites of Ancient and Primitive Masonry for the Grand Orient of France and its Dependencies at Paris." For his part, Encausse assisted Reuss in the formation of the O.T.O. Gnostic Catholic Church as a child of l'Église Gnostique de France, thus forming the E.G.C. within the tradition of French neo-gnosticism.

When John Yarker died in 1913, Encausse was elected as his successor to the office of Grand Hierophant (international head) of the Antient and Primitive Rites of Memphis and Mizraim.

8.3   Death

When World War I broke out, Encausse joined the French army medical corps. While working in a military hospital, he contracted tuberculosis and died in Paris on October 25, 1916, at the age of 51.

8.4   Partial bibliography

The written works of Papus (Gerard Encausse) include:

- Papus (Gerard Encausse). *L'Occultisme Contemporain.* 1887. PDF scans from Gallica

- Papus (Gerard Encausse). *L'Occultisme.* 1890.

- Papus (Gerard Encausse). *La Science Des Mages.* 1892. PDF scans from Gallica

- Papus (Gerard Encausse). *Anarchie, Indolence et Synarchie.* 1894. PDF scans from Gallica

- Papus (Gerard Encausse). *Le Diable et l'occultisme.* 1895.

- Papus (Gerard Encausse). *Traite Méthodique De La Magie Pratique.* 1898. PDF scans from Gallica

- Niet (Gerard Encausse and Jean Carrère). *La Russie Aujourd'hui.* 1902.

- Papus (Gerard Encausse). *La Kabbale.* 1903.

- Papus (Gerard Encausse). *Le Tarot Divinataire.* 1909. PDF scans from Internet Archive

8.5   See also

8.6   External links

- T. Apiryon, brief biography

- Complete bibliography of the writings of Papus

Chapter 9

Gerald Gardner (Wiccan)

This article is about the English Wiccan. For other notable figures with the same name, see Gerald Gardner. "Scire" redirects here. For the Italian submarines, see Italian submarine Scirè.

Gerald Brosseau Gardner (1884–1964), also known by the craft name **Scire**, was an English Wiccan, as well as an author and an amateur anthropologist and archaeologist. He was instrumental in bringing the Contemporary Pagan religion of Wicca to public attention, writing some of its definitive religious texts and founding the tradition of Gardnerian Wicca.

Born into an upper-middle-class family in Blundellsands, Lancashire, Gardner spent much of his childhood abroad in Madeira. In 1900, he moved to colonial Ceylon, and then in 1911 to Malaya, where he worked as a civil servant, independently developing an interest in the native peoples and writing papers and a book about their magical practices. After his retirement in 1936, he traveled to Cyprus, penning the novel *A Goddess Arrives* before returning to England. Settling down near the New Forest, he joined an occult group, the Rosicrucian Order Crotona Fellowship, through which he claimed to have encountered the New Forest coven into which he was initiated in 1939. Believing the coven to be a survival of the pre-Christian Witch-Cult discussed in the works of Margaret Murray, he decided to revive the faith, supplementing the coven's rituals with ideas borrowed from Freemasonry, ceremonial magic and the writings of Aleister Crowley to form the Gardnerian tradition of Wicca.

Moving to London in 1945, following the repeal of the Witchcraft Act of 1736 he became intent on propagating this religion, attracting media attention and writing about it in *High Magic's Aid* (1949), *Witchcraft Today* (1954) and *The Meaning of Witchcraft* (1959). Founding a Wiccan group known as the Bricket Wood coven, he introduced a string of High Priestesses into the religion, including Doreen Valiente, Lois Bourne, Patricia Crowther and Eleanor Bone, through which the Gardnerian community spread throughout Britain and subsequently into Australia and the United States in the late 1950s and early 1960s. Involved for a time with Cecil Williamson, Gardner also became director of the Museum of Magic and Witchcraft on the Isle of Man, which he ran until his death.

Gardner is internationally recognised as the "Father of Wicca" among the Pagan and occult communities. His claims regarding the New Forest coven have been widely scrutinised, with Gardner being the subject of investigation for historians and biographers such as Aidan Kelly, Ronald Hutton and Philip Heselton.

9.1 Early life

9.1.1 Childhood: 1884–99

Gardner's family was wealthy and upper middle class, running a family firm, Joseph Gardner and Sons, which described itself as "the oldest private company in the timber trade within the British Empire." Specialising in the import of hardwood, the company had been founded in the mid-18th century by Edmund Gardner (b. 1721), an entrepreneur who would subsequently become a Freeman of Liverpool.[1] Gerald's father, William Robert Gardner (1844–1935) had been the youngest son of Joseph Gardner (b. 1791), after whom the firm had been renamed, and who with his wife Maria had had five sons and three daughters. In 1867, William had been sent to New York City, in order to further the interests of the family firm. Here, he had met an American, Louise Burguelew Ennis, the daughter of a wholesale stationer; entering a relationship, they were married in Manhattan on 25 November 1868. After a visit to England, the couple returned to the US, where they settled in Mott Haven, Morrisania in New York State.[2] It was here that their first child, Harold Ennis Gardner, was born in 1870. At some point in the next two years they moved back to England, by 1873 settling into The Glen, a large Victorian house in Blundellsands in Lancashire, north-west England, which was developing into a wealthy suburb of Liverpool. It was here that their second child, Robert "Bob" Marshall Gardner, was born in 1874.[3]

In 1876 the family moved into one of the neighbouring houses, Ingle Lodge, and it was here that the couple's third son, Gerald Brosseau Gardner, was born on Friday 13 June 1884.[4][5] A fourth child, Francis Douglas Gardner, was then born in 1886.[6] Gerald would rarely see Harold, who went on to study Law at the University of Oxford, but saw more of Bob, who drew pictures for him, and Douglas, with whom he shared his nursery.[7][8] The Gardners employed an Irish nursemaid named Josephine "Com" McCombie, who was entrusted with taking care of the young Gerald; she would subsequently become the dominant figure of his childhood, spending far more time with him than his parents.[9][10] Gardner suffered with asthma from a young age, having particular difficulty in the cold Lancashire winters. His nursemaid offered to take him to warmer climates abroad at his father's expense in the hope that this condition would not be so badly affected.[9][11] Subsequently, in summer 1888, Gerald and Com traveled via London to Nice in the south of France.[12] After several more years spent in the Mediterranean, in 1891 they went to the Canary Islands, and it was here that Gardner first developed his lifelong interest in weaponry.[13][14] From there, they then went on to Accra in the Gold Coast (modern Ghana).[15][16] Accra was followed by a visit to Funchal on the Portuguese colony of Madeira; they would spend most of the next nine years on the island, only returning to England for three or four months in the summer.[17][18]

According to Gardner's first biographer, Jack Bracelin, Com was very flirtatious and "clearly looked on these trips as mainly manhunts", viewing Gardner as a nuisance.[15][19] As a result, he was largely left to his own devices, which he spent going out, meeting new people and learning about foreign cultures.[20] In Madeira, he also began collecting weapons, many of which were remnants from the Napoleonic Wars, displaying them on the wall of his hotel room.[21] As a result of his illness and these foreign trips, Gardner ultimately never attended school, or gained any formal education.[22] He taught himself to read by looking at copies of *The Strand Magazine* but his writing betrayed his poor education all his life, with highly eccentric spelling and grammar.[23][24] A voracious reader, one of the books that most influenced him at the time was Florence Marryat's *There Is No Death* (1891), a discussion of spiritualism, and from which he gained a firm belief in the existence of an afterlife.[25][26]

9.1.2   Ceylon and Borneo: 1900–11

In 1900, Com married David Elkington, one of her many suitors who owned a tea plantation in the British colony of Ceylon (modern Sri Lanka).[27][28] It was agreed with the Gardners that Gerald would live with her on a tea plantation named Ladbroke Estate in Maskeliya district, where he could learn the tea trade.[29][30] In 1901 Gardner and the Elkingtons lived briefly in a bungalow in Kandy, where a neighbouring bungalow had just been vacated by the occultists Aleister Crowley and Charles Henry Allan Bennett.[29][31] At his father's expense, Gardner trained as a "creeper", or trainee planter, learning all about the growing of tea; although he disliked the "dreary endlessness" of the work, he enjoyed being outdoors and near to the forests.[29][32] He lived with the Elkingtons until 1904, when he moved into his own bungalow and began earning a living working on the Non Pareil tea estate below the Horton Plains. He spent much of his spare time hunting deer and trekking through the local forests, becoming acquainted with the Singhalese natives and taking a great interest in their Buddhist beliefs.[33][34] In December 1904, his parents and younger brother visited, with his father asking him to invest in a pioneering rubber plantation which Gardner was to manage; located near the village of Belihil Oya, it was known as the Atlanta Estate, but allowed him a great deal of leisure time.[35][36] Exploring his interest in weaponry, in 1907 Gardner joined the Ceylon Planters Rifle Corps, a local volunteer force composed of European tea and rubber planters intent on protecting their interests from foreign aggression or domestic insurrection.[37][38]

In 1907 Gardner returned to Britain for several months' leave, spending time with his family and joining the Legion of Frontiersmen, a militia founded to repel the threat of German invasion.[39] During his visit, Gardner spent a lot of time with family relations known as the Sergenesons. Gardner became very friendly with this side of his family, whom his Anglican parents avoided because they were Methodists. According to Gardner, the Surgenesons readily talked about the paranormal with him; the patriarch of the family, Ted Surgeneson, believed that fairies were living in his garden and would say "I can often feel they're there, and sometimes I've seen them", though he readily admitted the possibility that it was all in his imagination.[40][41] It was from the Sergenesons that Gardner claimed to have discovered a family rumour that his grandfather, Joseph, had been a practicing witch, after being converted to the practice by his mistress.[42][43] Another unconfirmed family belief repeated by Gardner was that a Scottish ancestor, Grissell Gairdner, had been burned as a witch in Newburgh in 1610.[44]

Gardner returned to Ceylon in late 1907 and settled down to the routine of managing the rubber plantation. In 1910 he was initiated as an Apprentice Freemason into the Sphinx Lodge No. 107 in Colombo, affiliated with the Irish Grand Lodge. Gardner placed great importance on this new activity; In order to attend masonic meetings, he had to arrange a weekend's leave, walk 15 miles to the nearest railway station in Haputale, and then catch a train to the city. He entered into the second and third degrees of Freemasonry within the next month, but this enthusiasm seems also to have waned, and he resigned the next year, probably because he intended to leave Ceylon.[45][46] The experiment with rubber growing at the Atlanta Estate had proved relatively unsuccessful, and Gardner's father decided to sell the property in 1911, leaving Gerald unemployed.[47][48]

That year, Gardner moved to Borneo, gaining employment as a rubber planter at the Mawo Estate at Membuket. However, he did not get on well with the plantation's manager, a racist named R. J. Graham who had wanted to deforest the entire local area.[49][50] Instead Gardner became friendly with many of the locals, including the Dyak and Dusun people.[51][52] An amateur anthropologist, Gardner was fascinated by the indigenous way of life, particularly the local forms of weaponry such as the *sumpitan*.[53][54] He was intrigued by the tattoos of the Dayaks and pictures of him in later life show large snake or dragon tattoos on his forearms, presumably obtained at this time.[55] Taking a great interest in indigenous religious beliefs, Gardner told his first biographer that he had attended Dusun séances or healing rituals.[56][57] He was unhappy with the working conditions and the racist attitudes of his colleagues, and when he developed malaria he felt that this was the last straw; he left Borneo and moved to Singapore, in what was then known as the Straits Settlements, part of British Malaya.[58][59]

9.1.3 Malaya and World War I: 1911–26

Arriving in Singapore, he initially planned to return to Ceylon, but was offered a job working as an assistant on a rubber plantation in Perak, northern Malaya, and decided to take it, working for the Borneo Company.[60][61] Arriving in the area, he decided to supplement this income by purchasing his own estate, Bukit Katho, on which he could grow rubber; initially sized at 450 acres, Gardner purchased various pieces of adjacent land until it covered 600 acres.[62] Here, Gardner made friends with an American man known as Cornwall, who had converted to Islam and married a local Malay woman.[63][64] Through Cornwall, Gardner was introduced to many locals, whom he soon befriended, including members of the Senoi and Malay peoples. Cornwall invited Gardner to make the *Shahada*, the Muslim confession of faith, which he did; it allowed him to gain the trust of locals, although would he would never become a practicing Muslim. Cornwall was however an unorthodox Muslim, and his interest in local peoples included their magical and spiritual beliefs, to which he also introduced Gardner, who took a particular interest in the *kris*, a ritual knife with magical uses.[65]

In 1915, Gardner again joined a local volunteer militia, the Malay States Volunteer Rifles. Although between 1914 and 1918 World War I was raging in Europe, its effects were little felt in Malaya, apart from the 1915 Singapore Mutiny.[66][67] Gardner was keen to do more towards the war effort and in 1916 once again returned to Britain. He attempted to join the British Navy, but was turned down due to ill health.[42][68] Unable to fight on the front lines, he began working as an orderly in the Voluntary Aid Detachment (VAD) in the First Western General Hospital, Fazakerley, located on the outskirts of Liverpool. He was working in the VAD when casualties came back from the Battle of the Somme and he was engaged in looking after patients and assisting in changing wound dressings. He soon had to give this up when his malaria returned, and so decided to return to Malaya in October 1916 because of the warmer climate.[69][70]

He continued to manage the rubber plantation but after the end of the war, commodity prices dropped and by 1921 it was difficult to make a profit.[71] He returned again to Britain, in what later biographer Philip Heselton speculated might have been an unsuccessful attempt to ask his father for money.[72] Returning to Malaya, Gardner found that the Borneo Company had sacked him, and he was forced to find work with the Public Works Department.[73][74] In September 1923 he successfully applied to the Office of Customs to become a government-inspector of rubber plantations, a job that involved a great amount of traveling around the country, something he enjoyed.[75][76] After a brief but serious illness, the Johore government reassigned Gardner to an office in the Lands Office while he recovered, eventually being promoted to Principal Officer of Customs. In this capacity, he was made an Inspector of Rubber Shops, overseeing the regulation and sale of rubber in the country. In 1926 he was placed in charge of monitoring shops selling opium, noting regular irregularities and a thriving illegal trade in the controlled substance; believing opium to be essentially harmless, there is evidence indicating that Gardner probably took many bribes in this position, earning himself a small fortune.[77][78]

9.1.4   Marriage and archaeology: 1927–36

Gardner's mother had died in 1920, but he had not returned to Britain on that occasion.[79] However, in 1927 his father became very ill with dementia, and Gardner decided to visit him. On his return to Britain, Gardner began to investigate spiritualism and mediumship. He soon had several encounters which he attributed to spirits of deceased family members. Continuing to visit Spiritualist churches and séances, he was highly critical of much of what he saw, although he encountered several mediums he considered genuine. One medium apparently made contact with a deceased cousin of Gardner's, an event which impressed him greatly. His first biographer Jack Bracelin reports that this was a watershed in Gardner's life, and that a previous academic interest in spiritualism and life after death thereafter became a matter of firm personal belief for him.[80][81] The very same evening (28 July 1927) after Gardner had met this medium, he met the woman he was to marry; Dorothea Frances Rosedale, known as Donna, a relation of his sister-in-law Edith. He asked her to marry him the next day and she agreed. Because his leave was coming to an end very soon, they married quickly on 16 August at St Jude's Church, Kensington, and then honeymooned in Ryde on the Isle of Wight, before heading via France to Malaya.[82][83]

Arriving in the country, the couple settled into a bungalow at Bukit Japon in Johore Bahru.[84] Here, he once more became involved in Freemasonry, joining the Johore Royal Lodge No. 3946, but had retired from it by April 1931.[85] Gardner also returned to his old interests in the anthropology of Malaya, witnessing the magical practices performed by the locals, and he readily accepted a belief in magic.[86] During his time in Malaya, Gardner became increasingly interested in local customs, particularly those involved in folk magic and weapons. Gardner was not only interested in the anthropology of Malaya, but also in its archaeology. He began excavations at the city of Johore Lama, alone and in secret, as the local Sultan considered archaeologists little better than grave-robbers. Prior to Gardner's investigations, no serious archaeological excavation had occurred at the city, though he himself soon unearthed four miles of earthworks, and uncovered finds that included tombs, pottery, and porcelain dating from Ming China.[87][88] He went on to begin further excavations at the royal cemetery of Kota Tinggi, and the jungle city of Syong Penang.[89][90] His finds were displayed as an exhibit on the "Early History of Johore", at the National Museum of Singapore, and several beads that he had discovered suggested that trade went on between the Roman Empire and the Malays, presumably, Gardner thought, via India.[91] He also found gold coins originating from Johore and he published academic papers on both the beads and the coins.[92][93]

By the early 1930s Gardner's activities had moved from those exclusively of a civil servant, and he began to think of himself more as a folklorist, archaeologist and anthropologist.[89][94] He was encouraged in this by the director of the Raffles Museum (now the National Museum of Singapore) and by his election to Fellowship of the Royal Anthropological Institute in 1936.[94] En route back to London in 1932 Gardner stopped off in Egypt and, armed with a letter of introduction, joined Sir Flinders Petrie who was excavating the site of Tall al-Ajjul in Palestine.[95][96] Arriving in London in August 1932 he attended a conference on prehistory and protohistory at King's College London, attending at least two lectures which described the cult of the Mother Goddess.[97] He also befriended the archaeologist and practising Pagan Alexander Keiller, known for his excavations at Avebury, who would encourage Gardner to join in with the excavations at Hembury Hill in Devon, also attended by Aileen Fox and Mary Leakey.[98][99]

Returning to East Asia, he took a ship from Singapore to Saigon in French Indo-China, from where he traveled to Phnom Penh, visiting the Silver Pagoda. He then took a train to Hangzhou in China, before continuing onto Shanghai; because of the ongoing Chinese Civil War, the train did not stop throughout the entire journey, something that annoyed the passengers.[100] In 1935, Gardner attended the Second Congress for Prehistoric Research in the Far East in Manila, Philippines, acquainting himself with several experts in the field.[101] His main research interest lay in the Malay *kris* blade, which he unusually chose to spell "keris"; he eventually collected 400 examples and talked to natives about their magico-religious uses. Deciding to author a book on the subject, he wrote *Keris and Other Malay Weapons*, being encouraged to do so by anthropologist friends; it would subsequently edited into a readable form by Betty Lumsden Milne and published by the Singapore-based Progressive Publishing Company in 1936.[102][103] It was well received by literary and academic circles in Malaya.[104] In 1935, Gardner heard that his father had died, leaving him a bequest of £3,000. This assurance of financial independence may have led him to consider retirement, and as he was due for a long leave in 1936 the Johore

Civil Service allowed him to retire slightly early, in January 1936. Gardner wanted to stay in Malaya, but he conceded to his wife Donna, who insisted that they return to England.[105][106]

9.1.5 Return to Europe: 1936–38

In 1936, Gardner and Donna left Malaya and headed for Europe. She proceeded straight to London, renting them a flat at 26 Charing Cross Road.[107] Gardner visited Palestine, becoming involved in the archaeological excavations run by J.L. Starkey at Lachish. Here he grew particularly interested in a temple containing statues to both the male deity of Judeo-Christian theology and the pagan goddess Ashtoreth.[108] From Palestine, Gardner went to Turkey, Greece, Hungary, and Germany. He eventually reached England, but soon went on a visit to Denmark to attend a conference on weaponry at the Christiansborg Palace, Copenhagen, during which he gave a talk on the *kris*.[109]

Returning to Britain, he found that the climate made him sick, leading him to register with a doctor, Edward A.Gregg, who recommended that he try nudism. Hesitant at first, Gardner first attended an in-door nudist club, the Lotus League in Finchley, North London, where he made several new friends and felt that the nudity cured his ailment. When summer came, he decided to visit an outdoor nudist club, that of Fouracres near the town of Bricket Wood in Hertfordshire, which he soon began to frequent.[110] Through nudism, Gardner made a number of notable friends, including James Laver (1899–1975), who became the Keeper of Prints and Drawings at the Victoria and Albert Museum, and Cottie Arthur Burland (1905–1983), who was the Curator of the Department of Ethnography at the British Museum.[111] Biographer Philip Heselton suggested that through the nudist scene Gardner may have also met Dion Byngham (1896–1990), a senior member of the Order of Woodcraft Chivalry who propounded a Contemporary Pagan religion known as Dionysianism.[112] By the end of 1936, Gardner was finding his Charing Cross Road flat to be cramped, and moved into the block of flats at 32a Buckingham Palace Mansions.[113]

Fearing the cold of the English winter, Gardner decided to sail to Cyprus in late 1936, remaining there into the following year. Visiting the Museum in Nicosia, he studied the Bronze Age swords of the island, successfully hafting one of them, on the basis of which he wrote a paper entitled "The Problem of the Cypriot Bronze Dagger Hilt", which would subsequently be translated into both French and Danish, being published in the journals of the Société Préhistorique Française and the Vaabenhistorisk Selskab respectively.[114] Back in London, in September 1937, Gardner applied for and received a Doctorate of Philosophy from the Meta Collegiate Extension of the National Electronic Institute, an organisation based in Nevada that was widely recognised by academic institutions as offering invalid academic degrees via post for a fee. He would subsequently style himself as "Dr. Gardner", despite the fact that academic institutions would not recognise his qualifications.[115]

Planning to return to the Palestinian excavations the following winter, he was prevented from doing so when Starkey was murdered. Instead he decided to return to Cyprus. A believer in reincarnation, Gardner came to believe that he had lived on the island once before, in a previous life, subsequently buying a plot of land in Famagusta, planning to build a house on it, although this never came about.[116] Influenced by his dreams, he wrote his first novel, *A Goddess Arrives*, over the next few years. Revolving around an Englishman living in 1930s London named Robert Denvers who has recollections of a previous life as a Bronze Age Cypriot – an allusion to Gardner himself – the primary plot of *A Goddess Arrives* is set in ancient Cyprus and featured a queen, Dayonis, who practices sorcery in an attempt to help her people defend themselves from invading Egyptians. Published in late 1939, biographer Philip Heselton noted that the book was "a very competent first work of fiction", with strong allusions to the build-up which proceeded World War II.[117] Returning to London, he helped to dig shelter trenches in Hyde Park as a part of the build-up to the war, also volunteering for the Air Raid Wardens' Service.[118][119] Fearing the bombing of the city, Gardner and his wife soon moved to Highcliffe, just south of the New Forest in Hampshire. Here, they purchased a house built in 1923 named Southridge, situated on the corner of Highland Avenue and Elphinstone Road.[120]

9.2   Involvement in Wicca

9.2.1 The Rosicrucian Order: 1938–39

Main article: Rosicrucian Order Crotona Fellowship

In Highcliffe, Gardner came across a building describing itself as the "First Rosicrucian Theatre in England."[121] Having an interest in Rosicrucianism, a prominent magico-religious tradition within Western esotericism, Gardner decided to attend one of the plays performed by the group; in August 1939, Gardner took his wife to a theatrical performance based on the life of Pythagoras. An amateur thespian, she hated the performance, thinking the quality of both actors and script terrible, and she refused to go again.[122] Unperturbed and hoping to learn more of Rosicrucianism, Gardner joined the group in charge of running the theatre, the Rosicrucian Order Crotona Fellowship, and began attending meetings held in their local *ashram*. Founded in 1920 by George Alexander Sullivan, the Order had been based upon a blend of Rosicrucianism, Theosophy, Freemasonry and his own personal innovation, and had moved to Christchurch in 1930.[123]

As time went by, Gardner became critical of many of the Rosicrucian Order's practices; Sullivan's followers claimed that he was immortal, having formerly been the famous historical figures Pythagoras, Cornelius Agrippa and Francis Bacon. Gardner facetiously asked if he was also the Wandering Jew, much to the annoyance of Sullivan himself. Another belief held by the group that Gardner found amusing was that a lamp hanging from one of the ceilings was the disguised holy grail of Arthurian legend.[124] Gardner's dissatisfaction with the group grew, particularly when in 1939, one of the group's leaders sent a letter out to all members in which she stated that war would not come. The very next day, Britain declared war on Germany, greatly unimpressing the increasingly cynical Gardner.[125]

Alongside Rosicrucianism, Gardner had also been pursuing other interests. In 1939, Gardner joined the Folk-Lore Society; his first contribution to its journal *Folk-Lore*, appeared in the June 1939 issue and described a box of witchcraft relics that he believed had belonged to the 17th century "Witch-Finder General", Matthew Hopkins. Subsequently, in 1946 he would go on to become a member of the society's governing council, although most other members of the society were wary of him and his academic credentials.[126] Gardner would also join the Historical Association, being elected Co-President of its Bournemouth and Christchurch branch in June 1944, following which he became a vocal supporter for the construction of a local museum for the Christchurch borough.[127] He also involved himself in preparations for the impending war, joining the Air Raid Precautions (ARP) as a warden, where he soon rose to a position of local seniority, with his own house being assigned as the ARP post.[128] In 1940, following the outbreak of conflict, he also tried to sign up for the Local Defence Volunteers, or "Home Guard", but was turned away because he was already an ARP warden. He managed to circumvent this restriction by joining his local Home Guard in the capacity as armourer, which was officially classified as technical staff.[129] Gardner took a strong interest in the Home Guard, helping to arm his fellows from his own personal weaponry collection and personally manufacturing molotov cocktails.[130][131]

9.2.2 The New Forest coven: 1939–44

Main article: New Forest coven

Although sceptical of the Rosicrucian Order, Gardner got on well with a group of individuals inside the group who were "rather brow-beaten by the others, kept themselves to themselves."[132] Gardner's biographer Philip Heselton theorised that this group consisted of Edith Woodford-Grimes (1887–1975), Susie Mason, her brother Ernie Mason, and their sister Rosetta Fudge, all of whom had originally come from Southampton before moving to the area around Highcliffe, where they joined the Order.[132] According to Gardner, "unlike many of the others [in the Order], [they] had to earn their livings, were cheerful and optimistic and had a real interest in the occult". Gardner became "really very fond of them", remarking that he "would have gone through hell and high water even then for any of them."[133] In particular he grew close to Woodford-Grimes, being invited over to her home to meet her daughter, and the two helped each other with their writing, Woodford-Grimes probably assisting Gardner edit *A Goddess Arrives* prior to publication. Gardner would subsequently give her the nickname "Dafo", for which she would become better known.[134]

According to Gardner's later account, one night in September 1939 they took him to a large house owned by "Old Dorothy" Clutterbuck, a wealthy local woman, where he was made to strip naked and taken through an initiation ceremony. Halfway through the ceremony, he heard the word "Wica", and he recognised it as an Old English word for "witch". He was already acquainted with Margaret Murray's theory of the Witch-cult, and that "I then knew then that which I had thought burnt out hundreds of years ago still survived."[135] This group, he claimed, were the New Forest coven, and he believed them to be one of the few surviving covens of the ancient, pre-Christian Witch-Cult religion. Subsequent research by the likes of Hutton and Heselton has shown that in fact the New Forest coven was probably only formed in the mid-1930s, based upon such sources as folk magic and the theories of Margaret Murray.[136]

Gardner only ever described one of their rituals in depth, and this was an event that he termed "Operation Cone of Power". According to his own account, it took place in 1940 in a part of the New Forest and was designed to ward off the Nazis from invading Britain by magical means. Gardner claimed that a "Great Circle" was erected at night, with a "great cone of power" – a form of magical energy – being raised and sent to Berlin with the command of "you cannot cross the sea, you cannot cross the sea, you cannot come, you cannot come".[137]

9.2.3   Bricket Wood and the Origins of Gardnerianism: 1945–50

Throughout his time in the New Forest, Gardner had regularly travelled to London, keeping his flat at Buckingham Palace Mansions until mid-1939 and regularly visiting the Spielplatz nudist club there.[138] At Spielplatz he befriended Ross Nichols, whom he would later introduce to the Pagan religion of Druidry; Nichols would become enamoured with this faith, eventually founding the Order of Bards, Ovates and Druids.[139] However, following the war, Gardner decided to return permanently to London, moving into 47 Ridgemount Gardens, Bloomsbury in late 1944 or early 1945.[140] Continuing his interest in nudism, in 1945 he purchased a plot of land in Fouracres, a nudist colony near to the village of Bricket Wood in Hertfordshire that would soon be renamed Five Acres. As a result, he would become one of the major shareholders at the club, exercising a significant level of power over any administrative decisions and was involved in a recruitment drive to obtain more members.[141]

Between 1936 and 1939, Gardner befriended the Christian mystic J.S.M. Ward, proprietor of the Abbey Folk Park, Britain's oldest open-air museum. One of the exhibits was a 16th-century cottage that Ward had found near to Ledbury, Herefordshire and had transported to his park, where he exhibited it as a "witch's cottage". Gardner made a deal with Ward exchanging the cottage for Gardner's piece of land near to Famagusta in Cyprus. The witch's cottage was dismantled and the parts transported to Bricket Wood, where they were reassembled on Gardner's land at Five Acres. In Midsummer 1947 he held a ceremony in the cottage as a form of house-warming, which Heselton speculated was probably based upon the ceremonial magic rites featured in *The Key of Solomon* grimoire.[142]

Furthering his interest in esoteric Christianity, in August 1946 Gardner was ordained as a priest in the Ancient British Church, a fellowship open to anyone who considered themselves a monotheist. There is no evidence that Gardner ever took an active part in any of the Church's rituals.[143] Gardner also took an interest in Druidry, joining the Ancient Druid Order (ADO) and attending its annual Midsummer rituals at Stonehenge.[144] He also joined the Folk-Lore Society, being elected to their council in 1946, and that same year giving a talk on "Art Magic and Talismans". Nevertheless, many fellows – including Katherine Briggs – were dismissive of Gardner's ideas and his fraudulent academic credentials.[145] In 1946 he also joined the Society for Psychical Research.[146]

On May Day 1947, Gardner's friend Arnold Crowther introduced him to Aleister Crowley, the ceremonial magician who founded the religion of Thelema in 1904. Shortly before his death, Crowley elevated Gardner to the VII° of Ordo Templi Orientis (O.T.O.) and issued a charter decreeing that Gardner could perform its preliminary initiation rituals. The charter itself was written in Gardner's handwriting and only signed by Crowley.[147] From November 1947 to March 1948, Gardner and his wife toured the United States visiting relatives in Memphis, also visiting New Orleans, where Gardner hoped to learn about Voodoo.[148] During his voyage, Crowley had died, and as a result Gardner considered himself the head of the OTO in Europe, a position accepted by Lady Frieda Harris. Meeting Crowley's US successor, Karl Germer, in New York, Gardner however would soon lose interest in leading the OTO, and in 1951 he was replaced by Frederic Mellinger as the O.T.O's European representative.[149]

Gardner hoped to spread Wicca, and described some of its practices in a fictional form as *High Magic's Aid*. Set in the twelfth-century, Gardner included scenes of ceremonial magic based on *The Key of Solomon*. Published by the Atlantis Bookshop in July 1949, Gardner's manuscript has been edited into a publishable form by astrologer Madeline Montalban.[150] Privately, he had also begun work on a scrapbook known as "Ye Bok of Ye Art Magical", in which he wrote down a number of Wiccan rituals and spells. This would prove to be the prototype for what he later termed a Book of Shadows.[151] He also gained some of his first initiates, Barbara and Gilbert Vickers, who were initiated at some point between autumn 1949 and autumn 1950.[152]

9.2.4   Doreen Valiente and the Museum of Magic and Witchcraft: 1950–57

Gardner also came into contact with Cecil Williamson, who was intent on opening his own museum devoted to witchcraft; the result would be the Folk-lore Centre of Superstition and Witchcraft, opened in Castletown on the Isle of Man in 1951. Gardner and his wife moved to the island, where he took up the position of "resident witch".[153] On 29 July, *The Sunday Pictorial* published an article about the museum in which Gardner declared "Of course I'm a witch. And I get great fun out of it."[154] The museum was not a financial success, and the relationship between Gardner and Williamson deteriorated. In 1954, Gardner bought the museum from Williamson, who returned to England to found the rival Museum of Witchcraft, eventually settling it in Boscastle, Cornwall. Gardner renamed his exhibition the Museum of Magic and Witchcraft and continued running it up until his death.[155] He also acquired a flat at 145 Holland Road, near Shepherd's Bush in West London, but nevertheless fled to warmed climates during the winter, where his asthma would not be so badly affected, for instance spending time in France, Italy, and the Gold Coast.[156] From his base in London, he would frequent Atlantis bookshop, thereby encountering a number of other occultists, including Austin Osman Spare and Kenneth Grant, and he also continued his communication with Karl Germer until 1956.[157]

In 1952, Gardner had begun to correspond with a young woman named Doreen Valiente. She eventually requested initiation into the Craft, and though Gardner was hesitant at first, he agreed that they could meet during the winter at the home of Edith Woodford-Grimes. Valiente got on well with both Gardner and Woodford-Grimes, and having no objections to either ritual nudity or scourging (which she had read about in a copy of Gardner's novel *High Magic's Aid* that he had given to her), she was initiated by Gardner into Wicca on Midsummer 1953. Valiente went on to join the Bricket Wood Coven. She soon rose to become the High Priestess of the coven, and helped Gardner to rewrite his Book of Shadows, cutting out Crowley's influence.[158]

In 1954, Gardner published a non-fiction book, *Witchcraft Today*, containing a preface by Margaret Murray, who had published her theory of a surviving Witch-Cult in her 1921 book, *The Witch-Cult in Western Europe*. In his book, Gardner not only espoused the survival of the Witch-Cult, but also his theory that a belief in faeries in Europe was due to a secretive pygmy race that lived alongside other communities, and that the Knights Templar had been initiates of the Craft.[159] Alongside this book, Gardner began to increasingly court publicity, going so far as to invite the press to write articles about the religion. Many of these turned out very negatively for the cult; one declared "Witches Devil-Worship in London!", and another accused him of whitewashing witchcraft in his luring of people into covens. Gardner continued courting publicity, despite the negative articles that many tabloids were producing, and believed that only through publicity could more people become interested in witchcraft, so preventing the "Old Religion", as he called it, from dying out.[160]

Gardner's increasingly overt attempts at garnering media attention was one of the major reasons for rifts in his coven (and others). Many Witches felt he was threatening their traditional vows of secrecy and bringing about too much bad publicity, which in turn led to ostracism and job losses. Gardner introduced the Wiccan Laws to his coven, which drastically limited the powers of the High Priestess and even allowed the High Priest to call for the retirement of the High Priestess when he considered her too old. Valiente and other members of the coven were furious and left in disgust. Valiente herself said "we had had enough of the gospel according to Gerald, but we still believed that the ancient religion of Witchcraft had existed".

9.2.5   Later life and death

In 1960, Gardner's official biography, entitled *Gerald Gardner: Witch*, was published. It was written by a friend of his, the Sufi mystic Idries Shah, but used the name of one of Gardner's High Priests, Jack L. Bracelin, because Shah was wary about being associated with Witchcraft.[161][162] In May of that year, Gardner travelled to Buckingham Palace, where he enjoyed a garden party in recognition of his years of service to the Empire in the Far East. Soon after his trip, Gardner's wife Donna died, and Gardner himself once again began to suffer badly from asthma. The following year he, along with Shah and Lois Bourne, travelled to the island of Majorca to holiday with the poet Robert Graves, whose *The White Goddess* would play a significant part in the burgeoning Wiccan religion. In 1963, Gardner decided to go to Lebanon over the winter. Whilst returning home on the ship, *The Scottish Prince* on 12 February 1964, he suffered a fatal heart attack at the breakfast table. He was buried in Tunisia, the ship's next port of call, and his funeral was attended only by the ship's captain.[163] He was 79 years old.

Though having bequeathed the museum, all his artifacts, and the copyright to his books in his will to one of his High Priestess', Monique Wilson, she and her husband sold off the artefact collection to the American Ripley's Believe It or

Not! organisation several years later. Ripley's took the collection to America, where it was displayed in two museums before being sold off during the 1980s. Gardner had also left parts of his inheritance to Patricia Crowther, Doreen Valiente, Lois Bourne and Jack Bracelin,[164] the latter inheriting the Fiveacres Nudist Club and taking over as full-time High Priest of the Bricket Wood coven.

Several years after Gardner's death, the Wiccan High Priestess Eleanor Bone visited North Africa and went looking for Gardner's grave. She discovered that the cemetery he was interred in was to be redeveloped, and so she raised enough money for his body to be moved to another cemetery in Tunis,[165] where it currently remains. In 2007, a new plaque was attached to his grave, describing him as being "Father of Modern Wicca. Beloved of the Great Goddess".[166]

9.3 Personal life

Gardner only married once, to Donna, and several who knew him made the claim that he was devoted to her. Indeed, after her death in 1960, he began to again suffer serious asthma attacks. Despite this, as many coven members slept over at his cottage due to living too far away to travel home safely, he was known to cuddle up to his young High Priestess, Dayonis, after rituals.[167] The author Philip Heselton, who largely researched Wicca's origins, came to the conclusion that Gardner had held a long-term affair with Dafo, a theory expanded upon by Adrian Bott.[168] Those who knew him within the modern witchcraft movement recalled how he was a firm believer in the therapeutic benefits of sunbathing.[169] He also had several tattoos on his body, depicting magical symbols such as a snake, dragon, anchor and dagger.[170] In his later life he wore a "heavy bronze bracelet... denoting the three degrees... of witchcraft"[171] as well as a "large silver ring with... signs on it, which... represented his witch-name 'Scire', in the letters of the magical Theban alphabet."[171]

According to Bricket Wood coven member Fred Lamond, Gardner also used to comb his beard into a narrow barbiche and his hair into two horn like peaks, giving him "a somewhat demonic appearance".[172] Lamond thought that Gardner was "surprisingly lacking in charisma" for someone at the forefront of a religious movement.[172]

Gardner was a supporter of the right wing Conservative Party, and for several years had been a member of the Highcliffe Conservative Association, as well as being an avid reader of the pro-Conservative newspaper, the *Daily Telegraph*.[173]

9.4 Criticisms

In a 1951 interview with a journalist from the Sunday Pictorial newspaper, Gardner claimed to be a doctor of philosophy from Singapore and also to have a doctorate in literature from Toulouse.[174] Later investigation by Doreen Valiente suggested that these claims were false. The University of Singapore did not exist at that time and the University of Toulouse had no record of him receiving a doctorate. Valiente suggests that these claims may have been a form of compensation for his lack of formal education.[175]

Valiente further criticises Gardner for his publicity-seeking – or at least his indiscretion. After a series of tabloid exposés[176] some members of his coven proposed some rules limiting what members of the Craft should say to non-members. Valiente reports that Gardner responded with a set of Wiccan laws of his own, which he claimed were original but others suspected he had made up on the spot. This led to a split in the coven, with Valiente and others leaving.[177] She recounted many years after his death:

> With all his faults (and who among us is faultless?), Gerald was a great person, and he did great work in bringing back the Old Religion to many people. I am glad to have known him.[178]

9.5 Legacy

Commenting on Gardner, Pagan studies scholar Ethan Doyle White commented that "There are few figures in esoteric history who can rival him for his dominating place in the pantheon of Pagan pioneers."[179]

In 2012, Philip Heselton published a two-volume biography of Gardner, titled *Witchfather*. The biography was reviewed by Pagan studies scholar Ethan Doyle White in *The Pomegranate* journal, where he commented that it was "more exhaustive with greater detail" than Heselton's prior tomes and was "excellent in most respects".[180]

9.6   See also

- Ashrama Hall and Christchurch Garden Theatre

9.7   References

9.7.1   Footnotes

[1] Heselton 2012a, pp. 6–9.

[2] Heselton 2012a, pp. 11–18.

[3] Heselton 2012a, pp. 18–19, 23.

[4] Bracelin 1960, p. 13.

[5] Heselton 2012a, p. 28.

[6] Heselton 2012a, pp. 29.

[7] Bracelin 1960. p. 13.

[8] Heselton 2012a. p. 29.

[9] Bracelin 1960. p. 14.

[10] Heselton 2012a. pp. 29–31.

[11] Heselton 2012a. p. 32.

[12] Heselton 2012a. pp. 32–33.

[13] Bracelin 1960. p. 15.

[14] Heselton 2012a. pp. 33–34.

[15] Bracelin 1960. p. 17.

[16] Heselton 2012a. pp. 35–36.

[17] Bracelin 1960. p. 18.

[18] Heselton 2012a. p. 36.

[19] Heselton 2012a. pp. 34–35.

[20] Heselton 2012a. p. 39.

[21] Heselton 2012a. pp. 39–40.

[22] Heselton 2012a. p. 31.

[23] Bracelin 1960. p. 19.

[24] Heselton 2012a. p. 40.

[25] Bracelin 1960. pp. 19–20.

[26] Heselton 2012a. pp. 40–41.

[27] Bracelin 1960. p. 20.

[28] Heselton 2012a. pp. 43–44.

[29] Bracelin 1960. pp. 22–23.

[30] Heselton 2012a. pp. 44, 46.

[31] Heselton 2012a. pp. 47–48.

[32] Heselton 2012a. pp. 48–49.

[33] Bracelin 1960. pp. 27,30.

[34] Heselton 2012a. pp. 50–52.

[35] Bracelin 1960. pp. 28–29.

[36] Heselton 2012a. pp. 52–53.

[37] Bracelin 1960. p. 34.

[38] Heselton 2012a. pp. 55–56.

[39] Heselton 2012a. pp. 57–59.

[40] Bracelin 1960 p. 121.

[41] Heselton 2012a. pp. 59–62.

[42] Bracelin 1960. p. 123.

[43] Heselton 2012a. pp. 62–66.

[44] Heselton 2012a. pp. 3–4.

[45] Bracelin 1960. p. 35.

[46] Heselton 2012a. pp. 66–67.

[47] Bracelin 1960. p. 36.

[48] Heselton 2012a. pp. 67–68.

[49] Bracelin 1960. pp. 38–39.

[50] Heselton 2012a. pp. 70–71.

[51] Bracelin 1960. p. 43.

[52] Heselton 2012a. p. 71.

[53] Bracelin 1960. p. 44.

[54] Heselton 2012a. pp. 72–73.

[55] Heselton 2012a. p. 72.

[56] Bracelin 1960. pp. 45–48.

[57] Heselton 2012a. pp. 74–76.

[58] Bracelin 1960. p. 51.

[59] Heselton 2012a. pp. 76–77.

[60] Bracelin 1960. pp. 56, 60–61.

[61] Heselton 2012a. p. 81.

[62] Heselton 2012a. p. 85.

[63] Bracelin 1960. pp. 57–60.

[64] Heselton 2012a. pp. 82–83.

[65] Heselton 2012a. pp. 83–84, 91–95.

[66] Bracelin 1960. pp. 63–64.

[67] Heselton 2012a. pp. 85–86.

[68] Heselton 2012a. pp. 86–87.

[69] Bracelin 1960. pp. 123–124.

[70] Heselton 2012a. pp. 87–89.

[71] Heselton 2012a. p. 95.

[72] Heselton 2012a. pp. 95–96.

[73] Bracelin 1960. pp. 64–65.

[74] Heselton 2012a. p. 96.

[75] Bracelin 1960. pp. 65–66.

[76] Heselton 2012a. pp. 96–98.

[77] Bracelin 1960. pp. 66–74.

[78] Heselton 2012a. pp. 99–102.

[79] Bracelin 1960. p. 125.

[80] Bracelin 1960. pp. 125–133.

[81] Heselton 2012a. pp. 104–109 .

[82] Bracelin 1960. pp. 133–137.

[83] Heselton 2012a. pp. 109–114.

[84] Heselton 2012a. p. 117.

[85] Heselton 2012a. p. 122.

[86] Bracelin 1960. p. 59.

[87] Bracelin 1960. pp. 102–103.

[88] Heselton 2012a. pp. 118–121.

[89] Bracelin 1960. p. 104.

[90] Heselton 2012a. p. 119.

[91] Bracelin 1960. p. 106.

[92] Gardner, G.B. (1937) "Ancient Beads from the Johore River as Evidence of an Early Link by Sea between Malaya and the Roman Empire", *Journal of the Royal Asiatic Society*, Vol 69, pp. 467-470.

[93] Gardner, GB (1933) "Notes on some Ancient Gold Coins, from the Johore River", *Journal of the Malayan Branch of the Royal Asiatic Society*, Vol XI, Part II, pp. 171-176.

[94] Heselton 2012a. p. 123.

[95] Bracelin 1960. pp. 137–138.

[96] Heselton 2012a. pp. 124–126.

[97] Heselton 2012a. pp. 126–128.

[98] Bracelin 1960. p. 139.

[99] Heselton 2012a. pp. 126, 128.

[100] Heselton 2012a. p. 130.

[101] Heselton 2012a. pp. 130–132.

[102] Heselton 2012a. pp. 133–141.

[103] Gardner (1936).

[104] Heselton 2012a. pp. 140–145.

[105] Bracelin 1960. p. 142.

[106] Heselton 2012a. p. 139.

[107] Bracelin 1960, p. 152; Heselton 2012a, p. 150.

[108] Bracelin 1960, p. 149; Heselton 2012a, pp. 149–151.

[109] Bracelin 1960, pp. 150–152; Heselton 2012a, pp. 150–151.

[110] Heselton 2012a. pp. 152–154.

[111] Heselton 2012a. pp. 156–157.

[112] Heselton 2012a. pp. 158–159.

[113] Heselton 2012a. p. 161.

[114] Heselton 2012a. pp. 163–165.

[115] Heselton 2012a. p. 166.

[116] Heselton 2012a. p. 170.

[117] Heselton 2012a. pp. 169–181.

[118] Bracelin 1960. p. 159.

[119] Heselton 2012a. p. 183.

[120] Heselton 2012a. pp. 184–185, 188–189.

[121] Heselton 2012a. pp. 186–187.

[122] Bracelin 1960, p. 162; Heselton 2012a, pp. 187–188, 195–196.

[123] Heselton 2012a, pp. 196–198.

[124] Bracelin 1960, p. 163; Heselton 2012a, p. 198.

[125] Bracelin 1960. p. 164.

[126] Heselton 2012a, pp. 192–194, 333–336.

[127] Heselton 2012b. pp. 296–297.

[128] Heselton 2012a. p. 229.

[129] Heselton 2012a. pp. 229–234.

[130] Bracelin 1960. pp. 161–167.

[131] Heselton 2012a. p. 235.

[132] Heselton 2012a. p. 198.

[133] Bracelin 1960. p. 165.

[134] Heselton 2012a. pp. 199–200, 205.

[135] Heselton 2012a, pp. 207–215.

[136] Heselton 2012a, pp. 225–228.

[137] Bracelin 1960, p. 167; Heselton 2012a, pp. 237–251.

[138] Heselton 2012b. pp. 293–294.

[139] Heselton 2012b. pp. 295–296.

[140] Heselton 2012b, p. 298.

[141] Heselton 2012b. pp. 299–309.

[142] Valiente 1989, p. 56; Heselton 2012b, pp. 315–324.

[143] Heselton 2012b.

[144] Heselton 2012b, pp. 327–332..

[145] Heselton 2012b, pp. 332–338.

[146] Heselton 2012b, p. 339.

[147] Bracelin 1960, p. 171; Valiente 1989, p. 57; Heselton 2012b, pp. 341–362.

[148] Heselton 2012b, pp. 363–366.

[149] Heselton 2012b, pp. 366–371.

[150] Heselton 2012b, pp. 373–374, 377–399.

[151] Heselton 2012b, pp. 375–377.

[152] Heselton 2012b, pp. 403–409.

[153] Heselton 2012b, pp. 410–442.

[154] New Page 2

[155] Heselton 2012b, pp. 474–478, 480–483.

[156] Heselton 2012b, pp. 450–455, 457, 470–473, 478–480.

[157] Heselton 2012b, pp. 505–515.

[158] Heselton 2012b, pp. 490–494.

[159] Heselton 2012b, pp. 494–503.

[160] Valiente 1989, p. 67; Heselton 2012b, pp. 517–520.

[161] Fifty Years of Wicca, Frederic Lamond, 2004, page 19

[162] Dancing with Witches, Lois Bourne, 1998, page 29

[163] Gardner's Passing

[164] - "Other beneficiaries of his estate were Patricia C. Crowther and Jack L. Bracelin, who authored an authoritative biography of Gardner, Gerald Gardner: Witch (1960)."

[165] *The Rebirth of Witchcraft*, Doreen Valiente, page 44

[166] New Page 2

[167] Lamond 2004, p. 11.

[168] Heselton 2003, p. 26.

[169] Valiente 1989.

[170] "Dispatch", *The Wica*, UK.

[171] Valiente 1989, p. 38.

[172] Lamond 2004, p. 9.

[173] Heselton 2012a, p. 230.

[174] Andrews, Allen (29 June 1951), "Calling all Witches", *Sunday Pictorial* (UK: The Wica).

[175] Valiente 2007, pp. 41–42.

[176] Hawkins, Pater (12 June 1955), "No Witchraft is fun", *Sunday Pictorial* (UK: The Wica).

[177] Valiente 2007, pp. 69–72.

[178] Valiente 1989, p. 80.

[179] Doyle White 2012, p. 171.

[180] Doyle White 2012, p. 172.

9.7.2 Bibliography

- Bracelin, Jack (1960), *Gerald Gardner: Witch*, Octagon Press.

- Gardner, Gerald (1936), *Keris and other Malay Weapons*, Singapore: Progressive.

- ——— (1939), *A Goddess Arrives* (fiction).

- ——— (2010) [1949], *High Magic's Aid* (fiction), Aurinia Books, ISBN 978-0-9566182-0-7.

- ——— (1954), *Witchcraft Today*, Rider.

- ——— (1959), *The Meaning of Witchcraft*.

- ———, *The Story of the famous Witches Museum at Castletown, Isle of Man* (guidebook).

- Heselton, Philip (2000). *Wiccan Roots*. Capall Bann. ISBN 978-1-86163-110-7.

- ——— (2003), *Gerald Gardner and the Cauldron of Inspiration: An Investigation Into the Sources of Gardnerian Witchcraft*, Capall Bann, ISBN 978-1-86163-164-0.

- Heselton, Philip (2012a), *Witchfather: A Life of Gerald Gardner*, 1: Into the Witch Cult, Loughborough, Leicestershire: Thoth, ISBN 978-1-870450-80-5.

- Heselton, Philip (2012b). *Witchfather: A Life of Gerald Gardner. Vol 2: From Witch Cult to Wicca.* Loughborough, Leicestershire: Thoth. ISBN 978-1-870450-79-9

- Hutton, Ronald (1999). *The Triumph of the Moon: A History of Modern Pagan Witchcraft.* Oxford University Press. ISBN 978-0-19-285449-0.

- Ruickbie, Leo (2004). *Witchcraft Out of the Shadows.* Hale.

- Lamond, Frederic (2004), *Fifty Years of Wicca*, Green Magic, ISBN 978-0-9547230-1-9.

- Valiente, Doreen (2007) [1989], *The Rebirth of Witchcraft*, London: Robert Hale, ISBN 978-0-7090-8369-6.

9.8   External links

- GeraldGardner.com, an online reference resource

- Historical documents and media reports about Gardner

- Biography at Controverscial.com

- Biography at About.com

- The Gardnerian Book of Shadows

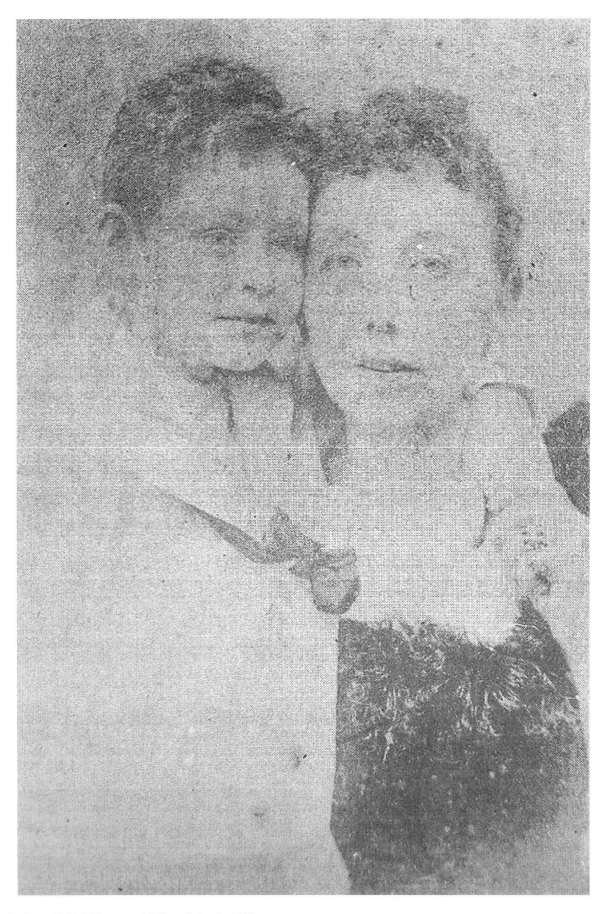

Gardner with his Irish nursemaid, Com, during the 1880s

While working in Borneo in 1911, Gardner eschewed the racist attitudes of his colleagues by befriending members of the Dayak indigenous community, fascinated by their magico-religious beliefs, tattoos and displays of weaponry.

A selection of kris *knives; Gardner took a great interest in such items, even authoring the definitive text on the subject,* Keris and Other Malay Weapons *(1936).*

A plaque erected to mark the house at Highcliffe where Gardner lived during the Second World War.

The Temple of the Rose Cross, *Teophilus Schweighardt Constantiens, 1618.*

The Mill House in Highcliffe, where Gardner was supposedly initiated into the Craft

The Witches' Cottage, where Gardner and his Bricket Wood coven performed their rituals

The Witches' Cottage in 2006

Chapter 10

Karl Germer

Karl Johannes Germer (22 January 1885 – 25 October 1962), also known as *Frater Saturnus*, was a German occultist and the successor of Aleister Crowley as the Outer Head of the Order (OHO) of Ordo Templi Orientis from 1947 until his death in 1962.[1] He was born in Elberfeld, Germany and died in West Point, California.

Germer studied in a university, worked as a military intelligence officer in the First World War and received first- and second class Iron Crosses for his service.[2] In 1923 he sold his Vienna property and founded the publishing house Pansophia Verlag in Munich. Germer stayed with his wife Maria at the Abbey of Thelema from January 10, 1926 until sometime in February.[3] In 1926, he moved to America with his wife and in 1927 founded the Thelema-Verlags-Gesellschaft, which published German versions of Crowley's works.[4]

Germer's visa gave out and he had to return to Germany in 1935. He was arrested by the Gestapo on 13 February 1935 for being an associate of the "High Grade Freemason Aleister Crowley".[5] He was first held at the Columbia-Haus in Berlin and was then moved to the Esterwegen concentration camp.[6]

As author and occultist Aleister Crowley's representative in Germany, Germer moved to America after being released from Nazi confinement. In 1942, Crowley appointed Germer as his successor, and he fulfilled that position after Crowley's death in 1947.[7]

10.1 References

[1] Melton, J. Gordon; Baumann, Martin (2010). *Religions of the World, Second Edition: A Comprehensive Encyclopedia of Beliefs and Practices*. ABC-CLIO. p. 2150. ISBN 1598842048.

[2] Kaczynski, Richard (2010). *Perdurabo: The Life of Aleister Crowley* (second edition). Berkeley, California: North Atlantic Books. ISBN 978-0-312-25243-4.

[3] Kaczynski 2010, p. 423

[4] Kaczynski 2010, p. 426

[5] Starr, Bro. Martin P. (1995). "Aleister Crowley: freemason!". In Gilbert, Robert A. *ARS QUATUOR CORONATORUM. Transactions of Quatuor Coronati Lodge N. 2076* (vol. 108 ed.). Frome and London: Butler & Tanner Ltd. pp. 150–161. ISBN 0-907655-32-7. Retrieved 2008-03-12.

[6] Churton, Tobias (2011). *Aleister Crowley: The Biography: Spiritual Revolutionary, Romantic Explorer, Occult Master and Spy*. Duncan Baird Publishers. ISBN 178028134X.

[7] Orpheus, Rodney (2009). "Gerald Gardner & Ordo Templi Orientis". *Pentacle Magazine* (30). pp. 14–18. ISSN 1753-898X.

Chapter 11

Kenneth Grant

For other people named Kenneth Grant, see Kenneth Grant (disambiguation).

Kenneth Grant (23 May 1924 – 15 January 2011) was an English ceremonial magician and prominent advocate of the Thelemite religion. A poet, novelist, and writer, with his wife Steffi Grant he founded his own Thelemite organisation, the Typhonian Ordo Templi Orientis, later renamed the Typhonian Order.

Born in Ilford, Essex, Grant took an interest in occultism in his teenage years. After several months serving in India with the British Army, he returned to Britain and became the personal secretary of Aleister Crowley, the ceremonial magician who had founded Thelema in 1904. Crowley taught Grant his esoteric practices, initiating him into his two active ceremonial magic orders, A∴A∴ and Ordo Templi Orientis (OTO). When Crowley died in 1947, Grant was seen as his heir apparent in Britain, and was appointed as such by the American head of the OTO, Karl Germer. Founding the New Isis Lodge in 1954, Grant added to many of Crowley's Thelemite teachings, bringing in extraterrestrial themes and influences from the work of H.P. Lovecraft. This was anathema to Germer, who excommunicated him from the OTO.

In 1949, Grant befriended the occult artist Austin Osman Spare. In 1969, Germer died and Grant proclaimed himself Outer Head of the OTO; this title was disputed by the American Grady McMurtry, who took control of the OTO in the U.S. Grant's Order became known as the Typhonian OTO, operating from his Golders Green home. In 1959 he began publishing on the subject of occultism, and proceeded to author the Typhonian Trilogies, as well as a number of novels, books of poetry, and publications devoted to propagating the work of Crowley and Spare.

Grant's writings and teachings have proved a significant influence over other British occultists. They also attracted academic interest within the study of western esotericism, particularly from Henrik Bogdan and Dave Evans.

11.1 Biography

11.1.1 Early life and Aleister Crowley: 1924–1947

Grant was born on 23 May 1928 in Ilford, Essex, the son of a Welsh clergyman.[1] By his early teenage years, Grant had read widely on the subject of western esotericism and eastern religions.[2] He had made use of a personal magical symbol ever since being inspired to do so in a visionary dream he experienced in 1939; he spelled its name variously as A'ashik, Oshik, or Aossic.[3] Aged 18, in the midst of the Second World War, Grant volunteered to join the British Army, later commenting that he hoped to be posted to British India, where he could find a spiritual guru to study under.[2] He was never posted abroad, and was ejected from the army aged 20 due to an unspecified medical condition.[4]

Grant was fascinated by the work of Aleister Crowley, having read a number of the occultist's books. Eager to meet Crowley, Grant unsuccessfully wrote to Crowley's publishers, asking them to give him his address; however, the publisher had moved address themselves, meaning that they never received his letter.[3] He also requested that Michael Houghton, proprietor of Central London's esoteric bookstore Atlantis Bookshop, introduce him to Crowley. Houghton refused, privately remarking that Grant was "mentally unstable."[3] Grant later stated his opinion that Houghton had refused because he didn't wish to "incur evil *karma*" from introducing the young man to Crowley,[5] but later suggested that it was because Houghton desired him for his own organisation, The Order of Hidden Masters, and thereby didn't want him to become Crowley's disciple.[6] Persisting, Grant wrote letters to the new address of Crowley's publishers, asking that they pass his letters on to Crowley himself.[7] These resulted in the first meeting between the two, in autumn 1944.[7]

After several further meetings and an exchange of letters, Grant agreed to work for Crowley as his secretary and personal assistant. Now living in relative poverty, Crowley was unable to pay Grant for his services in money, instead paying him in magical instruction.[8] In March 1945, Grant moved into a lodge cottage in the grounds of Netherwood, a Sussex boarding house where Crowley was living.[9] He continued living there with Crowley for several months, dealing with the old man's correspondences and needs. In turn, he was allowed to read from Crowley's extensive library on occult subjects, and performed ceremonial magic workings with him, becoming a high initiate of Crowley's magical group, the Ordo Templi Orientis (OTO).[10] Crowley saw Grant as his potential successor, writing in his diary, "value of Grant. If I die or go to the USA, there must be a trained man to take care of the English OTO."[10] However, they also argued, with Grant trying to convince Crowley to relocate to London.[11] On one occasion Crowley shouted at him: "You are the most consummate BORE that the world has yet known. And this at 20!"[11]

Grant's family disliked that he was working for no wage, and pressured him to resign, which he did in June 1945, leaving Netherwood.[10] Crowley wrote to Grant's father, stating that he was "very sorry to part with Kenneth" and that he felt that Grant was "giving up his real future."[10] To David Curwen, an OTO member who was another of his correspondents, he related his opinion that "I may have treated him too severely."[12] Crowley put Curwen in contact with Grant, with Grant later asserting that he learned much from Curwen, particularly regarding the Kaula school of Tantra; in his later writings he made reference to Curwen using his Order name of Frater Ani Abthilal.[13] Although they continued to correspond with one another, Crowley and Grant never met again, for the former died in December 1947.[14] Grant attended his funeral at Brighton crematorium along with his wife Steffi.[15]

11.1.2   The New Isis Lodge and Austin Osman Spare: 1947–1969

Steffi Grant met the occult artist Austin Osman Spare in 1949, shortly before introducing him to Kenneth.[16] At the time, Spare had fallen into poverty, living in obscurity in a South London flat. Although making some money as an artist and art tutor, he was largely financially supported by his friend Frank Letchford, whom he affectionately referred to as his "son".[16] There was some animosity between Letchford and Grant, although it is apparent that Spare preferred the former, having known him for 12 years longer, and placing him first in his will.[17] Grant desired a closer relationship, and in 1954 began signing his letters to Spare "thy son."[17] Letchford claimed that Spare often told the Grants "white lies... to boost a flagging ego."[18]

Grant had continued studying Crowley's work, and a year after Crowley's death was acknowledged as a Ninth Degree member of the OTO by Karl Germer, Crowley's successor as Head of the OTO.[19] Grant then successfully applied to Germer for a charter to operate the first three OTO degrees and run his own lodge, which was granted in March 1951.[20][21] As this would mean that his lodge would be the only chartered OTO body in England at the time, Grant believed that it meant that he was now head of the OTO in Britain.[19] Germer put Grant in contact with Wilfred Talbot Smith, an English Thelemite based in California who had founded the Agape Lodge, knowing that Smith was the only man who had practical knowledge of the OTO degree work. Smith was eager to help, and wrote an length on his experiences in founding a lodge, although he was made uneasy by Grant's magical seal of "Aossic" for reasons that have never been ascertained, and their correspondence soon petered out.[22]

In 1954, Grant began the work of founding the New Isis Lodge. The lodge became operational in April 1955 when Grant issued a manifesto announcing his discovery of an extraterrestrial "Sirius/Set current" upon which the lodge was to be based.[23] Germer however deemed it "blasphemy" that Grant had identified a single planet with Nuit, the goddess associated with infinite space in Thelemic theology. On 20 July 1955, Germer issued a "Note of Expulsion" expelling Grant from the O.T.O.,[24][21] and naming Noel Fitzgerald as the leader of the British section of the Order.[25] Grant however ignored Germer's letter of expulsion, continuing to operate the New Isis Lodge under the claim that he had powers from the "Inner Plane".[19] Upon learning of Grant's expulsion, Smith feared that the OTO would split up into warring factions much as the Theosophical Society had done following the death of Helena Blavatsky.[26] Grant's Lodge continued to operate until 1962.[27]

Grant believed that the OTO's sex magic teachings needed to be refashioned along tantric principles from India. This was part of his growing interest in Asian religious traditions; in the 1950s he became a follower of Bhagavan Sri Ramana Maharshi, "the Sage of Arunchala", and from 1953 to 1961 immersed himself in the study of Hinduism, authoring articles on Advaita Vedanta for Indian journals like the Bombay-based *The Call Divine*.[28]

After both Crowley and Spare's death, Grant began to focus more on his own writing career.[29] From 1959 to 1963, Grant published the *Carfax Monographs*, a series of short articles on magic published in ten installments, each at a limited print run of 100. They would eventually be assembled together and published as *Hidden Lore* in 1989.[29]

In 1969, Grant co-edited *The Confessions of Aleister Crowley* for publication with Crowley's literary executor John Symonds.[30] At this point, Grant began describing himself as O.H.O. (Outer Head of the Order) of Ordo Templi Orientis, asserting that he deserved this title not by direct succession from Crowley but because he displayed the inspiration and innovation that Germer lacked.[30] A document purportedly by Crowley naming Grant as his successor was subsequently exposed as a hoax created by Robert Taylor, a Typhonian OTO member.[31] His competing organisation was commonly called the "Typhonian" Ordo Templi Orientis, but is now officially renamed the Typhonian Order. The *New Isis Lodge* was absorbed into Grant's Order in 1962.[21]

11.1.3   Publications and growing fame: 1970–2011

In 1972, Grant published the first book in his "Typhonian Trilogies" series, *The Magical Revival*, in which he discussed various historic events in Western esotericism and also encouraged future interest in the subject.[32] He followed this with a sequel published in 1973, *Aleister Crowley and the Hidden God*, in which he examined Crowley's sex magick practices and the Tantra.[33] This was followed in 1975 by *Cults of the Shadow*, which brought the first Typhonian Trilogy to an end with a discussion of the Left Hand Path in magic, making reference to both Crowley and Spare's work, as well as to Voodoo and Tantra.[33] That same year, Grant also published *Images and Oracles of Austin Osman Spare*, a collection of his late friend's images based on 20 years of research. The volume did not sell well, with much of the stock being remaindered, although became a rare collector's item in later years.[33]

Of all OHO contenders, [Grant] made the greatest effort to expand and build upon Crowley's work rather than confine himself to the letter of the law. During the 1970s, he was only one of a handful of people editing material by Crowley and Austin Spare, and he was practically alone in offering new contributions to the literature of magick. While his system differs considerably from Crowley's, he gets high marks for originality."

– Crowley biographer Richard Kaczynski, 2010.[30]

In 1977, Grant began the second Typhonian Trilogy with *Nightside of Eden*, in which he discussed some of his own personal magical ideas, outlining magical formulae with which to explore a dark, dense realm that he variously called 'Universe B' and 'the Tunnels of Set', conceived as a 'dark side' of the Qabalistic Tree of Life. Grant made connections between this realm and the extramundane deities of H.P. Lovecraft's horror fiction. The book proved controversial among occultists and Thelemites, and starkly divided opinion.[34] The sequel appeared in 1980 as *Outside the Circles of Time*, and introduced Grant's thoughts on the relevance of Ufology and insectoid symbolism for occultism.[35] This would prove to be the final Grant volume published by Muller, and his next book would not appear for another eleven years.[35]

In 1991, Skoob Books published Grant's *Remembering Aleister Crowley*, a volume containing his memoirs of Crowley alongside reproductions of diary entries, photographs, and letters.[35] In the next few years, Skoob reissued a number of Grant's earlier books,[35] and in 1992 published the sixth volume in the Typhonian Trilogies, *Hecate's Fountain*, in which Grant provided many anecdotes about working in the New Isis Lodge and focused on describing accidents and fatalities that he believed were caused by magic.[36] The seventh volume of the Typhonian Trilogies, *Outer Gateways*, followed in 1994, discussing Grant's ideas of older Typhonian traditions from across the world, with reference to the work of Crowley, Spare, and H.P. Lovecraft. It ends with the text of *The Wisdom of S'lba*, a work that Grant claimed he had received clairvoyantly from a supernatural source.[37]

Switching to the Typhonian OTO's own imprint, Starfire, as a publisher, in 1997 he published his first novel, *Against the Light: A Nightside Narrative*, which involved a character also named "Kenneth Grant". He asserted that the work was "quasi-autobiographical", but never specified which parts ere based on his life and which were fictional.[37] In 1998, Starfire published a book co-written by Grant and his wife Steffi, titled *Zos Speaks! Encounters with Austin Osman*

Spare, in which they included 7 years' worth of diary entries, letters, and photographs pertaining to their relationship with the artist.[38] The following year, the next volume in the Typhonian Trilogies, *Beyond the Mauve Zone* was published, explaining Grant's ideas on a realm known as the Mauve Zone that he claimed to have explored.[39] A book containing two novellas, *Snakewand and the Darker Strain*, was published in 2000, while the final volume of the Typhonian Trilogies, *The Ninth Arch*, was published in 2003. It offered further Qabalistic interpretations of the work of Crowley, Spare, and Lovecraft, and the text of another work that Grant claimed had been given to him from a supernatural source, *Book of the Spider*.[39] That same year, Grant also published two further volumes of fictional stories, *Gamaliel and Dance, Doll, Dance!*, which told the story of a vampire and a Tantric sex group, and *The Other Child, and Other Tales*, which contained six short stories.[40]

Grant died on 15 January 2011 after a period of illness.[1]

11.2   Personal life

Grant was largely reclusive;[2] however, he was married for many years to his artist wife Steffi who worked magick with him.

11.3   Legacy

Historian Dave Evans noted that Grant was "certainly unique" in the history of British esotericism because of his "close dealings" with Crowley, Spare, and Gardner, the "three most influential Western occultists of the 20th century."[41] The occultist and comic book author Alan Moore thought it "hard to name" any other living individual who "has done more to shape contemporary western thinking with regard to Magic" than Grant,[42] thinking him "a schoolboy gone berserk on brimstone aftershave."[43]

The historian of Western esotericism Henrik Bogdan thought that Grant was "perhaps (the) most original and prolific English author of the post-modern occultist genre."[44] Grant was a significant influence over various ceremonial magical traditions, including chaos magic.[2]

Occult writer Peter Levenda discussed Grant's work in his 2013 book, *The Dark Lord*. Here, he asserted that Grant's importance was in attempting to create "a more global character for Thelema" by introducing ideas from Indian Tantra, Yezidism, and Afro-Caribbean syncretic religions.[45]

11.4   Bibliography

Grant published his work over a period of five decades, providing both a synthesis of Crowley and Spare's work and new, often idosyncratic interpretations of them.[41] Evans described Grant as having "an often confusing, oblique, and sanity-challenging writing style" that blends fictional stories with accounts of real-life people.[2]

11.4.1   The Typhonian Trilogies

11.4.2   Other works on the occult

- *Remembering Aleister Crowley* Skoob Books, 1992. ISBN 1-871438-12-8

- *Zos Speaks! Encounters with Austin Osman Spare*, Fulgur Limited, 1998.

- *Images and Oracles of Austin Osman Spare*, Fulgur Limited, 2003.

- *Borough Satyr, The Life and Art of Austin Osman Spare*, (includes a contribution from Steffi Grant), Fulgur Limited, 2005.

- *At the Feet of the Guru: Twenty Five Essays*, Starfire Publications, 2006. ISBN 0-9543887-6-3

- *Hidden Lore: The Carfax Monographs* by Kenneth & Steffi Grant, Fulgur Limited, 2006.

- *Dearest Vera* Holograph letters from Austin Osman Spare to Vera Wainwright, edited by Kenneth & Steffi Grant, Fulgur Limited, 2010.

11.4.3 Poetry

- *The Gulls Beak*

- *Black to Black*

- *Convolvulus*

11.4.4 Novellas and short stories

- *The Stellar Lode*

- *Against the Light* ISBN 0-9527824-1-3

- *Snakewand and the Darker Strain* ISBN 0-9527824-7-2

- *The Other Child and other tales*

- *Gamaliel Diary of a Vampire and Dance, Doll, Dance* ISBN 0-9543887-2-0

11.5 References

11.5.1 Footnotes

[1] O'Neill 2011.

[2] Evans 2007, p. 285.

[3] Evans 2007, p. 286; Kaczynski 2010, p. 533.

[4] Evans 2007, p. 285; Kaczynski 2010, p. 533.

[5] Grant 1980, p. 87.

[6] Grant 1991, p. 1; Kaczynski 2010, p. 533.

[7] Evans 2007, p. 286.

[8] Evans 2007, p. 286; Kaczynski 2010, p. 533–534.

[9] Evans 2007, p. 286; Kaczynski 2010, p. 534.

[10] Evans 2007, p. 287.

[11] Kaczynski 2010, p. 534.

[12] Evans 2007, p. 288.

[13] Bogdan 2013, pp. 188–189.

[14] Evans 2007, p. 289.

[15] Evans 2007, p. 289; Kaczynski 2010, p. 549.

[16] Evans 2007, p. 293.

[17] Evans 2007, pp. 293–294.

[18] Evans 2007, p. 297.

[19] Bogdan 2013, p. 196.

[20] Starr 2003, p. 324; Kaczynski 2010, p. 555; Bogdan 2013, p. 196.

[21] Koenig, P.R. (1991). *Kenneth Grant and the Typhonian Ordo Templi Orientis.*

[22] Starr 2003, p. 324.

[23] Starr 2003, p. 324; O'Neill 2011.

[24] Starr 2003, pp. 324–325; Kaczynski 2010, p. 556; Bogdan 2013, p. 196.

[25] Orpheus, Rodney (2009). "Gerald Gardner & Ordo Templi Orientis". *Pentacle Magazine* (30). pp. 14–18. ISSN 1753-898X.

[26] Starr 2003, p. 325.

[27] Bogdan 2013, p. 197.

[28] Bogdan 2013, pp. 196–197.

[29] Evans 2007, p. 306.

[30] Kaczynski 2010, p. 557.

[31] Staley 2008, p. 121.

[32] Evans 2007, pp. 306–307.

[33] Evans 2007, p. 307.

[34] Evans 2007, pp. 307–308.

[35] Evans 2007, p. 308.

[36] Evans 2007, pp. 308–309.

[37] Evans 2007, p. 309.

[38] Evans 2007, pp. 309–310.

[39] Evans 2007, p. 310.

[40] Evans 2007, pp. 310–311.

[41] Evans 2007, p. 284.

[42] Moore 2002, p. 162.

[43] Moore 2002, p. 156.

[44] Bogdan 2003, p. viii.

[45] Levenda 2013, p. 60.

11.5.2 Bibliography

Baker, Phil (2011). *Austin Osman Spare: The Life and Legend of London's Lost Artist*. London: Strange Attractor Press. ISBN 978-1907222016.

Bogdan, Henrik (2003). *Kenneth Grant: A Bibliography from 1948*. Gothenburg: Academia Esoterica.

Bogdan, Henrik (2013). "Reception of Occultism in India: The Case of the Holy Order of Krishna". *Occultism in a Global Perspective*. Henrik Bogdan and Gordan Djurdjevic (editors). Durham: Acumen. pp. 177–201. ISBN 978-1844657162.

Evans, Dave (2004). "Trafficking with an onslaught of compulsive weirdness: Kenneth Grant and the Magickal Revival". In Dave Evans. *Journal for the Academic Study of Magic: Issue 2*. Oxford: Mandrake. pp. 226–259. ISBN 978-1869928728.

Evans, Dave (2007). *The History of British Magick After Crowley*. n.p.: Hidden Publishing. ISBN 978-0-9555237-0-0.

Kaczynski, Richard (2010). *Perdurabo: The Life of Aleister Crowley* (second edition). Berkeley, California: North Atlantic Books. ISBN 978-0-312-25243-4.

Levenda, Peter (2013). *The Dark Lord: H.P. Lovecraft, Kenneth Grant and the Typhonian tradition in Magic*. Lake Worth, FL: Ibis Press. ISBN 978-0-89254-207-9.

Moore, Alan (2002). "Beyond our Ken" (PDF). *Kaos* (Babalon Press) **14**: 155–162.

O'Neill, Declan (4 March 2011). "Kenneth Grant: Writer and occultist who championed Aleister Crowley and Austin Osman Spare". *The Independent*. Retrieved 8 October 2013.

Staley, Michael (2008). "Instrument of Succession: An Apology". *Starfire: A Journal of the New Aeon* **2** (3). London: Starfire Publishing. p. 121.

Starr, Martin P. (2003). *The Unknown God: W.T. Smith and the Thelemites*. Bollingbrook, Illinois: Teitan Press. ISBN 0-933429-07-X.

11.6 External links

- Fulgur Limited: Bibliography, Biography and Articles

- Obituary in The Independent by Declan O'Neill

Frontispiece

Crowley, who became Grant's guru.

Chapter 12

Lady Frieda Harris

Marguerite Frieda Harris (née Bloxam, 1877, London, England — 11 May 1962, Srinagar, India) was an artist, and, after she met him when aged 60, an associate of the occultist Aleister Crowley. She is best known for her design of Crowley's Thoth tarot deck.

12.1 Family

Frieda Bloxam was a daughter of surgeon John Astley Bloxam, F.R.C.S.[1] She married Percy Harris in April 1901. Percy Harris served as a Liberal Party MP 1916-18 and 1922–45, and was Chief Whip for his party. After her husband was created a baronet in 1932 she was entitled to style herself **Lady Harris** but preferred to use **Lady Frieda Harris**.

Frieda and Percy Harris had two sons: Jack (born 1906, later Sir Jack Harris) and Thomas (born 1908).

12.2 Introduction to Crowley

Aleister Crowley had asked playwright and author Clifford Bax to help him find an artist for a Tarot project. On 9 June 1937 Bax invited Frieda Harris after two artists did not show up for an appointment.

As well as reading books by Crowley, Harris' study of Rudolf Steiner's Anthroposophy was to be a critical aspect in the creation of the Thoth deck. Crowley's friend Greta Valentine, a London socialite, also knew Harris and Harris and Crowley did much of their work on the Thoth tarot deck at Valentine's house in Hyde Park Crescent, London.

In 1937 Harris began taking lessons in projective synthetic geometry, based upon the ideas of Goethe as reflected in the teachings of Steiner, from Olive Whicher and George Adams.

John Symonds writes:

> [Crowley] helped her through the portals of the mystical Order of the A∴A∴ (Argenteum Astrum) She took the name of Tzaba "Hosts", which adds up to 93, the number of the Thelema current which she was trying to tap."[2]

According to Crowley's unpublished *Society of Hidden Masters*,[3] on 11 May 1938, Lady Harris became his "disciple" and also became a member of Ordo Templi Orientis, entering directly to the IV° (Fourth Degree) of that Order due to her previous initiation into Co-Masonry.[4]

Crowley also began to teach her divination - she had a choice of discipline and opted for the I Ching:

> "The Yi was your own choice from several. I approved highly, because it is the key to the kind of painting

after which you were groping when I met you." ... "If you are to make a new mark in art, you need a new mind, a mind enlightened from the Supernal Triangle."[5]

12.3   Harris visits Crowley

The author William Holt in his autobiography describes how he accompanied Harris to Crowley's lodgings at 93 Jermyn Street, Piccadilly. While Harris drew some charcoal sketches, there was a discussion on *The Book of Thoth* that Crowley was writing.

12.4   Creating the Tarot

By Crowley's own admission, the deck was originally intended to be traditional but Harris encouraged him to commit his occult, magical, spiritual and scientific views to the project.

Harris sent Crowley a regular stipend throughout the project. She also used her society contacts to find financial backers for the exhibition of the paintings, the catalogues, and for the publication of the Tarot deck. The pressure may have taken its toll on Harris and Crowley was sufficiently concerned to call in the lawyers to protect his 66% investment in the project. Crowley gives Harris praise in the introduction to the *Book of Thoth*:

> She devoted her genius to the Work. With incredible rapidity she picked up the rhythm, and with inexhaustible patience submitted to the correction of the fanatical slave-driver that she had invoked, often painting the same card as many as eight times until it measured up to his Vanadium Steel yardstick!

Throughout the project she insisted on her own anonymity but she revelled in working for such a notorious man. The *Book of Thoth* was then published in a 200 copy limited edition, but neither Crowley or Harris lived to see the deck itself printed.

12.5   Crowley's last days

The surviving letters between Frieda Harris and Crowley show the level of their devotion to each other. On 29 May 1942 Crowley wrote to Pearson, the photoengraver of the Thoth deck:

> I should like to emphasise that I am absolutely devoted to Lady Harris, and have the evidence of countless acts of kindness on her part, indicating that her feelings toward me are similar.[3]

There is break in the Harris - Crowley letters after the exhibition in July 1942 but she was in close contact with him, particularly towards the end of his life, and visited him frequently. A pencil sketch she made of Crowley on his deathbed survives.

After Crowley's death she wrote to Frederic Mellinger, an O.T.O. member in Germany, on 7 December 1947:

> He was well taken care of. I made him have a nurse about 3 months ago as he was dirty & neglected & he had Watson who was most devoted & the Symonds were as nice as they knew how to be. At the last Mrs. McAlpine & the boy were there. I saw him the day he died, but he did not recognize me. I think Mrs. McAlpine was with him but she says there was no struggle, just stopped breathing
> > I shall miss him terribly
> > An irreplaceable loss
> > Love is the law, love under will
> > Yours Sincerely
> > Frieda Harris

She also corresponded with Gerald Gardner and Karl Germer, Crowley's successor as head of O.T.O., in an attempt to assist with the Order's structure in Europe, which had been thrown into some confusion after Crowley's death.

Frieda Harris and Louis Wilkinson were the executors of Crowley's Will.

12.6 After Crowley

Harris had plans to do a lecture tour in the United States and exhibit the original paintings of the Thoth tarot deck in 1948 but this never materialised.

After her husband's death in 1952, she moved to India. She died in Srinagar on 11 May 1962. She bequeathed the original paintings of her Tarot cards to fellow Thelemite Gerald Yorke, who in turned placed them with the Warburg Institute along with much other Crowley material that he had collected over the years. However, Yorke retained several alternative versions of the cards and some preliminary studies which he later sold through bookdealer Harold Mortlake.[6]

Her legacy can be found in a later reprinting of *The Book of Thoth*:[7]

> May the passionate "love under will" which she has stored in this Treasury of Truth and Beauty flow forth from the Splendour and Strength of her work to enlighten the world; may this Tarot serve as a chart for the bold seamen of the New Aeon, to guide them across the Great Sea of Understanding to the City of the Pyramids!

12.7 References

[1] BMJ obituary 23 January 1926; 1(3395): 171

[2] Symonds, John (1973). *The Great Beast: the life and magick of Aleister Crowley*. St Albans, Herts.: Mayflower.

[3] Crowley, Aleister; Harris, Frieda. "Correspondence between Aleister Crowley and Frieda Harris". Retrieved 2009-05-25.

[4] "The Tracing Boards of Lady Frieda Harris". *Mill Valley Lodge*. Retrieved 2009-05-25.

[5] Letter from AC to FH, 17 December. The date is 1936, but should be 1938

[6] "Lady Frieda Harris". *Occult Art Gallery*. Retrieved 2009-05-25.

[7] Crowley, Aleister (1969). *The Book of Thoth: A short essay on the Tarot of the Egyptians*. Samuel Weiser, Inc.

Chapter 13

L. Ron Hubbard

Lafayette Ronald Hubbard (March 13, 1911 – January 24, 1986), better known as **L. Ron Hubbard** (/ɛl rɒn ˈhʌˌbərd/, *ELL-ron-HUB-ərd*[2]) and often referred to by his initials, **LRH**, was an American author and the founder of the Church of Scientology. After establishing a career as a writer, becoming best known for his science fiction and fantasy stories, he developed a system called Dianetics which was first expounded in book form in May 1950. He subsequently developed his ideas into a wide-ranging set of doctrines and rituals as part of a new religious movement that he called Scientology. His writings became the guiding texts for the Church of Scientology and a number of affiliated organizations that address such diverse topics as business administration, literacy and drug rehabilitation.

Although many aspects of Hubbard's life story are disputed, there is general agreement about its basic outline.[3] Born in Tilden, Nebraska, he spent much of his childhood in Helena, Montana. He traveled in Asia and the South Pacific in the late 1920s after his father, an officer in the United States Navy, was posted to the U.S. naval base on Guam. He attended George Washington University in Washington, D.C. at the start of the 1930s, before dropping out and beginning his career as a prolific writer of pulp fiction stories. He served briefly in the United States Marine Corps Reserve and was an officer in the United States Navy during World War II, briefly commanding two ships, the USS *YP-422* and USS *PC-815*. He was removed both times when his superiors found him incapable of command.[4] The last few months of his active service were spent in a hospital, being treated for a duodenal ulcer.[5]

After the war, Hubbard developed Dianetics, which he called "the modern science of mental health". He founded Scientology in 1952 and oversaw the growth of the Church of Scientology into a worldwide organization. During the late 1960s and early 1970s, he spent much of his time at sea on his personal fleet of ships as "Commodore" of the Sea Organization, an elite inner group of Scientologists. His expedition came to an end when Britain, Greece, Spain, Portugal, and Venezuela all closed their ports to his fleet. At one point, a court in Australia revoked the church's status as a religion. Similarly, a high court in France convicted Hubbard of fraud *in absentia*. He returned to the United States in 1975 and went into seclusion in the California desert. In 1983 L. Ron Hubbard was named as an unindicted co-conspirator in an international information infiltration and theft project called "Operation Snow White". He spent the remaining years of his life on his ranch near Creston, California, where he died in 1986.

The Church of Scientology describes Hubbard in hagiographic terms,[6] and he portrayed himself as a pioneering explorer, world traveler, and nuclear physicist with expertise in a wide range of disciplines, including photography, art, poetry, and philosophy. His critics, including his own son, have characterized him as a liar, a charlatan, and mentally unstable. Though many of his autobiographical statements have been proven to be fictitious,[7] the Church rejects any suggestion that its account of Hubbard's life is not historical fact.[8][9]

13.1 Early life

Main article: Early life of L. Ron Hubbard

Lafayette Ronald Hubbard was born in 1911, in Tilden, Nebraska.[10] He was the only child of Ledora May (née Waterbury), who had trained as a teacher, and Harry Ross Hubbard, a former United States Navy officer.[11][12] After moving to Kalispell, Montana, they settled in Helena in 1913.[12] Hubbard's father rejoined in the Navy in April 1917, during World War I, while his mother May worked as a clerk for the state government.[13]

Biographical accounts published by the Church of Scientology describe Hubbard as "a child prodigy of sorts" who rode a horse before he could walk and was able to read and write by the age of four.[14] A Scientology profile says that he was brought up on his grandfather's "large cattle ranch in Montana"[15] where he spent his days "riding, breaking broncos, hunting coyote and taking his first steps as an explorer".[16] His grandfather is described as a "wealthy Western cattleman" from whom Hubbard "inherited his fortune and family interests in America, Southern Africa, etc."[17] Scientology claims that Hubbard became a "blood brother" of the Native American Blackfeet tribe at the age of six through his friendship with a Blackfeet medicine man.[12][18]

Queen Anne High School, Seattle, which L. Ron Hubbard attended in 1926–1927

However, contemporary records show that his grandfather, Lafayette Waterbury, was a veterinarian, not a rancher, and was not wealthy. Hubbard was actually raised in a townhouse in the center of Helena.[19] According to his aunt, his family did not own a ranch but did own one cow and four or five horses on a few acres of land outside the city.[16] Hubbard lived over a hundred miles from the Blackfeet reservation. The tribe did not practice blood brotherhood and no evidence has been found that he had ever been a Blackfeet blood brother.[20]

During the 1920s the Hubbards repeatedly relocated around the United States and overseas. After Hubbard's father Harry rejoined the Navy, his posting aboard the USS *Oklahoma* in 1921 required the family to relocate to the ship's home ports, first San Diego, then Seattle.[21] During a journey to Washington, D.C. in 1923 Hubbard learned of Freudian psychology from Commander Joseph "Snake" Thompson, a U.S. Navy psychoanalyst and medic.[21][22] Scientology biographies describe this encounter as giving Hubbard training in a particular scientific approach to the mind, which he found unsatisfying.[23] Hubbard was active in the Boy Scouts in Washington, D.C. and earned the rank of Eagle Scout in 1924, two weeks after his 13th birthday. In his diary, Hubbard claimed he was the youngest Eagle Scout in the U.S.[24]

The following year, Harry Ross Hubbard was posted to Puget Sound Naval Shipyard at Bremerton, Washington.[25] His son was enrolled at Union High School, Bremerton,[25] and later studied at Queen Anne High School in Seattle.[26] In 1927 Hubbard's father was sent to the U.S. Naval Station on Guam in the Mariana Islands of the South Pacific. Although

Hubbard's mother also went to Guam, Hubbard himself did not accompany them but was placed in his grandparents' care in Helena, Montana to complete his schooling.[26]

Between 1927 and 1929 Hubbard traveled to Japan, China, the Philippines and Guam. Scientology texts present this period in his life as a time when he was intensely curious for answers to human suffering and explored ancient Eastern philosophies for answers, but found them lacking.[27] He is described as traveling to China "at a time when few Westerners could enter"[28] and according to Scientology, spent his time questioning Buddhist lamas and meeting old Chinese magicians.[27] According to church materials, his travels were funded by his "wealthy grandfather".[29]

Hubbard's unofficial biographers present a very different account of his travels in Asia. Hubbard's diaries recorded two trips to the east coast of China. The first was made in the company of his mother while traveling from the United States to Guam in 1927. It consisted of a brief stop-over in a couple of Chinese ports before traveling on to Guam, where he stayed for six weeks before returning home. He recorded his impressions of the places he visited and disdained the poverty of the inhabitants of Japan and China, whom he described as "gooks" and "lazy [and] ignorant". His second visit was a family holiday which took Hubbard and his parents to China via the Philippines in 1928.[30][31]

Aerial view of Qingdao, China, taken in 1930, two years after Hubbard's visit

After his return to the United States in September 1927, Hubbard enrolled at Helena High School but earned only poor grades.[32] He abandoned school the following May and went back west to stay with his aunt and uncle in Seattle. He joined his parents in Guam in June 1928. His mother took over his education in the hope of putting him forward for the entrance examination to the United States Naval Academy at Annapolis, Maryland.

Between October and December 1928 a number of naval families, including Hubbard's, traveled from Guam to China aboard the cargo ship USS *Gold Star*. The ship stopped at Manila in the Philippines before traveling on to Qingdao (Tsingtao) in China. Hubbard and his parents made a side trip to Beijing before sailing on to Shanghai and Hong Kong, from where they returned to Guam.[33] Scientology account say that Hubbard "made his way deep into Manchuria's Western Hills and beyond — to break bread with Mongolian bandits, share campfires with Siberian shamans and befriend the last in the line of magicians from the court of Kublai Khan".[34]

However, Hubbard did not record these events in his diary.[35] He remained unimpressed with China and the Chinese, writing: "A Chinaman can not live up to a thing, he always drags it down." He characterized the sights of Beijing as "rubberneck stations" for tourists and described the palaces of the Forbidden City as "very trashy-looking" and "not worth mentioning". He was impressed by the Great Wall of China near Beijing,[36] but concluded of the Chinese: "They smell of all the baths they didn't take. The trouble with China is, there are too many chinks here."[37]

Back on Guam, Hubbard spent much of his time writing dozens of short stories and essays[38] and failed the Naval Academy entrance examination. In September 1929 Hubbard was enrolled at the Swavely Preparatory School in Manassas, Virginia, to prepare him for a second attempt at the examination.[39] However, he was ruled out of consideration due to his near-sightedness.[40] He was instead sent to Woodward School for Boys in Washington, D.C. to qualify for admission to George Washington University. He successfully graduated from the school in June 1930 and entered the university the following September.[41]

13.2 University and explorations

Professor's Gate at George Washington University

Hubbard studied civil engineering during his two years at George Washington University at the behest of his father, who "decreed that I should study engineering and mathematics".[42] While he did not graduate from George Washington, his time there subsequently became important because, as George Malko puts it, "many of his researches and published conclusions have been supported by his claims to be not only a graduate engineer, but 'a member of the first United States course in formal education in what is called today nuclear physics.'"[43] However, a Church of Scientology biography describes him as "never noted for being in class" and says that he "thoroughly detest[ed] his subjects".[44] He earned poor grades, was placed on probation in September 1931 and dropped out altogether in the fall of 1932.[43][45]

Scientology accounts say that he "studied nuclear physics at George Washington University in Washington, D.C., before he started his studies about the mind, spirit and life"[46] and Hubbard himself stated that he "set out to find out from nuclear physics a knowledge of the physical universe, something entirely lacking in Asian philosophy".[44] His university records indicate that his exposure to "nuclear physics" consisted of one class in "atomic and molecular phenomena" for which he earned an "F" grade.[47]

Scientologists claim he was more interested in extracurricular activities, particularly writing and flying. According to church materials, "he earned his wings as a pioneering barnstormer at the dawn of American aviation"[18] and was "recognized as one of the country's most outstanding pilots. With virtually no training time, he takes up powered flight and barnstorms throughout the Midwest."[48] His airman certificate, however, records that he qualified to fly only gliders rather than powered aircraft and gave up his certificate when he could not afford the renewal fee.[49]

During Hubbard's final semester he organized an expedition to the Caribbean for "fifty young gentleman rovers" aboard the schooner *Doris Hamlin* commencing in June 1932. The aims of the "Caribbean Motion Picture Expedition" were stated as being to explore and film the pirate "strongholds and bivouacs of the Spanish Main" and to "collect whatever one collects for exhibits in museums".[50] It ran into trouble even before it left the port of Baltimore: Ten participants quit and storms blew the ship far off course to Bermuda. Eleven more members of the expedition quit there and more left when the ship arrived at Martinique.[51] With the expedition running critically short of money, the ship's owners ordered it to return to Baltimore.[52]

Hubbard blamed the expedition's problems on the captain: "the ship's dour Captain Garfield proved himself far less than a Captain Courageous, requiring Ron Hubbard's hand at both the helm and the charts."[53] Specimens and photographs collected by the expedition are said by Scientology accounts to have been acquired by the University of Michigan, the U.S. Hydrographic Office, an unspecified national museum and the *New York Times*,[53][54] though none of those institutions have any record of this.[55] Hubbard later wrote that the expedition "was a crazy idea at best, and I knew it, but I went ahead anyway, chartered a four-masted schooner and embarked with some fifty luckless souls who haven't stopped their cursings yet."[56] He called it "a two-bit expedition and financial bust",[57] which resulted in some of its participants making legal claims against him for refunds.[58]

Luquillo, Puerto Rico, near where scientologists say Hubbard carried out the "West Indies Mineralogical Survey" in 1932

After leaving university Hubbard traveled to Puerto Rico on what the Church of Scientology calls the "Puerto Rican Mineralogical Expedition".[59] Scientologists claim he "made the first complete mineralogical survey of Puerto Rico"[54] as a means of "augmenting his [father's] pay with a mining venture", during which he "sluiced inland rivers and crisscrossed the island in search of elusive gold" as well as carrying out "much ethnological work amongst the interior villages and native hillsmen".[59] Hubbard's unofficial biographer Russell Miller writes that neither the United States Geological Survey nor the Puerto Rican Department of Natural Resources have any record of any such expedition.[55]

According to Miller, Hubbard traveled to Puerto Rico in November 1932 after his father volunteered him for the Red Cross relief effort following the devastating 1932 San Ciprian hurricane.[55] In a 1957 lecture Hubbard said that he had been "a field executive with the American Red Cross in the Puerto Rico hurricane disaster".[60] According to his own account, Hubbard spent much of his time prospecting unsuccessfully for gold. Towards the end of his stay on Puerto Rico he appears to have done some work for a Washington, D.C. firm called West Indies Minerals Incorporated, accompanying a surveyor in an investigation of a small property near the town of Luquillo, Puerto Rico.[58] The survey was unsuccessful. A few years later, Hubbard wrote:

> Harboring the thought that the Conquistadores might have left some gold behind, I determined to find it
> ... Gold prospecting in the wake of the Conquistadores, on the hunting grounds of the pirates in the islands which still reek of Columbus is romantic, and I do not begrudge the sweat which splashed in muddy rivers, and the bits of khaki which have probably blown away from the thorn bushes long ago ...
> After a half year or more of intensive search, after wearing my palms thin wielding a sample pack, after assaying a few hundred sacks of ore, I came back, a failure.[56]

13.3 Early literary career and Alaskan expedition

See also: Golden Age of Science Fiction and Excalibur (L. Ron Hubbard)
Hubbard became a well-known and prolific writer for pulp fiction magazines during the 1930s. Scientology texts describe him as becoming "well established as an essayist" even before he had concluded college. Scientology claims he "solved his finances, and his desire to travel by writing anything that came to hand"[44] and to have earned an "astronomical" rate of pay for the times.[62]

His literary career began with contributions to the George Washington University student newspaper, *The University Hatchet*, as a reporter for a few months in 1931.[41] Six of his pieces were published commercially during 1932 to 1933.[49] The going rate for freelance writers at the time was only a cent a word, so Hubbard's total earnings from these articles would have been less than $100.[63] The pulp magazine *Thrilling Adventure* became the first to publish one of his short stories, in February 1934.[64] Over the next six years, pulp magazines published around 140 of his short stories[65] under a variety of pen names, including Winchester Remington Colt, Kurt von Rachen, René Lafayette, Joe Blitz and Legionnaire 148.[66]

Although he was best known for his fantasy and science fiction stories, Hubbard wrote in a wide variety of genres, including adventure fiction, aviation, travel, mysteries, westerns and even romance.[67] Hubbard knew and associated with writers such as Isaac Asimov, Robert A. Heinlein, L. Sprague de Camp and A. E. van Vogt.[68] His first full-length novel, *Buckskin Brigades*, was published in 1937.[69] He became a "highly idiosyncratic" writer of science fiction after being taken under the wing of editor John W. Campbell,[70] who published many of Hubbard's short stories and also serialized a number of well-received novelettes that Hubbard wrote for Campbell's magazines *Unknown* and *Astounding*. These included *Fear*, *Final Blackout* and *Typewriter in the Sky*.[71]

According to the Church of Scientology, Hubbard was "called to Hollywood" to work on film scripts in the mid-1930s, although Scientology accounts differ as to exactly when this was (whether 1935,[72] 1936[44] or 1937[48]). He wrote the script for *The Secret of Treasure Island*, a 1938 Columbia Pictures movie serial.[73] The Church of Scientology claims he also worked on the Columbia serials *The Mysterious Pilot* (1937), *The Great Adventures of Wild Bill Hickok* (1938) and *The Spider Returns* (1941),[48] though his name does not appear on the credits. Hubbard also claimed to have written *Dive Bomber* (1941),[74][75] Cecil B. DeMille's *The Plainsman* (1936) and John Ford's *Stagecoach* (1939).[76]

Hubbard's literary earnings helped him to support his new wife, Margaret "Polly" Grubb. She was already pregnant when they married on April 13, 1933, but had a miscarriage shortly afterwards; a few months later, she became pregnant again.[77] On May 7, 1934, she gave birth prematurely to a son who was named Lafayette Ronald Hubbard, Jr. and the nickname "His Nibs", invariably shortened to "Nibs".[78] Their second child, Katherine May, was born on January 15, 1936.[79] The Hubbards lived for a while in Laytonsville, Maryland, but were chronically short of money.[80]

In the spring of 1936 they moved to Bremerton, Washington. They lived there for a time with Hubbard's aunts and grandmother before finding a place of their own at nearby South Colby. According to one of his friends at the time, Robert MacDonald Ford, the Hubbards were "in fairly dire straits for money" but sustained themselves on the income from Hubbard's writing.[81] Hubbard spent an increasing amount of time in New York City,[82] working out of a hotel room where his wife suspected him of carrying on affairs with other women.[83][84]

Hubbard's authorship in mid-1938 of a still-unpublished manuscript called *Excalibur* is highlighted by the Church of Scientology as a key step in developing the principles of Scientology and Dianetics. The manuscript is said by Scientologists to have outlined "the basic principles of human existence"[44] and to have been the culmination of twenty years of research into "twenty-one races and cultures including Pacific Northwest Indian tribes, Philippine Tagalogs and, as he was wont to joke, the people of the Bronx".[85]

According to Arthur J. Cox, a contributor to John W. Campbell's *Astounding* magazine, Hubbard told a 1948 convention of science fiction fans that *Excalibur* 's inspiration came during an operation in which he "died" for eight minutes.[86] (Gerry Armstrong, Hubbard's archivist, explains this as a dental extraction performed under nitrous oxide, a chemical known for its hallucinogenic effects[87]):

> Hubbard realized that, while he was dead, he had received a tremendous inspiration, a great Message which he must impart to others. He sat at his typewriter for six days and nights and nothing came out. Then, *Excalibur* emerged.[88]

Arthur J. Burks, the President of the American Fiction Guild, wrote that an excited Hubbard called him and said: "I want to see you right away. I have written THE book." Hubbard believed that *Excalibur* would "revolutionize everything" and that "it was somewhat more important, and would have a greater impact upon people, than the Bible."[89] It proposed that all human behavior could be explained in terms of survival and that to understand survival was to understand life.[90] As Hubbard biographer Jon Atack notes, "the notion that everything that exists is trying to survive became the basis of Dianetics and Scientology."[87]

According to Burks, Hubbard "was so sure he had something 'away out and beyond' anything else that he had sent telegrams to several book publishers, telling them that he had written 'THE book' and that they were to meet him at Penn Station, and he would discuss it with them and go with whomever gave him the best offer." However, nobody bought the manuscript.[89] Forrest J Ackerman, later Hubbard's literary agent, recalled that Hubbard told him "whoever read it either went insane or committed suicide. And he said that the last time he had shown it to a publisher in New York, he walked into the office to find out what the reaction was, the publisher called for the reader, the reader came in with the manuscript, threw it on the table and threw himself out of the skyscraper window."[91] Hubbard's failure to sell *Excalibur* depressed him; he told his wife in an October 1938 letter: "Writing action pulp doesn't have much agreement with what I want to do because it retards my progress by demanding incessant attention and, further, actually weakens my name. So you see I've got to do something about it and at the same time strengthen the old financial position."[92] He went on:

> Sooner or later *Excalibur* will be published and I may have a chance to get some name recognition out of it so as to pave the way to articles and comments which are my ideas of writing heaven ... Foolishly perhaps, but determined none the less, I have high hopes of smashing my name into history so violently that it will take a legendary form even if all books are destroyed. That goal is the real goal as far as I am concerned.[92]

The manuscript later became part of Scientology mythology.[87] An early 1950s Scientology publication offered signed "gold-bound and locked" copies for the sum of $1,500 apiece (equivalent to about $29,000 now). It warned that "four of the first fifteen people who read it went insane" and that it would be "[r]eleased only on sworn statement not to permit other readers to read it. Contains data not to be released during Mr. Hubbard's stay on earth."[93]

Hubbard joined The Explorers Club in February 1940 on the strength of his claimed explorations in the Caribbean and survey flights in the United States.[94] He persuaded the club to let him carry its flag on an "Alaskan Radio-Experimental Expedition" to update the U.S. Coast Pilot guide to the coastlines of Alaska and British Columbia and investigate new methods of radio position-finding.[95] The expedition consisted of Hubbard and his wife—the children were left at South Colby—aboard his ketch *Magician*.[96]

Scientology accounts of the expedition describe "Hubbard's recharting of an especially treacherous Inside Passage, and his ethnological study of indigenous Aleuts and Haidas" and tell of how "along the way, he not only roped a Kodiak Bear, but braved seventy-mile-an-hour winds and commensurate seas off the Aleutian Islands."[97] They are divided about how far Hubbard's expedition actually traveled, whether 700 miles (1,100 km)[48] or 2,000 miles (3,200 km).[97]

Hubbard told *The Seattle Star* in a November 1940 letter that the expedition was plagued by problems and did not get any further than Ketchikan near the southern end of the Alaska Panhandle, far from the Aleutian Islands.[98] *Magician's* engine broke down only two days after setting off in July 1940. The Hubbards reached Ketchikan on August 30, 1940, after many delays following repeated engine breakdowns. The *Ketchikan Chronicle* reported—making no mention of the expedition—that Hubbard's purpose in coming to Alaska "was two-fold, one to win a bet and another to gather material for a novel of Alaskan salmon fishing".[96] Having underestimated the cost of the trip, he did not have enough money to repair the broken engine. He raised money by writing stories and contributing to the local radio station[99] and eventually earned enough to fix the engine,[94] making it back to Puget Sound on December 27, 1940.[99]

13.4 Military career

Main article: Military career of L. Ron Hubbard

After returning from Alaska, Hubbard applied to join the United States Navy. His Congressman, Warren G. Magnuson, wrote to President Roosevelt to recommend Hubbard as "a gentleman of reputation" who was "a respected explorer" and had "marine masters papers for more types of vessels than any other man in the United States". Hubbard was described as "a key figure" in writing organizations, "making him politically potent nationally". The Congressman concluded: "Anything you can do for Mr Hubbard will be appreciated." His friend Robert MacDonald Ford, by now a State Representative for Washington, sent a letter of recommendation describing Hubbard as "one of the most brilliant men I have ever known". It called Hubbard "a powerful influence" in the Northwest and said that he was "well known in many parts of the world and has considerable influence in the Caribbean and Alaska". The letter declared that "for courage and ability I cannot too strongly recommend him." Ford later said that Hubbard had written the letter himself: "I don't know why Ron wanted a letter. I just gave him a letter-head and said, 'Hell, you're the writer, you write it!'"[100]

Hubbard was commissioned as a Lieutenant (junior grade) in the U.S. Naval Reserve on July 19, 1941. His military service forms a major element of his public persona as portrayed by Scientologists.[101] The Church of Scientology presents him as a "much-decorated war hero who commanded a corvette and during hostilities was crippled and wounded".[102] Scientology publications say he served as a "Commodore of Corvette squadrons" in "all five theaters of World War II" and was awarded "twenty-one medals and palms" for his service.[103] He was "severely wounded and was taken crippled and blinded" to a military hospital, where he "worked his way back to fitness, strength and full perception in less than two years, using only what he knew and could determine about Man and his relationship to the universe".[72] He said that he had seen combat repeatedly, telling A. E. van Vogt that he had once sailed his ship "right into the harbor of a Japanese occupied island in the Dutch East Indies. His attitude was that if you took your flag down the Japanese would not know one boat from another, so he tied up at the dock, went ashore and wandered around by himself for three days."[104]

According to The Los Angeles Times, Hubbard's official Navy service records indicate that "his military performance was, at times, substandard" and he received only four campaign medals rather than twenty-one. He was never recorded as being injured or wounded in combat and so never received a Purple Heart.[16] Most of his military service was spent ashore in the continental United States on administrative or training duties. He served for a short time in Australia but was sent home after quarreling with his superiors. He briefly commanded two anti-submarine vessels, the USS *YP-422* and USS *PC-815*, in coastal waters off Massachusetts, Oregon and California in 1942 and 1943 respectively.[16]

After Hubbard reported that the *PC-815* had attacked and crippled or sunk two Japanese submarines off Oregon in May 1943, his claim was rejected by the commander of the Northwest Sea Frontier.[16] Hubbard and Thomas Moulton, his second in command on the *PC-815*, later said the Navy wanted to avoid panic on the mainland.[105] A month later Hubbard unwittingly sailed the *PC-815* into Mexican territorial waters and conducted gunnery practice off the Coronado Islands, in the belief that they were uninhabited and belonged to the United States. The Mexican government complained and Hubbard was relieved of command. A fitness report written after the incident rated Hubbard as unsuitable for independent duties and "lacking in the essential qualities of judgment, leadership and cooperation".[106] He served for a while as the Navigation and Training Officer for the USS *Algol* while it was based at Portland. A fitness report from this period recommended promotion, describing him as "a capable and energetic officer, [but] very temperamental", and an "above average navigator".[107] However, he never held another such position and did not serve aboard another ship after the *Algol*.

Hubbard's war service has great significance in the history and mythology of the Church of Scientology, as he is said to have cured himself through techniques that would later underpin Scientology and Dianetics. According to Moulton, Hubbard told him that he had been machine-gunned in the back near the Dutch East Indies. Hubbard asserted that his eyes had been damaged as well, either "by the flash of a large-caliber gun" or when he had "a bomb go off in my face".[16] Scientology texts say that he returned from the war "[b]linded with injured optic nerves, and lame with physical injuries to hip and back" and was twice pronounced dead.[9]

He told his doctors that he was suffering from lameness caused by a hip infection[16] and he told *Look* magazine in December 1950 that he had suffered from "ulcers, conjunctivitis, deteriorating eyesight, bursitis and something wrong with my feet".[57] He was still complaining in 1951 of eye problems and stomach pains, which had given him "continuous trouble" for eight years, especially when "under nervous stress". This came well after Hubbard had promised that Dianetics would provide "a cure for the very ailments that plagued the author himself then and throughout his life, including allergies, arthritis, ulcers and heart problems".[16]

The Church of Scientology says that Hubbard's key breakthrough in the development of Dianetics was made at Oak Knoll Naval Hospital in Oakland, California. According to the Church,

> In early 1945, while recovering from war injuries at Oak Knoll Naval Hospital, Mr. Hubbard conducts a series of tests and experiments dealing with the endocrine system. He discovers that, contrary to long-standing beliefs, function monitors structure. With this revolutionary advance, he begins to apply his theories to the field of the mind and thereby to improve the conditions of others.[108]

An October 1945 Naval Board found that Hubbard was "considered physically qualified to perform duty ashore, preferably within the continental United States".[109] He was discharged from hospital on December 4, 1945, and transferred to inactive duty on February 17, 1946. He resigned his commission with effect from October 30, 1950.[110] The Church of Scientology says he quit because the U.S. Navy "attempted to monopolize all his researches and force him to work on a project 'to make man more suggestible' and when he was unwilling, tried to blackmail him by ordering him back to active duty to perform this function. Having many friends he was able to instantly resign from the Navy and escape this trap."[111] The Navy said in a statement in 1980: "There is no evidence on record of an attempt to recall him to active duty."[110]

The Church disputes the official record of Hubbard's naval career. It asserts that the records are incomplete and perhaps falsified "to conceal Hubbard's secret activities as an intelligence officer".[16] In 1990 the Church provided the *Los Angeles Times* with a document that was said to be a copy of Hubbard's official record of service. The U.S. Navy told the *Times* that "its contents are not supported by Hubbard's personnel record."[16] *The New Yorker* reported in February 2011 that the Scientology document was considered by federal archivists to be a forgery.[9]

Nevertheless, the German Protestant theologian and history of religion scholar Marco Frenschkowski wrote in the *Marburg Journal of Religion* that the publically available copies of Hubbard's military records (of which Frenschkowski has a complete collection) are "much nearer" in his assessment to Hubbard's statements about his military career than Miller's *Bare-Faced Messiah*.[67]

13.5   Occult involvement in Pasadena

See also: Scientology and the occult

Hubbard's life underwent a turbulent period immediately after the war. According to his own account, he "was abandoned by family and friends as a supposedly hopeless cripple and a probable burden upon them for the rest of my days".[112] His daughter Katherine presented a rather different version: his wife had refused to uproot their children from their home in

Bremerton, Washington, to join him in California. Their marriage was by now in terminal difficulties and he chose to stay in California.[113]

In August 1945 Hubbard moved into the Pasadena mansion of John "Jack" Whiteside Parsons. A leading rocket propulsion researcher at the California Institute of Technology and a founder of the Jet Propulsion Laboratory, Parsons led a double life as an avid occultist and Thelemite, follower of the English ceremonial magician Aleister Crowley and leader of a lodge of Crowley's magical order, Ordo Templi Orientis (OTO).[9][114] He let rooms in the house only to tenants who he specified should be "atheists and those of a Bohemian disposition".[115]

Hubbard befriended Parsons and soon became sexually involved with Parsons's 21-year-old girlfriend, Sara "Betty" Northrup.[116] Despite this Parsons was very impressed with Hubbard and reported to Crowley:

> [Hubbard] is a gentleman; he has red hair, green eyes, is honest and intelligent, and we have become great friends. He moved in with me about two months ago, and although Betty and I are still friendly, she has transferred her sexual affection to Ron. Although he has no formal training in Magick, he has an extraordinary amount of experience and understanding in the field. From some of his experiences I deduced that he is in direct touch with some higher intelligence, possibly his Guardian Angel. He describes his Angel as a beautiful winged woman with red hair whom he calls the Empress and who has guided him through his life and saved him many times. He is the most Thelemic person I have ever met and is in complete accord with our own principles.[117]

Parsons and Hubbard collaborated on the "Babalon Working", a sex magic ritual intended to summon an incarnation of Babalon, the supreme Thelemite Goddess. It was undertaken over several nights in February and March 1946 in order to summon an "elemental" who would participate in further sex magic.[118] As Richard Metzger describes it,

> Parsons used his "magical wand" to whip up a vortex of energy so the elemental would be summoned. Translated into plain English, Parsons jerked off in the name of spiritual advancement whilst Hubbard (referred to as "The Scribe" in the diary of the event) scanned the astral plane for signs and visions.[119]

The "elemental" arrived a few days later in the form of Marjorie Cameron, who agreed to participate in Parsons' rites.[118] Soon afterwards, Parsons, Hubbard and Sara agreed to set up a business partnership, "Allied Enterprises", in which they invested nearly their entire savings—the vast majority contributed by Parsons. The plan was for Hubbard and Sara to buy yachts in Miami and sail them to the West Coast to sell for a profit. Hubbard had a different idea; he wrote to the U.S. Navy requesting permission to leave the country "to visit Central & South America & China" for the purposes of "collecting writing material"—in other words, undertaking a world cruise.[120] Aleister Crowley strongly criticized Parsons's actions, writing: "Suspect Ron playing confidence trick—Jack Parsons weak fool—obvious victim prowling swindlers." Parsons attempted to recover his money by obtaining an injunction to prevent Hubbard and Sara leaving the country or disposing of the remnants of his assets.[121] They attempted to sail anyway but were forced back to port by a storm. A week later, Allied Enterprises was dissolved. Parsons received only a $2,900 promissory note from Hubbard and returned home "shattered". He had to sell his mansion to developers soon afterwards to recoup his losses.[122]

Hubbard's fellow writers were well aware of what had happened between him and Parsons. L. Sprague de Camp wrote to Isaac Asimov on August 27, 1946, to tell him:

> The more complete story of Hubbard is that he is now in Fla. living on his yacht with a man-eating tigress named Betty-alias-Sarah, another of the same kind ... He will probably soon thereafter arrive in these parts with Betty-Sarah, broke, working the poor-wounded-veteran racket for all its worth, and looking for another easy mark. Don't say you haven't been warned. Bob [Robert Heinlein] thinks Ron went to pieces morally as a result of the war. I think that's fertilizer, that he always was that way, but when he wanted to conciliate or get something from somebody he could put on a good charm act. What the war did was to wear him down to where he no longer bothers with the act.[123]

Scientology accounts do not mention Hubbard's involvement in occultism. He is instead described as "continu[ing] to write to help support his research" during this period into "the development of a means to better the condition of man".[124] The Church of Scientology has nonetheless acknowledged Hubbard's involvement with the OTO; a 1969 statement, written by Hubbard himself,[125] said:

Hubbard broke up black magic in America ... L. Ron Hubbard was still an officer of the U.S. Navy, because he was well known as a writer and a philosopher and had friends amongst the physicists, he was sent in to handle the situation. He went to live at the house and investigated the black magic rites and the general situation and found them very bad ...

Hubbard's mission was successful far beyond anyone's expectations. The house was torn down. Hubbard rescued a girl they were using. The black magic group was dispersed and destroyed and has never recovered.[126]

The Church of Scientology says Hubbard was "sent in" by his fellow science fiction author Robert Heinlein, "who was running off-book intelligence operations for naval intelligence at the time". However, Heinlein's authorized biographer has said that he looked into the matter at the suggestion of Scientologists but found nothing to corroborate claims that Heinlein had been involved, and his biography of Heinlein makes no mention of the matter.[9]

On August 10, 1946, Hubbard bigamously married Sara, while still married to Polly. It was not until 1947 that his first wife learned that he had remarried. Hubbard agreed to divorce Polly in June that year and the marriage was dissolved shortly afterwards, with Polly given custody of the children.[127]

13.6   Origins of *Dianetics*

After Hubbard's wedding to Sara, the couple settled at Laguna Beach, California, where Hubbard took a short-term job looking after a friend's yacht[128] before resuming his fiction writing to supplement the small disability allowance that he was receiving as a war veteran.[129] Working from a trailer in a run-down area of North Hollywood,[127] Hubbard sold a number of science fiction stories that included his *Ole Doc Methuselah* series and the serialized novels *The End Is Not Yet* and *To the Stars*.[70] However, he remained short of money and his son, L. Ron Hubbard Jr, testified later that Hubbard was dependent on his own father and Margaret's parents for money and his writings, which he was paid at a penny per word, never garnered him any more than $10,000 prior to the founding of Scientology.[130] He repeatedly wrote to the Veterans Administration (VA) asking for an increase in his war pension. In October 1947 he wrote:

After trying and failing for two years to regain my equilibrium in civil life, I am utterly unable to approach anything like my own competence. My last physician informed me that it might be very helpful if I were to be examined and perhaps treated psychiatrically or even by a psychoanalyst. Toward the end of my service I avoided out of pride any mental examinations, hoping that time would balance a mind which I had every reason to suppose was seriously affected. I cannot account for nor rise above long periods of moroseness and suicidal inclinations, and have newly come to realize that I must first triumph above this before I can hope to rehabilitate myself at all.[131]

The VA eventually did increase his pension,[132] but his money problems continued. On August 31, 1948, he was arrested in San Luis Obispo, California, and subsequently pled guilty to a charge of petty theft, for which he was ordered to pay a $25 fine.[133] According to the Church of Scientology, around this time he "accept[ed] an appointment as a Special Police Officer with the Los Angeles Police Department and us[ed] the position to study society's criminal elements"[48] and also "worked with neurotics from the Hollywood film community".[134]

Hubbard has been quoted as telling a science fiction convention in 1948: "Writing for a penny a word is ridiculous. If a man really wants to make a million dollars, the best way would be to start his own religion."[135]

In late 1948 Hubbard and Sara moved to Savannah, Georgia.[136] Here, Scientology sources say, he "volunteer[ed] his time in hospitals and mental wards, saving the lives of patients with his counseling techniques".[137] Hubbard began to make the first public mentions of what was to become Dianetics. He wrote in January 1949 that he was working on a "book of psychology" about "the cause and cure of nervous tension", which he was going to call *The Dark Sword*, *Excalibur* or *Science of the Mind*.[138] In April 1949, Hubbard wrote to several professional organizations to offer his research.[139] None were interested, so he turned to his editor John W. Campbell, who was more receptive due to a long-standing fascination with fringe psychologies and psychic powers ("psionics") that "permeated both his fiction and non-fiction".[140]

Campbell invited Hubbard and Sara to move into a cottage at Bay Head, New Jersey, not far from his own home at Plainfield. In July 1949, Campbell recruited an acquaintance, Dr. Joseph Winter, to help develop Hubbard's new therapy of "Dianetics". Campbell told Winter:

> With cooperation from some institutions, some psychiatrists, [Hubbard] has worked on all types of cases. Institutionalized schizophrenics, apathies, manics, depressives, perverts, stuttering, neuroses—in all, nearly 1000 cases. But just a brief sampling of each type; he doesn't have proper statistics in the usual sense. But he has one statistic. He has cured every patient he worked with. He has cured ulcers, arthritis, asthma.[141]

Hubbard collaborated with Campbell and Winter to refine his techniques,[142] testing them on science fiction fans recruited by Campbell.[143] The basic principle of Dianetics was that the brain recorded every experience and event in a person's life, even when unconscious. Bad or painful experiences were stored as what he called "engrams" in a "reactive mind". These could be triggered later in life, causing emotional and physical problems. By carrying out a process he called "auditing", a person could be regressed through his engrams to re-experiencing past experiences. This enabled engrams to be "cleared". The subject, who would now be in a state of "Clear", would have a perfectly functioning mind with an improved IQ and photographic memory.[144] The "Clear" would be cured of physical ailments ranging from poor eyesight to the common cold,[145] which Hubbard asserted were purely psychosomatic.[146]

Winter submitted a paper on Dianetics to the *Journal of the American Medical Association* and the *American Journal of Psychiatry* but both journals rejected it.[147] Hubbard and his collaborators decided to announce Dianetics in Campbell's *Astounding Science Fiction* instead. In an editorial, Campbell said: "Its power is almost unbelievable; it proves the mind not only can but does rule the body completely; following the sharply defined basic laws set forth, physical ills such as ulcers, asthma and arthritis can be cured, as can all other psychosomatic ills."[148] The birth of Hubbard's second daughter Alexis Valerie, delivered by Winter on March 8, 1950, came in the middle of the preparations to launch Dianetics.[149] A "Hubbard Dianetic Research Foundation" was established in April 1950 in Elizabeth, New Jersey, with Hubbard, Sara, Winter and Campbell on the board of directors. Dianetics was duly launched in *Astounding's* May 1950 issue and on May 9, Hubbard's companion book *Dianetics: The Modern Science of Mental Health* was published.[150]

13.7 From Dianetics to Scientology

Main article: History of Dianetics
Hubbard called Dianetics "a milestone for man comparable to his discovery of fire and superior to his invention of the wheel and the arch". It was an immediate commercial success and sparked what Martin Gardner calls "a nationwide cult of incredible proportions".[151] By August 1950, Hubbard's book had sold 55,000 copies, was selling at the rate of 4,000 a week and was being translated into French, German and Japanese. Five hundred Dianetic auditing groups had been set up across the United States.[152]

Dianetics was poorly received by the press and the scientific and medical professions.[152] The American Psychological Association criticized Hubbard's claims as "not supported by empirical evidence".[57] *Scientific American* said that Hubbard's book contained "more promises and less evidence per page than any publication since the invention of printing",[153] while *The New Republic* called it a "bold and immodest mixture of complete nonsense and perfectly reasonable common sense, taken from long acknowledged findings and disguised and distorted by a crazy, newly invented terminology".[154] Some of Hubbard's fellow science fiction writers also criticized it; Isaac Asimov considered it "gibberish"[68] while Jack Williamson called it "a lunatic revision of Freudian psychology".[155]

Several famous individuals became involved with Dianetics. Aldous Huxley received auditing from Hubbard himself;[156] the poet Jean Toomer[157] and the science fiction writers Theodore Sturgeon[158] and A. E. van Vogt became trained Dianetics auditors. Van Vogt temporarily abandoned writing and became the head of the newly established Los Angeles branch of the Hubbard Dianetic Research Foundation. Other branches were established in New York, Washington, D.C., Chicago, and Honolulu.[159][160]

Although Dianetics was not cheap, a great many people were nonetheless willing to pay; van Vogt later recalled "doing little but tear open envelopes and pull out $500 checks from people who wanted to take an auditor's course".[159] Financial controls were lax. Hubbard himself withdrew large sums with no explanation of what he was doing with it. On one occasion, van Vogt saw Hubbard taking a lump sum of $56,000 (equivalent to $0.5 million at 2010 prices) out of the Los Angeles Foundation's proceeds.[159] One of Hubbard's employees, Helen O'Brien, commented that at the Elizabeth, N.J.

branch of the Foundation, the books showed that "a month's income of $90,000 is listed, with only $20,000 accounted for".[161]

Hubbard played a very active role in the Dianetics boom, writing, lecturing and training auditors. Many of those who knew him spoke of being impressed by his personal charisma. Jack Horner, who became a Dianetics auditor in 1950, later said, "He was very impressive, dedicated and amusing. The man had tremendous charisma; you just wanted to hear every word he had to say and listen for any pearl of wisdom."[162] Isaac Asimov recalled in his autobiography how, at a dinner party, he, Robert Heinlein, L. Sprague de Camp and their wives "all sat as quietly as pussycats and listened to Hubbard. He told tales with perfect aplomb and in complete paragraphs."[68] As Atack comments, he was "a charismatic figure who compelled the devotion of those around him".[163] Christopher Evans described the personal qualities that Hubbard brought to Dianetics and Scientology:

> He undoubtedly has charisma, a magnetic lure of an indefinable kind which makes him the centre of attraction in any kind of gathering. He is also a compulsive talker and pontificator ... His restless energy keeps him on the go throughout a long day—he is a poor sleeper and rises very early—and provides part of the drive which has allowed him to found and propagate a major international organization.[164]

Hubbard's supporters soon began to have doubts about Dianetics. Winter became disillusioned and wrote that he had never seen a single convincing Clear: "I have seen some individuals who are supposed to have been 'clear,' but their behavior does not conform to the definition of the state. Moreover, an individual supposed to have been 'clear' has undergone a relapse into conduct which suggests an incipient psychosis."[165] He also deplored the Foundation's omission of any serious scientific research.[166] Dianetics lost public credibility in August 1950 when a presentation by Hubbard before an audience of 6,000 at the Shrine Auditorium in Los Angeles failed disastrously.[167] He introduced a Clear named Sonya Bianca and told the audience that as a result of undergoing Dianetic therapy she now possessed perfect recall. However, Gardner writes, "in the demonstration that followed, she failed to remember a single formula in physics (the subject in which she was majoring) or the color of Hubbard's tie when his back was turned. At this point, a large part of the audience got up and left."[168]

Hubbard also faced other practitioners moving into leadership positions within the Dianetics community. It was structured as an open, public practice in which others were free to pursue their own lines of research and claim that their approaches to auditing produced better results than Hubbard's.[169] The community rapidly splintered and its members mingled Hubbard's ideas with a wide variety of esoteric and even occult practices.[170] By late 1950, the Elizabeth, N.J. Foundation was in financial crisis and the Los Angeles Foundation was more than $200,000 in debt.[171] Winter and Art Ceppos, the publisher of Hubbard's book, resigned under acrimonious circumstances.[156] Campbell also resigned, criticizing Hubbard for being impossible to work with, and blamed him for the disorganization and financial ruin of the Foundations.[172] By the summer of 1951, the Elizabeth, N.J. Foundation and all of its branches had closed.[161]

The collapse of Hubbard's marriage to Sara created yet more problems. He had begun an affair with his 20-year-old public relations assistant in late 1950, while Sara started a relationship with Dianetics auditor Miles Hollister.[173] Hubbard secretly denounced the couple to the FBI in March 1951, portraying them in a letter as communist infiltrators. According to Hubbard, Sara was "currently intimate with [communists] but evidently under coercion. Drug addiction set in fall 1950. Nothing of this known to me until a few weeks ago." Hollister was described as having a "sharp chin, broad forehead, rather Slavic". He was said to be the "center of most turbulence in our organization" and "active and dangerous".[174] The FBI did not take Hubbard seriously: an agent annotated his correspondence with the comment, "Appears mental."[135]

Three weeks later, Hubbard and two Foundation staff seized Sara and his year-old daughter Alexis and forcibly took them to San Bernardino, California, where he attempted unsuccessfully to find a doctor to examine Sara and declare her insane.[175] He let Sara go but took Alexis to Havana, Cuba. Sara filed a divorce suit on April 23, 1951, that accused him of marrying her bigamously and subjecting her to sleep deprivation, beatings, strangulation, kidnapping and exhortations to commit suicide.[176] The case led to newspaper headlines such as "Ron Hubbard Insane, Says His Wife."[177] Sara finally secured the return of her daughter in June 1951 by agreeing to a settlement with her husband in which she signed a statement, written by him, declaring:

> The things I have said about L. Ron Hubbard in courts and the public prints have been grossly exaggerated or entirely false. I have not at any time believed otherwise than that L. Ron Hubbard is a fine and brilliant man.[178]

Dianetics appeared to be on the edge of total collapse. However, it was saved by Don Purcell, a millionaire businessman and Dianeticist who agreed to support a new Foundation in Wichita, Kansas. Their collaboration ended after less than a year when they fell out over the future direction of Dianetics.[179] The Wichita Foundation became financially non-viable after a court ruled that it was liable for the unpaid debts of its defunct predecessor in Elizabeth, N.J. The ruling prompted Purcell and the other directors of the Wichita Foundation to file for voluntary bankruptcy in February 1952.[173] Hubbard resigned immediately and accused Purcell of having been bribed by the American Medical Association to destroy Dianetics.[179] Hubbard established a "Hubbard College" on the other side of town where he continued to promote Dianetics while fighting Purcell in the courts over the Foundation's intellectual property.[180]

Only six weeks after setting up the Hubbard College and marrying a staff member, 18-year-old Mary Sue Whipp, Hubbard closed it down and moved with his new bride to Phoenix, Arizona. He established a Hubbard Association of Scientologists International to promote his new "Science of Certainty"—Scientology.[181]

13.8 Rise of Scientology

Main article: Scientology
See also: Timeline of Scientology

The Church of Scientology attributes its genesis to Hubbard's discovery of "a new line of research", first set out in his book *Science of Survival*—"that man is most fundamentally a spiritual being".[182] Non-Scientologist writers have suggested alternative motives: that he aimed "to reassert control over his creation",[170] that he believed "he was about to lose control of Dianetics",[179] or that he wanted to ensure "he would be able to stay in business even if the courts eventually awarded control of Dianetics and its valuable copyrights to ... the hated Don Purcell."[183]

Hubbard expanded upon the basics of Dianetics to construct a spiritually oriented (though at this stage not religious) doctrine based on the concept that the true self of a person was a thetan—an immortal, omniscient and potentially omnipotent entity.[184] Hubbard taught that the thetans, having created the material universe, had forgotten their god-like powers and become trapped in physical bodies.[185] Scientology aimed to "rehabilitate" each person's thetan to restore its original capacities and become once again an "Operating Thetan".[183][184] Hubbard insisted humanity was imperiled by the forces of "aberration", which were the result of engrams carried by the immortal thetans for billions of years.[179]

Hubbard introduced a device called an E-meter that he presented as having, as Miller puts it, "an almost mystical power to reveal an individual's innermost thoughts".[186] He promulgated Scientology through a series of lectures, bulletins and books such as *A History of Man* ("a cold-blooded and factual account of your last sixty trillion years")[186] and *Scientology: 8-8008* ("With this book, the ability to make one's body old or young at will, the ability to heal the ill without physical contact, the ability to cure the insane and the incapacitated, is set forth for the physician, the layman, the mathematician and the physicist.")[187]

Scientology was organized in a very different way from the decentralized Dianetics movement. The Hubbard Association of Scientologists (HAS) was the only official Scientology organization. Training procedures and doctrines were standardized and promoted through HAS publications, and administrators and auditors were not permitted to deviate from Hubbard's approach.[170] Branches or "orgs" were organized as franchises, rather like a fast food restaurant chain. Each franchise holder was required to pay ten percent of income to Hubbard's central organization. They were expected to find new recruits, known as "raw meat", but were restricted to providing only basic services. Costlier higher-level auditing was only provided by Hubbard's central organization.[188]

Although this model would eventually be extremely successful, Scientology was a very small-scale movement at first. Hubbard started off with only a few dozen followers, generally dedicated Dianeticists; a seventy-hour series of lectures in Philadelphia in December 1952 was attended by just 38 people.[189] Hubbard was joined in Phoenix by his 18-year-old son Nibs, who had been unable to settle down in high school.[190] Nibs had decided to become a Scientologist, moved into his father's home and went on to become a Scientology staff member and "professor".[191] Hubbard also traveled to the United Kingdom to establish his control over a Dianetics group in London. It was very much a shoestring operation; as Helen O'Brien later recalled, "there was an atmosphere of extreme poverty and undertones of a grim conspiracy over all. At 163 Holland Park Avenue was an ill-lit lecture room and a bare-boarded and poky office some eight by ten feet—mainly infested by long haired men and short haired and tatty women."[192] On September 24, 1952, only a few weeks after arriving in London, Hubbard's wife Mary Sue gave birth to her first child, a daughter whom they named Diana

Meredith de Wolfe Hubbard.[193]

In February 1953, Hubbard acquired a doctorate from the unaccredited Sequoia University. According to a Scientology biography, this was "given in recognition of his outstanding work on Dianetics" and "as an inspiration to the many people ... who had been inspired by him to take up advanced studies in this field ..."[111] The British government concluded in the 1970s that Sequoia University was a "degree mill" operated by Joseph Hough, a Los Angeles chiropractor.[194] Miller cites a telegram sent by Hubbard on February 27, 1953, in which he instructed Scientologist Richard de Mille to procure him a Ph.D. from Hough urgently—"FOR GOSH SAKES EXPEDITE. WORK HERE UTTERLY DEPENDANT ON IT."[195] Hough's "university" was closed down by the Californian authorities in 1971. British government officials noted in a report written in 1977: "It has not and never had any authority whatsoever to issue diplomas or degrees and the dean is sought by the authorities 'for questioning'."[194]

A few weeks after becoming "Dr." Hubbard, he wrote to Helen O'Brien—who had taken over the day-to-day management of Scientology in the United States—proposing that Scientology should be transformed into a religion.[196] As membership declined and finances grew tighter, Hubbard had reversed the hostility to religion he voiced in *Dianetics*.[197] His letter to O'Brien discussed the legal and financial benefits of religious status.[197] The idea may not have been new; Hubbard has been quoted as telling a science fiction convention in 1948: "Writing for a penny a word is ridiculous. If a man really wants to make a million dollars, the best way would be to start his own religion."[135][198][199] Scholar J. Gordon Melton notes, "There is no record of Hubbard having ever made this statement, though several of his science fiction colleagues have noted the broaching of the subject on one of their informal conversations."[200] The Church of Scientology has denied that Hubbard said this and insists that it is a misattributed quote that was said instead by George Orwell.[201] Hubbard outlined plans for setting up a chain of "Spiritual Guidance Centers" charging customers $500 for twenty-four hours of auditing ("That is real money ... Charge enough and we'd be swamped."). He wrote:

> I await your reaction on the religion angle. In my opinion, we couldn't get worse public opinion than we have had or have less customers with what we've got to sell. A religious charter would be necessary in Pennsylvania or NJ to make it stick. But I sure could make it stick.[202]

O'Brien was not enthusiastic and resigned the following September, worn out by work.[203] She criticized Hubbard for creating "a temperate zone voodoo, in its inelasticity, unexplainable procedures, and mindless group euphoria".[204] He nonetheless pressed ahead and on December 18, 1953, he incorporated the Church of Scientology, Church of American Science and Church of Spiritual Engineering in Camden, New Jersey.[205] Hubbard, his wife Mary Sue and his secretary John Galusha became the trustees of all three corporations.[206] Hubbard later denied founding the Church of Scientology, and to this day, Scientologists maintain that the "founding church" was actually the Church of Scientology of California, established on February 18, 1954, by Scientologist Burton Farber.[207] The reason for Scientology's religious transformation was explained by officials of the HAS:

> [T]here is little doubt but what [*sic*] this stroke will remove Scientology from the target area of overt and covert attacks by the medical profession, who see their pills, scalpels, and appendix-studded incomes threatened ... [Scientologists] can avoid the recent fiasco in which a Pasadena practitioner is reported to have spent 10 days in that city's torture chamber for "practicing medicine without a license."[208]

Scientology franchises became Churches of Scientology and some auditors began dressing as clergymen, complete with clerical collars. If they were arrested in the course of their activities, Hubbard advised, they should sue for massive damages for molesting "a Man of God going about his business".[205] A few years later he told Scientologists: "If attacked on some vulnerable point by anyone or anything or any organization, always find or manufacture enough threat against them to cause them to sue for peace ... Don't ever defend, always attack."[209] Any individual breaking away from Scientology and setting up his own group was to be shut down:

> The purpose of the suit is to harass and discourage rather than to win. The law can be used very easily to harass, and enough harassment on somebody who is simply on the thin edge anyway, well knowing that he is not authorized, will generally be sufficient to cause his professional decease. If possible, of course, ruin him utterly.[210]

The 1950s saw Scientology growing steadily. Hubbard finally achieved victory over Don Purcell in 1954 when the latter, worn out by constant litigation, handed the copyrights of Dianetics back to Hubbard.[211] Most of the formerly independent Scientology and Dianetics groups were either driven out of business or were absorbed into Hubbard's organizations.[212] Hubbard marketed Scientology through medical claims, such as attracting polio sufferers by presenting the Church of Scientology as a scientific research foundation investigating polio cases.[213] One advertisement during this period stated:

> Plagued by illness? We'll make you able to have good health. Get processed by the finest capable auditors in the world today [...] Personally coached and monitored by L. Ron Hubbard.[214]

Scientology became a highly profitable enterprise for Hubbard.[215] He implemented a scheme under which he was paid a percentage of the Church of Scientology's gross income and by 1957 he was being paid about $250,000 annually—equivalent to $1.9 million at 2010 prices.[216] His family grew, too, with Mary Sue giving birth to three more children—Geoffrey Quentin McCaully on January 6, 1954;[203] Mary Suzette Rochelle on February 13, 1955;[217] and Arthur Ronald Conway on June 6, 1958.[218] In the spring of 1959, he used his new-found wealth to purchase Saint Hill Manor, an 18th-century country house in Sussex, formerly owned by Sawai Man Singh II, the Maharaja of Jaipur. The house became Hubbard's permanent residence and an international training center for Scientologists.[213]

13.9 Controversies and crises

By the start of the 1960s, Hubbard was the leader of a worldwide movement with thousands of followers. A decade later, however, he had left Saint Hill Manor and moved aboard his own private fleet of ships as the Church of Scientology faced worldwide controversy.

The Church of Scientology says that the problems of this period were due to "vicious, covert international attacks" by the United States government, "all of which were proven false and baseless, which were to last 27 years and finally culminated in the Government being sued for 750 million dollars for conspiracy."[111] Behind the attacks, stated Hubbard, lay a vast conspiracy of "psychiatric front groups" secretly controlling governments: "Every single lie, false charge and attack on Scientology has been traced directly to this group's members. They have sought at great expense for nineteen years to crush and eradicate any new development in the field of the mind. They are actively preventing any effectiveness in this field."[219]

Hubbard believed that Scientology was being infiltrated by saboteurs and spies and introduced "security checking"[209] to identify those he termed "potential trouble sources" and "suppressive persons". Members of the Church of Scientology were interrogated with the aid of E-meters and were asked questions such as "Have you ever practiced homosexuality?" and "Have you ever had unkind thoughts about L. Ron Hubbard?"[220] For a time, Scientologists were even interrogated about crimes committed in past lives: "Have you ever destroyed a culture?" "Did you come to Earth for evil purposes?" "Have you ever zapped anyone?"[221]

He also sought to exert political influence, advising Scientologists to vote against Richard Nixon in the 1960 presidential election and establishing a Department of Government Affairs "to bring government and hostile philosophies or societies into a state of complete compliance with the goals of Scientology". This, he said, "is done by high-level ability to control and in its absence by a low-level ability to overwhelm. Introvert such agencies. Control such agencies."[222]

The U.S. Government was already well aware of Hubbard's activities. The FBI had a lengthy file on him, including a 1951 interview with an agent who considered him a "mental case".[172] Police forces in a number of jurisdictions began exchanging information about Scientology through the auspices of Interpol, which eventually led to prosecutions.[223] In 1958, the U.S. Internal Revenue Service withdrew the Washington, D.C. Church of Scientology's tax exemption after it found that Hubbard and his family were profiting unreasonably from Scientology's ostensibly non-profit income.[215] The Food and Drug Administration took action against Scientology's medical claims, seizing thousands of pills being marketed as "radiation cures"[224] as well as publications and E-meters. The Church of Scientology was required to label them as being "ineffective in the diagnosis or treatment of disease".[225]

Following the FDA's actions, Scientology attracted increasingly unfavorable publicity across the English-speaking world.[226] It faced particularly hostile scrutiny in Victoria, Australia, where it was accused of brainwashing, blackmail, extortion and damaging the mental health of its members.[227] The Victorian state government established a Board of Inquiry into

Scientology in November 1963.[228] Its report, published in October 1965, condemned every aspect of Scientology and Hubbard himself. He was described as being of doubtful sanity, having a persecution complex and displaying strong indications of paranoid schizophrenia with delusions of grandeur. His writings were characterized as nonsensical, abounding in "self-glorification and grandiosity, replete with histrionics and hysterical, incontinent outbursts".[229] Sociologist Roy Wallis comments that the report drastically changed public perceptions of Scientology:

> The former conception of the movement as a relatively harmless, if cranky, health and self-improvement cult, was transformed into one which portrayed it as evil, dangerous, a form of hypnosis (with all the overtones of Svengali in the layman's mind), and brainwashing.[227]

The report led to Scientology being banned in Victoria,[230] Western Australia and South Australia,[231] and led to more negative publicity around the world. Newspapers and politicians in the UK pressed the British government for action against Scientology. In April 1966, hoping to form a remote "safe haven" for Scientology, Hubbard traveled to the southern African country Rhodesia (today Zimbabwe) and looked into setting up a base there at a hotel on Lake Kariba. Despite his attempts to curry favour with the local government—he personally delivered champagne to Prime Minister Ian Smith's house, but Smith refused to see him—Rhodesia promptly refused to renew Hubbard's visa, compelling him to leave the country.[232] In July 1968, the British Minister of Health, Kenneth Robinson, announced that foreign Scientologists would no longer be permitted to enter the UK and Hubbard himself was excluded from the country as an "undesirable alien".[233] Further inquiries were launched in Canada, New Zealand and South Africa.[231]

Hubbard took three major new initiatives in the face of these challenges. "Ethics Technology" was introduced to tighten internal discipline within Scientology. It required Scientologists to "disconnect" from any organization or individual—including family members—deemed to be disruptive or "suppressive".[234] Scientologists were also required to write "Knowledge Reports" on each other, reporting transgressions or misapplications of Scientology methods. Hubbard promulgated a long list of punishable "Misdemeanors", "Crimes", and "High Crimes".[235] The "Fair Game" policy was introduced, which was applicable to anyone deemed an "enemy" of Scientology: "May be deprived of property or injured by any means by any Scientologist without any discipline of the Scientologist. May be tricked, sued or lied to or destroyed."[236][237]

At the start of March 1966, Hubbard created the Guardian's Office (GO), a new agency within the Church of Scientology that was headed by his wife Mary Sue.[238] It dealt with Scientology's external affairs, including public relations, legal actions and the gathering of intelligence on perceived threats.[239] As Scientology faced increasingly negative media attention, the GO retaliated with hundreds of writs for libel and slander; it issued more than forty on a single day.[240] Hubbard ordered his staff to find "lurid, blood sex crime actual evidence [sic] on [Scientology's] attackers".[241]

Finally, at the end of 1966, Hubbard acquired his own fleet of ships.[9] He established the "Hubbard Explorational Company Ltd" which purchased three ships—the *Enchanter*, a forty-ton schooner,[242] the *Avon River*, an old trawler,[243] and the *Royal Scotman* [sic], a former Irish Sea cattle ferry that he made his home and flagship.[244] The ships were crewed by the Sea Organization or Sea Org, a group of Scientologist volunteers, with the support of a couple of professional seamen.[9][245]

13.10   Commodore of the Sea Org

Main article: Sea Org
 After Hubbard created the Sea Org "fleet" in early 1967 it began an eight-year voyage, sailing from port to port in the Mediterranean Sea and eastern North Atlantic. The fleet traveled as far as Corfu in the eastern Mediterranean and Dakar and the Azores in the Atlantic, but rarely stayed anywhere for longer than six weeks. Ken Urquhart, Hubbard's personal assistant at the time, later recalled:

> [Hubbard] said we had to keep moving because there were so many people after him. If they caught up with him they would cause him so much trouble that he would be unable to continue his work, Scientology would not get into the world and there would be social and economic chaos, if not a nuclear holocaust.[246]

When Hubbard established the Sea Org he publicly declared that he had relinquished his management responsibilities. According to Miller, this was not true. He received daily telex messages from Scientology organizations around the world reporting their statistics and income. The Church of Scientology sent him $15,000 a week and millions of dollars were transferred to his bank accounts in Switzerland and Liechtenstein.[247] Couriers arrived regularly, conveying luxury food for Hubbard and his family[248] or cash that had been smuggled from England to avoid currency export restrictions.[249]

Along the way, Hubbard sought to establish a safe haven in "a friendly little country where Scientology would be allowed to prosper", as Miller puts it.[250] The fleet stayed at Corfu for several months in 1968–1969. Hubbard renamed the ships after Greek gods—the *Royal Scotman* was rechristened *Apollo*—and he praised the recently established military dictatorship.[249] The Sea Org was represented as "Professor Hubbard's Philosophy School" in a telegram to the Greek government.[251] In March 1969, however, Hubbard and his ships were ordered to leave.[252] In mid-1972, Hubbard tried again in Morocco, establishing contacts with the country's secret police and training senior policemen and intelligence agents in techniques for detecting subversives.[253] The program ended in failure when it became caught up in internal Moroccan politics, and Hubbard left the country hastily in December 1972.[254]

At the same time, Hubbard was still developing Scientology's doctrines. A Scientology biography states that "free of organizational duties and aided by the first Sea Org members, L. Ron Hubbard now had the time and facilities to confirm in the physical universe some of the events and places he had encountered in his journeys down the track of time."[54] In 1965, he designated several existing Scientology courses as confidential, repackaging them as the first of the esoteric "OT levels".[255] Two years later he announced the release of OT3, the "Wall of Fire", revealing the secrets of an immense disaster that had occurred "on this planet, and on the other seventy-five planets which form this Confederacy, seventy-five million years ago".[256] Scientologists were required to undertake the first two OT levels before learning how Xenu, the leader of the Galactic Confederacy, had shipped billions of people to Earth and blown them up with hydrogen bombs, following which their traumatized spirits were stuck together at "implant stations", brainwashed with false memories and eventually became contained within human beings.[257] The discovery of OT3 was said to have taken a major physical toll on Hubbard, who announced that he had broken a knee, an arm, and his back during the course of his research.[258] A year later, in 1968, he unveiled OT levels 4 to 6 and began delivering OT training courses to Scientologists aboard the *Royal Scotman*.[259]

Scientologists around the world were presented with a glamorous picture of life in the Sea Org and many applied to join Hubbard aboard the fleet.[259] What they found was rather different from the image. Most of those joining had no nautical experience at all.[259] Mechanical difficulties and blunders by the crews led to a series of embarrassing incidents and near-disasters. Following one incident in which the rudder of the *Royal Scotman* was damaged during a storm, Hubbard ordered the ship's entire crew to be reduced to a "condition of liability" and wear gray rags tied to their arms.[260] The ship itself was treated the same way, with dirty tarpaulins tied around its funnel to symbolize its lower status. According to those aboard, conditions were appalling; the crew was worked to the point of exhaustion, given meagre rations and forbidden to wash or change their clothes for several weeks.[261] Hubbard maintained a harsh disciplinary regime aboard the fleet, punishing mistakes by confining people in the *Royal Scotman*'s bilge tanks without toilet facilities and with food provided in buckets.[262] At other times erring crew members were thrown overboard with Hubbard looking on and, occasionally, filming.[263] David Mayo, a Sea Org member at the time, later recalled:

> We tried not to think too hard about his behavior. It was not rational much of the time, but to even consider such a thing was a discreditable thought and you couldn't allow yourself to have a discreditable thought. One of the questions in a sec[urity] check was, "Have you ever had any unkind thoughts about LRH?" and you could get into very serious trouble if you had. So you tried hard not to.[264]

From about 1970, Hubbard was attended aboard ship by the children of Sea Org members, organized as the Commodore's Messenger Organization (CMO). They were mainly young girls dressed in hot pants and halter tops, who were responsible for running errands for Hubbard such as lighting his cigarettes, dressing him or relaying his verbal commands to other members of the crew.[265][266] In addition to his wife Mary Sue, he was accompanied by all four of his children by her, though not his first son Nibs, who had defected from Scientology in late 1959.[267] The younger Hubbards were all members of the Sea Org and shared its rigors, though Quentin Hubbard reportedly found it difficult to adjust and attempted suicide in mid-1974.[268]

13.11 Life in hiding

During the 1970s, Hubbard faced an increasing number of legal threats. French prosecutors charged him and the French Church of Scientology with fraud and customs violations in 1972. He was advised that he was at risk of being extradited to France.[269] Hubbard left the Sea Org fleet temporarily at the end of 1972, living incognito in Queens, New York,[270] until he returned to his flagship in September 1973 when the threat of extradition had abated.[271] Scientology sources say that he carried out "a sociological study in and around New York City".[272]

Hubbard's health deteriorated significantly during this period. A chain-smoker, he also suffered from bursitis and excessive weight, and had a prominent growth on his forehead.[273] He suffered serious injuries in a motorcycle accident in 1973 and had a heart attack in 1975 that required him to take anticoagulant drugs for the next year.[274] In September 1978, Hubbard had a pulmonary embolism, falling into a coma, but recovered.[275]

He remained active in managing and developing Scientology, establishing the controversial Rehabilitation Project Force in 1974[276] and issuing policy and doctrinal bulletins.[277] However, the Sea Org's voyages were coming to an end. The *Apollo* was banned from several Spanish ports[277] and was expelled from Curaçao in October 1975.[278] The Sea Org came to be suspected of being a CIA operation, leading to a riot in Funchal, Madeira, when the *Apollo* docked there. At the time, *The Apollo Stars*, a musical group founded by Hubbard and made up entirely of shipbound members of the Sea Org, was offering free on-pier concerts in an attempt to promote Scientology, and the riot occurred at one of these events. Hubbard decided to relocate back to the United States to establish a "land base" for the Sea Org in Florida.[279] The Church of Scientology attributes this decision to the activities on the *Apollo* having "outgrow[n] the ship's capacity".[272]

In October 1975, Hubbard moved into a hotel suite in Daytona Beach. The Fort Harrison Hotel in Clearwater, Florida, was secretly acquired as the location for the "land base".[279] On December 5, 1975, Hubbard and his wife Mary Sue moved into a condominium complex in nearby Dunedin.[280] Their presence was meant to be a closely guarded secret but was accidentally compromised the following month.[281] Hubbard immediately left Dunedin and moved to Georgetown, Washington, D.C., accompanied by a handful of aides and messengers, but not his wife.[282] Six months later, following another security alert in July 1976, Hubbard moved to another safe house in Culver City, California. He lived there for only about three months, relocating in October to the more private confines of the Olive Tree Ranch near La Quinta.[283] His second son Quentin committed suicide a few weeks later in Las Vegas.[284][285]

Throughout this period, Hubbard was heavily involved in directing the activities of the Guardian's Office (GO), the legal bureau/intelligence agency that he had established in 1966. He believed that Scientology was being attacked by an international Nazi conspiracy, which he termed the "Tenyaka Memorial", through a network of drug companies, banks and psychiatrists in a bid to take over the world.[286] In 1973, he instigated the "Snow White Program" and directed the GO to remove negative reports about Scientology from government files and track down their sources.[287] The GO was ordered to "get all false and secret files on Scientology, LRH ... that cannot be obtained legally, by all possible lines of approach ... i.e., job penetration, janitor penetration, suitable guises utilizing covers." His involvement in the GO's operations was concealed through the use of codenames. The GO carried out covert campaigns on his behalf such as Operation Bulldozer Leak, intended "to effectively spread the rumor that will lead Government, media, and individual [Suppressive Persons] to conclude that LRH has no control of the C of S and no legal liability for Church activity". He was kept informed of GO operations, such as the theft of medical records from a hospital, harassment of psychiatrists and infiltrations of organizations that had been critical of Scientology at various times, such as the Better Business Bureau, the American Medical Association, and American Psychiatric Association.[288]

Members of the GO infiltrated and burglarized numerous government organizations, including the U.S. Department of Justice and the Internal Revenue Service.[289] After two GO agents were caught in the Washington, D.C. headquarters of the IRS, the FBI carried out simultaneous raids on GO offices in Los Angeles and Washington, D.C. on July 7, 1977. They retrieved wiretap equipment, burglary tools and some 90,000 pages of incriminating documents. Hubbard was not prosecuted, though he was labeled an "unindicted co-conspirator" by government prosecutors. His wife Mary Sue was indicted and subsequently convicted of conspiracy. She was sent to a federal prison along with ten other Scientologists.[290]

Hubbard's troubles increased in February 1978 when a French court convicted him in absentia for obtaining money under false pretenses. He was sentenced to four years in prison and a 35,000FF ($7,000) fine.[291] He went into hiding in April 1979, moving to an apartment in Hemet, California, where his only contact with the outside world was via ten trusted Messengers. He cut contact with everyone else, even his wife, whom he saw for the last time in August 1979.[292] Hubbard faced a possible indictment for his role in Operation Freakout, the GO's campaign against New York journalist Paulette

Cooper, and in February 1980 he disappeared into deep cover in the company of two trusted Messengers, Pat and Anne Broeker.[293][294]

For the first few years of the 1980s, Hubbard and the Broekers lived on the move, touring the Pacific Northwest in a recreational vehicle and living for a while in apartments in Newport Beach and Los Angeles.[295] Hubbard used his time in hiding to write his first new works of science fiction for nearly thirty years—*Battlefield Earth* (1982) and *Mission Earth*, a ten-volume series published between 1985 and 1987.[296] They received mixed responses; as writer Jeff Walker puts it, they were "treated derisively by most critics but greatly admired by followers".[297] Hubbard also wrote and composed music for three of his albums, which were produced by the Church of Scientology. The book soundtrack *Space Jazz* was released in 1982.[298] *Mission Earth* and *The Road to Freedom* were released posthumously in 1986.[299]

In Hubbard's absence, members of the Sea Org staged a takeover of the Church of Scientology and purged many veteran Scientologists. A young Messenger, David Miscavige, became Scientology's *de facto* leader. Mary Sue Hubbard was forced to resign her position and her daughter Suzette became Miscavige's personal maid.[300]

13.12 Death and legacy

For the last two years of his life, Hubbard lived in a luxury Blue Bird motorhome on Whispering Winds, a 160-acre ranch near Creston, California. He remained in deep hiding while controversy raged in the outside world about whether he was still alive and if so, where. He spent his time "writing and researching", according to a spokesperson, and pursued photography and music, overseeing construction work and checking on his animals.[301] He repeatedly redesigned the property, spending millions of dollars remodeling the ranch house—which went virtually uninhabited—and building a quarter-mile horse-racing track with an observation tower, which reportedly was never used.[295]

He was still closely involved in managing the Church of Scientology via secretly delivered orders[295] and continued to receive large amounts of money, of which *Forbes* magazine estimated "at least $200 million [was] gathered in Hubbard's name through 1982." In September 1985, the IRS notified the Church that it was considering indicting Hubbard for tax fraud.[302]

Hubbard suffered further ill-health, including chronic pancreatitis, during his residence at Whispering Winds. He suffered a stroke on January 17, 1986, and died a week later.[290][303] His body was cremated following an autopsy and the ashes were scattered at sea.[304] Scientology leaders announced that his body had become an impediment to his work and that he had decided to "drop his body" to continue his research on another planet,[305] having "learned how to do it without a body".[306]

Hubbard was survived by his wife Mary Sue and all of his children except his second son Quentin. His will provided a trust fund to support Mary Sue; her children Arthur, Diana and Suzette; and Katherine, the daughter of his first wife Polly.[307] He disinherited two of his other children.[308] L. Ron Hubbard, Jr. had become estranged, changed his name to "Ronald DeWolf" and, in 1982, sued unsuccessfully for control of his father's estate.[309] Alexis Valerie, Hubbard's daughter by his second wife Sara, had attempted to contact her father in 1971. She was rebuffed with the implied claim that her real father was Jack Parsons rather than Hubbard, and that her mother had been a Nazi spy during the war.[310] Both later accepted settlements when litigation was threatened.[308] In 2001, Diana and Suzette were reported to still be Church members, while Arthur had left and become an artist. Hubbard's great-grandson, Jamie DeWolf, is a noted slam poet.[311]

The copyrights of his works and much of his estate and wealth were willed to the Church of Scientology.[312] In a bulletin dated May 5, 1980, Hubbard told his followers to preserve his teachings until an eventual reincarnation when he would return "not as a religious leader but as a political one".[7] The Church of Spiritual Technology (CST), a sister organization of the Church of Scientology, has engraved Hubbard's entire corpus of Scientology and Dianetics texts on steel tablets stored in titanium containers. They are buried at the Trementina Base in a vault under a mountain near Trementina, New Mexico, on top of which the CST's logo has been bulldozed on such a gigantic scale that it is visible from space.[313][314]

Hubbard is the Guinness World Record holder for the most published author, with 1,084 works,[315] most translated book (70 languages for *The Way to Happiness*)[316] and most audiobooks (185 as of April 2009).[317] According to Galaxy Press, Hubbard's *Battlefield Earth* has sold over 6 million copies and *Mission Earth* a further 7 million, with each of its ten volumes becoming *New York Times* bestsellers on their release;[28] however, the *Los Angeles Times* reported in 1990 that Hubbard's followers had been buying large numbers of the books and re-issuing them to stores, so as to boost sales figures.[318] Opinions are divided about his literary legacy. Scientologists have written of their desire to "make Ron the most acclaimed and widely known author of all time".[318] The sociologist William Sims Bainbridge writes that even at his peak in the late 1930s Hubbard was regarded by readers of *Astounding Science Fiction* as merely "a passable, familiar author but not one of the best", while by the late 1970s "the [science fiction] subculture wishes it could forget him" and fans gave him a worse rating than any other of the "Golden Age" writers.[319]

In 2004, eighteen years after Hubbard's death, the Church claimed eight million followers worldwide. According to religious scholar J. Gordon Melton, this is an overestimate, counting as Scientologists people who had merely bought a book.[320] The City University of New York's American Religious Identification Survey found that by 2009 only 25,000 Americans identified as Scientologists.[321] Hubbard's presence still pervades Scientology. Every Church of Scientology maintains an office reserved for Hubbard, with a desk, chair and writing equipment, ready to be used.[312] Lonnie D. Kliever notes that Hubbard was "the only source of the religion, and he has no successor". Hubbard is referred to simply as "Source" within Scientology and the theological acceptability of any Scientology-related activity is determined by how closely it adheres to Hubbard's doctrines.[322] Hubbard's name and signature are official trademarks of the Religious Technology Center, established in 1982 to control and oversee the use of Hubbard's works and Scientology's trademarks and copyrights. The RTC is the central organization within Scientology's complex corporate hierarchy and has put much effort into re-checking the accuracy of all Scientology publications to "ensur[e] the availability of the pure unadulterated writings of Mr. Hubbard to the coming generations".[322]

The Danish historian of religions Mikael Rothstein describes Scientology as "a movement focused on the figure of Hubbard". He comments: "The fact that [Hubbard's] life is mythologized is as obvious as in the cases of Jesus, Muhammad or Siddartha Gotama. This is how religion works. Scientology, however, rejects this analysis altogether, and goes to great lengths to defend every detail of Hubbard's amazing and fantastic life as plain historical fact." Hubbard is presented as "the master of a multitude of disciplines" who performed extraordinary feats as a photographer, composer, scientist, therapist, explorer, navigator, philosopher, poet, artist, humanitarian, adventurer, soldier, scout, musician and many other fields of endeavor.[8] The Church of Scientology portrays Hubbard's life and work as having proceeded seamlessly, "as if they were a continuous set of predetermined events and discoveries that unfolded through his lifelong research" even up to and beyond his death.[3]

According to Rothstein's assessment of Hubbard's legacy, Scientology consciously aims to transfer the charismatic authority of Hubbard to institutionalize his authority over the organization, even after his death. Hubbard is presented as a virtually superhuman religious ideal just as Scientology itself is presented as the most important development in human history.[323] As Rothstein puts it, "reverence for Scientology's scripture is reverence for Hubbard, the man who in the Scientological perspective single-handedly brought salvation to all human beings."[8] David G. Bromley of the University of Virginia comments that the real Hubbard has been transformed into a "prophetic persona", "LRH", which acts as the basis for his prophetic authority within Scientology and transcends his biographical history.[3]

13.13   Biographies

Following Hubbard's death, Bridge Publications has published several stand-alone biographical accounts of his life. Marco Frenschkowski notes that "non-Scientologist readers immediately recognize some parts of Hubbard's life are here systematically left out: no information whatsoever is given about his private life (his marriages, divorces, children), his legal affairs and so on."[324] The Church maintains an extensive website presenting the official version of Hubbard's life.[325] It also owns a number of properties dedicated to Hubbard including the Los Angeles-based L. Ron Hubbard Life Exhibition (a presentation of Hubbard's life), the Author Services Center (a presentation of Hubbard's writings),[326] and the L. Ron Hubbard House in Washington, D.C.

In late 2012, Bridge published a comprehensive official biography of Hubbard, titled *The L. Ron Hubbard Series: A Biographical Encyclopedia*, written primarily by Dan Sherman, the official Hubbard biographer at the time. This most recent official Church of Scientology biography of Hubbard is a 17 volume series, with each volume focusing on a different aspect of Hubbard's life, including his music, photography, geographic exploration, humanitarian work, and nautical career. It is advertised as a "Biographic Encyclopedia" and is primarily authored by the official biographer, Dan Sherman.[327]

To date, there has not been a single volume comprehensive official biography published[327] [328] During his lifetime, a number of brief biographical sketches were also published in his Scientology books. The Church of Scientology issued "the only authorized LRH Biography" in October 1977 (it has since been followed by the Sherman "Biographic Encyclopedia").[111] His life was illustrated in print in *What Is Scientology?*, a glossy publication published in 1978 with paintings of Hubbard's life contributed by his son Arthur.[329]

In the late 1970s two men began to assemble a very different picture of Hubbard's life. Michael Linn Shannon, a resident of Portland, Oregon, became interested in Hubbard's life story after an encounter with a Scientology recruiter. Over the next four years he collected previously undisclosed records and documents. He intended to write an exposé of Hubbard and sent a copy of his findings and key records to a number of contacts but was unable to find a publisher.[330]

Shannon's findings were acquired by Gerry Armstrong, a Scientologist who had been appointed Hubbard's official archivist.[330] He had been given the job of assembling documents relating to Hubbard's life for the purpose of helping Omar V. Garrison, a non-Scientologist who had written two books sympathetic to Scientology, to write an official biography. However, the documents that he uncovered convinced both Armstrong and Garrison that Hubbard had systematically misrepresented his life. Garrison refused to write a "puff piece" and declared that he would not "repeat all the falsehoods they [the Church of Scientology] had perpetuated over the years". He wrote a "warts and all" biography while Armstrong quit Scientology, taking five boxes of papers with him. The Church of Scientology and Mary Sue Hubbard sued for the return of the documents while settling out of court with Garrison, requiring him to turn over the nearly completed manuscript of the biography.[331] In October 1984 Judge Paul G. Breckenridge ruled in Armstrong's favor, saying:

> The evidence portrays a man who has been virtually a pathological liar when it comes to his history, background and achievements. The writings and documents in evidence additionally reflect his egoism, greed, avarice, lust for power, and vindictiveness and aggressiveness against persons perceived by him to be disloyal or hostile. At the same time it appears that he is charismatic and highly capable of motivating, organizing, controlling, manipulating and inspiring his adherents. He has been referred to during the trial as a "genius," a "revered person," a man who was "viewed by his followers in awe." Obviously, he is and has been a very complex person and that complexity is further reflected in his alter ego, the Church of Scientology.[332]

In November 1987, the British journalist and writer Russell Miller published *Bare-faced Messiah*, the first full-length biography of L. Ron Hubbard. He drew on Armstrong's papers, official records and interviews with those who had known Hubbard including ex-Scientologists and family members. The book was well-received by reviewers but the Church of Scientology sought unsuccessfully to prohibit its publication on the grounds of copyright infringement.[333] Other critical biographical accounts are found in Bent Corydon's *L. Ron Hubbard, Messiah or Madman?* (1987) and Jon Atack's *A Piece of Blue Sky* (1990).

13.14   In popular culture

Hubbard appears as a major character in Paul Malmont's historical novel *The Astounding, the Amazing, and the Unknown* (2011).

The title character in the 2012 film *The Master* drew comparisons with Hubbard.[334][335][336]

13.15   Bibliography

Main article: L. Ron Hubbard bibliography
See also: Bibliography of Scientology and Written works of L. Ron Hubbard

According to the Church of Scientology, Hubbard produced some 65 million words on Dianetics and Scientology, contained in about 500,000 pages of written material, 3,000 recorded lectures and 100 films. His works of fiction included some 500 novels and short stories.[313]

13.16   Notes

[1] Von Dehsen, Christian D. "L. Ron Hubbard," in *Philosophers and religious leaders*, p. 90. Westport, Conn.: Greenwood Publishing Group, 1999. ISBN 978-1-57356-152-5

[2] Church of Scientology International. *L. Ron Hubbard: A Profile*. Retrieved November 26, 2012.

[3] Bromley, p. 89

[4] Sappel, Joel; Welkos, Robert W. (June 24, 1990). "The Mind Behind the Religion, Chapter 2: Creating the Mystique: Hubbard's Image Was Crafted of Truth, Distorted by Myth". *Los Angeles Times*. Archived from the original on June 12, 2008. Retrieved July 14, 2009.

[5] http://web.archive.org/web/20080612145705/http://www.latimes.com/business/la-scientology062490,0,2050131,full.story

[6] Christensen, p. 228

[7] Urban, Hugh B. "Fair Game: Secrecy, Security, and the Church of Scientology in Cold War America." *Journal of the American Academy of Religion* **74**:2 (2006)

[8] Rothstein, p. 21.

[9] Wright, Lawrence (February 14, 2011)."The Apostate: Paul Haggis vs. the Church of Scientology." *The New Yorker*, retrieved February 8, 2011.

[10] Hall, Timothy L. *American religious leaders*, p. 175. New York: Infobase Publishing, 2003. ISBN 978-0-8160-4534-1

[11] Miller, Russell. Bare-faced Messiah: the true story of L. Ron Hubbard, p. 11. London: Joseph, 1987. ISBN 0-7181-2764-1, OCLC 17481843

[12] Christensen, pp. 236–237

[13] Miller, p. 19

[14] Tucker, p. 300

[15] "About The Author," in Hubbard, L. Ron: *Have You Lived Before This Life?: A Scientific Survey: A Study of Death and Evidence of Past Lives*, p. 297. Los Angeles: Church of Scientology Publications Organization, 1977. ISBN 978-0-88484-055-8

[16] Sappell, Joel; Welkos, Robert (June 24, 1990). "The Making of L. Ron Hubbard: Creating the Mystique." *Los Angeles Times*, p. A38:1

[17] Quoted in Rolph, p. 17

[18] "L. Ron Hubbard and American Pulp Fiction," in Hubbard, L. Ron: "The Great Secret," p. 107–108. Hollywood, CA: Galaxy Press, 2008. ISBN 978-1-59212-371-1

[19] Atack, p. 48

[20] Sappell, Joel; Welkos, Robert (June 24, 1990). "The Making of L. Ron Hubbard: Staking a Claim to Blood Brotherhood." *Los Angeles Times*, p. A38:5

[21] Miller, p. 23

[22] Whitehead, p. 46

[23] Christensen, p. 238

[24] Miller, p. 25

[25] Miller, p. 27

[26] Miller, p. 28

[27] Christensen, pp. 239–240

[28] "About the Author," in Hubbard, L. Ron: *Battlefield Earth*. (No page number given.) Los Angeles: Galaxy Press, 2005. ISBN 978-1-59212-007-9

[29] "Appendix" in Hubbard, L. Ron: *Hymn of Asia*. (No page number given.) Los Angeles : Church of Scientology of California, Publications Organization, 1974. ISBN 0-88404-035-6

[30] Atack, p. 54

[31] Miller, p. 31

[32] Miller, p. 34

[33] Miller, p. 41

[34] "L. Ron Hubbard Biographical Profile: Asia and the South Pacific." Church of Scientology International, 2010, retrieved February 17, 2011.

[35] Atack, p. 57

[36] Miller, p. 42

[37] Miller, p. 43

[38] Miller, p. 44

[39] Miller, p. 45

[40] Miller, p. 46

[41] Miller, p. 47

[42] Atack, p. 59

[43] Malko, p. 31

[44] "A Brief Biography of L. Ron Hubbard," *Ability*, Church of Scientology Washington, D.C. Issue 111, January 1959.

[45] Wallis, p. 18

[46] "Foreword," in Hubbard, L. Ron: *Scientology: The Fundamentals of Thought*, p. vii. Los Angeles: Bridge Publications, 2007. ISBN 978-1-4031-4420-1

[47] Streeter, p. 206

[48] L. Ron Hubbard: A Chronicle, 1930–1940." Church of Scientology International, 2007, retrieved February 17, 2011.

[49] Atack, p. 64

[50] Miller, p. 52

[51] Miller, p. 54

[52] Miller, p. 55

[53] L. Ron Hubbard Biographical Profile — Caribbean Motion Picture Expedition." Church of Scientology International, 2010, retrieved February 17, 2011.

[54] Hubbard, L. Ron. *Mission into Time*, p. 7. Copenhagen: AOSH DK Publications Department A/S, 1973. ISBN 87-87347-56-3

[55] Miller, p. 56

[56] Hubbard, L. Ron, "The Camp-Fire," *Adventure* magazine, vol. 93 no. 5, October 1, 1935. Quoted in Atack, p. 62

[57] Maisel, Albert (December 5, 1950). "Dianetics — Science or Hoax?" *Look* magazine, p. 79

[58] Atack, p. 63

[59] "L. Ron Hubbard Biographical Profile — Puerto Rican Mineralogical Expedition." Church of Scientology, 2010, retrieved February 8, 2011.

[60] Hubbard, L. Ron. "Creating a Third Dynamic / United Survival Action Clubs," lecture of December 30, 1957. Ability Congress, 5th lecture.

[61] Nicholls, Peter. *Encyclopedia of Science Fiction*, 1978, p.108, ISBN 0-586-05380-8

[62] *L. Ron Hubbard, the writer*. Los Angeles, CA : Bridge Publications, 1989. (No page number in original.)

[63] Miller, p. 63

[64] "About L. Ron Hubbard — Master Storyteller." Galaxy Press, 2010, retrieved February 8, 2011.

[65] "L. Ron Hubbard Biographical Profile — L. Ron Hubbard's Fiction Books." Church of Scientology International, 2010, retrieved February 8, 2011.

[66] Miller, p. 72

[67] Frenschkowski, Marco (July 1999). "L. Ron Hubbard and Scientology: An annotated bibliographical survey of primary and selected secondary literature" (PDF). *Marburg Journal of Religion:* **4** (1): 15. Retrieved 13 May 2015.

[68] Asimov, Isaac. *In Memory Yet Green: The Autobiography of Isaac Asimov, 1920-1954*, p. 413. New York: Doubleday, 1979. ISBN 978-0-385-13679-2

[69] Staff (July 30, 1937). "Books Published Today". *The New York Times* (The New York Times Company). p. 17.

[70] Stableford, Brian. *Historical dictionary of science fiction literature*, p. 164. Lanham, MD: Scarecrow Press, 2004. ISBN 978-0-8108-4938-9

[71] Miller, p. 86

[72] "About the Author" in Hubbard, L. Ron: *Dianetics Today*, p. 989. Los Angeles: Church of Scientology of California, 1975. ISBN 0-88404-036-4

[73] Harmon, Jim; Donald F. Glut. *The Great Movie Serials: Their Sound and Fury*, p. 329. London: Routledge, 1973. ISBN 978-0-7130-0097-9

[74] Hubbard, L. Ron. "The Story of Dianetics and Scientology," lecture of October 18, 1958

[75] Atack, p. 65

[76] Miller, p. 69

[77] Miller, p. 61

[78] Miller, p. 64

[79] Miller, p. 70

[80] Miller, p. 62

[81] Miller, p. 74

[82] Miller, p. 71

[83] Miller, p. 75

[84] Miller, p. 84

[85] "L. Ron Hubbard Biographical Profile — Founder." Church of Scientology International, 2010, retrieved February 17, 2011.

[86] Gardner, p. 272

[87] Atack, p. 66

[88] Malko, p. 40

[89] Burks, Arthur J (December 1961). "Excalibur." *The Aberree*.

[90] Miller, p. 80

[91] Ackerman, Forrest J (November 19, 1997) *Secret Lives: L. Ron Hubbard*. Channel 4 Television.

[92] Letter from L. Ron Hubbard, October 1938, quoted in Miller, p. 81

[93] Quoted in Malko, p. 39

[94] Miller, p. 85

[95] Miller, p. 88

[96] Miller, p. 89

[97] "L. Ron Hubbard Biographical Profile — Alaskan Radio-Experimental Expedition" Church of Scientology International, 2010, retrieved February 17, 2011.

[98] Atack, p. 68

[99] Miller, p. 91

[100] Miller, p. 93

[101] Atack, p. 70

[102] Lamont, pp. 19–20

[103] Rolph, p. 16

[104] Miller, p. 141

[105] Streeter, p. 208

[106] Miller, p. 107

[107] Atack, p. 81; Streeter, p. 208

[108] "L. Ron Hubbard: A Chronicle, 1941–1949. Church of Scientology International, 2007, retrieved February 17, 2011.

[109] Atack, p. 84

[110] Stafford, Charles L.; Orsini, Bette (January 9, 1980). "Church moves to defend itself against 'attackers". *St. Petersburg Times*.

[111] Flag Information Letter 67, "L.R.H. Biography." Sea Organization, October 31, 1977.

[112] Hubbard, L. Ron. "My Philosophy," Church of Scientology International, 1965, retrieved February 17, 2011.

[113] Miller, p. 125

[114] Miller, p. 113

[115] Miller, p. 114

[116] Miller, p. 117

[117] Quoted in Symonds, John. *The Great Beast: the life and magick of Aleister Crowley*, p. 392. London: Macdonald and Co., 1971. ISBN 0-356-03631-6

[118] Urban, Hugh B. *Magia sexualis: sex, magic, and liberation in modern Western esotericism*, p. 137. Berkeley, CA: University of California Press, 2006. ISBN 978-0-520-24776-5

[119] Metzger, Richard. *Book of Lies: The Disinformation Guide to Magick and the Occult*, p. 200. New York: The Disinformation Company, 2008. ISBN 978-0-9713942-7-8

[120] Pendle, p. 268

[121] Pendle, p. 269

[122] Pendle, p. 270

[123] De Camp, L. Sprague, letter of August 26, 1946. Quoted by Pendle, p. 271

[124] "L. Ron Hubbard: A Chronicle, 1941–1949." Church of Scientology International, retrieved February 8, 2011.

[125] Atack, p. 90

[126] "Scientology: New Light on Crowley." *The Sunday Times*, December 28, 1969

[127] Miller, p. 134

[128] Miller, p. 132

[129] Streeter, p. 210

[130] Video on YouTube

[131] Hubbard, L. Ron, letter to Veterans Administration, October 15, 1947; quoted in Miller, p. 137

[132] Miller, p. 139

[133] Miller, p. 142

[134] "Letters from the Birth of Dianetics." Church of Scientology International, 2004, retrieved February 8, 2011

[135] Methvin, Eugene H. (May 1990). "Scientology: Anatomy of a Frightening Cult." *Reader's Digest*. pp. 16.

[136] Miller, p. 143

[137] "L. Ron Hubbard: A Chronicle, 1941–1949" Church of Scientology International, 2007, retrieved February 14, 2011.

[138] Miller, p. 144

[139] One such letter can be found on the Church of Scientology's official L. Ron Hubbard website. See "Letters from the Birth of Dianetics," Church of Scientology International, 2004, retrieved February 8, 2011.

[140] Luckhurst, Roger. *Science Fiction*, p. 74. Malden, MA: Polity, 2005. ISBN 978-0-7456-2893-6

[141] Miller, p. 149

[142] Atack, p. 106

[143] Miller, p. 150

[144] Streeter, pp. 210–211

[145] Atack, p. 108

[146] Miller, Timothy (1995). *America's Alternative Religions*. Albany: State University of New York Press. pp. 385–386. ISBN 978-0-7914-2398-1. OCLC 30476551.

[147] Winter, p. 18

[148] Quoted in Miller, p. 145

[149] Miller, p. 152

[150] Atack, p. 107

[151] Gardner, p. 265

[152] Staff (August 21, 1950). "Dianetics book review; Best Seller." *Newsweek*

[153] Rabi, Isaac Isador. "Book Review." *Scientific American*, January 1951

[154] Gumpert, Martin. (August 14, 1950) "*Dianetics*: book review by Martin Gumpert." *The New Republic*

[155] Miller, p. 153

[156] Atack, p. 113

[157] Kerman, Cynthia Earl; Eldridge, Richard. *The lives of Jean Toomer: a hunger for wholeness*, pp. 317–318. Baton Rouge: Louisiana State University Press, 1989. ISBN 978-0-8071-1548-0

[158] Sturgeon, Theodore; Williams, Paul. *Baby is three*, p. 414. Berkeley, CA: North Atlantic Books, 1999. ISBN 978-1-55643-319-1

[159] Miller, p. 166

[160] Melton, p. 190

[161] O'Brien, p. 27

[162] Miller, pp. 159–160

[163] Atack, p. 377

[164] Evans, p. 26

[165] Winter, p. 34

[166] Miller, p. 169

[167] Whitehead, p. 67

[168] Gardner, p. 270

[169] Stark, Rodney; Bainbridge, William Sims. *The future of religion: secularization, revival, and cult formation*, pp. 268–269. Berkeley: University of California Press, 1986. ISBN 978-0-520-05731-9

[170] Marshall, Gordon. *In praise of sociology*, p. 186. London: Routledge, 1990. ISBN 978-0-04-445688-9

[171] Miller, p. 173

[172] Miller, p. 181

[173] Miller, p. 170

[174] Miller, p. 180

[175] Atack, p. 117

[176] Martin, Walter Ralston; Zacharias, Ravi K. (ed.). *The Kingdom of the Cults*, p. 338. Minneapolis: Bethany House, 2003. ISBN 978-0-7642-2821-6

[177] Staff (April 24, 1951). "Ron Hubbard Insane, Says His Wife." *San Francisco Chronicle*

[178] Quoted in Miller, p. 192

[179] Streissguth, p. 71

[180] Miller, p. 200

[181] Atack, p. 129

[182] "L. Ron Hubbard: A Chronicle, 1950–1959. Church of Scientology International, 2007, retrieved February 8, 2011.

[183] Miller, p. 203

[184] DeChant, Dell; Danny L. Jorgensen. "The Church of Scientology: A Very New American Religion" in Neusner, Jacob. *World Religions in America: An Introduction*, p. 226. Westminster John Knox Press, 2003. ISBN 0-664-22475-X

[185] Bromley, p. 91

[186] Miller, p. 204

[187] Miller, p. 206

[188] Tucker, p. 304

[189] Miller, p. 210

[190] Miller, p. 207

[191] Miller, p. 232

[192] O'Brien, p. 49

[193] Miller, p. 208

[194] Smith, Graham (August 7, 2009). "Scientology founder L. Ron Hubbard exposed as a 'fraud' by British diplomats 30 years ago." *Daily Mail*, retrieved February 8, 2011.

[195] Miller, p. 212

[196] Streeter, p. 215; Miller, p. 213

[197] Kent, Stephen A. "The Creation of 'Religious' Scientology." *Religious Studies and Theology* **18**:2, pp. 97–126. 1999. ISSN 1747-5414

[198] Lawrence, Sara. (April 18, 2006) "The Secrets of Scientology" *The Independent*. Retrieved February 17, 2011.

[199] Staff. (April 5, 1976). "Religion: A Sci-Fi Faith." *Time*. Retrieved February 17, 2011.

[200] Melton, J. Gordon (2000). *Studies in Contemporary Religion: The Church of Scientology* (1 ed.). Torino, Italy: Elle Di Ci, Leumann. pp. 55, 74. ISBN 978-1-56085-139-4. The actual quote seems to have come from a cynical remark in a letter written by Orwell published in *The Collected Essays, Journalism, and Letters of George Orwell*.

[201] Did L. Ron Hubbard state that the way to make money was to start a religion? Church of Scientology International, 2003, retrieved February 8, 2011.

[202] Hubbard, L. Ron. Letter of April 10, 1953. Quoted in Miller, p. 213

[203] Miller, p. 214

[204] O'Brien, p. vii

[205] Williams, Ian. *The Alms Trade: Charities, Past, Present and Future*, p. 127. New York: Cosimo, 2007. ISBN 978-1-60206-753-0

[206] Voltz, Tom. *Scientology und (k)ein Ende*, p. 75. Solothurn: Walter, 1995. ISBN 978-3-530-89980-1

[207] Atack, p. 137

[208] Staff (April 1954). "Three Churches Are Given Charters in New Jersey." *The Aberree*, volume 1, issue 1, p. 4

[209] Miller, p. 239

[210] Hubbard, L. Ron. "The Scientologist: A Manual on the Dissemination of Material," 1955. Quoted in Atack, p. 139

[211] Atack, p. 138

[212] Atack, p. 139

[213] Streissguth, p. 74

[214] Staff (Hubbard?) (November 1957). *Ability*, Issue 58, p. 5.

[215] Atack, p. 142

[216] Miller, p. 227

[217] Miller, p. 221

[218] Miller, p. 230

[219] Hubbard, L. Ron. "Constitutional Destruction." June 9, 1969, retrieved February 8, 2011.

[220] Atack, p. 150

[221] Hubbard, L. Ron. "Sec Check Whole Track," HCO Bulletin of June 19, 1961; quoted in Atack, p. 152

[222] Hubbard, L. Ron. "Department of Government Affairs," HCO Policy Letter of August 15, 1960; quoted in Miller, p. 241

[223] Fooner, Michael. *Interpol: issues in world crime and international criminal justice*, p. 13. New York: Plenum Press, 1989. ISBN 978-0-306-43135-7

[224] Miller, p. 228

[225] Atack, p. 154

[226] Wallis, p. 192

[227] Wallis, p. 215

[228] Miller, p. 250

[229] Miller, pp. 252–253

[230] Wallis, p. 193

[231] Wallis, p. 196

[232] Reitman (2011), pp. 80–81

[233] Atack, p. 183

[234] Atack, p. 155

[235] Atack, p. 156

[236] Hubbard, L. Ron. "Penalties for Lower Conditions." HCO Policy Letter of October 18, 1967, Issue IV. Quoted in Atack, pp. 175–176

[237] Wallis, pp. 144–145

[238] Atack, p. 161

[239] Atack, p. 165

[240] Atack, p. 189

[241] Atack, p. 160

[242] Miller, p. 264

[243] Miller, p. 265

[244] Miller, p. 269

[245] Miller, p. 272

[246] Quoted in Miller, p. 297

[247] Miller, p. 299

[248] Miller, p. 300

[249] Miller, p. 290

[250] Miller, p. 310

[251] Miller, p. 295

[252] Miller, p. 296

[253] Miller, p. 311

[254] Miller, p. 312

[255] Atack, p. 159

[256] Hubbard, L. Ron. "Ron's Journal '67," quoted in Atack, p. 173.

[257] Atack, p. 32

[258] Atack, p. 173

[259] Atack, p. 177

[260] Miller, p. 285

[261] Miller, p. 286

[262] Atack, p. 180

[263] Atack, p. 186

[264] Miller, p. 289

[265] Miller, p. 301

[266] Sappell, Joel; Welkos, Robert (June 24, 1990). "The Mind Behind the Religion : Life With L. Ron Hubbard." *Los Angeles Times*, retrieved February 20, 2011.

[267] Miller, p. 236

[268] Miller, p. 325

[269] Corydon, Bent. *L. Ron Hubbard: Messiah or Madman?*, p. 94. Fort Lee, N.J.: Barricade Books, 1992. ISBN 978-0-942637-57-1

[270] Miller, p. 314

[271] Miller, p. 318

[272] "L. Ron Hubbard: A Chronicle, 1970–1979." Church of Scientology International, 2007, retrieved February 8, 2011.

[273] Miller, p. 316

[274] Atack, p. 255

[275] Atack, p. 256

[276] Atack, p. 206

[277] Atack, p. 204

[278] Atack, p. 209

[279] Miller, p. 334

[280] Miller, p. 336

[281] Miller, p. 338

[282] Miller, p. 340

[283] Miller, p. 343

[284] Miller, p. 344

[285] Sappell, Joel; Robert W. Welkos (June 24, 1990). "The Mind Behind the Religion : Life With L. Ron Hubbard : Aides indulged his eccentricities and egotism". *Los Angeles Times*. Retrieved February 19, 2011.

[286] Beresford, David (February 7, 1980). "Snow White's dirty tricks." London: *The Guardian*

[287] Miller, pp. 317–318

[288] Marshall, John (January 24, 1980). "The Scientology Papers: Hubbard still gave orders, records show." Toronto: *Globe and Mail*

[289] Streissguth, p. 75

[290] Reitman (2007), p. 323

[291] Marshall, John (January 26, 1980). "The Scientology Papers: The hidden Hubbard." Toronto: *Globe and Mail*

[292] Atack, p. 258

[293] Atack, p. 259

[294] Miller, p. 364

[295] Sappell, Joel; Welkos, Robert W. (June 24, 1990). The Mind Behind the Religion : Chapter Four : The Final Days : Deep in hiding, Hubbard kept tight grip on the church." *Los Angeles Times*, retrieved February 8, 2011.

[296] Queen, Edward L.; Prothero, Stephen R.; Shattuck, Gardiner H. *Encyclopedia of American religious history*, Volume 1, p. 493. New York: Infobase Publishing, 2009. ISBN 978-0-8160-6660-5

[297] Walker, Jeff. *The Ayn Rand Cult*, p. 275. Chicago: Open Court, 1999. ISBN 978-0-8126-9390-4

[298] Garchik, Leah (March 17, 2006). "Leah Garchik (Daily Datebook)". *San Francisco Chronicle* (The Chronicle Publishing Co.). p. E16.

[299] Goldstein, Patrick (September 21, 1986). "Hubbard Hymns". *Los Angeles Times*. p. 40.

[300] Miller, p. 366

[301] Brown, Mark (January 30, 1986). "Creston provided quiet retreat for controversial church leader." *The County Telegram-Tribune*, San Luis Obispo, pp. 1A/5A.

[302] Behar, Richard (October 27, 1986). "The prophet and profits of Scientology." Forbes 400 (Forbes)

[303] Church of Scientology. L. Ron Hubbard's death. Image of Death Certificate. Retrieved on: 2012-06-15.

[304] Miller, p. 375

[305] Petrowsky, Marc. *Sects, cults, and spiritual communities: a sociological analysis*, p. 144. Westport, Conn.: Praeger, 1998. ISBN 978-0-275-95860-2

[306] Atack, p. 354

[307] [Staff] (February 7, 1986). "Hubbard Left Most of Estate to Scientology Church; Executor Appointed." The Associated Press

[308] Atack, p. 356

[309] Lamont, p. 154

[310] Miller, p. 306

[311] Lattin, Don (February 12, 2001). "Scientology Founder's Family Life Far From What He Preached." *San Francisco Chronicle*, retrieved February 12, 2011.

[312] Reitman (2007), p. 324

[313] Gallagher, Eugene V.; Ashcraft, Michael. *African Diaspora Traditions and Other American Innovations*, p. 172; vol 5 of *Introduction to New and Alternative Religions in America*. Westport, Conn.: Greenwood Publishing Group, 2006. ISBN 978-0-275-98717-6

[314] "Google Map".

[315] "Most published works by one author". *GuinnessWorldRecords.com*. Guinness World Records. Retrieved February 12, 2011.

[316] "Most translated author, same book". *GuinnessWorldRecords.com*. Guinness World Records. Retrieved February 22, 2011.

[317] "Most audio books published for one author". *GuinnessWorldRecords.com*. Guinness World Records. Retrieved February 22, 2011.

[318] Sappell, Joel; Welkos, Robert W. (June 28, 1990). "Costly Strategy Continues to Turn Out Bestsellers." *Los Angeles Times*, retrieved February 15, 2011.

[319] Bainbridge, William Sims. "Science and Religion: The Case of Scientology," in Bromley, David G.; Hammond, Phillip E. (eds). *The Future of new religious movements*, p. 63. Macon, GA: Mercer University Press, 1987. ISBN 978-0-86554-238-9

[320] Jarvik, Elaine (September 20, 2004). "Scientology: Church now claims more than 8 million members". *Deseret Morning News*. Retrieved February 13, 2011.

[321] Associated Press. "Defections, court fights test Scientology." *MSNBC.com*, November 1, 2009, retrieved February 14, 2011

[322] Rothstein, p. 24

[323] Rothstein, p. 20

[324] Frenschkowski, Marco. "L. Ron Hubbard and Scientology: An annotated bibliographical survey of primary and selected secondary literature," *Marburg Journal of Religion*, **4**:1, July 1999, retrieved February 8, 2011.

[325] Available at www.lronhubbard.org

[326] Cowan, Douglas E.; Bromley, David G. *Cults and new religions: a brief history*, p. 30. Oxford: Blackwell, 2008. ISBN 978-1-4051-6128-2

[327] http://www.lronhubbard.org/books/ron-series/biographical-encyclopedia.html

[328] Gallagher, Eugene V. *The new religious movements experience in America*, p. 216. Greenwood Publishing Group, 2004. ISBN 978-0-313-32807-7

[329] Miller, p. 350

[330] Atack, p. 46

[331] Shelor, George-Wayne. "Writer tells of Hubbard's 'faked past'." *Clearwater Sun*, May 10, 1984

[332] Breckenridge Jr., Paul G. (October 24, 1984). *Memorandum of Intended Decision*, Church of Scientology of California vs. Gerald Armstrong. Quoted by Miller, pp. 370-71

[333] Murtagh, Peter (October 10, 1987). "Scientologists fail to suppress book about church's founder." *The Guardian*.

[334] Brown, Lane (December 3, 2010). "So This New Paul Thomas Anderson Movie Is Definitely About Scientology, Right?". *NYMag.com*. New York Media Holdings. Retrieved June 5, 2011.

[335] Brown, Lane (March 17, 2010). "Universal Passes on Paul Thomas Anderson's Scientology Movie". *NYMag.com*. New York Media Holdings. Retrieved June 5, 2011.

[336] Pilkington, Ed (April 26, 2011). "Church of Scientology snaps up Hollywood film studio". *Guardian.co.uk*. Guardian News and Media Limited. Retrieved June 12, 2011.

13.17 References

- Atack, Jon. *A Piece of Blue Sky: Scientology, Dianetics, and L. Ron Hubbard exposed.* Carol Publishing Group, 1990. ISBN 978-0-8184-0499-3, OCLC 20934706

- Behar, Richard *Pushing Beyond the U.S.: Scientology makes its presence felt in Europe and Canada*

- Bromley, David G. "Making Sense of Scientology: Prophetic, Contractual Religion," in Lewis, James R. (ed.), *Scientology.* Oxford: Oxford University Press, 2009. ISBN 978-0-19-533149-3 OCLC 232786014

- Christensen, Dorthe Refslund. "Inventing L. Ron Hubbard: On the Construction and Maintenance of the Hagiographic Mythology of Scientology's Founder," pp. 227–258 in Lewis, James R.; Petersen, Jesper Aagaard: *Controversial new religions.* Oxford: Oxford University Press, 2005. ISBN 978-0-19-515683-6, OCLC 53398162, available through *Oxford Scholarship Online*, doi:10.1093/019515682X.003.0011

- Evans, Christopher. *Cults of Unreason.* New York: Farrar, Straus and Giroux, 1974. ISBN 0-374-13324-7, OCLC 863421

- Gardner, Martin. *Fads and fallacies in the name of science.* New York: Courier Dover Publications, 1957. ISBN 978-0-486-20394-2, OCLC 18598918

- Jacobsen, Jeff Day, Robert RJ. *What the Church of Scientology Doesn't Want You To Know*

- Lamont, Stewart. *Religion Inc.: The Church of Scientology.* London: Harrap, 1986. ISBN 978-0-245-54334-0, OCLC 23079677

- Malko, George. *Scientology: The Now Religion.* New York: Delacorte Press, 1970. OCLC 115065

- Melton, J. Gordon. *Encyclopedic handbook of cults in America.* Taylor & Francis; 1992. ISBN 978-0-8153-1140-9

- Miller, Russell. *Bare-faced Messiah: the true story of L. Ron Hubbard.* London: Joseph, 1987. ISBN 0-7181-2764-1, OCLC 17481843

- O'Brien, Helen. *Dianetics in Limbo: A Documentary About Immortality.* Philadelphia: Whitmore Publishing, 1966. OCLC 4797460

- Pendle, George. *Strange Angel: The Otherworldly Life of Rocket Scientist John Whiteside Parsons.* Orlando, FL: Houghton Mifflin Harcourt, 2006. ISBN 978-0-15-603179-0, OCLC 55149255

- Reitman, Janet. "Inside Scientology," pp. 305–348 of American Society of Magazine Editors (Ed.) *The Best American Magazine Writing 2007.* New York: Columbia University Press, 2007. ISBN 978-0-231-14391-2, OCLC 154711228

- Reitman, Janet. *Inside Scientology: The Story of America's Most Secretive Religion.* Boston, MA: Houghton Mifflin Harcourt, 2011. ISBN 978-0-618-88302-8, OCLC 651912263

- Rolph, Cecil Hewitt *Believe What You Like: what happened between the Scientologists and the National Association for Mental Health.* London: Deutsch, 1973. ISBN 978-0-233-96375-4, OCLC 815558

- Rothstein, Mikael. "Scientology, scripture and sacred traditions," in Lewis, James R.; Hammer, Olav (eds.): *The invention of sacred tradition.* Cambridge: Cambridge University Press, 2007. ISBN 978-0-521-86479-4, OCLC 154706390

- Streeter, Michael. *Behind closed doors: the power and influence of secret societies.* London: New Holland Publishers, 2008. ISBN 978-1-84537-937-7, OCLC 231589690

- Streissguth, Thomas. *Charismatic cult leaders.* Minneapolis: The Oliver Press, 1995. ISBN 978-1-881508-18-2, OCLC 30892074

- Tucker, Ruth A. *Another Gospel: Cults, Alternative Religions, and the New Age Movement.* Grand Rapids, MI: Zondervan, 2004. ISBN 978-0-310-25937-4, OCLC 19354219

- Wallis, Roy. *The road to total freedom: a sociological analysis of Scientology.* New York: Columbia University Press, 1977. ISBN 978-0-231-04200-0, OCLC 2373469

- Whitehead, Harriet. *Renunciation and reformulation: a study of conversion in an American sect.* Ithaca, NY: Cornell University Press, 1987. ISBN 978-0-8014-1849-5, OCLC 14002616

- Winter, Joseph A. *A Doctor's Report on Dianetics: Theory and Therapy.* New York: Julian Press, 1951. OCLC 1572759

13.18 External links

Sites run by Church of Scientology International

- Official L. Ron Hubbard site

- Biographical Profile of L. Ron Hubbard

- L. Ron Hubbard: A Chronicle

Publishers' sites

- Author Services Inc. Publisher of L. Ron Hubbard's fiction

- Bridge Publications Inc. Publisher of L. Ron Hubbard's Scientology and Dianetics works

- Writers of the Future A contest founded in the early 1980s by L. Ron Hubbard to encourage upcoming fiction and fantasy writers

Further mention of Hubbard

- *Bare Faced Messiah* by Russell Miller

- Biographical documentation from *The New Yorker*

- Operation Clambake. Critical material on Hubbard and Scientology

- U.S. Government FBI Files for Hubbard via *The Smoking Gun*

- 'The Shrinking World of L. Ron Hubbard': Rare interview with Hubbard by an external documentary team on YouTube - World in Action, Granada TV, directed & produced by Charlie Nairn, 1967.

- Frenschkowski, Marco, L. Ron Hubbard and Scientology: An annotated bibliographical survey of primary and selected secondary literature, *Marburg Journal of Religion*, Vol. 1. No. 1. July 1999, ISSN 1612-2941

- L. Ron Hubbard at the Internet Movie Database

- L. Ron Hubbard at the Internet Speculative Fiction Database

- L. Ron Hubbard at the Internet Book List

- Hubbard, L Ron at the Encyclopedia of Science Fiction

- Hubbard, , L Ron at the Encyclopedia of Fantasy

Illustration by Edd Cartier for Hubbard's story "Fear"[611]

Ketchikan, Alaska, where Hubbard and his wife were stranded during the "Alaskan Radio-Experimental Expedition"

Lts (jg) L. Ron Hubbard and Thomas S. Moulton in Portland, Oregon in 1943

The USS PC-815, *Hubbard's second and final command*

Masters of Sleep, *one of Hubbard's last works of pulp fiction, on the cover of the October 1950 issue of* Fantastic Adventures

Hubbard conducting a Dianetics seminar in Los Angeles, 1950

Hubbard established an "Academy of Scientology" at this Northwest, Washington, D.C. building in 1955. It is now the L. Ron Hubbard House museum.

The L. Ron Hubbard House at Camelback in Phoenix, Az. The house is listed in the National Register of Historic Places.

L. Ron Hubbard's car, a 1947 Buick Super 8. The car is parked behind the house.

Corfu town, where the Sea Org moored in 1968–1969

The Internal Revenue Service building in Washington D.C., one of the targets of Hubbard's "Snow White Program"

The ranch in San Luis Obispo County, California where Hubbard spent his final years

Gerry Armstrong, formerly Hubbard's official biographical researcher, whose trial disclosed many details of Hubbard's life

Chapter 14

Christopher Hyatt

Christopher Hyatt (July 12, 1943 – February 9, 2008), born **Alan Ronald Miller**, was an American occultist, author, and founder of the Extreme Individual Institute (EII). He is best known as president of New Falcon Publications.

14.1 Early life

A native of Chicago, Alan Miller, the son of police lieutenant Leonard Miller and his wife, Bertha Freidman, was born during what he described as the "roaring war years". Writing and speaking as Christopher Hyatt, he gave two different accounts of the end of his high school career. In the first account, he claimed that he dropped out of high school at the age of sixteen, working instead as a dishwasher and cook, roaming around the United States.[1]

14.2 Occultist

Hyatt's interest in the occult began in his early twenties. His desire to further pursue his studies in magick resulted in meeting Israel Regardie in Studio City in the 1970s. Regardie introduced Hyatt to Reichian therapy, which he insisted Hyatt learn prior to any magickal pursuits. Regardie further instructed Hyatt in the magical system of the Hermetic Order of the Golden Dawn. Hyatt was a Ninth Degree member of occult Order Ordo Templi Orientis,[2] and once headed the Thelemic Golden Dawn.[1][3]

14.3 Academic career

Hyatt was trained in experimental and clinical psychology and practiced as a psychotherapist for many years. As Alan Miller, he used the 18 units earned from his military GED towards his first academic career at Los Angeles City College, where he studied accounting for two years. He later changed his graduate to General Psychology, earning Masters Degrees in experimental psychology and medical education and Counselling. He was a member of a Freudian clinic in Southern California. He spent almost a year studying hypnosis at the Hypnosis Motivation Institute in Los Angeles and also studied hypnosis at the University of California, Irvine. Miller possessed Ph.D.s in both clinical psychology and human behavior[2] and was a Postdoctoral researcher in Criminal Justice.[4] Some of his techniques blended Reichian physiotherapy and tantric yoga. He also incorporated hypnosis alongside his body work with patients and students. According to his website: "He left academia and state sponsored psychology to become an explorer of the human mind."

Christopher Hyatt died of cancer in Scottsdale, Arizona at the age of 64.

14.4   Notes and references

[1] Hyatt, Christopher; Zehm Aloim. *The Magic of Israel Regardie*. New Falcon Publishing. ISBN 1-56184-230-3.

[2] Hymenaeus Beta (2008-02-12). "Alan Ronald Miller, Ph.D., IX° O.T.O. (1943-2008)". *Ordo Tempi Orientis International Headquarters*. Retrieved 2011-06-01.

[3] Greer, John Michael (2003). *The New Encyclopedia of the Occult*. Llewellyn Worldwide. p. 205. ISBN 978-1-56718-336-8. Several of these new Golden Dawn orders were created by friends and students of Regardie in the United States.... [A]nother emerged in Arizona under the leadership of Christopher Hyatt.

[4] Hyatt, Christopher; S. Jason Black; Zehm Aloim; Israel Regardie. *Techniques for Undoing Yourself*. New Falcon Publishing. ISBN 1-56184-280-X.

14.5   External links

- Tribute site to Christopher Hyatt by New Falcon Publications

- www.originalfalcon.com

- New Falcon Publications Official Website

Chapter 15

Richard Kaczynski

For the Polish politician, see Ryszard Kaczyński.

Richard Kaczynski is an American writer and lecturer in the fields of social psychology, metaphysical beliefs and new religious movements. He is known for his biography *Perdurabo: The Life of Aleister Crowley*, described by the Times Literary Supplement as "the major biography to date",[1] and by the Norwegian daily *Aftenposten* as being regarded as the best biography of Crowley.[2]

Kaczynski is also a keyboard player for the band *House of Usher*.[3]

15.1 Academic background

Kaczynski holds a Bachelor of Science degree, Master's degrees, and a PhD in social psychology from Wayne State University, where his doctoral dissertation focused on the nature of metaphysical beliefs.[4] He is currently a staff affiliate at Yale University's Department of Psychiatry.[5] He is also an adjunct instructor of orthodontics at the University of Detroit Mercy School of Dentistry.[6]

He has published dozens of articles in a variety of academic peer-reviewed journals in areas ranging from national program evaluation of comprehensive work therapy, and multi-site clinical trials of treatment efficacy for bipolar disorder (STEP-BD), schizophrenia (CATIE) and Alzheimer's (CATIE). Other areas of experience include mental health, caregiving, substance abuse, prenatal health, orthodontics, violent crime, emergency room utilization, and PTSD in Holocaust survivors.[7]

15.2 Metaphysical background

Kaczynski has been a student of Thelema since 1977, a member of Ordo Templi Orientis since 1987, and a lecturer on magick since 1990.[8] Within OTO he has been a very active member, and has done editorial duties on several publications including *Neshamah*[9] and the proceedings books for its US biennial national conference. He appeared on Canada's Drew Marshall radio show on June 25, 2011, where he was described as the "world's leading expert on Aleister Crowley"[10]

15.3 Works

Kaczynski's occult writings have appeared in various magazines including *High Times*,[11] *The Magical Link*, *Neshamah*, *Cheth*, *Mezlim*, *Eidolon*, and *Different Worlds*.[12] His medical and psychological writing has appeared in several publications in those fields.[7]

15.3.1 Books

- *The Revival of Magick and Other Essays* by Aleister Crowley. Hymenaeus Beta and Richard Kaczynski, ed. New Falcon, 1998. ISBN 978-1-56184-133-2.

- *Perdurabo: The Life of Aleister Crowley.* New Falcon Publications, 2002. ISBN 1-56184-170-6

- *Perdurabo Outtakes.* Blue Equinox, 2005.

- *Panic in Detroit: The Magician and the Motor City.* Blue Equinox, 2006.

- *The Weiser Concise Guide to Aleister Crowley* (co-authored with James Wasserman). Weiser Books, 2009. ISBN 978-1-57863-456-9

- *Beauty and Strength: Proceedings of the Sixth Biennial National Ordo Templi Orientis Conference* R. Kaczynski, ed., BookSurge Publishing, 2009. ISBN 1-4392-4734-X

- *Perdurabo, Revised and Expanded Edition: The Life of Aleister Crowley* 2nd ed., North Atlantic Books. ISBN 978-1-55643-899-8

- *Forgotten Templars, The Untold Origins of the Ordo Templi Orientis*, 2012

15.3.2 Metaphysical articles

- Kaczynski, R. (1989). *Preface to J.F.C. Fuller's Bibliotheca Crowleyana.* Edmonds, WA: Sure Fire Press.

- Kaczynski, R. (1993). "The Structure and Correlates of Metaphysical Beliefs Among a Sample of Behaviorally Committed Participants". Doctoral dissertation, Wayne State University, Detroit.

- "Foreword" to *People of the Earth: The New Pagans Speak Out* by Ellen Evert Hopman, Lawrence Bond. Inner Traditions, 1995. ISBN 0-89281-559-0 reissued and renamed *Being a Pagan: Druids, Wiccans, and Witches Today* Destiny Books 2001 ISBN 0-89281-904-9, ISBN 978-0-89281-904-1

- "Daybreak: Early History and Origins of the British Golden Dawn" in *Golden Dawn Sourcebook* by Darcy Kuntz. Holmes Publishing, (1996). ISBN 1-55818-332-9

- "Taboo and Transformation in the Works of Aleister Crowley" in *Rebels & Devils: The Psychology of Liberation*, edited by Christopher S. Hyatt. New Falcon Publications, (1996). ISBN 1-56184-153-6

- Kaczynski, R. (1996). *Barking up the wrong tree: The Kabbalah that the western Hermetic tradition overlooked.* In P. Kershaw (Ed.), Proceedings of Convocation '96. Magical Education Council of Ann Arbor: Ann Arbor, MI.

- Kaczynski, R. (1998). *Equidistant letter sequences: A guide for the perplexed.* In P. Kershaw (Ed.), Proceedings of Convocation '98. Magical Education Council of Ann Arbor: Ann Arbor, MI.

- Kaczynski, R. (1999). *An introduction to "The Revival of Magick"* In Proceedings of Convocation '99. Magical Education Council of Ann Arbor: Ann Arbor, MI.

- Kaczynski, R. (2001). *One is the magus, twain his biographies.* The Magical Link, 3:8-9.

- Kaczynski, R. (2003). *Wine and strange drugs: Aleister Crowley's quest for enlightenment.* High Times, November, 339:64-66.

- Kaczynski, R. (2005). *The Satanic ritual abuse controversy: A case of groupthink?* Neshamah, 1(1), 7-10.

- Kaczynski, R. (2005). *Metaphysical belief correlates in a behaviorally committed sample.* Neshamah, 1(1), 34-38.

- Kaczynski, R. (2008). *Foreword.* In Colin D. Campbell (ed.), A Concordance to the Holy Books of Thelema. York Beach, ME: Teitan Press.

- Kaczynski, R. (2009). *Carl Kellner's occult roots: Sex and sex magick in the Victorian age.* In Richard Kaczynski (ed.), Beauty & Strength: Proceedings of the Sixth Biennial National Conference of Ordo Templi Orientis. Riverside, CA: Ordo Templi Orientis

- Kaczynski, R. (2009). *Iconic or iconoclastic? The Thoth Tarot and the Western esoteric tradition.* Tarosophist International #4 (September).

- Kaczynski, R. (2010). *The Method of Science: Ten Steps toward Scientific Illuminism.* Neshamah (fall 2010).

- Kaczynski, R. (2011), *Introducing Perdurabo*, Watkins Review, summer, 2011 issue.

15.3.3 Films

- Donna Zuckerbrot (2007). *Engima: Aleister Crowley: The Beast 666* (Television production). Vision TV.[13]

15.3.4 Music

House of Usher

- Body of Mind (1998) - House of Usher

- Fanfare for the Pirates (1998) Mellow Records

- Live Encore? (40 minutes live from Progday 1999) (2001)

Page

- *Giant for a Life: A Tribute to Gentle Giant* - Mellow Records

- *Zarathustra's Revenge* - Mellow Records

- *Fanfare for the Pirates* - (1998) Mellow Records

15.4 See also

- William Breeze
- Lon Milo DuQuette
- Rodney Orpheus
- Lionel Snell
- James Wasserman

15.5 References

[1] Baker, Phil (2011-11-09). "Beastly Aleister Crowley". *Times Literary Supplement* (London). Retrieved 2011-12-07.

[2] (Norwegian) Sønderlind, Didrik (29 November 2006). "Verdens ondeste mann". *Aftenposten*. Retrieved December 8, 2011. Many biographies are written about Crowley, but connoisseurs of new religious movements believe that *Perdurabo* by American Richard Kaczynski is best.

[3] AllMusic Website

[4] Kaczynski, Richard (1993). "The structure and correlates of metaphysical beliefs among a sample of behaviorally committed participants". Wayne State University. Retrieved 2011-12-07.

[5] "Richard P Kaczynski". *Yale Phonebook.*

[6] University of Detroit Mercy Website

[7] Kaczynski, Richard. "Academia C.V.". Retrieved 2011-12-07.

[8] ""Crowley Without Tears" lecture offered by Richard Kaczynski at the 1990 Starwood Festival" (PDF). Retrieved 2013-12-27.

[9] "Neshamah". Retrieved 2011-12-07.

[10] "Richard Kaczynski - Author, World's Leading Expert on Aleister Crowley". (Joy 1250). 2011-06-25. Retrieved 2011-12-08. Missing or empty |series= (help)

[11] Kaczynski, Richard (November 2003). "Wine and strange drugs: Aleister Crowley's quest for enlightenment.". *High Times* (339): 64–66.

[12] "Different Worlds Publications - DW#37-47". *Diffworlds.com.* Retrieved December 7, 2011.

[13] "Kaczynski is credited for "Stock footage" and "Special thanks"". Reeltimeimages.ca. 2013-08-13. Retrieved 2013-12-27.

15.6 Further reading

Reviews

- *The Neverendingly Told Story: Recent Biographies of Aleister Crowley* by M. Pasi in Aries 3(2, 2003):224-45.

- *Perdurabo: The Life of Aleister Crowley* by Leni Austine in newWitch 6 (Spring, 2004):72.

- *Perdurabo: The Life of Aleister Crowley* by Robert Dean Lurie in Blurt, 2010, issue 9, p. 94-5.

- *Perdurabo: The Life of Aleister Crowley* in Midwest Book Review, December 2010

- *The Compleat Beast* by Richard McNeff - review of *The Weiser Concise Guide to Aleister Crowley* in the Fortean Times, June 2009, issue 249, page 63.

- *The Weiser Concise Guide to Aleister Crowley* review by Psyche in Spiral Nature

15.7 External links

- Official website

Chapter 16

Carl Kellner (mystic)

For other people of the same name, see Carl Kellner (disambiguation).

Carl Kellner (1 September 1851 – June 7, 1905) was a chemist, inventor, and industrialist. He made significant improvements to the sulfite process and was co-inventor of the Castner-Kellner process. He was a student of Freemasonry, Rosicrucianism, and Eastern mysticism. He was the putative founder of Ordo Templi Orientis.

16.1 Career

Carl Kellner is reputed to have developed the Ritter-Kellner process while working for Baron Hector Von Ritter-Zahony in 1876.[1] In 1889 he established the Kellner-Partington paper pulp Co[2] in association with Edward Partington.

The process for making caustic soda and chlorine by electrolysis of brine using a mercury electrode was developed independently by Mr Hamilton Y. Castner and Dr Carl Kellner in 1892. They established the Castner Kellner company jointly to exploit their patents in 1895.[3][4]

It is not known when he obtained his doctorate but he used the title of PhD from 1895.[5]

16.2 Freemasonry and esotericism

Kellner had become a Freemason in 1873, being initiated at the Humanitas Lodge on the Austro-Hungarian border, taking the motto of Brother Renatus.[6] In 1885, Kellner met the Theosophical and Rosicrucian scholar, Dr. Franz Hartmann (1838–1912). He and Hartmann later collaborated on the development of the "ligno-sulphite" inhalation therapy for tuberculosis, which formed the basis of treatment at Hartmann's sanitarium near Saltzburg. During this period Kellner became interested in the more esoteric aspects of Freemasonry, joining John Yarker's Rite of Memphis-Misraim. Hartmann's obituary of Kellner describes that in 1902 Kellner

> "...was personally initiated in Manchester by Brother Yarker into the 96°, and made Sovereign Honorary General Grand Master of our Order"

During extensive travels in Europe, America, and Asia Minor, Kellner claimed to have come into contact with three adepts (a Sufi, Soliman ben Aifa, and two Hindu Tantrics, Bhima Sena Pratapa of Lahore and Sri Mahatma Agamya Paramahamsa), and an organization called the Hermetic Brotherhood of Light. These adepts are attributed with having initiated Kellner into the use of sexual magick (sometimes referred to as 'the sexual current' by ritual magicians). Kellner was also influenced by a French followers of the American occultist Paschal Beverly Randolph.

During the course of his esoteric studies, Kellner believed that he had discovered a "key" which offered a clear explanation of all the complex symbolism of Freemasonry, and, Kellner believed, opened the mysteries of nature. Kellner developed a desire to form an Academia Masonica which would enable Freemasons to become familiar with all existing Masonic degrees and systems.

16.3 Ordo Templi Orientis

In 1895, Kellner began to discuss his idea for founding this Academia Masonica with his associate Theodor Reuss (aka Frater Merlin or Peregrinus). During these discussions, Kellner decided that the Academia Masonica should be called Ordo Templi Orientis (Oriental Templar Order). The occult inner circle of this order (O.T.O. proper) would be organized parallel to the highest degrees of the Rite of Memphis-Misraim and would teach the esoteric Rosicrucian doctrines of the Hermetic Brotherhood of Light, and Kellner's "key" to Masonic symbolism. Both men and women would be admitted at all levels to this order, but possession of the various degrees of Craft and high-grade Freemasonry would be a prerequisite for admission to the inner circle of O.T.O.

Due to the regulations of the established grand lodges which governed Regular Masonry, women could not be made Masons and would therefore be excluded by default from membership in Ordo Templi Orientis. Reforming the Masonic system to allow the admission of women may have been one of the reasons that Kellner and his associates resolved to obtain control over one of the many rites of Masonry; possibly because of wishing to incorporate the practice of sex magic. They may have believed that sex magic was "...the key to all the secrets of the universe and to all the symbolism ever used by secret societies and religions."[7]

The discussions between Reuss and Kellner did not lead to any positive results at the time, because Reuss was very busy with a revival of the Order of Illuminati along with his associate Leopold Engel of Dresden. Kellner did not approve of the revived Illuminati Order or of Engel. According to Reuss, upon his final separation with Engel in June 1902, Kellner contacted him and the two agreed to proceed with the establishment of Ordo Templi Orientis by seeking authorizations to work the various rites of high-grade Masonry. Reuss and Kellner together prepared a brief manifesto for their order in 1903, which was published the next year in The Oriflamme. However whether Kellner ever lived to see O.T.O. becoming more than just these early plans is debatable, since he died in 1905, not long after the first announcements were made.

16.4 Notes

[1] http://www.parareligion.ch/reuss.htm

[2] http://www.gracesguide.co.uk/Kellner-Partington_Paper_Pulp_Co

[3] http://www.gracesguide.co.uk/Castner_Kellner_Co

[4] North Eastern Daily Gazette, 21 Oct 1895 via 19th Century British Library newspapers

[5] http://www.parareligion.ch/sunrise/kellner.htm

[6] Dvorak, Josef (December 1998). "Carl Kellner". *Flensburger Hefte* (63). Retrieved 2011-04-26.

[7] Neil Powell *Alchemy, the Ancient Science*, p. 127, Aldus Books Ltd., 1976 SBN 490-00346-X

16.5 References

* Free Encyclopedia of Thelema (2005). *Carl Kellner*. Retrieved May 24, 2005.

* U.S. Grand Lodge, Ordo Templi Orientis. *Carl Kellner*. Retrieved 6 October 2004.

Chapter 17

Liber OZ

"Liber OZ" (or **"Book 77"**) is a single page by English author and occultist Aleister Crowley purporting to declare mankind's basic and intrinsic rights according to Crowley's philosophy of Thelema. Written in 1941[1] (though based on a much earlier O.T.O. initiation lecture), the work consists of five succinct and concise paragraphs, being one of the last and shortest of Crowley's many "libri," or books.[2]

Crowley wrote the piece for Louis Wilkinson[1] in order to convey as simply as possible the "O.T.O. plan in words of one syllable" broken down into "five sections: moral, bodily, mental, sexual, and the safeguard tyrannicide...".[3]

17.1   See also

- Libri of Aleister Crowley

17.2   References

[1] Sabazius X°. "Observations on Liber OZ".

[2] *The Equinox*: The Review of Scientific Illuminism, Samuel Weiser, 1990, page 144

[3] Crowley, Aleister; Desti, Mary & Waddell, Leila (2004) [1997]. "Editor's note to p. 689 Appendix VIII". In Hymenaeus Beta. *Magick : Liber ABA, Book 4, parts I-IV* (2nd. revised ed.). York Beach, Maine: S. Weiser. p. 788. ISBN 978-0-87728-919-7. OCLC 316894481. Retrieved 2009-09-13.

17.3   External links

- Full text of Liber OZ (Book 77)

Chapter 18

Liber XV, The Gnostic Mass

Aleister Crowley wrote **The Gnostic Mass** — technically called Liber XV or "Book 15" — in 1913 while travelling in Moscow, Russia. The structure is copied from the Mass of the Eastern Orthodox Church and Roman Catholic Church, replacing Christian tenets of faith with the principles of Crowley's Thelema. It is the central rite of Ordo Templi Orientis and its ecclesiastical arm, Ecclesia Gnostica Catholica.

The ceremony calls for five officers: a Priest, a Priestess, a Deacon, and two acolytes, called Children (though current practice is that the part is usually performed by adults). The end of the ritual culminates in the consummation of the eucharist, consisting of a goblet of wine and a Cake of Light, after which the congregant proclaims "There is no part of me that is not of the gods!"

Crowley explains why he wrote the Gnostic Mass in his *Confessions*:

> While dealing with this subject I may as well outline its scope completely. Human nature demands (in the case of most people) the satisfaction of the religious instinct, and, to very many, this may best be done by ceremonial means. I wished therefore to construct a ritual through which people might enter into ecstasy as they have always done under the influence of appropriate ritual. In recent years, there has been an increasing failure to attain this object, because the established cults shock their intellectual convictions and outrage their common sense. Thus their minds criticize their enthusiasm; they are unable to consummate the union of their individual souls with the universal soul as a bridegroom would be to consummate his marriage if his love were constantly reminded that its assumptions were intellectually absurd.

> I resolved that my Ritual should celebrate the sublimity of the operation of universal forces without introducing disputable metaphysical theories. I would neither make nor imply any statement about nature which would not be endorsed by the most materialistic man of science. On the surface this may sound difficult; but in practice I found it perfectly simple to combine the most rigidly rational conceptions of phenomena with the most exalted and enthusiastic celebration of their sublimity.[1]

18.1   Publications of the Mass

Crowley published the text of the Gnostic Mass three times: in 1918 in a publication called *The International*, in 1919 in *The Equinox (III:1)*, and in 1929 in *Magick in Theory and Practice*. It was privately performed while Crowley was at the Abbey of Thelema in Sicily, Italy,[2] and its first public performance was March 19, 1933 by Wilfred T. Smith and Regina Kahl in Hollywood, California at the first Agape Lodge.[3]

18.2   The Temple

There are four main pieces of furniture in a Gnostic Mass temple:

The High Altar: the dimensions are 7 feet (2.1 m) long by 3 feet (0.91 m) wide by 44 inches (1,100 mm) high. It is covered with a crimson cloth. It is situated in the East, or in the direction of Boleskine House—Crowley's former estate—on the shores of Loch Ness in Scotland ("Temple East"). The two-tiered super-altar sits on top of the High Altar. It all holds 22 candles, the Stele of Revealing, the Book of the Law, the Cup, and two bunches of roses. There is room for the Paten, and the Priestess to sit.

The High Altar is contained within a great Veil, and sits on a dais with three steps. On either side of the High Altar are two pillars, countercharged in black and white.

The Altar of Incense: to the West of the Dais is a black altar made of superimposed cubes.

The Font: this is a small circular item which is able to contain or hold water.

The Tomb: this is generally a small, enclosing space with an entrance that is covered by a veil. It should be big enough to hold the Priest, Deacon and the two Children.

18.3   Structure

There are six component ceremonies within the Gnostic Mass:

18.3.1   The Ceremony of the Introit

The congregation enters the temple, the Deacon presents the Law of Thelema, and the Gnostic Creed is recited. The Priestess and the Children enter from a side room. The Priestess raises the Priest from his Tomb, then purifies, consecrates, robes and crowns him.

18.3.2   The Ceremony of the Rending of the Veil

The Priestess is enthroned at the High Altar and the veil is closed. The Priest circumambulates the temple and he ascends to the veil. The officers give their orations, including the Calendar by the Deacon. The Priest then opens the veil and kneels at the High Altar.

18.3.3   The Collects

Eleven prayers addressed to the Sun, Moon, Lord, Lady, Gnostic Saints, Earth, Principles, Birth, Marriage, Death, and The End.

18.3.4   The Consecration of the Elements

The preparation of the Eucharist.

18.3.5   The Anthem

Of the Anthem, Crowley writes in *Confessions*:

> *During this period [i.e. around 1913] the full interpretation of the central mystery of freemasonry became clear in consciousness, and I expressed it in dramatic form in* The Ship. *The lyrical climax is in some respects*

my supreme achievement in invocation; in fact, the chorus beginning: "Thou who art I beyond all I am..."
seemed to me worthy to be introduced as the anthem into the Ritual of the Gnostic Catholic Church.

18.3.6 The Mystic Marriage and Consummation of the Elements

The Eucharist is perfected and consumed. The Priest gives the final benediction. The Priest, Deacon, and Children exit. The People exit.

18.4 The narrative of the Gnostic Mass [4]

The People enter into the ritual space, where the Deacon stands at the Altar of Incense (symbolic of Tiphareth on the Tree of Life). She takes the Book of the Law and places it on the super-altar within the great Veil, and proclaims the Law of Thelema in the name of IAO. Returning, she leads the People in the Gnostic Creed, which announces a belief (or value) in the Lord, the Sun, Chaos, Air, Babalon, Baphomet, the Gnostic Catholic Church, the communion of Saints, the Miracle of the Mass (i.e. the Eucharist), as well as confessions of their birth as incarnate beings and the eternal cycle of their individual lives.

The Virgin then enters with the two Children, and greets the People. She moves in a serpentine manner around the Altar of Incense and the Font (symbolizing the unwinding of the Kundalini Serpent which is twined around the base of the spine)[5] before stopping at the Tomb. She tears down the veil with her Sword, and raises the Priest to life by the power of Iron, the Sun, and the Lord. He is lustrated and consecrated with the four elements (water and earth, fire and air), and then invested with his scarlet Robe and crowned with the golden Uraeus serpent of wisdom. Finally, she gently strokes his Lance eleven times, invoking the Lord.

The Priest lifts up the Virgin and takes her to the High Altar, seating her "upon the summit of the Earth." After he purifies and consecrates her, he closes the Veil and circumambulates the temple three times, followed by the remaining officers. They take their place before the Altar of Incense, kneeling in adoration (along with all the People), while the Priest takes the first step upon the Dais before the Veil. In this symbolic crossing of the Abyss, the Priest begins with his first oration, invoking Nuit, the goddess of the infinite night sky. The Priestess calls to him as Nuit, enticing the Priest to ascend to her. He then takes the second step, and identifies as Hadit, the infinitely condensed center of all things — the Fire of every star and the Life in every person. The Deacon leads the congregation to rise and he delivers the Calendar. The Priest takes his third and final step before the Veil, invoking Ra-Hoor-Khuit, the Crowned and Conquering Child of the New Aeon. With his Lance, he parts the Veil, revealing the Priestess who sits (sometimes naked) upon the High Altar. He greets her with the masculine powers of Pan and she returns it with eleven kisses on the Lance. He kneels in adoration.

The Deacon then recites the eleven Collects, which include the Sun, Moon, Lord, Lady, Saints, Earth, Principles, Birth, Marriage, Death, and the End.

The Elements are then consecrated by the Virtue of the Lance, transforming the bread into the Body of God and the wine into the Blood of God. Of these, the Priest makes a symbolic offering to On, being our Lord the Sun.

The Priest and all the People then recite the Anthem, which was taken from Crowley's allegorical play "The Ship", and represents the legend of the Third Degree of Masonry.

The Priest blesses the Elements in the name of the Lord, and also states the essential function of the entire operation, which is to bestow health, wealth, strength, joy, peace, and the perpetual happiness that is the successful fulfillment of will. He breaks off a piece of one of the hosts, and, placing it on the tip of the Lance, both he and the Priestess depress it into the Cup, crying "Hriliu" (which Crowley translated as "the shrill scream of orgasm").

The Priest entreats Baphomet—"O Lion and O Serpent"—to be "mighty among us." He then declares the Law of Thelema to the People—"Do what thou wilt shall be the whole of the Law"—who respond with "Love is the law, love under will." He finally partakes of the Eucharist with the words, "In my mouth be the essence of the life of the Sun" (with the Host) and "In my mouth be the essence of the joy of the earth" (with the Wine). He turns to the People and declares, "There is no part of me that is not of the Gods."

The People then follow in Communication, one at a time, much as the Priest did, by partaking of a whole goblet of wine and a Cake of Light. They make the same proclamation of godhood as did the Priest. Afterwards, the Priest encloses the Priestess within the Veil, and delivers the final benediction:

+ The LORD bless you.

+ The LORD enlighten your minds and comfort your hearts and sustain your bodies.

+ The LORD bring you to the accomplishment of your true Wills, the Great Work, the Summum Bonum, True Wisdom and Perfect Happiness.

The Priest, Deacon, and Children then retire to the Tomb and return the torn veil. The People exit.

18.5   See also

- Works of Aleister Crowley

- Libri of Aleister Crowley

- Sex magick

18.6   References

[1] Crowley, Aleister (1989). *The Confessions of Aleister Crowley: An autohagiography*. London: Arkana. ISBN 978-0-14-019189-9.

[2] Crowley, Aleister (1933-07-02). "Black Magic is Not a Myth". *The London Sunday Dispatch* (London). Retrieved 2011-12-18.

[3] Apiryon, T. "The Invisible Basilica: Introduction to the Gnostic Mass". Retrieved 2009-05-24.

[4] The text of The Gnostic Mass

[5] IAO131. "The Journal of Thelemic Studies: The Mysteries of the Gnostic Mass". Retrieved 2015-04-20.

18.7   External links

- The Gnostic Mass, full text with hyperlinked annotations

- A First Look at the Gnostic Mass, by Dionysos Thriambos

- Original Essays and Propaganda of Dionysos Thriambos regarding the Gnostic Mass & the E.G.C.

- Apiryon, T. "The Invisible Basilica: Introduction to the Gnostic Mass". Retrieved 2009-05-24.

- The Gnostic Mass: Annotations and Commentary by Helena and Tau Apiryon

- The Gnostic Mass: An Appreciation by A.T. Dennis

- GnosticMass.org

Chapter 19

Grady Louis McMurtry

Grady Louis McMurtry (October 18, 1918 – July 12, 1985) was a student of author and occultist Aleister Crowley and an adherent of Thelema. He is best known for reviving the fraternal organization, Ordo Templi Orientis, which he headed from 1971 until his death in 1985.

19.1 Early life and career

He lived in various parts of Oklahoma and the Midwest, and graduated from high school in Valley Center, Kansas in 1937. He then moved to Southern California to study engineering at Pasadena Junior College, where he made friends with some students at nearby Caltech. Among them was Jack Parsons, who shared his enthusiasm for science fiction, and who introduced him to Thelema. In 1941 McMurtry was initiated into the *Minerval* and *I°* of Ordo Templi Orientis (O.T.O.), a secret society headed at the time by Aleister Crowley.

In February 1942, two months after the Japanese attack on Pearl Harbor, McMurtry's entire R.O.T.C. (Reserve Officers Training Corps) class was called to active duty, and he served as an officer in Ordnance. He took part in the Normandy invasion, the liberation of France and Belgium, and the occupation of Germany. He was recalled to active duty to serve in the Korean War, eventually reaching the rank of Major. He was recalled again for another tour of duty in Korea in the early 1960s, then six months prior to completing 30 years Reserve service, he was mustered out during a RIF (Reduction In Force), thus losing what would have been an earned pension. McMurtry's "retired" rank was Lieutenant Colonel. He continued his studies as a civilian between tours of duty, with both a bachelor's degree and a master's degree in Political Science from the University of California, Berkeley.

During World War II, especially when he was stationed in England in 1943 and the first half of 1944, McMurtry was able to meet with and become a personal student of Aleister Crowley, who elevated him to *IX°* of O.T.O., giving him the name *Hymenaeus Alpha* (which enumerates to 777) in November 1943.

In September and November 1944 (and once again in June 1947), he received letters from Crowley referring to him as Crowley's "Caliph" (or eventual successor). When McMurtry returned to California after the war he was appointed Crowley's O.T.O. representative in the United States (April 1946), subject only to the authority of Crowley's viceroy and heir apparent, Karl Germer.

Crowley died in December 1947, and Germer was recognized as the head of O.T.O. At the time the only functioning Thelemic O.T.O. body in the world was Agape Lodge in Southern California, which was headed for a time by McMurtry's friend Jack Parsons. McMurtry planned to start a lodge in Northern California, but his deteriorating relationship with Karl Germer (based on Germer's refusal to initiate new members) put an end to his plans. He tried to organize other O.T.O. members in California to lobby Germer to change his policy, but the situation came to a head at a meeting in 1959 in which Dr. Gabriel Montenegro (Germer's representative) "ordered" McMurtry to cease his efforts. This order was reiterated in writing in November 1960. McMurtry unwillingly complied with the order, and he was disillusioned enough by this turn of events that he ended his direct involvement with O.T.O. In 1961 he moved to Washington, D.C., where he soon became completely out of touch with other O.T.O. members.

19.2   Re-establishing O.T.O.

In October 1962 Germer died from complications following a prostate operation at the age of 77, without naming a successor as head of O.T.O. His widow, who was not a member of O.T.O., retained material possession of the O.T.O.'s extensive archives (her co-executor in Germany, Frederick Mellinger, lost interest in the O.T.O. within a few years). Though individual members carried on with their spiritual activities, the central organization, for all intents and purposes, ceased to function.

There were a few individuals, notably Kenneth Grant of Britain, Hermann Metzger of Switzerland, and later, Marcelo Ramos Motta of Brazil, who claimed succession to Germer. McMurtry was unaware of any of these developments until 1968, when he received a letter from Phyllis Seckler, a fellow Agape Lodge O.T.O. initiate.

Seckler's letter was to inform McMurtry that the archives in Germer's widow's care (including Aleister Crowley's library) had been burglarized the previous year by persons unknown. When he became aware of the situation he decided to take charge of what remained of O.T.O. In 1969 he left his job at the United States Department of Labor and returned to California to investigate the burglary. Though the crime was never officially solved, McMurtry felt that it had probably been carried out by a group, falsely claiming affiliation with O.T.O., that called itself "Solar Lodge". McMurtry had moved into Seckler's home in Dublin, California, and soon they were married.

At this time, McMurtry decided to restore the Order by invoking his emergency orders from Crowley which gave him authority (subject to Karl Germer's approval) to "take charge of the whole work of the Order in California to reform the Organization", and he assumed the title "Caliph of O.T.O.," as specified in Crowley's letters to McMurtry from the 1940s. His witnesses were Dr. Israel Regardie (1907–1985) and Gerald Yorke, who both offered their support.

Along with Seckler and two other surviving members, Mildred Burlingame and Helen Parsons Smith, he slowly began performing O.T.O. initiations again. They also eventually succeeded in their efforts to find a publisher for the Thoth tarot deck designed by Aleister Crowley. O.T.O. was registered with the State of California on December 28, 1971 as a legal organization.

In 1974 McMurtry and Seckler separated, and he moved to Berkeley, California. Germer's widow died in 1975, and in 1976 the surviving members of O.T.O. were enabled by court order to claim the still considerable archives. In October 1977 McMurtry founded Thelema Lodge in Berkeley to serve as the headquarters of his resuscitated O.T.O. Many initiations were performed, and a weekly celebration of the Gnostic Mass was soon established in the San Francisco Bay area. McMurtry, and other initiators chartered by him, established O.T.O. groups in many other areas in the United States and internationally. By 1985 O.T.O., by its own report, had more than seven hundred members in several different countries. In that year McMurtry, in failing health, successfully sued Motta in United States district court over the possession of the O.T.O. trademarks and copyrights. He died in a Martinez, California convalescent hospital on the day that the U.S. court clerk released the text of the decision that set the seal on McMurtry's efforts to reestablish O.T.O. Since then O.T.O. has, by its own report, grown to over three thousand members in more than fifty countries.

19.3   Bibliography

- "Hymenaeus Alpha: In Memoriam" in *The Equinox* Vol. III, No. 10, March 1986

- *The O.T.O. Newsletter* Vol. I, Nos.1-4, May 1977 - March 1978

- Transcript of an interview with McMurtry about his early life, serialized in the *Thelema Lodge Calendar*, November 2000 - September 2001

- Transcript of *U.S. District Court Proceedings*, D.C. No. 83-5434-CAL, GRADY McMURTRY, *et al.*, Plaintiffs-Appellees, *v.* SOCIETY ORDO TEMPLI ORIENTIS, *et al.*, Defendants-Appellants.

- Biography Abstract of McMurtry by Nathan W. Bjorge, serialized in the *Thelema Lodge Calendar*, September 1999

- A comprehensive collection of 134 poems was published as "The Poetry of Grady Louis McMurtry" *Red Flame* No. 1, September 2001

- In The Name of The Beast, A two volume Biography of Grady Louis McMurtry, a disciple of Aleister Edward Crowley' Vol.One 1918-1962. Vol.Two 1962-1985, by J. Edward Cornelius (Red Flame, A Thelemic Research Journal 2005)

19.4 See also

- Ordo Templi Orientis

- Thelema

19.5 External links

- "On Knowing Aleister Crowley Personally" by Grady Louis McMurtry

- "On Technical Information and On Curriculum" a series of essays by McMurtry

- Luminist Archive collection of McMurtry articles

- Ordo Templi Orientis

Chapter 20

Noname Jane

This article is about the pornographic film actress formerly known as Violet Blue. For other uses, see Violet blue (disambiguation).

Noname Jane, born **Ada Mae Johnson** (March 27, 1977), is an American pornographic actress.[1] In the majority of the pornographic films in which she appeared, she used the stage name **Violet Blue**. In October 2007, a lawsuit brought by author Violet Blue charged that Jane had adopted the author's name and persona,[2] prompting Jane to change her stage name to **Violetta Blue**,[3] and then to **Noname Jane**, in response to an injunction in the case.[4]

20.1 Early life

Noname Jane was born in Aberdeen, Washington and she is of Cherokee, Dutch, English, and French descent.[1] She claims that she began having sexual experiences at around age 7[5] and that she had sexual intercourse for the first time at age 13 while her parents were out playing bingo.[6] She began studying magick and witchcraft at the age of 16[7] and was initiated into Ordo Templi Orientis, a Thelemic religious organization, at age 21.[7]

20.2 Career

Prior to making pornographic films, she claimed, in an interview, to have worked as a stripper in Salt Lake City, UT, and she only started acting in pornographic movies in Los Angeles, CA after pornographic magazines were not interested in her.[5] She appeared in over 300 pornographic films under the name "Violet Blue", several of which were produced by Wicked Pictures and Vivid Entertainment. The films became popular in Japan, and she performed in two pornographic films with Japanese men. She was represented by the Gold Star Modeling talent agency.[8]

20.2.1 Retirement

In April 2005, Noname Jane announced that in May, she would return to her home state of Washington and that her husband would stay in Los Angeles to continue working for pornographer Stoney Curtis. Her mother had bought a house for her to live in.[6] She expressed that she wanted to help care for her sick father and to give her son a healthier environment. Jane announced that she would continue to be represented by Gold Star Modeling, and she also said, "I'll be anxious to come back and visit my porn valley friends so let me know when you have me in mind for a project."

In August 2006, Noname Jane announced by email that she would no longer perform in pornographic scenes with men, stating her reasons as a desire to be monogamous with her boyfriend, Dick Danger. She gave birth to her second child, a girl whom she named "Clover", in May 2007. She also hosts an Internet radio show called *Recipes for Sex* on KSEX.

In July 2007, she announced a "memorabilia sale", offering the clothing she had worn and sex toys that she had used in photo shoots and films.[9]

In January 2009, Noname Jane announced on her Myspace blog that she would resume working with male talent.[10] In August 2010, Noname Jane announced on her MySpace blog that she would only be performing with one male actor, Dick Danger, and that, in spite of her earlier announcement, she had not subsequently worked with any other male talent.[11]

20.3 Trademark infringement issue

In October 2007, author Violet Blue filed suit in federal court[2] alleging trademark violation and dilution, as well as unfair business practices with [12] author Blue's persona and belatedly-trademarked name being used.[13] The pornographic actress had used the name since 2000[12] and was financially unable to properly defend herself.[13] The court issued a preliminary injunction that forced her to stop using the name "Violet Blue" or anything confusingly similar; the stage name Noname Jane was adopted instead.[4]

20.4 Awards and nominations

- 2002 AVN Award **winner** - Best New Starlet[14]

20.5 References

[1] "Noname Jane". Retrieved 17 December 2014.

[2] Ryan Singel (2007-10-24). "Sex Writer Violet Blue Sues Porn Star Violet Blue Over Name". *Wired News*. Retrieved 2007-10-24.

[3] Pornstar Violet Blue Changes Name"; Adult Industry News; November 3, 2007

[4] Mark Kernes (2008-05-16). "Noname Jane, The Best Performer You Never Heard Of". *AVN*. Retrieved 2008-05-18.

[5] Violet Blue Interview, Rogreviews.com

[6] "Violet Blue Interview". Adult DVD Talk. Retrieved 17 December 2014.

[7] "Official bio". Noname Jane's Official Site. Retrieved 2012-06-12.

[8] Violet Blue Goes to Washington. Adult Industry News (April 19, 2005).

[9] Violet Blue Memorabilia Sale. Adult Entertainment News (July 31, 2007).

[10] Myspace.com Blog (January 14, 2009).

[11] Myspace.com Blog (August 05, 2010).

[12] "S.M.U.T. 14 (Video 1999)". *IMDb*. 1 July 1999. Retrieved 17 December 2014.

[13] US Patent and Trademark Office (search for Violet Blue)

[14] "2002 AVN Award Winners". 2002. Retrieved January 1, 2014.

20.6   External links

- Official website

- Noname Jane at the Internet Movie Database

- Noname Jane at the Internet Adult Film Database

- Noname Jane at the Adult Film Database

- Noname Jane Interview on (re)Search my Trash

Chapter 21

Sara Northrup Hollister

Sara Elizabeth Bruce Northrup Hollister (April 8, 1924 – December 19, 1997) was an occultist who played a major role in the creation of Dianetics, which evolved into the religious movement Scientology. Sara was the second wife of science-fiction author L. Ron Hubbard, who would become the leader of the Church of Scientology.[1]

Sara Northrup was a major figure in the Pasadena branch of the Ordo Templi Orientis (OTO), a secret society founded by the English occultist Aleister Crowley, where she was known as "Soror [Sister] Cassap". She joined as a teenager. From 1941 to 1945 she had a turbulent relationship with her sister's husband John Whiteside Parsons, the head of the Pasadena branch. Though a committed and popular member, she acquired a reputation for disruptiveness that prompted Crowley to denounce her as a "vampire". She began a relationship with L. Ron Hubbard, whom she met through the OTO, in 1945. She and Hubbard eloped, taking with them a substantial amount of Parsons' life savings and marrying bigamously a year later while Hubbard was still married to his first wife, Margaret Grubb.

Sara played a significant role in the development of Dianetics, Hubbard's "modern science of mental health", between 1948 and 1951. She was Hubbard's personal auditor and along with Hubbard, one of the seven members of the Dianetics Foundation's Board of Directors. However, their marriage was deeply troubled; Hubbard was responsible for a prolonged campaign of domestic violence against her and kidnapped both her and her infant daughter. Hubbard spread allegations that she was a Communist secret agent and repeatedly denounced her to the FBI. The FBI declined to take any action, characterizing Hubbard as a "mental case". The marriage broke up in 1951 and prompted lurid headlines in the Los Angeles newspapers. She subsequently married one of Hubbard's former employees, Miles Hollister, and moved to Hawaii and later Massachusetts, where she died in 1997.

21.1 Early life

Sara was one of five children born to Olga Nelson, the daughter of a Swedish immigrant to the United States.[2] She was the granddaughter of Russian emigrant Malacon Kosadamanov (later Nelson) who emigrated to Sweden.[3] Sara's mother first married Thomas Cowley, an Englishman working for the Standard Oil Company. The couple had three daughters. In 1923 the family moved to Pasadena, a destination said to have been chosen by Olga using a Oujia board.[2] Although she later remembered her childhood with warmth, Sara's upbringing was marred by her sexually abusive father, who was imprisoned in 1928 for financial fraud.[4] She was sexually active from an unusually young age and often claimed to have lost her virginity at the age of ten.[5]

21.2 Relationship with Jack Parsons

In 1933, Sara's 22-year-old sister Helen met the 18-year-old Jack Parsons, a chemist who went on to be a noted expert in rocket propulsion. Jack Parsons was also an avid student and practitioner of the occult. Helen and Jack were engaged in July 1934[6] and married in April 1935.[2] Parsons' interest in the occult led in 1939 to him and Helen joining the

Jack Parsons in 1938

Pasadena branch of the Ordo Templi Orientis (OTO).

At age 15, Sara moved in with sister Helen and her husband Jack, while she finished high school.[1] Parsons had subdivided the house, a rambling mansion next door to the estate of Adolphus Busch (which later became the first Busch Gardens), into 19 apartments which he populated with a mixture of artists, writers, scientists and occultists.[7] Her parents not only knew about her unconventional living arrangements but supported Parsons' group financially.[8]

Sara joined the OTO in 1941, at Parsons' urging, and was given the title of Soror [Sister] Cassap.[1] She soon rose to the rank of a second degree member, or "Magician", of the OTO.[9]

In June 1941, at the age of seventeen, she began a passionate affair with Parsons while her sister Helen was away on vacation. She made a striking impression on the other lodgers; George Pendle describes her as "feisty and untamed, proud and self-willed, she stood five foot nine, had a lithe body and blond hair, and was extremely candid."[10] When Helen returned, she found Sara wearing Helen's own clothes and calling herself Parsons' "new wife." Such conduct was expressly permitted by the OTO, which followed Crowley's disdain of marriage as a "detestable institution" and accepted as commonplace the swapping of wives and partners between OTO members.[10]

Although both were committed OTO members, Sara's usurpation of Helen's role led to conflict between the two sisters. The reactions of Parsons and Helen towards Sara were markedly different. Parsons told Helen to her face that he preferred Sara sexually: "This is a fact that I can do nothing about. I am better suited to her temperamentally – we get on well. Your character is superior. You are a greater person. I doubt that she would face what you have with me – or support me as well."[11] Some years later, addressing himself as "You", Parsons told himself that his affair with Sara (whom he called Betty) marked a key step in his growth as a practitioner of magick: "Betty served to affect a transference from Helen at a critical period ... Your passion for Betty also gave you the magical force needed at the time, and the act of adultery tinged with incest, served as your magical confirmation in the law of Thelema."[11]

Helen was far less sanguine, writing in her diary of "the sore spot I carried where my heart should be",[11] and had furious – sometimes violent – rows with both Parsons and Sara. She began an affair with Wilfred Smith, Parsons' mentor in the OTO[11] and had a son in 1943 who bore Parsons' surname but who was almost certainly fathered by Smith.[11] Sara also became pregnant but had an abortion on April 1, 1943, arranged by Parsons and carried out by Dr. Zachary Taylor Malaby, a prominent Pasadena doctor and Democratic politician.[12]

Sara's hostility towards other members of the OTO caused further tensions in the house, which Aleister Crowley heard about from communications from her housemates. He dubbed her "the alley-cat" after an unnamed mutual acquaintance told him that Parsons's attraction to her was like "a yellow pup bumming around with his snout glued to the rump of an alley-cat."[13] Concluding that she was a vampire, which he defined as "an elemental or demon in the form of a woman" who sought to "lure the Candidate to his destruction," he warned that Sara was a grave danger to Parsons and to the "Great Work" which the OTO was carrying out in California.[13]

Similar concerns were expressed by other OTO members. The OTO's US head, Karl Germer, labeled her "an ordeal sent by the gods". Her disruptive behavior appalled Fred Gwynn, a new OTO member living in the commune at 1003 South Orange Avenue: "Betty went to almost fantastical lengths to disrupt the meetings [of the OTO] that Jack did get together. If she could not break it up by making social engagements with key personnel she, and her gang, would go out to a bar and keep calling in asking for certain people to come to the telephone."[14]

21.3 Relationship with L. Ron Hubbard

L. Ron Hubbard in 1950

In August 1945, Sara met L. Ron Hubbard for the first time. He had visited 1003 South Orange Avenue at the behest of Lou Goldstone, a well-known science fiction illustrator, while on leave from his service in the US Navy. Parsons took an immediate liking to Hubbard and invited him to stay in the house for the duration of his leave.[15] Hubbard soon began an affair with Sara after beginning "affairs with one girl after another in the house."[8] He was a striking figure who habitually wore dark glasses and carried a cane with a silver handle, the need for which he attributed to his wartime service: as Sara later put it, "He was not only a writer but he was the captain of a ship that had been downed in the Pacific and he was weeks on a raft and had been blinded by the sun and his back had been broken."[8] She believed all of it, though none of his claims of wartime action or injuries were true.[8]

Parsons was deeply dismayed but tried to put a brave face on the situation, informing Aleister Crowley:

> About three months ago I met Captain L. Ron Hubbard, a writer and explorer of whom I had known for some time ... He is a gentleman; he has red hair, green eyes, is honest and intelligent, and we have become great friends. He moved in with me about two months ago, and although Betty and I are still friendly, she has transferred her sexual affection to Ron.

> I think I have made a great gain and as Betty and I are the best of friends, there is little loss. I cared for her rather deeply but I have no desire to control her emotions, and I can, I hope, control my own. I need a magical partner. I have many experiments in mind.[16]

Hubbard became Parsons' "magical partner" for a sex magic ritual involving that was intended to summon an incarnation of a goddess.[17] Although they got on well as fellow occultists, tensions between the two men were apparent in more domestic settings. Hubbard and Sara made no secret of their relationship; another lodger at Parsons' house described how he saw Hubbard "living off Parsons' largesse and making out with his girlfriend right in front of him. Sometimes when the two of them were sitting at the table together, the hostility was almost tangible."[8] Despite the tensions between them, Hubbard, Sara and Parsons agreed at the start of 1946 that they would go into business together, buying yachts on the East Coast and sailing them to California to sell at a profit. They set up a business partnership on January 15, 1946 under the name of "Allied Enterprises", with Parsons putting up $20,000 of capital, Hubbard adding $1,200 and Sara contributing nothing.[18] Hubbard and Sara left for Florida towards the end of April, taking with him $10,000 drawn from the Allied Enterprises account to fund the purchase of the partnership's first yacht. Weeks passed without word from Hubbard. Louis Culling, another OTO member, wrote to Karl Germer to explain the situation:

> As you may know by this time, Brother John signed a partnership agreement with this Ron and Betty whereby all money earned by the three for life is equally divided between the three. As far as I can ascertain, Brother John has put in all of his money ... Meanwhile, Ron and Betty have bought a boat for themselves in Miami for about $10,000 and are living the life of Riley, while Brother John is living at Rock Bottom, and I mean *Rock Bottom*. It appears that originally they never secretly intended to bring this boat around to the California coast to sell at a profit, as they told Jack, but rather to have a good time on it on the east coast.[19]

Germer informed Crowley, who wrote back to opine: "It seems to me on the information of our brethren in California that Parsons has got an illumination in which he has lost all his personal independence. From our brother's account he has given away both his girl and his money. Apparently it is the ordinary confidence trick." [19]

Parsons initially attempted to obtain redress through magical means, carrying out a "Banishing Ritual of the Pentagram" to curse Hubbard and Sara. He credited it with causing the couple to abort an attempt to evade him:

> Hubbard attempted to escape me by sailing at 5 P.M., and I performed a full evocation to Bartzabel [the spirit of Mars or War] within the circle at 8 P.M. At the same time, so far as I can check, his ship was struck by a sudden squall off the coast, which ripped off his sails and forced him back to port, where I took the boat in custody... Here I am in Miami pursuing the children of my folly; they cannot move without going to jail. However I am afraid that most of the money has already been dissipated.[20]

Sara later recalled that the boat had been caught in a hurricane in the Panama Canal, damaging it too badly to be able to continue the voyage to California.[21] Parsons subsequently resorted to more conventional means of obtaining redress and sued the couple on July 1 in the Circuit Court for Dade County. His lawsuit accused Hubbard and Sara of breaking the terms of their partnership, dissipating the assets and attempting to abscond. The case was settled out of court eleven days later, with Hubbard and Sara agreeing to refund some of Parsons' money while keeping a yacht, the *Harpoon*, for themselves. The boat was soon sold to ease the couple's shortage of cash.[22] Sara was able to dissuade Parsons from pressing his case by threatening to expose their past relationship, which had begun when she was under the legal age of consent.[23] Hubbard's relationship with Sara, while legal, had already caused alarm among those who knew him; Virginia Heinlein, the wife of the science fiction writer Robert Heinlein, regarded Hubbard as "a very sad case of post-war breakdown" and Sara as his "latest Man-Eating Tigress".[24]

Hubbard's financial troubles were reflected in his attempts to persuade the Veterans Administration to increase his pension award on the grounds of a variety of ailments which he said were preventing him finding a job. He persuaded Sara to pose as an old friend writing in support of his appeals; in one letter, she claimed untruthfully to have "known Lafayette Ronald Hubbard for many years" and described his supposed pre-war state of health.[19] His health and emotional difficulties were reflected in another, much more private, document which has been dubbed "The Affirmations". It is thought to have been written around 1946–7 as part of an attempted program of self-hypnotism. His sexual difficulties with Sara, for which he was taking testosterone supplements, are a significant feature of the document.[25] He wrote:

> Sara, my sweetheart, is young, beautiful, desirable. We are very gay companions. I please her physically until she weeps about any separation. I want her always. But I am 13 years older than she. She is heavily sexed. My libido is so low I hardly admire her naked.[25][26]

Around the same time, Hubbard proposed marriage to Sara. According to Sara's later recollections she repeatedly refused him but relented after he threatened to kill himself. She told him: "All right, I'll marry you, if that's going to save you."[24] They were married in the middle of the night of August 10, 1946 at Chestertown, Maryland after awakening a minister and roping in his wife and housekeeper to serve as witnesses.[24] It was not until much later that Sara discovered that Hubbard had never been divorced from his first wife, Margaret "Polly" Grubb; the marriage was bigamous. Ironically, the wedding took place only 30 miles from the town where Hubbard had married his first wife thirteen years previously.[27] The wedding attracted criticism from L. Sprague de Camp, another science fiction colleague of Hubbard's, who suggested to the Heinleins that he supposed "Polly was tiresome about not giving him his divorce so he could marry six other gals who were all hot & moist over him. How many girls is a man entitled to in one lifetime, anyway? Maybe he should be reincarnated as a rabbit."[24]

The couple moved repeatedly over the following year – first to Laguna Beach, California,[28] then to Santa Catalina Island, California,[29] New York City,[30] Stroudsburg, Pennsylvania[31] and ultimately to Hubbard's first wife's home at South Colby, Washington. Polly Hubbard had filed for divorce on the grounds of desertion and non-support, and was not even aware that Hubbard was living with Sara, let alone that he had married her. The arrival of Hubbard and Sara three weeks after the divorce was filed scandalized Hubbard's family, who deeply disapproved of his treatment of Polly.[32] Sara had no idea of Hubbard's first marriage or why people were treating her so strangely until his son L. Ron Hubbard Jr. told her that his parents were still married. She attempted to flee on a ferry but Hubbard caught up with her and convinced her to stay, claiming that he was in the process of getting a divorce and that an attorney had told him that the marriage with Sara was legal.[33] The couple moved to a rented trailer in North Hollywood in July 1947, where Hubbard spent much of his time writing stories for pulp magazines.[32]

The relationship was not an easy one. According to Sara, Hubbard began beating her when they were in Florida in the summer of 1946. Her father had just died and her grief appeared to aggravate Hubbard, who was attempting to restart his pre-war career of writing pulp fiction. He was struggling with constant writers' block and leaned heavily on Sara to provide plot ideas and even to help write some of his stories.[33] She later recalled: "I would often entertain him with plots so he could write. I loved to make plots. The *Ole Doc Methuselah* series was done that way."[34] One night while they were living beside a frozen lake in Stroudsburg, Hubbard hit her across the face with his .45 pistol. She recalled that "I got up and left the house in the night and walked on the ice of the lake because I was terrified." Despite her shock and humiliation, she felt compelled to return to Hubbard. He was severely depressed and repeatedly threatened suicide, and Sara believed "he must be suffering or he wouldn't act that way".[33]

After Hubbard was convicted of petty theft in San Luis Obispo in August 1948,[32] the couple moved again to Savannah, Georgia.[35] Hubbard told his friend Forrest J. Ackerman that he had acquired a Dictaphone machine which Sara was "beating out her wits on" transcribing not only fiction but his book on the "cause and cure of nervous tension".[36] This eventually became the first draft of Hubbard's book *Dianetics: The Modern Science of Mental Health*, which marked the foundation of Dianetics and ultimately of Scientology.

21.4   The Dianetics years

The final version of *Dianetics* was written at Bay Head, New Jersey in a cottage which the science fiction editor John W. Campbell had found for the Hubbards. Sara, who was beginning a pregnancy, was said to have been delighted with the location. In three years of marriage to Hubbard, she had set up home in seven different states and had never stayed in one place for more than a few months.[37] She gave birth on March 8, 1950 to a daughter, Alexis Valerie. A month later Sara was made a director of the newly established Hubbard Dianetic Research Foundation in Elizabeth, New Jersey, an organization founded to disseminate knowledge of Dianetics. The Hubbards moved to a new house in Elizabeth to be near the Foundation.[38] Sara became Hubbard's personal auditor (Dianetic counselor)[39] and was hailed by him as one of the first Dianetic "Clears".[40]

Dianetics became an immediate bestseller when it was published in May 1950. Only two months later, over 55,000 copies had been sold and 500 Dianetics groups had been set up across the United States.[41] The Dianetics Foundation was making a huge amount of money, but problems were already evident: money was pouring out as fast as it was coming in, due to lax financial management and Hubbard's own free spending.[42] Sara recalled that "he used to carry huge amounts of cash around in his pocket. I remember going past a Lincoln dealer and admiring one of those big Lincolns they had then. He walked right in there and bought it for me, cash!"[43]

By October, the Foundation's financial affairs had reached a crisis point. According to his public relations assistant, Barbara Klowdan, Hubbard became increasingly paranoid and authoritarian due to "political and organizational problems with people grabbing for power."[42] He began an affair with the twenty-year-old Klowdan, much to the annoyance of Sara, who was clearly aware of the liaison.[44] Klowdan recalled that Sara "was very hostile to me. We were talking about guns and she said to me that I was the type to use a Saturday night special" (a very cheap "junk gun").[45] One evening he arranged a double-date with his wife and Klowdan, who was accompanied by Miles Hollister, an instructor in the Los Angeles Dianetic Foundation. The dinner party backfired drastically; Sara began an affair with Hollister, a handsome 22-year-old who was college-educated and a noted sportsman.[46]

The marriage was in the process of breaking down rapidly. Sara and Hubbard had frequent rows and his violent behaviour towards her continued unabated. On one occasion, while Sara was pregnant, Hubbard kicked her several times in the stomach in an apparent – though unsuccessful – attempt to induce an abortion. She recalled that "with or without an argument, there'd be an upsurge of violence. The veins in his forehead would engorge" and he would hit her "out of the blue", breaking her eardrum in one attack. Despite this, she still "felt so guilty about the fact that he was so psychologically damaged. I felt as though he had given so much to our country and I couldn't even bring him peace of mind. I believed thoroughly that he was a man of great honor, had sacrificed his well being to the country ... It just never occurred to me he was a liar."[47] He told her that he didn't want to be married "for I can buy my friends whenever I want them" but could not divorce either, as the stigma would hurt his reputation. Instead, he said, if Sara really loved him she should kill herself.[47]

Klowdan recalled later that "he was very down in the dumps about his wife. He told me how he had met Sara. He said he went to a party and got drunk and when he woke up in the morning he found Sara was in bed with him. He was having a lot of problems with her. I remember he said to me I was the only person he knew who would set up a white silk tent for him. I was rather surprised when we were driving back to LA on Sunday evening, he stopped at a florist to buy some flowers for his wife."[46] She In November 1950, Sara attempted suicide by taking sleeping pills. Hubbard blamed Klowdan for the suicide bid and told her to forget about him and the Foundation, but resumed the affair with her again within a month.[48]

Hubbard attempted to patch up the marriage in January 1951 by inviting Sara and baby Alexis to Palm Springs, California where he had rented a house.[49] The situation soon became tense again; Richard de Mille, nephew of the famous director Cecil B. de Mille, recalled that "there was a lot of turmoil and dissension in the Foundation at the time; he kept accusing Communists of trying to take control and he was having difficulties with Sara. It was clear their marriage was breaking up – she was very critical of him and he told me she was fooling around with Hollister and he didn't trust her."[50] Hubbard enlisted de Mille and another Dianeticist, Dave Williams, in an attempt to convince her to stay with him. John Sanborne, who worked with Hubbard for many years, recalled:

> Earlier on (before the divorce) he made this stupid attempt to get Sara brainwashed so she'd do what
> he said. He kept her sitting up in a chair, denying her sleep, trying to use Black Dianetic principles on her,
> repeating over and over again whatever he wanted her to do. Things like, "Be his wife, have a family that

looks good, not have a divorce." Or whatever. He had Dick de Mille reciting this sort of thing day and night to her.[51]

Sara went to a psychiatrist to obtain advice about Hubbard's increasingly violent and irrational behaviour, and was told that he probably needed to be institutionalized and that she was in serious danger. She gave Hubbard an ultimatum: get treatment or she would leave with the baby. He was furious and threatened to kill Alexis rather than let Sara care for her: "He didn't want her to be brought up by me because I was in league with the doctors. He thought I had thrown in with the psychiatrists, with the devils."[52] She left Palm Springs on February 3, leaving Hubbard to complain that Sara "had hypnotized him in his sleep and commanded him not to write."[50]

21.5   Kidnapped by Hubbard

Three weeks later, Hubbard abducted both Sara and Alexis. On the night of February 24, 1951, Alexis was being looked after by John Sanborne while Sara had a night at the movies. Hubbard turned up and took the child. A few hours later, he returned with two of his Dianetics Foundation staff and told Sara, who was now back at her apartment: "We have Alexis and you'll never see her alive unless you come with us."[53] She was bundled into the back of a car and driven to San Bernardino, California, where Hubbard attempted to find a doctor to examine his wife and declare her insane. His search was unsuccessful and he released her at Yuma Airport across the state line in Arizona. He promised that he would tell her where Alexis was if she signed a piece of paper saying that she had gone with him voluntarily. Sara agreed but Hubbard reneged on the deal and flew to Chicago, where he found a psychologist who wrote a favorable report about his mental condition to refute Sara's accusations.[39] Rather than telling Sara where Alexis was, he called her and said that "he had cut [Alexis] into little pieces and dropped the pieces in a river and that he had seen little arms and legs floating down the river and it was my fault, I'd done it because I'd left him."[53]

Hubbard subsequently returned to the Foundation in Elizabeth, New Jersey. There he wrote a letter informing the FBI that Sara and her lover Miles Hollister – whom he had fired from the Foundation's staff and, according to Hollister, had also threatened to kill[54] – were among fifteen "known or suspected Communists" in his organization.[55] He listed them as:

> SARA NORTHRUP (HUBBARD): formerly of 1003 S. Orange Grove Avenue, Pasadena, Calif. 25 yrs. of age, 5'10", 140 lbs. Currently missing somewhere in California. Suspected only. Had been friendly with many Communists. Currently intimate with them but evidently under coercion. Drug addiction set in fall 1950. Nothing of this known to me until a few weeks ago. Separation papers being filed and divorce applied for.
> MILES HOLLISTER: Somewhere in the vicinity of Los Angeles. Evidently a prime mover but very young. About 22 yrs, 6', 180 lbs. Black hair. Sharp chin, broad forehead, rather Slavic. Confessedly a member of the Young Communists. Center of most turbulence in our organization. Dissmissed [sic] in February when affiliations discovered. Active and dangerous. Commonly armed. Outspokenly disloyal to the U.S.[56]

In another letter sent in March, Hubbard told the FBI that Sara was a Communist and a drug addict, and offered a $10,000 reward to anyone who could resolve Sara's problems through the application of Dianetics techniques.[57]

Sara filed a kidnapping complaint with the Los Angeles Police Department on her return home but was rebuffed by the police, who dismissed the affair as a mere domestic dispute.[58] After a fruitless six-week search she finally filed a writ of habeas corpus at the Los Angeles Superior Court in April 1951, demanding the return of Alexis. The dispute immediately became front-page news: the newspapers ran headlines such as "Cult Founder Accused of Tot Kidnap", "'Dianetic' Hubbard Accused of Plot to Kidnap Wife", and "Hiding of Baby Charged to Dianetics Author".[59] Hubbard fled to Havana, Cuba, where he wrote a letter to Sara:

> Dear Sara,
> I have been in the Cuban military hospital and I am being transferred to the United States next week as a classified scientist immune from interference of all kinds.

Though I will be hospitalized probably a long time, Alexis is getting excellent care. I see her every day. She is all I have to live for.

My wits never gave way under all you did and let them do but my body didn't stand up. My right side is paralyzed and getting more so. I hope my heart lasts. I may live a long time and again I may not. But Dianetics will last 10,000 years – for the Army and Navy have it now.

My Will is all changed. Alexis will get a fortune unless she goes to you as she would then get nothing. Hope to see you once more. Goodbye – I love you.

Ron.[60] [note 1]

In reality, Hubbard had made an unsuccessful request for assistance from the US military attaché to Havana. The attaché did not act on the request; having asked the FBI for background information, he was told that Hubbard had been interviewed but the "agent conducting interview considered Hubbard to be [a] mental case."[59] On April 19, as Barbara Klowdan recorded in her journal, Hubbard telephoned her from Wichita and told her "he was not legally married. His first wife had not obtained divorce until '47 and he was married in '46. According to him, Sara had served a stretch at Tahatchapie (in a desert woman's prison) and was a dope addict."[45] A few days later – while still married to Sara – he proposed marriage to Klowdan.[61]

21.6   Divorced from Hubbard

Sara filed for divorce on April 23, charging Hubbard with causing her "extreme cruelty, great mental anguish and physical suffering". Her allegations produced more lurid headlines: not only was Hubbard accused of bigamy and kidnapping, but she had been subjected to "systematic torture, including loss of sleep, beatings, and strangulations and scientific experiments". Because of his "crazy misconduct" she was in "hourly fear of both the life of herself and of her infant daughter, who she has not seen for two months".[62] She had consulted doctors who "concluded that said Hubbard was hopelessly insane, and, crazy, and that there was no hope for said Hubbard, or any reason for her to endure further; that competent medical advisers recommended that said Hubbard be committed to a private sanatorium for psychiatric observation and treatment of a mental ailment known as paranoid schizophrenia."[62]

Her lawyer, a flamboyant fixture of the California bar named Caryl Warner, also worked the media on her behalf so that Sara's story received maximum publicity. He briefed the divorce court reporters for the *Los Angeles Times* and the *Examiner*, who were both women and early feminists, to ensure that "they knew what a bastard this guy Hubbard was."[62] He later told Hubbard's unofficial biographer, Russell Miller:

I liked Sara and Miles a lot. They eventually married and got a house in Malibu and we became friends; I remember they introduced me to pot. I believed Sara absolutely; there was no question about the truth in my opinion. When she first came to me with this wild story about how her husband had taken her baby I was determined to help her all I could. I telephoned Hubbard's lawyer in Elizabeth and warned him: "Listen, asshole, if you don't get that baby back I'm going to burn you."[63]

The divorce writ prompted a deluge of bad publicity for Hubbard and elicited an unexpected letter to Sara from his first wife, Polly, who wrote: "If I can help in any way I'd like to—You must get Alexis in your custody—Ron is not normal. I had hoped that you could straighten him out. Your charges sound fantastic to the average person—but I've been through it—the beatings, threats on my life, all the sadistic traits you charge—twelve years of it ... Please do believe I do so want to help you get Alexis."[64]

In May 1951, Sara filed a further complaint against Hubbard, accusing him of having fled to Cuba to evade the divorce papers that she was seeking to serve. By that time, however, he had moved to Wichita, Kansas. Sara's attorney filed another petition asking for Hubbard's assets to be frozen as he had been found "hiding" in Wichita "but that he would probably leave town upon being detected".[65] Hubbard wrote to the FBI to further denounce Sara as a Communist secret agent. He accused Communists of destroying his business, ruining his health and withholding material of interest to the US Government. His misfortunes had been caused by "a woman known as Sara Elizabeth Northrup . . . whom I believed to be my wife, having married her and then, after some mix-up about a divorce, believed to be my wife in common law."[65] He accused Sara of having conspired in a bid to assassinate him and described how he had found love letters to his wife from Miles Hollister, a "member of the Young Communists." Her real motive in filing for divorce, he claimed, was to seize control of Dianetics. He urged the FBI to start a "round-up" of "vermin Communists or ex-Communists", starting with Sara, and declared:

> I believe this woman to be under heavy duress. She was born into a criminal atmosphere, her father having a criminal record. Her half-sister was an inmate of an insane asylum. She was part of a free love colony in Pasadena. She had attached herself to a Jack Parsons, the rocket expert, during the war and when she left him he was a wreck. Further, through Parsons, she was strangely intimate with many scientists of Los Alamo Gordos [Alamogordo in New Mexico was where the first atomic bomb was tested]. I did not know or realize these things until I myself investigated the matter. She may have a record . . . Perhaps in your criminal files or on the police blotter of Pasadena you will find Sara Elizabeth Northrop, age about 26, born April 8, 1925, about 5'9", blond-brown hair, slender . . . I have no revenge motive nor am I trying to angle this broader than it is. I believe she is under duress, that they have something on her and I believe that under a grilling she would talk and turn state's evidence.[66]

Fortunately for Sara – as it was the peak of the McCarthyite "Red Scare" – Hubbard's allegations were apparently ignored by the FBI, which filed his letter but took no further action. In June 1951, she finally secured the return of Alexis by agreeing to cancel her receivership action and divorce suit in California in return for a divorce "guaranteed by L. Ron Hubbard".[67] She met him in Wichita to resolve the situation. He told her that she was "in a state of complete madness" due to being dictated to and hypnotized by Hollister and his "communist cell". Playing along, she told Hubbard that he was right and that the only way she could break free of their power was by going through with the divorce. He replied, "You know, I'm a public figure and you're nobody, so if you have to go through the divorce, I'll accuse you of desertion so it won't look so bad on my public record."[68] She agreed to sign a statement, written by Hubbard himself, that retracted the allegations that she had made against him:

> I, Sara Northrup Hubbard, do hereby state that the things I have said about L. Ron Hubbard in courts and the public prints have been grossly exaggerated or entirely false.
>
> I have not at any time believed otherwise than that L. Ron Hubbard is a fine and brilliant man.
>
> I make this statement of my own free will for I have begun to realize that what I have done may have injured the science of Dianetics, which in my studied opinion may be the only hope of sanity in future generations.
>
> I was under enormous stress and my advisers insisted it was necessary for me to carry through an action as I have done.
>
> There is no other reason for this statement than my own wish to make atonement for the damage I may have done. In the future I wish to lead a quiet and orderly existence with my little girl far away from the enturbulating influences which have ruined my marriage.
>
> Sara Northrup Hubbard.[67]

Interviewed more than 35 years later, Sara stated that she had signed the statement because "I thought by doing so he would leave me and Alexis alone. It was horrible. I just wanted to be free of him!"[69]

On June 12, Hubbard was awarded a divorce in the County Court of Sedgwick County, Kansas on the basis of Sara's "gross neglect of duty and extreme cruelty", which had caused him "nervous breakdown and impairment to health."[70] She did not give evidence but was awarded custody of Alexis and $200 a month in child support.[43] She left Wichita as soon as Alexis was returned to her.[70] Her reunion with her daughter was uncertain to the last, as Hubbard had second thoughts about letting her go as he drove Sara and Alexis to the local airport. She persuaded him that the compulsion instilled by the communists would be dissipated by going ahead with the flight: "Well, I have to follow their dictates. I'll just go to the airplane."[71] She was so desperate to leave by the time she got to the airport that she left behind her daughter's clothes and her own suitcase and one of Alexis's shoes fell off as she dashed to the plane. "I just ran across the airfield, across the runways, to the airport and got on the plane. And it was the nineteenth of June and it was the happiest day of my life."[72]

21.7   Life after Hubbard

After divorcing Hubbard, Sara married Miles Hollister and bought a house in Malibu, California.[63] Hubbard continued to develop Dianetics (and ultimately Scientology), through which he met his third and last wife, Mary Sue, in late 1951 – only a few months after his divorce.[73] The controversy surrounding the divorce had severely dented his reputation. He sought to explain it to his followers as being the result of his victimization by his ex-wife. Speaking to Dianeticists following the divorce, Hubbard blamed shadowy outside forces for the bad publicity: "We have just been through the saw mill, through the public presses. Every effort was made to butcher my personal reputation. A young girl is nearly dead because of this effort. My wife Sara."[74] Around the summer of 1951, he explained his flight to Cuba as being a bid to escape Sara's depredations: "He talked a lot about Sara. When she ran off with another man Ron followed them and they locked him in a hotel room and pushed drugs up his nose, but he managed to escape and went to Cuba."[73] He publicly portrayed his marital problems as being entirely the fault of Sara and her lover Miles:

> The money and glory inherent in Dianetics was entirely too much for those with whom I had the bad misfortune to associate myself ... including a woman who had represented herself as my wife and who had been cured of severe psychosis by Dianetics, but who, because of structural brain damage would evidently never be entirely sane. ... Fur coats, Lincoln cars and a young man without any concept of honor so far turned the head of the woman who had been associated with me that on discovery of her affairs, she and these others, hungry for money and power, sought to take over and control all of Dianetics.[75]

Many years later, another of his followers, Virginia Downsborough, recalled that during the mid-1960s he "talked a lot about Sara Northrup and seemed to want to make sure that I knew he had never married her. I didn't know why it was so important to him; I'd never met Sara and I couldn't have cared less, but he wanted to persuade me that the marriage had never taken place. When he talked about his first wife, the picture he put out of himself was of this poor wounded fellow coming home from the war and being abandoned by his wife and family because he would be a drain on them."[76] As Downsborough put it, he portrayed himself as "a constant victim of women".[76]

The writer Christopher Evans has noted that "So painful do the memories of these incidents appear to be that L. Ron has more than once denied that he was ever married to Sarah [*sic*] Northrup at all."[77] He notes as an example of "this apparent erasure of Sarah Northrup from his mind"[77] a 1968 interview with the British broadcaster Granada Television, in which Hubbard denied that he had had a second wife in between his first, Polly, and the present one, Mary Sue:[77]

> HUBBARD: "How many times have I been married? I've been married twice. And I'm very happily married just now. I have a lovely wife, and I have four children. My first wife is dead."
> INTERVIEWER: "What happened to your second wife?"
> HUBBARD: "I never had a second wife." [78]

Granada's reporter commented: "What Hubbard said happens to be untrue. It's an unimportant detail but he's had three wives... What is important is that his followers were there as he lied, but no matter what the evidence they don't believe it."[79] Hubbard also gave a new explanation of why he had been involved with Jack Parsons and the OTO. After the British *Sunday Times* newspaper published an exposé of Hubbard's membership of the OTO in October 1969, the newspaper printed a statement attributed to the Church of Scientology (but written by Hubbard himself[80]) that asserted:

> Hubbard broke up black magic in America... L. Ron Hubbard was still an officer of the US Navy because he was well known as a writer and a philosopher and had friends amongst the physicists, he was sent in to handle the situation. He went to live at the house and investigated the black magic rites and the general situation and found them very bad. Hubbard's mission was successful far beyond anyone's expectations. The house was torn down. Hubbard rescued a girl they were using. The black magic group was dispersed and destroyed and has never recovered.[81]

Only a couple of months later, he highlighted Sara to his staff as a participant in a "full complete covert operation" mounted against Dianetics and Scientology by a "Totalitarian Communistic" enemy. In a memo of December 2, 1969, he wrote that the operation had started with bad reviews of *Dianetics*, "pushed then by the Sara Komkovadamanov [*sic*] (alias Northrup) "divorce" actions ... At the back of it was Miles Hollister (psychology student) Sara Komkosadamanov [*sic*] (housekeeper at the place nuclear physicists stayed near Caltech) ..."[82]

By 1970, Sara and Hollister had moved to Maui, Hawaii. Sara's daughter Alexis, who was by now twenty-one years old, attempted to contact her father but was rebuffed in a handwritten statement in which Hubbard denied that he was her father: "Your mother was with me as a secretary in Savannah in late 1948 . . . In July 1949 I was in Elizabeth, New Jersey, writing a movie. She turned up destitute and pregnant."[83] He claimed that Sara had been a Nazi spy during the war and accused her and Hollister of using the divorce case to seize control of Dianetics: "They obtained considerable newspaper publicity, none of it true, and employed the highest priced divorce attorney in the US to sue me for divorce and get the foundation in Los Angeles in settlement. This proved a puzzle since where there is no legal marriage, there can't be any divorce."[83] Despite clearly being written by Hubbard, who spoke in the first person in the letter, it was signed "Your good friend, J. Edgar Hoover".[84] Even his own staff were shocked by the contents of Hubbard's letter; he ended his instructions to them with the statement, "Decency is not a subject well understood".[85]

Neither Sara nor Alexis made any further attempt to contact Hubbard, who disinherited Alexis in his will, written in January 1986 on the day before he died.[86] In June 1986 the Church of Scientology and Alexis agreed a financial settlement under which she was compelled not to write or speak on the subject of L. Ron Hubbard and her relationship to him. An attempt was made to have her sign an affidavit stating that she was in fact the daughter of L. Ron Hubbard's first son, her half-brother L. Ron Hubbard, Jr.[87]

As the United Press International news agency noted, Church of Scientology biographies of Hubbard's life do not mention either of his first two wives.[88] In one publication the Church has airbrushed Sara out of a photograph of the couple that appeared in the *Miami Daily News* issue of June 30, 1946. The news story which the photograph accompanied has been republished by the Church with all mention of Sara edited out from the text.[89]

The church continues to promulgate Hubbard's claims about their relationship. The writer Lawrence Wright was told in September 2010 by Tommy Davis, the then spokesman for the Church of Scientology, that Hubbard "was never married to Sara Northrup. She filed for divorce in an effort to try and create a false record that she had been married to him." She had been part of Jack Parson's group because "she had been sent in there by the Russians. I can never pronounce her name. Her actual true name is a Russian name. That was one of the reasons L. Ron Hubbard never had a relationship with her. He never had a child with her. He wasn't married to her. But he did save her life and pull her out of that whole black magic ring."[90] After the documentary-maker Alex Gibney directed the film *Going Clear*, based on Wright's book of the same name and citing Sara's words about Hubbard, the Church published a video calling Sara a "failed gold digger" and "self admitted perjurer" who was responsible for "a get-rich-quick scheme [concocted] by the woman and her publicity starved lawyer to try to shake down Mr. Hubbard for money and take over the Hubbard Dianetics Foundation after Dianetics soared to the top of national bestseller lists."[91]

Although Sara did not speak out publicly against her ex-husband following their divorce, she broke her silence in 1972. She wrote privately to Paulette Cooper, the author of the book *The Scandal of Scientology* who was subsequently targeted by the Church's Operation Freakout. Sara told Cooper that Hubbard was a dangerous lunatic, and that although her own life had been transformed when she left him, she was still afraid both of him and of his followers,[92] whom she later described as looking "like Mormons, but with bad complexions."[51] In July 1986 she was interviewed by the ex-Scientologist Bent Corydon several months after Hubbard's death, which had reduced her fear of retaliation. Excerpts from the interview were published in Corydon's 1987 book, *L. Ron Hubbard: Messiah or Madman?*.[54] She died of breast cancer in 1997 but in the last few months of her life she dictated a tape-recorded account of her relationship with Hubbard. It is now in the Stephen A. Kent Collection on Alternative Religions at the University of Alberta.[93] Rejecting any suggestion that she was some kind of "pathetic person who has suffered through the years because of my time with Ron", Sara spoke of her relief that she had been able to put it behind her.[51] She stated that she was "not interested in revenge; I'm interested in the truth"[94]

21.8 Notes

[1] The Church of Scientology claims that this letter was forged by Sara's attorney, Carol Warner

21.9   References

[1] Starr, p. 254

[2] Pendle, pp. 85–87

[3] Wright, p. 414

[4] Starr, p. 235

[5] Wright, p. 42

[6] Starr, p. 256

[7] Rasmussen, Cecilia (March 19, 2000). "Life as Satanist Propelled Rocketeer". *The Los Angeles Times*.

[8] Wright, p. 43

[9] Starr, p. 366

[10] Pendle, p. 203.

[11] Pendle, p. 204.

[12] Starr, p. 288 fn. 31

[13] Starr, pp. 302–303

[14] Pendle, p. 247

[15] Miller, p. 116

[16] Miller, p. 118

[17] Urban, p. 137

[18] Miller, p. 120

[19] Miller, p. 126

[20] Corydon, p. 258

[21] Wright, p. 47

[22] Miller, p. 127

[23] Pendle, p. 270

[24] Wright, p. 48

[25] Wright, pp. 51–2

[26] Ortega, Tony (February 22, 2012). "Scientology and the Occult: Hugh Urban's new exploration of L. Ron Hubbard and Aleister Crowley". *Village Voice*. Retrieved August 11, 2015.

[27] Miller, p. 129

[28] Miller, p. 131

[29] Miller, p. 132

[30] Miller, p. 133

[31] Miller, p. 134

[32] Miller, p. 142

[33] Wright, p. 49

[34] Corydon, p. 290

[35] Miller, p. 143

[36] Miller, p. 144

[37] Miller, p. 147

[38] Miller, p. 152

[39] Atack, p. 117

[40] Lamont, p. 24

[41] Miller, p. 161

[42] Miller, p. 166

[43] Corydon, p. 284

[44] Miller, p. 168

[45] Miller, Russell. Interviews with Barbara Klowdan

[46] Miller, p. 170

[47] Wright, p. 70

[48] Miller, p. 172-173

[49] Miller, p. 174

[50] Miller, p. 175

[51] Corydon, p. 294

[52] Wright, p. 71

[53] Wright, p. 72

[54] Corydon, p. 287

[55] Miller, pp. 177–179

[56] Miller, p. 180

[57] Atack, p. 118

[58] Miller, p. 179

[59] Miller, p. 183

[60] "Letter indicates Dianetics founder, baby fled to Cuba". *Los Angeles Daily News.* May 1, 1951.

[61] Miller, p. 188

[62] Miller, p. 184

[63] Miller, p. 185

[64] Wright, p. 73

[65] Miller, p. 189

[66] Miller, pp. 190–191

[67] Miller, p. 192

[68] Wright, pp. 75–6

[69] Corydon, p. 285.

[70] Miller, p. 193

[71] Wright, p. 76

[72] Wright, p. 77

[73] Miller, p. 195

[74] Hubbard, L. Ron (June 28, 1951). *The Completed Auditor, Part I: The Dynamics – Interior and Exterior* (Taped lecture no. 5106C28 CAC). First Annual Conference of Hubbard Dianetic Auditors.

[75] Hubbard, L. Ron (October 1951). *Dianetics: Axioms*. Wichita, KS: Hubbard Dianetic Research Foundation. OCLC 14677877.

[76] Miller, p. 267

[77] Evans, p. 27

[78] Secret Lives: L. Ron Hubbard

[79] The Shrinking World of L Ron Hubbard

[80] Atack, p. 90

[81] "Scientology: New Light on Crowley". *Sunday Times*. December 28, 1969.

[82] Wright, p. 414 fn. 348, quoting Hubbard, "Intelligence Actions Covert Intelligence Data Collection", December 2, 1969

[83] Miller, pp. 305–306

[84] Wright, p. 118

[85] Miller, p. 305

[86] Wright, p. 356

[87] Corydon, p. 290-291

[88] UPI staff (May 21, 1982). "*Untitled*". *United Press International*. Official biographies of Hubbard do not mention Margaret Grubb or Sara Northrup

[89] Ortega, Tony (November 11, 2014). "Scientology Photoshopping: Erasing L. Ron Hubbard's second wife from 'The RON Series'". *The Underground Bunker*. Retrieved August 6, 2015.

[90] Wright, pp. 347–8

[91] "Alex Gibney: Stacking The Deck". *Freedom (magazine)*. Church of Scientology.

[92] Atack, p. 122

[93] Wright, pp. 348, 414

[94] Wright, p. 348

Bibliography

- Atack, Jon (1990). *A Piece of Blue Sky*. New York: Carol Publishing Group. ISBN 978-0-8184-0499-3.

- Corydon, Bent (1987). *L. Ron Hubbard: Messiah or Madman?*. Secaucus, NJ: Lyle Stuart. ISBN 978-0-8184-0444-3.

- Evans, Christopher (1974). *Cults of Unreason*. New York: Farrar, Straus and Giroux. ISBN 978-0-374-13324-5.

- Lamont, Stewart (1986). *Religion Inc.* London: Harrap. ISBN 978-0-245-54334-0.

- Miller, Russell (1987). *Bare-faced Messiah, The True Story of L. Ron Hubbard* (First American ed.). New York: Henry Holt and Company. ISBN 978-0-8050-0654-4.

    - Miller, Russell. "Interviews with "Barbara Kaye", Los Angeles, July 28 & August 21, 1986". Retrieved August 22, 2015.

- Pendle, George (2006). *Strange Angel: The Otherworldly Life of Rocket Scientist John Whiteside Parsons*. Orlando, FL: Houghton Mifflin Harcourt. ISBN 978-0-15-603179-0.

- *Secret Lives: L. Ron Hubbard* (Television). United Kingdom: Channel 4 Television. November 19, 1997.

- *World in Action: The Shrinking World of L Ron Hubbard* (Television). United Kingdom: Granada Television. July 1968.

- Starr, Martin P. (2003). *The Unknown God: W.T. Smith and the Thelemites*. Bolingbrook, IL: Teitan Press. ISBN 978-0-933429-07-9.

- Urban, Hugh B (2006). *Magia Sexualis: Sex, Magic, and Liberation in Modern Western Esotericism*. Berkeley, CA: University of California Press. ISBN 978-0-520-24776-5.

- Wright, Lawrence (2013). *Going Clear: Scientology, Hollywood, and the Prison of Belief*. New York: Alfred A. Knopf. ISBN 978-0-307-70066-7.

Hubbard and Sara aboard the schooner Blue Water II *in Miami, Florida, June 1946. The Church of Scientology has republished this photograph with Sara airbrushed out.*

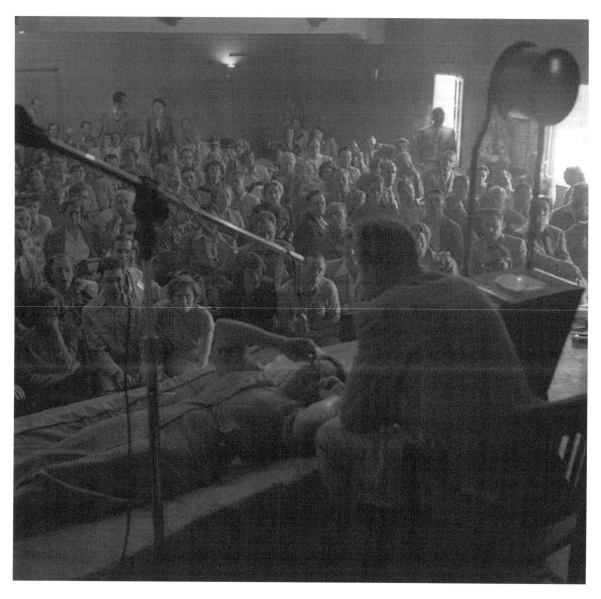

Hubbard conducting a Dianetics seminar in 1950

The Hubbard Dianetic Research Foundation, Inc.
275 MORRIS AVENUE
P. O. BOX 502, ELIZABETH, N. J.
ELIZABETH 2-2991

Office of the President

March 3, 1951

FEDERAL BUREAU OF INVESTIGATION
WASHINGTON, D.C.
Attn: Mr. Parrish.

Gentlemen:

The following is a list of Communist Party
members or suspects in our organization.

LEO WEST: In charge Chicago office. Known.
DAVE VROOMAN: Employee our Chicago office. Suspect.
ROSS LAMEREAUX: "   "   "   "   "   "   "   "
SARA NORTHRUP (HUBBARD), formerly of 1003 S. Orange
    Grove Avenue, Pasadena, Calif. 25 yrs. of age,
    5'10", 140 lbs. Currently missing somewhere
    in California. Suspected only. Had been
    friendly with many Communists. Currently
    intimate with them but evidently under coercion.
    Drug addiction set in fall 1950. Nothing of
    this known to me until a few weeks ago.
    Separation papers being filed and divorce applied
    for.
MILES HOLLISTER: Somewhere in vicinity of Los Angeles.
    Evidently a prime mover but very young. About 22 y
    6'. 180 lbs. Black hair. Sharp chin, broad
    forehead, rather Slavic. Confessedly a member
    of the Young Communists. Center of most turbulence
    in our organization. Dismissed in February when
    affiliations discovered. Active and dangerous.
    Commonly armed. Outspokenly disloyal to the U.S.
GENE BENTON: Somewhere in Los Angeles. Permitted
    to resign when discovered to be a member of the
    Young Communists. Center of much turbulence
    in organization. Was living at Doane Apts.
    on North Carondolet. May still be there. Squat,
    beefy, about 5'8", about 30. Possibly a member of
    the Lincoln Brigade but not very probable.
    Right name, Weinberger.
PEGGY BENTON: Member Young Communists by statement.
    28 yrs. old, wife of Gene Benton.
LYN HITE: Friend of Bentons and Hollister. Suspected
    840 N. Western, Los Angeles, Hempstead 1316. Very
    intimate with none but Communists or suspects.
HENRY HUNTER: Mathematician from Berkeley. One arm.
    Left arm severed at shoulder. Supposed to have had
    trouble with government before. About 28 yrs.
    Blond hair. Blue-grey eyes. Suspected only.
MARGE HUNTER: Wife of Henry. States she is a

Letter sent by L. Ron Hubbard to the FBI on March 3, 1951, denouncing his wife and her lover as Communists

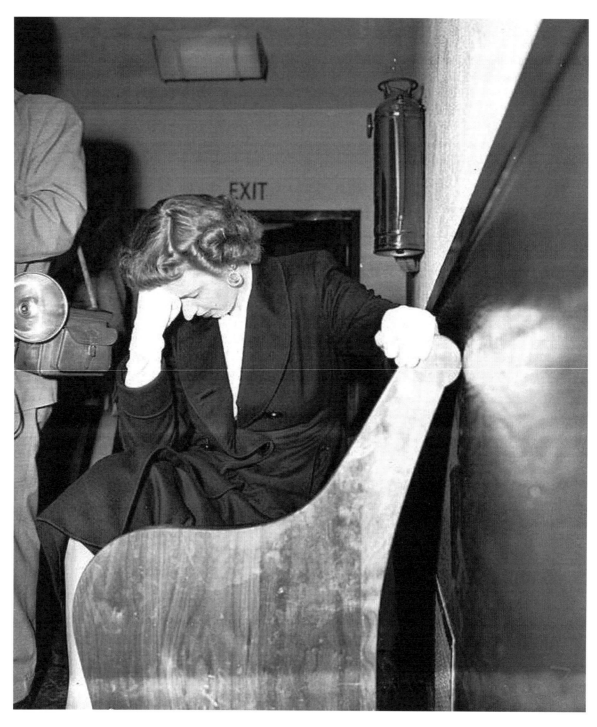

Sara at a custody hearing, April 24, 1951

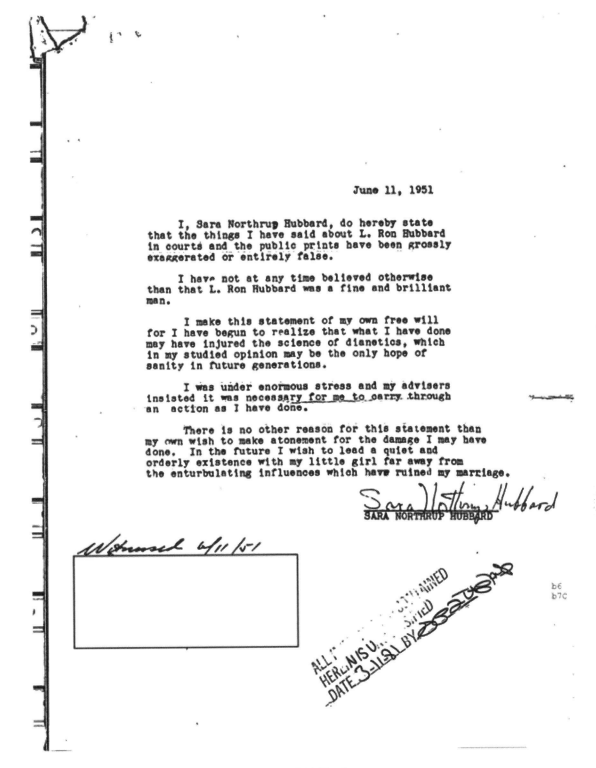

June 11, 1951

    I, Sara Northrup Hubbard, do hereby state
that the things I have said about L. Ron Hubbard
in courts and the public prints have been grossly
exaggerated or entirely false.

    I have not at any time believed otherwise
than that L. Ron Hubbard was a fine and brilliant
man.

    I make this statement of my own free will
for I have begun to realize that what I have done
may have injured the science of dianetics, which
in my studied opinion may be the only hope of
sanity in future generations.

    I was under enormous stress and my advisers
insisted it was necessary for me to carry through
an action as I have done.

    There is no other reason for this statement than
my own wish to make atonement for the damage I may have
done. In the future I wish to lead a quiet and
orderly existence with my little girl far away from
the enturbulating influences which have ruined my marriage.

SARA NORTHRUP HUBBARD

The statement made by Sara as part of her divorce settlement with Hubbard

Chapter 22

Rodney Orpheus

Rodney Orpheus is a Northern Irish musician, record producer, writer, lecturer, and a leading member of the Thelemic organisation Ordo Templi Orientis (O.T.O.). He is known for his work with the musical group The Cassandra Complex and for his book on the magick of Aleister Crowley, *Abrahadabra*.

22.1 Early life

Rodney Orpheus was born William Rodney Campbell on 8 July 1960 in Moneymore, Northern Ireland, and attended Rainey Endowed School on a scholarship. He became interested in music during the punk rock movement of the late 70s and led one of Ireland's first experimental punk bands, The Spare Mentals. In 1980 he migrated to Leeds, England where he formed The Cassandra Complex with Paul Dillon in 1984.[1] The two, who met when Orpheus gatecrashed Dillon's 21st birthday party, originally financed the band by working at The Sorcerer's Apprentice occult store.

After the release of The Cassandra Complex's first records Orpheus spent several years touring Europe, and while living in Aachen, Germany he joined Ordo Templi Orientis. Orpheus had studied the works of Aleister Crowley and other occult writers since his teenage years, and had previously founded and edited the UK occult newspaper *Pagan News* along with writer Phil Hine.[2]

While in Aachen he began work on the book *Abrahadabra*, published by Looking Glass Press in Sweden and later republished by Weiser Books. The *Ashe Journal* described the book as "a significant contribution to the field of Thelemic, or Crowleyan if you will, magick,"[3] and the *Tree of Light* journal said it was "one of the very few competent and readable introductory texts to Thelemic magick."[2]

22.2 Hamburg

Orpheus moved to Hamburg, Germany in 1990 where he formed the Makhashanah Oasis (later Lodge) of O.T.O. During this period he also formed the band Sun God,[1][4] based on Santería initiation he had received from Baba Raul Canizares on a visit to New York and inspired by the work of Vodou artist Sallie Ann Glassman. He set up a recording studio where The Cassandra Complex recorded their next albums, as well as producing and remixing several records for other German alternative artists, including Die Krupps and Girls Under Glass.[5] Orpheus had a role in the German vampire movie *Kiss My Blood*,[6] and toured with The Sisters of Mercy.[7] He was described as a "technopagan" in Mark Dery's 1996 overview of cyberculture *Escape Velocity*:

> To Rodney Orpheus the ease with which such metaphors are turned upside down underscores his belief that there's nothing oxymoronic about the term *technopagan* in end-of-the-century cyberculture. "People say 'pagans sit in the forest worshipping nature; what are you doing drinking diet coke in front of a Macintosh?' " says Orpheus, who in addition to being a card-carrying Crowleyite is a hacker and a mind machine aficionado.

"But when you use a computer, you're using your imagination to manipulate the computer's reality. Well, that's *exactly* what sorcery is all about – changing the plastic quality of nature on a nuts-and-bolts level. And that's why magickal techniques dating back hundreds of years are totally valid in a cyberpunk age."[8]

22.3   Los Angeles

Orpheus had used Steinberg's computer music software in the studio for some time, and soon after moving to Hamburg he joined the company to pioneer their Internet Services division. He became a well-known figure presenting the company's software at trade shows, and in 1999 relocated to Los Angeles, to design one of the first Web 2.0 community sites, Cubase.net.[9][10] While based in L.A., Orpheus served as a member of the US Grand Lodge O.T.O. Supreme Grand Council. He was still writing literature as well as music during this period: his horror short story "Gothic Blood Dream" and his poem "Poison Butterflies" would be published in the *Gothic II* anthology in 2002.

22.4   Return to the UK

In Los Angeles Orpheus spent time working within the movie sound industry[11] and became a strong supporter of surround sound. This led to him moving to Henley-on-Thames and becoming Business Development Manager for the DTS Entertainment surround record label in 2004.[12] During this period he produced the surround albums *Planet Earth* for LTJ Bukem and *A Gigantic Globular Burst of Anti-Static* for The Future Sound of London.

In 2007 he reformed the original line-up of The Cassandra Complex.

Orpheus has always been fascinated by games, and has written supplements for the tabletop game *Car Wars* from Steve Jackson Games. During a long period of recuperation after an operation in 2001 he started designing modules for the computer game *Neverwinter Nights*, eventually running an online server called *The Hidden Tradition* and winning a Neverwinter Vault Hall of Fame award.[13] This led him to spend time lecturing in games design at South Gloucestershire and Stroud College from 2008–2010.

22.5   Current work

Rodney Orpheus was appointed Deputy National Grand Master General for UK Grand Lodge of O.T.O.. at the Spring equinox 2009,[14] and appeared on the O.T.O. podcast *Thelema NOW!* in September of that year;[15] where he would make a second appearance in the August 2011 edition.[16]

He appeared with Nick Margerrison on Kerrang Radio representing O.T.O. in May 2009:

> We're chatting to a bloke, Rodney Orpheus, who is part of the religion which Crowley left behind after he died, it's called O.T.O. I'm asking him what would happen if we were to play out Crowley's magical spell ritual designed to call out demons. He tells me probably nothing, "If demons were to come out of the radio I'd be very surprised, if they're going to come out of anywhere, they'll come out of people's heads". Awesome. Great bit of radio. Hit play on the song. Two minutes in the station has a major technical glitch. The consoles in all three studios stop working. The mic won't turn on and then won't turn off. We play three songs in a row as we try to sort it out. Chaos as broadcast assistants and producers run about like headless chickens trying to sort it out. Technical response team on the phone. Finally we're back on air. Not the most impressive bit of radio ever. An example of Crowley's curse?[17]

His most recent book on magick, *Grimoire of Aleister Crowley*, was published by Abrahadabra Press in August 2011. It has been described as "a truly exceptional modern grimoire" by magical scholar and editor Colin Campbell.[18]

22.6 Bibliography

- Orpheus, Rodney (1988). "Convoy Tactics.". *Autoduel Quarterly* **6** (4). Retrieved 4 June 2009.

- Orpheus, Rodney; Phil Hine (ed.) (1988–1992) *Pagan News*

- Orpheus, Rodney (1989). *Trojan Horses – The Cassandra Complex Lyrics 1984–1989 e.v.* Aachen, Germany: Complex Music.

- Orpheus, Rodney (1995). *Abrahadabra: A Beginners Guide to Thelemic Magick*. Stockholm: Looking Glass Press. ISBN 91-88708-01-2.

- Orpheus, Rodney (1999). "Car Wars – Death Rally". *Pyramid Magazine* (April 1999). Retrieved 26 November 2009.

- Orpheus, Rodney (2002). "Gothic Blood Dream". In Matzke & Seeliger (ed.). *Gothic II. Die internationale Szene aus der Sicht ihrer Macher.* Schwarzkopf & Schwarzkopf. ISBN 3-89602-396-9.

- Orpheus, Rodney (2002). "Poison Butterflies". In Matzke & Seeliger (ed.). *Gothic II. Die internationale Szene aus der Sicht ihrer Macher.* Schwarzkopf & Schwarzkopf. ISBN 3-89602-396-9.

- Orpheus, Rodney (2005). *Abrahadabra: Understanding Aleister Crowley's Thelemic Magick (2nd Edition)*. Red Wheel/Weiser. ISBN 1-57863-326-5.

- Orpheus, Rodney (2009). "Gerald Gardner & Ordo Templi Orientis". *Pentacle Magazine* (30). pp. 14–18. ISSN 1753-898X.

- Orpheus, Rodney; Cathryn Orchard (30 November 2009). "Baptism in the Thelemic Tradition". In Kim Huggens (ed.). *From a Drop of Water*. Avalonia. ISBN 1-905297-34-3.

- Orpheus, Rodney (12 August 2011). *Grimoire of Aleister Crowley*. Manchester: Abrahadabra Press. ISBN 978-0-9569853-0-9.

- Orpheus, Rodney (2011). "Thelemic Morality". In Carl Abrahamssson (ed.). *The Fenris Wolf 1–3*. Stockholm: Edda Publishing. ISBN 978-91-979534-1-2.

22.7 Discography

1984

- *The Cassandra Complex – March* (Vocals, Instruments, producer, Songwriter)

1985

- *The Cassandra Complex – Moscow, Idaho* (Vocals, Instruments, producer, Songwriter)

- *Third Circle – Last Night* (Producer)

1986

- *The Cassandra Complex – Datakill* (Vocals, Instruments, producer, Songwriter)

- *The Cassandra Complex – Grenade* (Vocals, Instruments, producer, Songwriter)

- *The Cassandra Complex – Hello America* (Vocals, Instruments, producer, Songwriter)

1987

- *The Cassandra Complex – Feel The Width* (Vocals, producer, Songwriter)
- *The Cassandra Complex – Kill Your Children* (Vocals, Instruments, producer, Songwriter)

1988

- *The Cassandra Complex – Theomania* (Vocals, Instruments, producer, Songwriter)
- *Set Fatale* (Producer)

1989

- *The Cassandra Complex – 30 Minutes of Death* (Vocals, Instruments, producer, Songwriter)
- *The Cassandra Complex – Satan, Bugs Bunny & Me* (Vocals, Instruments, producer, Songwriter)
- *The Cassandra Complex – Penny Century* (Vocals, Instruments, producer, Songwriter)

1990

- *The Cassandra Complex – Cyberpunx* (Vocals, Instruments, producer, Songwriter)
- *The Cassandra Complex – Finland* (Vocals, Instruments, producer, Songwriter)
- *Girls Under Glass – Positive* (Producer)

1991

- *The Cassandra Complex – The War Against Sleep* (Vocals, Instruments, producer, Songwriter)

1992

- *The Cassandra Complex – Beyond The Wall of Sleep* (Vocals, producer, Songwriter)

1993

- *The Cassandra Complex – Sex & Death* (Vocals, Instruments, producer, Songwriter)
- *Sisters of Mercy – Under The Gun* (Keyboards/Top of the Pops appearance)
- *Catastrophe Ballet – Transition* (Producer)

1994

- *Die Krupps – Fatherland* (Remixer w/ Andrew Eldritch)

1995

- *Sun God – Sun God* (Vocals, Instruments, producer, Songwriter)

- *Asylum – Vent* (Producer)

1996

- *Aurora Sutra – Passing Over in Silence Unto Nuit* (Producer)
- *INRI – The Whole of Nature is Renewed by Fire* (Producer)
- *Still Silent* (Vocals, Lyrics)

2000

- *The Cassandra Complex – Wetware* (Vocals, Instruments, producer, Songwriter)
- *The Cassandra Complex – Twice As Good* (Vocals, Instruments, producer, Songwriter)

2001

- *Faith & the Muse – Vera Causa* (Remixer)

2002

- *Soil & Eclipse – Purity* (Remixer)

2003

- *Kraftwerk – Tour de France Soundtracks* (Technical Adviser)

2004

- *LTJ Bukem – Planet Earth* (Producer)
- *Beborn Beton – Another World* (Remixer)

2005

- *London Symphony Orchestra – Beethoven Classics* (Creative Director)
- *London Symphony Orchestra – Handel's Water Music* (Creative Director)
- *London Symphony Orchestra – Mozart Classics* (Creative Director)
- *London Symphony Orchestra – Tchaikovsky's The Nutcracker* (Creative Director)
- *London Symphony Orchestra – Bach Classics* (Creative Director)
- *London Symphony Orchestra – Tchaikovsky Classics* (Creative Director)

2006

- *Future Sound of London – A Gigantic Globular Burst of Anti-Static* (Producer)

2015

- *Within Temptation - And We Run ft Xzibit (WholeWorldBand Edition)* (Remixer)

22.8   Notes

[1]   Strong, Martin C. (2003) *The Great Indie Discography*, Canongate, ISBN 1-84195-335-0, p. 256

[2]   "Tree of Light: Biographies". *Tree of Life*. Retrieved 8 December 2011.

[3]   "Ashé Journal: Book Reviews". *Ashe Journal* **5** (2): 247–256. 2006. Retrieved 5 June 2009.

[4]   Jester (January 1996). "Sun God Interview". Retrieved 31 May 2009.

[5]   "Rodney Orpheus Discography". Retrieved 29 May 2009.

[6]   Jazay, David (Director). *Kiss My Blood (1998)*. Retrieved 29 May 2009.

[7]   "1996/07/14, Stadthalle, Offenbach, Germany". Retrieved 29 May 2009.

[8]   Dery, Mark (1 January 1996). *Escape Velocity: Cyberculture at the End of the Century*. New York, Grove Press, Inc. ISBN 0-340-67202-1.

[9]   "Sonic State – News Steinberg unveils Cubase.Net, A new web community for Cubase users". 12 November 1999. Retrieved 29 May 2009.

[10]   Fassett, Mark (2001). "Audio Notes From Macworld Expo". *XLR8YOURMAC* (64). Retrieved 5 June 2009.

[11]   Border, W.K. (Director). *Sex, Death & Eyeliner (2000)*. Retrieved 29 May 2009.

[12]   "DTS Expands DTS Entertainment in Europe; Company Appoints Business Development Manager". *Business Wire*. 22 June 2004. Retrieved 29 May 2009.

[13]   Savicki, Steve (2006). "Hall of Fame Interview – Rodney Orpheus (Hidden Tradition)". *Neverwinter Nights 2 Vault*. Retrieved 4 June 2009.

[14]   "Current News – UK Grand Lodge, Ordo Templi Orientis". 20 March 2009. Retrieved 29 May 2009.

[15]   "US Grand Lodge, OTO: Thelema NOW! podcast". Retrieved 28 February 2010.

[16]   Frater Puck. "US Grand Lodge, OTO: Thelema NOW! podcast" (Podcast). Thelema Now!. Event occurs at 85 minutes. Retrieved 12 September 2011.

[17]   Margerrison, Nick. "Straight From The Nicholarse". Retrieved 3 June 2009.

[18]   Campbell, Colin. "Grimoire of Aleister Crowley". *Colin Campbell's De Arte Magica*. Retrieved 8 December 2011.

22.9   External links

- Official website

Chapter 23

Jack Parsons (rocket engineer)

John Whiteside Parsons (born **Marvel Whiteside Parsons**;[nb 1] October 2, 1914 – June 17, 1952), better known as **Jack Parsons**, was an American rocket engineer and rocket propulsion researcher, chemist, inventor, businessman, expert witness, writer, socialite, and Thelemite occultist. Parsons was associated with the California Institute of Technology (Caltech), and was one of the principal founders of both the Jet Propulsion Laboratory (JPL) and the Aerojet Engineering Corporation. He invented the first castable, composite solid rocket propellant,[1] and pioneered the advancement of both liquid-fuel and solid-fuel rockets.

Born in Los Angeles, California, Parsons was raised by a wealthy family on Orange Grove Avenue in Pasadena. Inspired by science fiction literature, he developed an interest in rocketry in his childhood and in 1928 began amateur rocket experiments with school friend Ed Forman. He was forced to drop out of Pasadena Junior College and Stanford University due to financial difficulties during the Great Depression, but in 1934 he united with Forman and graduate student Frank Malina to form the Caltech-affiliated GALCIT Rocket Research Group, supported by Guggenheim Aeronautical Laboratory chairman Theodore von Kármán. In 1939 the Group gained funding from the National Academy of Sciences (NAS) to work on Jet-Assisted Take Off (JATO) for the U.S. military. In 1942 they founded Aerojet to develop and sell their JATO technology in response to American involvement in World War II; the Group became JPL in 1943.

After a brief involvement in Marxism, in 1939 Parsons began practising magick and converted to Thelema, the English occultist Aleister Crowley's new religious movement. In 1941, alongside his first wife Helen Northrup, Parsons joined the Agape Lodge, the Californian branch of the Thelemite Ordo Templi Orientis (OTO). At Crowley's bidding, he replaced Wilfred Talbot Smith as its leader in 1942 and ran the Lodge from his mansion on Orange Grove Avenue. Inciting criminal investigations into allegedly illicit activities, Parsons was expelled from JPL and Aerojet in 1944 in part due to the Lodge's infamy, along with his quixotic working practices as a scientist. In 1945 Parsons separated from Helen after having an affair with her sister Sara; when Sara left him for his friend L. Ron Hubbard he conducted the Babalon Working, a series of rituals designed to invoke the Thelemic goddess Babalon to Earth. He and Hubbard continued the procedure with Marjorie Cameron, whom Parsons married in 1946. After Hubbard and Sara defrauded him of his life savings, Parsons resigned from the OTO and went through various jobs while acting as a consultant for the Israeli rocket program. Amid the climate of McCarthyism he was accused of espionage and left unable to work in rocketry. In 1952 Parsons died at the age of 37 in a home laboratory explosion that attracted national media attention; the police ruled it an accident, but many associates suspected suicide or assassination.

Parsons' occult and libertarian polemical writings were published posthumously, reigniting intrigue in his status as a Thelemite among Western esoteric and countercultural circles, with occultists citing him as one of the most significant figures in propagating Thelema across North America. Although academic interest in his scientific career was negligible following his death, in subsequent decades scientific historians came to recognize Parsons' contributions to rocket propulsion chemistry and design. For these innovations, his advocacy of space exploration and human spaceflight, and his role in the founding of JPL and Aerojet, Parsons is regarded as among the most important figures in the history of the U.S. space program. He has been the subject of several biographies and fictionalized portrayals.

23.1   Biography

23.1.1   Early life: 1914–34

Marvel Whiteside Parsons was born on October 2, 1914, at the Good Samaritan Hospital in Los Angeles.[2] His parents, Ruth Virginia Whiteside (c. 1893–1952) and Marvel H. Parsons (c. 1894–1947), had moved to California from Massachusetts the previous year, purchasing a house on Scarf Street in downtown Los Angeles. Although their son was his father's namesake, he was known in the household as Jack.[3] Their marriage broke down soon after Jack's birth, when Ruth discovered that his father had made numerous visits to a prostitute, and she filed for divorce in March 1915. Parsons' father returned to Massachusetts after being publicly exposed as an adulterer, with Ruth forbidding him from having any contact with Jack.[4] Parsons' father would later join the armed forces, reaching the rank of major, and marry a woman with whom he had a son named Charles — a half-brother whom Jack would only meet once.[5] Although she retained her ex-husband's surname, Ruth started calling her son John; many friends throughout his life knew him as Jack.[6] Ruth's parents Walter and Carrie Whiteside moved to California to be with Jack and their daughter, using their wealth to buy an up-market house on Orange Grove Avenue in Pasadena — known locally as "Millionaire's Mile" — where they could live together.[7] Jack was surrounded by domestic servants.[8] Having few friends, he lived a solitary childhood and spent much time reading; he took a particular interest in works of mythology, Arthurian legend, and the *Arabian Nights*.[8] Through the works of Jules Verne he became interested in science fiction and a keen reader of pulp magazines like *Amazing Stories*, which led to his early interest in rocketry.[8][9]

At age twelve, Parsons began attending Washington Junior High School, where he performed poorly — something biographer George Pendle attributed to undiagnosed dyslexia — and was bullied for his upper-class status and perceived effeminacy.[10] Although unpopular, he formed a strong friendship with Edward Forman, a boy from a poor working class family who defended him from bullies and shared his interest in science fiction and rocketry, with the well-read Parsons enthralling Forman with his literary prowess. In 1928 the pair — adopting the Latin motto *per aspera ad astra* (*through hardship to the stars*) — began engaging in homemade gunpowder-based rocket experiments in the nearby Arroyo Seco canyon, as well as the Parsons family's back garden, which left it pockmarked with craters from explosive test failures. They incorporated commonly available fireworks such as cherry bombs into their rockets, and Parsons suggested using glue as a binding agent to reduce the rocket fuel's volatility, which was noted by Forman as early example of Parsons' inventiveness. This research became more complex when they began using materials such as aluminium foil to enhance the castability of the gunpowder.[10][11][12] Parsons had also begun to investigate occultism, and performed a ritual intended to invoke the Devil into his bedroom; he worried that the invocation was successful and was frightened into ceasing these activities.[13] In 1929 he began attending John Muir High School, where he maintained an insular friendship with Forman and was a keen participant in the sports of fencing and archery. After receiving poor school results, Parsons' mother sent him away to study at a private boarding school in San Diego — the Brown Military Academy for Boys — but he was expelled for blowing up the toilets.[14]

The Parsons family spent the summer of 1929 on a tour of Europe before returning to Pasadena, where they moved into a house on San Rafael Avenue. With the onset of the Great Depression their fortune began to dwindle, and in July 1931 Jack's grandfather Walter died.[15] Parsons began studying at the privately-run University School, a liberal institution that took an unconventional approach to teaching. He flourished academically, becoming editor of the school's newspaper *El Universitano* and winning an award for literary excellence, while teachers that had trained at the nearby California Institute of Technology (Caltech) honed his attentions on the study of chemistry.[16] With the family's financial difficulties deepening, Parsons began working during weekends and school holidays at the offices of the Hercules Powder Company, where he learned more about explosives and their potential use in rocket propulsion.[17] He and Forman continued to independently explore the subject in their spare time, building and testing different rockets — sometimes with materials that Parsons had stolen from work. Parsons soon constructed a solid-fuel rocket engine, and with Forman corresponded with pioneer rocket engineers including Robert H. Goddard, Russians Hermann Oberth and Konstantin Tsiolkovsky, and Germans Willy Ley and Wernher von Braun. Parsons and von Braun talked for hours over the telephone about rocketry in their respective countries as well as their own research. Pendle attributes the sudden dissipation of their conversations to the men's mutual reticence about disclosing the technical details of their discoveries.[18][19][11][20]

Graduating from University School in the summer of 1933, Parsons moved with his mother and grandmother to a more modest house on St. John Avenue, where he continued to pursue his interests in literature and poetry.[21] In the autumn he enrolled in Pasadena Junior College with the hope of earning an associate degree in physics and chemistry, but dropped

The young Parsons spoke for hours with Wernher von Braun in phone correspondence about rocketry. Wernher von Braun.

out after only a term because of his financial situation and he took up permanent employment at the Hercules Powder Company.[22] His employers then sent him to work at their manufacturing plant in Pinole on San Francisco Bay, where he earned a relatively high wage of $100 a month; however, he was plagued by headaches caused by exposure to nitroglycerin.

He saved money in the hope of continuing his academic studies and began a degree in chemistry at Stanford University, but again found the tuition fees unaffordable and returned to Pasadena.[23]

23.1.2   GALCIT Rocket Research Group and the Kynette trial: 1934–38

Parsons (center) and GALCIT colleagues in the Arroyo Seco, Halloween 1936. JPL marks this experiment as its foundation.[24][25]

In the hope of gaining access to the state-of-the-art resources of Caltech to use in their rocketry research, Parsons and Forman attended a lecture on the work of Austrian rocket engineer Eugen Sänger and hypothetical above-stratospheric aircraft by the institute's William Bollay— a PhD student specializing in rocket-powered aircraft — and approached him to express their interest in designing a liquid-fuel rocket motor.[26][27] Bollay redirected them to another PhD student named Frank Malina, a mathematician and mechanical engineer composing a thesis on rocket propulsion who shared their interests and soon befriended the pair.[28] Parsons, Forman, and Malina applied for funding from Caltech together; they did not mention that their ultimate objective was to develop rockets for space exploration, realizing that most of the scientific establishment then relegated such ideas to science fiction. While Caltech's Clark Blanchard Millikan immediately rebuffed them, Malina's doctoral advisor Theodore von Kármán saw more promise in their proposal and agreed to allow them to operate under the auspices of the university's Guggenheim Aeronautical Laboratory (GALCIT).[29] Naming themselves the GALCIT Rocket Research Group, they gained access to Caltech's specialist equipment, though the economics of the Great Depression left von Kármán unable to finance them.[30]

The trio focused their distinct skills on collaborative rocket development; Parsons was the chemist, Forman the machinist, and Malina the technical theoretician. Malina wrote in 1968 that the self-educated Parsons "lacked the discipline of a formal higher education, [and] had an uninhibited and fruitful imagination."[31] The informally trained Parsons and Forman who, as described by Geoffrey A. Landis, "were eager to try whatever idea happened to spring to mind", contrasted with the approach of Malina, who insisted on the need for scientific discipline as informed by von Kármán. Landis writes that their creativity, however, "kept Malina focused toward building actual rocket engines, not just solving equations on paper".[32] Sharing socialist values, they operated on an egalitarian basis; Malina taught the others about scientific procedure and they taught him about the practical elements of rocketry. They often socialized, smoking marijuana and drinking, while Malina and Parsons set about writing a semiautobiographical science fiction screenplay they planned to pitch to Hollywood with strong anti-capitalist and pacifist themes.[33]

GALCIT Group members in the Arroyo Seco, November 1936. Left foreground to right: Rudolph Schott, Amo Smith, Frank Malina, Ed Forman, and Jack Parsons.

Parsons had met Helen Northup at a local church dance and proposed marriage in July 1934. She accepted and they were married in April 1935 at the Little Church of the Flowers in Forest Lane Memorial Park, Glendale, before undertaking a brief honeymoon in San Diego.[34] They moved into a house on South Terrace Drive, Pasadena, while Parsons gained employment for the explosives manufacturer Halifax Powder Company at their facility in Saugus. Much to Helen's dismay, Parsons spent most of his wages funding the GALCIT Rocket Research Group.[35] For extra money he manufactured nitroglycerin in their home, constructing a home laboratory on their front porch, and at one point he pawned Helen's engagement ring and would often ask her family for loans.[36]

Malina recounted that "Parsons and Forman were not too pleased with an austere program that did not include at least the launching of model rockets",[31] but the Group reached the consensus of developing a working static rocket-motor before embarking on more complex research. They contacted liquid-fuel rocket pioneer Robert H. Goddard and he invited Malina to his facility in Roswell, New Mexico, but he was not interested in cooperating — reticent about sharing his research and having been subjected to widespread derision for his work in rocketry.[37] They were instead joined by Caltech graduate students Apollo M. O. "Amo" Smith, Carlos C. Wood, Mark Muir Mills, Fred S. Miller, William C. Rockefeller, and Rudolph Schott; Schott was relied upon for the use of his pickup truck to transport equipment.[38] Their first liquid-fuel motor test took place near the Devil's Gate Dam in the Arroyo Seco on Halloween 1936.[39][40] Parsons' biographer John Carter described the layout of the contraption as showing[41]

> oxygen flowing from one side, with methyl alcohol (the fuel) and nitrogen flowing from the other side. Water cooled the rocket during the burn. Thrust pulled down a spring which measured force. The deflection of the spring measured the force applied to it. A small diamond tip on the apparatus scratched a glass plate

to mark the furthest point of deflection. The rocket and mount were protected by sandbags, with the tanks (and the experimenters) well away from it.

Three attempts to fire the rocket failed; on the fourth the oxygen line was accidentally ignited and perilously billowed fire at the Group, but they viewed this experience as formative.[42] They continued their experiments throughout the final quarter of 1936; after the final test was successfully completed in January 1937 von Kármán agreed that they could perform their future experiments at an exclusive rocket testing facility on campus.[43][44][45]

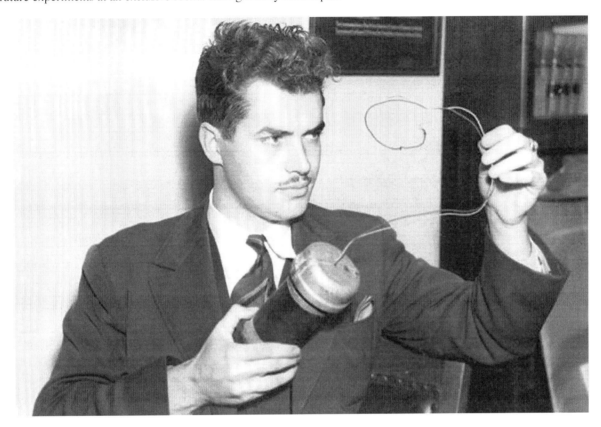

Parsons in 1938, holding the replica car bomb used in the murder trial of police officer Captain Earl Kynette.

In April 1937 Caltech mathematician Qian Xuesen (a Chinese citizen) joined the Group. Several months later Weld Arnold, a Caltech laboratory assistant who worked as the Group's official photographer, also joined. The main reason for Arnold's appointment to this position was his provision of a donation to the Group on behalf of an anonymous benefactor whose identity was never revealed.[46] They became well known on campus, earning the moniker of the "Suicide Squad" for the dangerous nature of some of their experiments and attracting attention from the local press.[47] Parsons himself gained further media publicity when he appeared as an expert explosives witness in the trial of Captain Earl Kynette, the head of police intelligence in Los Angeles who was accused of conspiring to set a car bomb in the attempted murder of private investigator Harry Raymond, a former LAPD detective who was fired after challenging corruption in the force. When Kynette was convicted largely on Parsons' testimony, which included his forensic reconstruction of the car bomb and its explosion, his identity as an expert scientist in the public eye was established despite his lack of a university education.[48][49] While working at Caltech, Parsons was admitted to evening courses in chemistry at the University of Southern California (USC), but distracted by his GALCIT workload he attended sporadically and received unexceptional grades.[50]

By early 1938 the Group had made their static rocket motor, which originally burned for three seconds, run for over a minute.[51][52] In May that year, Parsons was invited by Forrest J Ackerman to lecture on his rocketry work at Chapter Number 4 of the Los Angeles Science Fiction League (LASFL). Although he never joined the society, he occasionally attended their talks, on one occasion conversing with a teenage Ray Bradbury.[53] Another scientist to become involved in the GALCIT project was Sidney Weinbaum, a Jewish refugee from Europe who was a vocal Marxist; he led Parsons,

Malina, and Qian in their creation of a largely secretive communist discussion group at Caltech, which became known as Professional Unit 122 of the Pasadena Communist Party. Although Parsons subscribed to the *People's Daily World* and joined the American Civil Liberties Union (ACLU), he refused to join the American Communist Party, causing a break in his and Weinbaum's friendship.[54] This coupled with the need to focus on paid employment led to the disintegration of much of the Rocket Research Group, leaving only its three founding members by late 1938.[55]

23.1.3 Embracing Thelema; advancing JATO and foundation of Aerojet: 1939–42

In January 1939 John and Frances Baxter, a brother and sister who had befriended Jack and Helen Parsons, took Jack to the Church of Thelema in Winona Boulevard, Hollywood, where he witnessed the performance of The Gnostic Mass. Notable attendees of the church had included Hollywood actor John Carradine and gay rights activist Harry Hay. Parsons was intrigued, having already heard of Thelema's founder and Outer Head of the Ordo Templi Orientis (OTO), Aleister Crowley, after reading a copy of Crowley's text *Konx om Pax* (1907).

Parsons was introduced to leading members Regina Kahl, Jane Wolfe, and Wilfred Talbot Smith at the mass. Feeling both "repulsion and attraction" for Smith, Parsons continued to sporadically attend the Church's events for a year.[56] He continued to read Crowley's works, which increasingly interested him, and encouraged Helen to read them.[57] Parsons came to believe in the reality of magic — or *magick* in Thelemic terms — as a force that could be explained through quantum physics.[57] He tried to interest his friends and acquaintances in Thelema, taking science fiction writers Jack Williamson and Cleve Cartmill to a performance of The Gnostic Mass. Although they were unimpressed, Parsons was more successful with Grady Louis McMurtry, a young Caltech student whom he had befriended, as well as McMurtry's fiancée Claire Palmer, and Helen's sister Sara "Betty" Northrup.[58]

Jack and Helen were initiated into the Agape Lodge, the renamed Church of Thelema, in February 1941. Parsons adopted the Thelemic motto of *Thelema Obtenteum Proedero Amoris Nuptiae*, a Latin mistranslation of "The establishment of Thelema through the rituals of love". The initials of this motto spelled out T.O.P.A.N., also serving as the declaration "To Pan".[59] Commenting on Parsons' errors of translation, in jest Crowley said that "the motto which you mention is couched in a language beyond my powers of understanding".[60] Parsons also adopted the Thelemic title *Frater T.O.P.A.N* — with *T.O.P.A.N* represented in Kabbalistic numerology as *210*—the name with which he frequently signed letters to occult associates — while Helen became known as *Soror Grimaud*.[61] Smith wrote to Crowley claiming that Parsons was "a really excellent man ... He has an excellent mind and much better intellect than myself ... JP is going to be very valuable".[62] Wolfe wrote to German OTO representative Karl Germer that Parsons was "an A1 man ... Crowleyesque in attainment as a matter of fact", and mooted Parsons as a potential successor to Crowley himself as Outer Head of the Order.[63] Crowley concurred with such assessments, informing Smith that Parsons "is the most valued member of the whole Order, with no exception!"[60]

At von Kármán's suggestion, Malina approached the National Academy of Sciences (NAS) Committee on Army Air Corps Research to request funding for research into what they referred to as "jet propulsion", a term chosen to avoid the stigma attached to rocketry. The military were interested in jet propulsion as a means of getting aircraft quickly airborne where there was insufficient room for a full-length runway, and gave the Rocket Research Group $1,000 to put together a proposal on the feasibility of Jet-Assisted Take Off (JATO) by June 1939, making Parsons *et al.* the first U.S. government-sanctioned rocket research group. Since their formation in 1934, they had also performed experiments involving model, black powder motor-propelled multistage rockets. In a research paper submitted to the American Institute of Aeronautics and Astronautics (AIAA), Parsons reported these rockets reaching velocities of 4,875 miles per hour, thereby demonstrating the potential of solid fuels as being significantly more effective than liquid types primarily preferred by researchers such as Goddard. In light of this progress, Caltech and the GALCIT Group received an additional $10,000 rocketry research grant from the AIAA.[64]

Although a quarter of their funding went on repairing damage to Caltech buildings caused by their experiments, in June 1940 they submitted a report to the NAS in which they showed the feasibility of the project for the development of JATO and requested $100,000 to continue; however, they only received $22,000.[65] Now known as GALCIT Project Number 1, they continued to be ostracized by other Caltech scientists who grew increasingly irritated by their accidents and noise pollution, and were made to relocate their experiments back to the Arroyo Seco, at a site with unventilated, corrugated iron sheds that served as both research facilities and administrative offices. It was here that JPL would be founded.[66] Parsons and Forman's rocket experiments were the cover story of the August 1940 edition of *Popular Mechanics*, in which the pair discussed the prospect of rockets being able to ascend above Earth's atmosphere and orbit around it for research purposes, as well as reaching the Moon.[67]

For the JATO project, they were joined by Caltech mathematician Martin Summerfield and 18 workers supplied by the Works Progress Administration. Former colleagues like Qian were prevented from returning to the project by the Federal Bureau of Investigation (FBI), who ensured the secrecy of the operation and restricted the involvement of foreign nationals and political extremists.[68] The FBI was satisfied that Parsons was not a Marxist but were concerned when Thelemite friend Paul Seckler used Parsons' gun in a drunken car hijacking, for which Seckler was imprisoned in San Quentin State Prison for two years. Englishman George Emerson replaced Arnold as the Group's official photographer.[69]

The Group's aim was to find a replacement for black-powder rocket motors — units consisting of charcoal, sulphur and potassium nitrate with dectin as a binding agent — the volatility of which frequently resulted in explosions damaging military aircraft.[70] The solid JATO fuel invented by Parsons consisted of amide, corn starch, and ammonium nitrate bound together in the JATO unit with glue and blotting paper. It was codenamed GALCIT-27, implying the previous invention of 26 new fuels. The first JATO tests using an Ercoupe plane took place in late July 1941; though effectively aiding propulsion, the units frequently exploded and damaged the aircraft. Parsons theorized that this was because the ammonium nitrate became dangerously combustible following overnight storage, during which temperature and consistency changes had resulted in a chemical imbalance. Parsons and Malina accordingly devised a method in which they would fill the JATOs with the fuel in the early mornings shortly before the tests, enduring sleep deprivation to do so. On August 21, 1941, Navy Captain Homer J. Boushey, Jr. — watched by such figures as Clark Millikan and William F. Durand — piloted the JATO-equipped Ercoupe at the March Air Force Base in Moreno Valley, California. It proved a success and reduced takeoff distance by 30%, but one of the JATOs partially exploded.[71] Over the following weeks 62 further tests took place, and the NAS increased their grant to $125,000. During a series of static experiments, an exploding JATO did significant damage to the fuselage in the Ercoupe's tail; one observer optimistically noted that "at least it wasn't a big hole", but necessary repairs delayed their efforts.[72]

The military ordered a flight test using liquid fuel rather than the pre-existing solid fuel in early 1942. Upon the United States' entry into the Second World War in December 1941, the Group realized they could be drafted directly into military service if they failed to provide viable JATO technology for the military. Informed by their left-wing politics, aiding the war effort against Nazi Germany and the Axis powers was as much of a moral vocation to Parsons, Forman and Malina as it was a practical one. Parsons, Summerfield and the GALCIT workers focused on the task and found success with a combination of gasoline with red fuming nitric acid as its oxidizer — with the latter, suggested by Parsons, proving to be an effective substitute for liquid oxygen.[70][73] The testing of this fuel resulted in another calamity, however, when the testing rocket motor exploded; the fire, containing iron shed fragments and shrapnel inexplicably left the experimenters unscathed. Malina solved the problem by replacing the gasoline with aniline, resulting in a successful test launch of a JATO-equipped A-20A plane at the Mura Auxiliary Air Field in the Mojave Desert. Providing a thrust five times more powerful than GALCIT-27, and again reducing takeoff distance by 30%, Malina wrote to his parents that "We now have something that really works and we should be able to help give the Fascists hell!"[74]

The Group then agreed to produce and sell 60 JATO engines to the United States Army Air Corps. To do so they formed the Aerojet Engineering Corporation in March 1942, into which Parsons, Forman, Malina, von Kármán, and Summerfield each invested $250, opening their offices on Colorado Boulevard and bringing in Amo Smith as their engineer. Andrew G. Haley was recruited by von Kármán as their lawyer and treasurer. Although Aerojet was a for-profit operation that provided technology for military means, the founders' mentality was rooted in the ideal of using rockets for peaceful space exploration. As Haley recounted von Kármán requesting: "we will make the rockets — you must make the corporation and obtain the money. Later on you will have to see that we all behave well in outer space."[75]

Despite these successes, Parsons — project engineer of Aerojet's Solid Fuel Department — remained motivated to address the malfunctions observed during the Ercoupe tests. In June 1942 — assisted by Mills and Miller — he focused his attention on developing an effective method of restricted burning when using solid rocket fuel, as the military demanded JATOs that could provide over 100 pounds of thrust without any risk of exploding. Although solid fuels such as GALCIT-27 were less volatile than their liquid counterparts, they were disfavored for military JATO use as they provided less immediate thrust and did not have the versatility of being turned on and off mid-flight. Parsons tried to resolve GALCIT-27's volatility issue with GACLIT-46, which replaced the former's ammonium nitrate with guanidine nitrate. To avoid the problems seen with ammonium nitrate, he had GALCIT-46 supercooled and then superheated prior to testing. When it failed the test, he realized that the fuel's binding black powders rather than the oxidizers which had resulted in their volatility, and in June that year had the idea of using liquidized asphalt as an appropriate binding agent with potassium perchlorate as its oxidizer.[39]

Malina recounted that Parsons was inspired to use asphalt by the ancient incendiary weapon Greek fire, while in a 1982 talk for the International Association of Astronomical Artists Captain Boushey stated that Parsons experienced an epiphany after watching manual workers using molten asphalt to fix tiles onto a roof. Known as GALCIT-53, this fuel proved to be significantly less volatile than the Group's earlier concoctions, fulfilling Parsons' aim of creating a restricted-burn rocket fuel inside a castable container, and providing a thrust 427% more powerful than that of GALCIT-27. This set a precedent which according to his biographer John Carter "changed the future of rocket technology": the thermoplastic asphalt casting — durable in all climates — allowing for mass-production and indefinite storage of the Group's invention and transforming solid-fuel agents into a safe and viable form of rocket propulsion. Plasticized variants of Parsons' solid-fuel design — invented by JPL's Charles Bartley — were later used by NASA in Space Shuttle Solid Rocket Boosters and by the Strategic Air Command in Polaris, Poseidon and Minuteman intercontinental ballistic missiles.[39][1][76]

23.1.4 Foundation of JPL and leading the Agape Lodge: 1942–44

Aerojet's first two contracts were from the U.S. Navy; the Bureau of Aeronautics requested a solid-fuel JATO and the Wilbur Wright Field requested a liquid-fuel unit. The Air Corps had requested two thousand JATOs from Aerojet by late 1943, committing $256,000 toward Parsons' solid-fuel type. Despite this drastically increased turnover, the company continued to operate informally and remained intertwined with the GALCIT project. Caltech astronomer Fritz Zwicky was brought in as head of the company's research department, and Haley replaced von Kármán as Aerojet chairman and imposed payroll cuts instead of reducing JATO output; the alternative was to cut staff numbers while maintaining more generous salaries, but Haley's priority was Aerojet's contribution to the war effort. However, company heads including Parsons were exempted from this austerity, drawing the ire of many personnel.[77][78]

Parsons' newfound credentials and financial security gave him the opportunity to travel more widely throughout the U.S. as an ambassador for Aerojet, meeting with other rocket enthusiasts. In New York he met with Karl Germer, the head of the OTO in North America and in Washington, D.C. he met Poet Laureate Joseph Auslander, donating some of Crowley's poetry books to the Library of Congress.[79] He also became a regular at the Mañana Literary Society, which met in Laurel Canyon at the home of Parsons' friend Robert A. Heinlein and included science fiction writers including Cleve Cartmill, Jack Williamson, and Anthony Boucher. Among Parsons' favorite works of fiction was Williamson's *Darker Than You Think*, a novelette published in the fantasy magazine *Unknown* in 1940, which inspired his later occult workings. Boucher used Parsons as a partial basis for the character of Hugo Chantrelle in his murder mystery *Rocket to the Morgue* (1942).[80]

Helen went away for a period in June 1941, during which Parsons, encouraged to do so by the sexually permissive attitude of the OTO, began a sexual relationship with her 17-year-old sister, Sara. Upon Helen's return, Sara asserted that she was Parsons' new wife, and Parsons himself admitted that he found Sara more sexually attractive than Helen.[81] Conflicted in her feelings, Helen sought comfort in Smith and began a relationship with him that would last for the rest of his life; the four remained friends.[82] The two couples, along with a number of other Thelemites (some of whom with their children), relocated to 1003 South Orange Grove Avenue, an American Craftsman-style mansion. They all contributed to the rent of $100 a month and lived communally in what replaced Winona Boulevard as the new base of the Agape Lodge, maintaining an allotment and slaughtering their own livestock for meat as well as blood rituals.[83] Parsons decorated his new room with a copy of the Stele of Revealing, a statue of Pan, and his collection of swords and daggers. He converted the garage and laundry room into a chemical laboratory and often held science fiction discussion meetings in the kitchen, and entertained the children with hunts for fairies in the 25 acre garden.[84]

"I height Don Quixote, I live on Peyote,
marihuana, morphine and cocaine.
I never knew sadness but only a madness
that burns at the heart and brain,"

Excerpt from an untitled poem published in Parsons' ill-fated *Oriflamme* journal[85]

Although there were arguments among the commune members, Parsons remained dedicated to Thelema. He gave almost all of his salary to the OTO while actively seeking out new members—including Forman—and financially supported Crowley in London through Germer.[86] Parsons' enthusiasm for the Lodge quickly began to impact on his professional life. He frequently appeared at Aerojet hungover and sleep deprived from late nights of Lodge activities, and invited many of his colleagues to them, drawing the ire of staff who previously tolerated Parsons' occultism as harmless eccentricity; known to von Kármán as a "delightful screwball", he was frequently observed reciting Crowley's poem "Hymn to Pan" in an ecstatic manner compared to the preaching of Billy Graham during rocket tests—and on request at parties to their great amusement. However, they disapproved of his hesitancy to separate his vocations; Parsons became more rigorously engaged in Aerojet's day-to-day business in an effort to resolve this weariness, but the Agape Lodge soon came under investigation by both the Pasadena Police Department and the FBI. Both had received allegations of a "black magic cult" involved in sexual orgies; one complainant was a 16-year-old boy who claimed that he was raped by lodge members, while neighbors reported a ritual involving a naked pregnant woman jumping through fire. After Parsons explained that the Lodge was simply "an organization dedicated to religious and philosophical speculation", neither agency found evidence of illegal activity and came to the conclusion that the Lodge constituted no threat to national security.[87] Having been a long-term heavy-user of alcohol and marijuana, Parsons now habitually used cocaine, amphetamines, peyote, mescaline and opiates as well.[88][52] He continued to have sexual relations with multiple women, including McMurtry's fiancee Claire. When Parsons paid for Claire to have an abortion, McMurtry was angered and their friendship broke down.[89]

Crowley and Germer wanted to see Smith removed as head of the Agape Lodge, believing that he had become a bad influence on its members. Parsons and Helen wrote to them to defend their mentor but Germer nevertheless ordered him to stand down and Parsons was appointed as temporary head of the Lodge.[90] Some veteran Lodge members disliked Parsons' influence, concerned that it encouraged excessive sexual polyandry that was religiously detrimental, but his charismatic orations at Lodge meetings assured his popularity among the majority of followers. Parsons soon created the Thelemite journal *Oriflamme*, in which he published his own poetry, but Crowley was unimpressed—particularly due to Parsons' descriptions of drug use—and the project was soon shelved.[91] Helen gave birth to Smith's son in April; the child was named Kwen Lanval Parsons.[92] Smith and Helen left with Kwen for a two-room cabin in Rainbow Valley in May.[93] Concurrently in England, Crowley undertook an astrological analysis of Smith's birth chart and came to the conclusion that Smith was the incarnation of a god, greatly altering his estimation of him. Smith remained skeptical as Crowley's analysis was seemingly deliberately devised in Parsons' favor, encouraging Smith to step down from his role in the Agape Lodge and instructing him to take a meditative retreat.[94] Refusing to take orders from Germer anymore, Smith resigned from the OTO. Parsons — who remained sympathetic and friendly to Smith during the conflict and was weary of Crowley's "appalling egotism, bad taste, bad judgement, and pedanticism" — ceased lodge activities and resigned as its head, but withdrew his resignation after receiving a pacifying letter from Crowley.[95]

By the summer of 1943 Aerojet was operating on a budget of $650,000. The same year Parsons and von Kármán traveled to Norfolk, Virginia to consult on a new JATO contract for the U.S. Navy on the invitation of Secretary of the Navy Frank Knox. Though JATOs were being mass-produced for military applications, JATO-propelled aircraft could not "keep up" with larger, bomber planes taking off from long aircraft carrier runways — which made Aerojet's industry at risk of becoming defunct.[96] Parsons demonstrated the efficacy of the newer JATOs to solve this issue by equipping a Grumman plane with solid-fuel units; its assisted takeoff from the USS *Charger* was successful, but produced smoke containing a noxious, yellow-colored residue. The Navy guaranteed Parsons a contract on the condition that this residue was removed; this led to the invention of *Aeroplex*, a technology for smokeless vapor trails developed at Aerojet by Parsons.[97]

As the U.S. became aware that Nazi Germany had developed the V-2 rocket, the military — following recommendations from von Kármán based upon research using British intelligence — placed a renewed impetus on its own rocket research, reinstating Qian to the GALCIT project. They gave the Group a $3 million grant to develop rocket-based weapons, and the Group was expanded and renamed the Jet Propulsion Laboratory (JPL).[98] By this point the Navy were ordering 20,000 JATOs a month from Aerojet, and in December 1944 Haley negotiated for the company to sell 51% of its stock to the General Tire and Rubber Company to cope with the increased demand. However, Aerojet's Caltech-linked employees — including Zwicky, Malina and Summerfield — would only agree to the sale on the condition that Parsons and Forman were removed from the company, viewing their occult activities as disreputable. JPL historian Erik M. Conway also attributes Parsons' expulsion to more practical concerns: he "still wanted to work in the same way as he'd done in his backyard, instinctive and without regard for safety".[70] Parsons and Forman were unfazed, informing Haley of their prediction that the rocket industry would become obsolete in the postwar age and seeing more financial incentive in starting a chain of laundromats. Haley persuaded them to sell their stock, resulting in Parsons leaving the company with $11,000.[99] With this money he bought the lease to 1003, which had come to be known as "the Parsonage" after him.[100]

23.1.5   L. Ron Hubbard and the Babalon Working: 1945–46

See also: L. Ron Hubbard § Occult involvement in Pasadena

Now disassociated from JPL and Aerojet, Parsons and Forman founded the Ad Astra Engineering Company, under which Parsons founded the chemical manufacturing Vulcan Powder Company.[101] Ad Astra was subject to an FBI investigation under suspicion of espionage when security agents from the Manhattan Project discovered that Parsons and Forman had procured a chemical used in a top secret project for a material known only as *x-metal*, but they were later acquitted of any wrongdoing.[102] Parsons continued to financially support Smith and Helen, although he asked for a divorce from her and ignored Crowley's commands by welcoming Smith back to the Parsonage when his retreat was finished.[103] Parsons continued to hold OTO activities at the Parsonage but began renting rooms at the house to non-Thelemites, including journalist Nieson Himmel, Manhattan Project physicist Robert Cornog, and science fiction artist Louis Goldstone.[104] Parsons attracted controversy in Pasadena for his preferred clientele. Parsonage resident Alva Rogers recalled in a 1962 article for an occultist fanzine: "In the ads placed in the local paper Jack specified that only bohemians, artists, musicians, atheists, anarchists, or any other exotic types need to apply for rooms — any mundane soul would be unceremoniously rejected".[105]

Science fiction writer and U.S. Navy officer L. Ron Hubbard soon moved in to the Parsonage; he and Parsons became close friends. Parsons wrote to Crowley that although Hubbard had "no formal training in Magick he has an extraordinary amount of experience and understanding in the field. From some of his experiences I deduce he is direct touch with some higher intelligence, possibly his Guardian Angel. ... He is the most Thelemic person I have ever met and is in complete accord with our own principles."[106]

Although Parsons and Sara were in an open relationship encouraged by the OTO's polyandrous sexual ethics, she became enamored with Hubbard; Parsons, despite attempting to repress his passions, became intensely jealous.[107] Motivated to find a new partner through occult means, Parsons began to devote his energies to conducting black magic, causing concern among fellow OTO members who believed that it was invoking troublesome spirits into the Parsonage; Jane Wolfe wrote to Crowley that "our own Jack is enamored with Witchcraft, the houmfort, voodoo. From the start he always wanted to evoke something — no matter what, I am inclined to think, as long as he got a result." He claimed to the residents that he was imbuing statues in the house with a magical energy in order to sell them to fellow occultists.[108] Parsons reported paranormal events in the house resulting from the rituals; including poltergeist activity, sightings of orbs and ghostly apparitions, alchemical (sylphic) effect on the weather, and disembodied voices. Pendle suggested that Parsons was particularly susceptible to these interpretations and attributed the voices to a prank by Hubbard and Sara.[108] One ritual allegedly brought screaming banshees to the windows of the Parsonage, an incident that disturbed Forman for the rest of his life.[109] In December 1945 Parsons began a series of rituals based on Enochian magic during which he masturbated onto magical tablets, accompanied by Sergei Prokofiev's Second Violin Concerto and using his own semen and blood for this purpose. Describing this magical operation as the Babalon Working, he hoped to bring about the incarnation of Thelemite goddess Babalon onto Earth. He allowed Hubbard to take part as his "scribe", believing that he was particularly sensitive to detecting magical phenomena.[110] As described by Richard Metzger, "Parsons jerked off in the name of spiritual advancement" while Hubbard "scanned the astral plane for signs and visions."[111]

Their final ritual took place in the Mojave Desert in late February 1946, during which Parsons abruptly decided that his undertaking was complete. On returning to the Parsonage he discovered that a woman named Marjorie Cameron — an unemployed illustrator and former Navy WAVE — had come to visit. Believing her to be the "elemental" woman and manifestation of Babalon that he had invoked, in early March Parsons began performing sex magic rituals with Cameron, who acted as his "Scarlet Woman", while Hubbard continued to participate as the amanuensis. Unlike the rest of the household, Cameron knew nothing at first of Parsons' magical intentions: "I didn't know anything about the OTO, I didn't know that they had invoked me, I didn't know anything, but the whole house knew it. Everybody was watching to see what was going on."[112] Despite this ignorance, and her skepticism about Parsons' magic, Cameron reported her sighting of a UFO to him which she believed was a materialization of its paranormal energy.[113] Through this sex magic, inspired by Crowley's novel *Moonchild* (1917), Parsons and Hubbard aimed to magically fertilize a "magickal child" through immaculate conception, which when born to a woman somewhere on Earth nine months following the working's completion would become the Thelemic messiah embodying Babalon.[114][115] To quote Metzger, the purpose of the Babalon Working was "a daring attempt to shatter the boundaries of space and time" facilitating, according to Parsons, the emergence of Thelema's Æon of Horus.[111] When Cameron departed for a trip to New York, Parsons retreated to the desert, where he believed that a preternatural entity psychographically provided him with *Liber 49*, which represented a fourth part of Crowley's *The Book of the Law*, the primary sacred text of Thelema, as well as part of a new sacred text he called the *Book of Babalon*.[116] Crowley was bewildered and concerned by the endeavor, complaining to Germer of being "fairly frantic when I contemplate the idiocy of these louts". Believing the Babalon Working was accomplished, Parsons sold the Parsonage to developers for $25,000 under the condition that he and Cameron could continue to live in the coach house, and he appointed Roy Leffingwell to head the Agape Lodge, which would now have to meet elsewhere for its rituals.[117]

Parsons decided to co-found a company called Allied Enterprises with Hubbard and Sara, into which Parsons invested his life savings of $20,970. Hubbard suggested that with this money they travel to Miami to purchase three yachts, which they would then sail through the Panama Canal to the West Coast, where they could sell them on for a profit. Parsons agreed, but many of his friends thought it was a bad idea. Hubbard had secretly requested permission from the U.S. Navy to sail to China and South and Central America on a mission to "collect writing material"; his real plans were for a world cruise. Left "flat broke" by this defrauding, Parsons was incensed when he discovered that Hubbard and Sara had left for Miami with $10,000 of the money; he suspected a scam but was placated by a telephone call from Hubbard and agreed to remain business partners. When Crowley, in a telegram to Germer, dismissed Parsons as a "weak fool" and victim to Hubbard and Sara's obvious confidence trick, Parsons changed his mind, flew to Miami and placed a temporary injunction and restraining order on them. Upon tracking them down to a harbor in County Causeway, Parsons discovered that the couple had purchased three yachts as planned; they tried to flee aboard one but hit a squall and were forced to return to port. Parsons was convinced that he had brought them to shore through a lesser banishing ritual of the pentagram containing an astrological, geomantic invocation of Bartzabel—a vengeful spirit of Mars. Allied Enterprises was dissolved and in a court settlement Hubbard was made to promise to reimburse Parsons. Parsons was discouraged from taking further action by Sara, who threatened to report him for statutory rape since their sexual relationship took place when she was under California's age of consent of 18. Parsons was ultimately compensated with only $2,900. Hubbard, already married to Margaret Grubb, bigamously married Sara and went on to found Dianetics and Scientology.[118]

The Sunday Times published an article about Hubbard's involvement with the OTO and Parsons' occult activities in December 1969. In response, the Church of Scientology released an unsubstantiated press statement which said that Hubbard had been sent as an undercover agent by the U.S. Navy to intercept and destroy Parsons' "black magic cult", and save Sara from its influence. The Church also claimed that Robert A. Heinlein was the clandestine Navy operative who "sent in" Hubbard to undertake this operation.[119] Returning to California, Parsons completed the sale of the Parsonage, which was then demolished, and resigned from the OTO. He wrote in his letter to Crowley that he did not believe that "as an autocratic organization, [the OTO] constitutes a true and proper medium for the expression and attainment" of Thelema.[120]

23.1.6   Work for Israelis and espionage accusations: 1946–52

Parsons obtained employment with North American Aviation at Inglewood, where he worked on the Navaho Missile Program.[121] He and Cameron moved into a house on Manhattan Beach, where her instructed her in occultism and esotericism.[122] When Cameron developed catalepsy, Parsons referred her to Sylvan Muldoon's books on astral projection, suggesting that she could manipulate her seizures to accomplish it.[123] They were married on October 19, 1946, four days after his divorce from Helen was finalized, with Forman as their witness.[124] Parsons continued to be seen as a specialist in rocketry; he acted as an expert consultant in numerous industrial tribunals and police and Army Ordnance investigations regarding explosions. In May 1947, Parsons gave a talk at the Pacific Rocket Society in which he predicted that rockets would take humans to the Moon.[125] Although he had become distant from the now largely defunct OTO and had sold much of his Crowleyan library, he continued to correspond with Crowley until the latter's death in December 1947.[126]

At the emergence of the Cold War, a Red Scare developed in the U.S. as the Congressional House Un-American Activities Committee began investigating and obstructing the careers of people with perceived communist sympathies. Many of Parsons' former colleagues lost their security clearances and jobs as a result, and eventually the FBI stripped Parsons of his clearance because of his "subversive" character, including his involvement in and advocacy of "sexual perversion" in the OTO. He speculated in a June 1949 letter to Germer that his clearance was revoked in response to his public dissemination of Crowley's *Liber OZ*, a 1941 tract summarizing the individualist moral principles of Thelema. Declassified FBI documents would reveal that the FBI's primary concern was Parsons' former connections to Marxists at Caltech and his membership of the also "subversive" ACLU. When they interviewed Parsons he denied communist sympathies but informed them of Sidney Weinbaum's "extreme communist views" and Frank Malina's involvement in Weinbaum's communist cell at Caltech, which resulted in Weinbaum's arrest for perjury since he had formally denied any involvement in communist groups, and Malina's security clearance being withdrawn. In reaction to this hostile treatment, Parsons sought work in the rocket industry abroad. He sought advice to do so in correspondence with von Kármán; whose advice he followed by enrolling in an evening course in advanced mathematics at USC to bolster his employability in the field — but again he neglected attendance and failed the course.[127] Parsons again resorted to bootlegging nitroglycerin for money, and managed to earn a wage as a car mechanic, a manual laborer at a gas station, and a hospital orderly; for two years he was also a faculty member at the USC Department of Pharmacology.[128] Relations between Parsons and Cameron became strained; they agreed to a temporary separation and she moved to Mexico to join an artists' commune in San Miguel de Allende.[129]

Unable to pursue his scientific career, without his wife and devoid of friendship, Parsons decided to return to occultism and embarked on sexually based magical operations with prostitutes. He was intent, informally following the ritualistic practice of Thelemite organization the A∴A∴, on performing "the Crossing of the Abyss", attaining union with the universal consciousness, or "All" as understood in Thelemic mysticism, and becoming the "Master of the Temple".[130] Following his apparent success in doing so, Parsons recounted having an out-of-body experience invoked by Babalon, who astrally transported him to the biblical City of Chorazin, an experience he referred to as a "Black Pilgrimage". Accompanying Parsons' "Oath of the Abyss" was his own "Oath of the AntiChrist", which was witnessed by Wilfred Talbot Smith. In this oath, Parsons professed to embody an entity named *Belarion Armillus Al Dajjal*, the Antichrist "who am come [*sic*] to fulfill the law of the Beast 666 [Aleister Crowley]".[130] Viewing these oaths as the completion of the Babalon Working, Parsons wrote an illeist autobiography titled *Analysis by a Master of the Temple* and an occult text titled *The Book of AntiChrist*. In the latter work, Parsons (writing as *Belarion*) prophesied within nine years Babalon would manifest on Earth and supersede the dominance of the Abrahamic religions.[131]

During this period, Parsons also wrote an essay on his individualist philosophy and politics — which he described as standing for "liberalism and liberal principles" — titled "Freedom is a Two-Edged Sword", in which he condemned the authoritarianism, censorship, corruption, antisexualism and racism he saw as prevalent in American society.[130] None of these works were published in his lifetime. Through Heinlein, Parsons received a visit from writer L. Sprague de Camp, with whom he discussed magic and science fiction, and disclosed that Hubbard had sent a letter offering him Sara back. De Camp later referred to Parsons as "An authentic mad genius if I ever met one", and based the character Courtney James on him in his time travel story *A Gun for Dinosaur* (1956). Parsons was also visited by Jane Wolfe, who unsuccessfully appealed for him to rejoin the dilapidated OTO. He entered a brief relationship with an Irishwoman named Gladis Gohan; they moved to a house on Redondo Beach, a building known by them as the "Concrete Castle".[132][126] Cameron returned to Redondo Beach from San Miguel de Allende and violently argued with Parsons upon discovering his infidelity, before she again left for Mexico. Parsons responded by initiating divorce proceedings against her on the grounds of "extreme cruelty".[133]

Parsons testified to a closed federal court that the moral philosophy of Thelema was both anti-fascist and anti-communist, emphasizing his belief in individualism. This along with references from his scientific colleagues resulted in his security clearance being reinstated by the Industrial Employment Review Board, which ruled that there was insufficient evidence that he had ever had communist sympathies. This allowed Parsons to obtain a contract in designing and constructing a chemical plant for the Hughes Aircraft Company in Culver City.[134] Von Kármán put Parsons in touch with Herbert T. Rosenfeld, President of the Southern Californian chapter of the American Technion Society—a Zionist group dedicated to supporting the newly created State of Israel. Rosenfeld offered Parsons a job with the Israeli rocket program and hired him to produce technical reports for them.[135] In November 1950, as the Red Scare intensified, Parsons decided to migrate to Israel to pursue Rosenfeld's offer, but a Hughes secretary whom Parsons had asked to type up a portfolio of technical documents reported him to the FBI. She accused Parsons of espionage and attempted theft of classified company documents on the basis of some of the reports that he had sought to submit to the Technion Society.[136]

Parsons was immediately fired from Hughes; the FBI investigated the complaint and were suspicious that Parsons was spying for the Israeli government. Parsons denied the allegations when interrogated; he insisted that his intentions were peaceful and had suffered an error of judgment in procurement of the documents. Some of Parsons' scientific colleagues rallied to his defense, but the case against him worsened when the FBI investigated Rosenfeld for being linked to Soviet agents, and more accounts of his occult and sexually permissive activities at the Parsonage came to light. In October 1951 the U.S. attorney decided that because the contents of the reports did not constitute state secrets, Parsons was not guilty of espionage.[136][137]

The Review Board, however, still considered Parsons a liability because of his historical Marxist affiliations and investigations by the FBI, and in January 1952 they permanently reinstated their ban on him working for classified projects, effectively prohibiting him from working in rocketry.[138] To make a living he founded the Parsons Chemical Manufacturing Company, which was based in North Hollywood and created pyrotechnics and explosives such as fog effects and imitation gunshot wounds for the film industry, and he also returned to chemical manufacturing at the Bermite Powder Company in Saugus.[139][140]

Reconciling with Cameron, they resumed their relationship and moved into a former coach house on Orange Grove Avenue. Parsons converted its large, first-floor laundry room into a home laboratory to work on his chemical and pyrotechnic projects, homebrew absinthe and stockpile his materials.[142] They let out the upstairs bedrooms and began holding parties that were attended largely by bohemians and members of the Beat Generation, along with old friends including Forman, Malina and Cornog. They also congregated at the home of Andrew Haley, who lived on the same street. Though Parsons in his mid-thirties was a "prewar relic" to the younger attendees, the raucous socials often lasted until dawn and frequently attracted police attention.[143] Parsons also founded a new Thelemite group known as "the Witchcraft", whose beliefs revolved around a simplified version of Crowley's Thelema and Parsons' own Babalon prophecies. He offered a course in its teachings for a ten dollar fee, which included a new Thelemic belief system called "the Gnosis", a version of Christian Gnosticism with Sophia as its godhead and the Christian God as its demiurge. He also collaborated with Cameron on *Songs for the Witch Woman*, a collection of poems which she illustrated that remained unpublished until 2014.[144][145]

23.1.7 Death: 1952

Parsons and Cameron decided to travel to Mexico for a few months, both for a vacation and for Parsons to take up a job opportunity establishing an explosives factory for the Mexican government. They hoped that this would facilitate a move to Israel, where they could start a family, and where Parsons could bypass the U.S. government to recommence his rocketry career. He was particularly disturbed by the presence of the FBI, convinced that they were spying on him.[146]

On June 17, 1952, a day before their planned departure, Parsons received a rush order of explosives for a film set and began to work on it in his home laboratory.[147] An explosion destroyed the lower part of the building, during which Parsons sustained mortal wounds. His right forearm was amputated, his legs and left arm were broken and a hole was torn in the right side of his face.[148] Despite these critical injuries, Parsons was found conscious by the upstairs lodgers. He tried to communicate with the arriving ambulance workers, who rushed him to the Huntingdon Memorial Hospital, where he was declared dead around thirty-seven minutes after the explosion. Parsons' last words are frequently said to have been "I wasn't done", but Cameron recited them as "Who will take care of me now?"[148] When his mother, Ruth, was informed of the events, she immediately committed suicide by taking an overdose of barbiturates. Cameron learned of her husband's death from reporters at the scene when she returned home from grocery shopping.[149][49]

Pasadena Police Department criminologist Don Harding led the official investigation; he concluded that Parsons had been mixing fulminate of mercury in a coffee can when he dropped it on the floor, causing the initial explosion, which worsened when it came into contact with other chemicals in the room.[150] Forman considered this likely, stating that Parsons often had sweaty hands and could easily have dropped the can.[151] Some of Parsons' colleagues rejected this explanation, saying that he was very attentive about safety. Two colleagues from the Bermite Powder Company described Parsons' work habits as "scrupulously neat" and "exceptionally cautious". The latter statement — from chemical engineer George Santymers — insisted that the explosion must have come from beneath the floorboards, implying an organized plot to kill Parsons. Harding accepted that these inconsistencies were "incongruous" but described the manner in which Parsons had stored his chemicals as "criminally negligent", and noted that Parsons had previously been investigated by the police for illegally storing chemicals at the Parsonage. He also found a morphine-filled syringe at the scene, indicating that Parsons was narcotized. The police saw insufficient evidence to continue the investigation and closed the case as an accidental death.[152]

"John W. Parsons, handsome 37-year-old rocket scientist killed Tuesday in a chemical explosion, was one of the founders of a weird semi-religious cult that flourished here about 10 years ago ... Old police reports yesterday pictured the former Caltech professor as a man who led a double existence — a down-to-earth explosives expert who dabbled in intellectual necromancy. Possibly he was trying to reconcile fundamental human urges with the inhuman, Buck Rogers type of innovations that sprang from his test tubes." Parsons' obituary in the June 19, 1952 edition of *The Pasadena Independent*[153]

Both Wolfe and Smith suggested that Parsons' death had been suicide, stating that he had suffered from depression for some time. Others theorized that the explosion was an assassination planned by Howard Hughes in response to Parsons' suspected theft of Hughes Aircraft Company documents.[154] Cameron became convinced that Parsons had been murdered

— either by police officers seeking vengeance for his role in the conviction of Earl Kynette or by anti-Zionists opposed to his work for Israel.[155] One of Cameron's friends, the artist Renate Druks, later stated her belief that Parsons had died in a rite designed to create a homunculus.[156] His death has never been definitively explained.[157]

The immediate aftermath of the explosion attracted the interest of the U.S. media, making headline news in the *Los Angeles Times*. These initial reports focused on Parsons' prominence in rocketry but neglected to mention his occult interests. When asked for comment, Aerojet secretary-treasurer T.E. Beehan said that Parsons "liked to wander, but he was one of the top men in the field".[158] However, within several days, journalists had discovered his involvement in Thelema and emphasized this in their reports.[158]

A private prayer service was held for Parsons at the funeral home where his body was cremated. Cameron scattered his ashes in the Mojave Desert, before burning most of his possessions.[159] She later tried to perform astral projection to commune with him.[160] The OTO also held a memorial service — with attendees including Helen and Sara — at which Smith led the Gnostic Mass.[161]

23.2 Personal life

23.2.1 Personality

Although considered effeminate as a child, in adult life Parsons was known to exhibit an attitude of machismo.[162] His FBI file described him as "potentially bisexual" and he once expressed experiencing a latent homosexuality.[61] The actor Paul Mathison claimed to have had a gay relationship with Parsons in the 1950s, though this was disputed by others who knew him and Cameron.[163] Parsons had the reputation of being a womanizer, and was notorious for frequently flirting and having sexual liaisons with female staff members at JPL and Aerojet.[164][165] He was also known for personal eccentricity such as greeting house guests with a large pet snake around his neck, driving to work in a rundown Pontiac, and using a mannequin dressed in a tuxedo with a bucket labelled "The Resident" as his mailbox.[29][166]

As well as a fencing and archery enthusiast, Parsons was also a keen shooter; he often hunted jack rabbits and cotton tails in the desert, and was amused by mock duelling with Forman while on test sites with rifles and shotguns. Upon proposing to his first wife Helen, he also gifted her with a pistol.[29][162][167] Parsons also enjoyed playing pranks on his colleagues, often through detonating explosives such as firecrackers and smoke bombs,[168] and was known to spend hours at a time in the bathtub playing with toy boats while living at the Parsonage.[169]

As well as intense bursts of creativity, Parsons suffered from what he described as "manic hysteria and depressing melancholy."[170] His father Marvel, after suffering a near-fatal heart attack, died as a psychiatric patient at St. Elizabeths Hospital in Washington D.C. diagnosed with severe clinical depression, a condition Pendle suggested the younger Parsons inherited.[5]

23.2.2 Professional associations

Parsons' obituary listed him as a member of the Army Ordnance Corps Association, the American Institute of Aeronautics and Astronautics, the American Chemical Society, the American Association for the Advancement of Science, and — despite his lack of an academic degree — the Sigma Xi fraternity. It also stated that he had turned down several honorary degrees.[171]

23.3 Philosophy

23.3.1 Religious beliefs

"[Parsons] treated magic and rocketry as different sides of the same coin: both had been disparaged, both derided as impossible, but because of this both presented themselves as challenges to be conquered. Rocketry postulated that we should no longer see ourselves as creatures chained to the earth but as beings capable of exploring the universe.

Similarly, magic suggested there were unseen metaphysical worlds that existed and could be explored with the right knowledge. Both rocketry and magic were rebellions against the very limits of human existence; in striving for one challenge he could not help but strive for the other."

George Pendle[172]

Parsons adhered to the occult philosophy of Thelema, which had been founded in 1904 by the English occultist Aleister Crowley following a spiritual revelation that he had in the city of Cairo, Egypt, when — according to Crowley's own accounts — a spirit being known as Aiwass dictated to him a prophetic text known as *The Book of the Law*.[173] Prior to becoming aware of Thelema and Crowley, Parsons' interest in esotericism was developed through his reading of *The Golden Bough* (1890), a work in comparative mythology by Scottish social anthropologist James George Frazer.[174] Parsons had also attended lectures on Theosophy by philosopher Jiddu Krishnamurti with his first wife Helen, but disliked the belief system's sentiment of "the good and the true".[175] During rocket tests, Parsons often recited Crowley's poem "Hymn to Pan" as a good luck charm.[165] He took to addressing Crowley as his "Most Beloved Father" and signed off to him as "thy son, John".[176]

In July 1945, Parsons gave a speech to the Agape Lodge, in which he attempted to explain how he felt that *The Book of the Law* could be made relevant to "modern life". In this speech, which was subsequently published under the title of "Doing your Will", he examined the Thelemite concept of True Will, writing that:

> The mainspring of an individual is his creative Will. This Will is the sum of his tendencies, his destiny, his inner truth. It is one with the force that makes the birds sing and flowers bloom; as inevitable as gravity, as implicit as a bowel movement, it informs alike atoms and men and suns.

> To the man who knows this Will, there is no why or why not, no can or cannot; he IS!

> There is no known force that can turn an apple into an alley cat; there is no known force that can turn a man from his Will. This is the triumph of genius; that, surviving the centuries, enlightens the world.

> This force burns in every man.[177]

Parsons identified four obstacles that prevented humans from achieving and performing their True Will, all of which he connected with fear: the fear of incompetence, the fear of the opinion of others, the fear of hurting others, and the fear of insecurity. He insisted that these must be overcome, writing that "The Will must be freed of its fetters. The ruthless examination and destruction of taboos, complexes, frustrations, dislikes, fears and disgusts hostile to the Will is essential to progress."[178]

Though Parsons was a lifelong devotee to Thelema, he grew weary of and eventually left the Ordo Templi Orientis — the religious organization that began propagating Thelema under Crowley's leadership from the 1910s — which Parsons viewed, despite the disagreement of Crowley himself, as excessively hierarchical and impeding upon the rigorous spiritual and philosophical practice of True Will, describing the OTO as "an excellent training school for adepts, but hardly an appropriate Order for the manifestation of Thelema". In this sense Parsons was described by Carter as an "almost fundamentalist" Thelemite who placed *The Book of the Law*'s dogma above all other doctrine.[131][179]

23.3.2 Politics

"[Parsons] had witnessed the blinding overnight successes achieved by the government-by-terror totalitarianism of Stalinist Russia and Nazi Germany. He had the foresight to see that [the United States of] America, once armed with the new powers of total destruction and surveillance that were sure to follow the swelling flood of new technologies, had the potential to become even more repressive unless its founding principles of individual liberty were religiously preserved and its leaders held accountable to them.

Two of the keys to redressing the balance were the freedom of women and an end to the state control of individual sexual expression. He knew that these potent forces, embodied as they are in a majority of the world's population, had the power, once unleashed, to change the world."

William Breeze (Hymenaeus Beta), current Frater Superior of Ordo Templi Orientis[180]

From early on in his career, Parsons took an interest in socialism and communism,[181] views that he shared with his friend Malina.[182] Under the influence of another friend, Sidney Weinbaum, the two joined a communist group in the late 1930s, with Parsons reading Marxist literature, but he remained unconvinced and refused to join the American Communist Party.[54] Malina asserted that this was because Parsons was a "political romantic", whose attitude was more anti-authoritarian than anti-capitalist.[183] Parsons would later become critical of the Marxist-Leninist government of the Soviet Union led by Joseph Stalin, sarcastically commenting that

> The dictatorship of the proletariat is merely temporary — the state will eventually wither away like a snark hunter, leaving us all free as birds. Meanwhile it may be necessary to kill, torture and imprison a few million people, but whose fault is it if they get in the way of progress?[184]

During the era of McCarthyism and the Second Red Scare in the early 1950s, Parsons was questioned regarding his former links to the communist movement, by which time he denied any connection to it, instead describing himself as "an individualist" who was both anti-communist and anti-fascist.[185] In reaction to the McCarthyite red-baiting of scientists, he expressed disdain that

> Science, that was going to save the world in H. G. Wells' time is regimented, straight-jacked, [and] scared shitless, its universal language diminished to one word: security.[186]

Parsons was politically influenced by Thelema — which holds to the ethical code of "Do what thou wilt" — equating this principle to the libertarian views of some of the Founding Fathers of the United States in his article "Freedom is a Lonely Star", claiming that by his own time these values had been "sold out by America, and for that reason the heart of America is sick and the soul of America is dead."[187] He proceeded to criticize many aspects of contemporary U.S. society, particularly the police force, remarking that "The police mind is usually of a sadistic and homicidal trend" and noting that they carried out the "ruthless punishment of symbolic scapegoats" such as African-Americans, prostitutes, alcoholics, homeless people and sociopolitical radicals, under the pretense of a country that upheld "liberty and justice for all."[188]

To bring about a freer future Parsons believed in liberalizing attitudes to sexual morality stating that, in his belief, the publication of the Kinsey report and development of the psychonautical sciences had as significant an influence on Western society as the creation of the atomic bomb and the development of nuclear physics. He also believed that in the future the restrictions on sexual morality within society should be abolished in order to bring about greater freedom and individuality. Parsons concluded that

> the liberty of the individual is the foundation of civilization. No true civilization is possible without this liberty and no state, national or international, is stable in its absence. The proper relation between individual liberty on the one hand and social responsibility on the other is the balance which will assure a stable society. The only other road to social equilibrium demands the total annihilation of individuality. There is not further evasion of nature's immemorial ultimatum: change or perish but the choice of change is ours.[189]

Jack Cashill, American studies professor at Purdue University, argues that "Although his literary career never got much beyond pamphleteering and an untitled anti-war, anti-capitalist manuscript", Parsons played a significant role — greater than that of Church of Satan founder Anton LaVey — in shaping the Californian counterculture of the 1960s and beyond through his influence on contemporaries such as Hubbard and Heinlein.[190] Hugh B. Urban, religious studies professor at Ohio State University, cites Parsons' Witchcraft group as precipitating the neopagan revival of the 1950s.[115][191]

Science fiction writer and occultist Robert Anton Wilson described Parsons' political writings as exemplifying an "ultra-individualist" who exhibited a "genuine sympathy for working people", strongly empathized with feminism and held an antipathy toward patriarchy comparable to that of John Stuart Mill, arguing in this context that Parsons was an influence on the American libertarian and anarchist movements of the 20th century.[192] Parsons was also supportive of the creation of the State of Israel, making plans to emigrate there when his military security clearance was revoked.[181]

23.4 Legacy and influence

In the decades following his death, Parsons would be better remembered among the Western esoteric community rather than their scientific counterpart, with his recognition in the latter frequently amounting to a footnote.[193] For instance, English Thelemite Kenneth Grant suggested that Parsons' Babalon Working marked the start of the appearance of flying saucers in the skies, leading to phenomena such as the Roswell UFO incident and Kenneth Arnold UFO sighting.[194] Cameron herself postulated that the 1952 Washington, D.C. UFO incident was a spiritual reaction to Parsons' death.[160] In 1954 she portrayed Babalon in American Thelemite Kenneth Anger's short film *Inauguration of the Pleasure Dome*, viewing this cinematic depiction of a Thelemic ritual as aiding the literal invocation of Babalon begun by Parsons' working, and later claimed that his *Book of the AntiChrist* prophecies were fulfilled through the manifestation of Babalon in her person.[195][196]

In December 1958 JPL was integrated into the newly established National Aeronautics and Space Administration, after having built the *Explorer 1* satellite that commenced America's Space Race with the Soviet Union.[197] Aerojet was contracted by NASA to build the main engine of the Apollo Command/Service Module, and the Space Shuttle Orbital Maneuvering System.[70] In a letter to Malina, von Kármán ranked Parsons first in a list of figures he viewed as most important to modern rocketry and the foundation of the American space program.[198] According to Richard Metzger, Wernher von Braun — who was nicknamed "The Father of Rocket Science" — once argued that Parsons was more worthy of this moniker.[111] In October 1968 Malina — himself a pioneer in sounding rocketry — gave a speech at JPL in which he highlighted Parsons' contribution to the U.S. rocket project, and lamented how it had come to be neglected, crediting him for making "key contributions to the development of storable propellants and of long duration solid propellant agents that play such an important role in American and European space technology."[199]

The same month JPL held an open access event to mark the 32nd anniversary of its foundation — which featured a "nativity scene" of mannequins reconstructing the November 1936 photograph of the GALCIT Group — and erected a monument commemorating their first rocket test on Halloween 1936.[25] Among the aerospace industry, JPL was nicknamed as standing for "Jack Parsons' Laboratory" or "Jack Parsons Lives".[157] The International Astronomical Union decided to name a crater on the far side of the Moon Parsons after him in 1972.[200] JPL would later credit him for making "distinctive technical innovations that advanced early efforts" in rocket engineering, with aerospace journalist Craig Covault stating that the work of Parsons, Qian Xuesen and the GALCIT Group "planted the seeds for JPL to become preeminent in space and rocketry."[20][201]

Many of Parsons' writings would see posthumous publication as *Freedom is a Two-Edged Sword* in 1989, a compilation co-edited by Cameron and OTO leader Hymenaeus Beta (ceremonial name of musician William Breeze), which incited a resurgence of interest in Parsons within occult and countercultural circles.[202] English comic book writer and occultist Alan Moore identified him as a creative influence in a 1998 interview with Clifford Meth, comparing Parsons to John Dee and Isaac Newton as a "distinguished scientist" who was inspired by esotericism.[203] The Cameron-Parsons Foundation was founded as an incorporated company in 2006, with the intention of conserving and promoting Parsons' writings and Cameron's artwork,[204] and in 2014 Fulger Esoterica published *Songs for the Witch Woman*—a limited edition book of poems by Parsons with illustrations by Cameron, released to coincide with his centenary. An exhibition of the same name was held at the Museum of Contemporary Art, Los Angeles.[145]

In 1999 Feral House published the biography *Sex and Rockets: The Occult World of Jack Parsons* by John Carter, who expressed the opinion that Parsons had accomplished more in under five years of research than Robert H. Goddard had in his lifetime, and noted that his role in the development of rocket technology had been neglected by historians of science;[198] conversely, Carter thought that Parsons' abilities and accomplishments as an occultist had been overestimated and exaggerated among Western esotericists, emphasizing his disowning by Crowley for practising magic beyond his grade.[205] Feral House republished the work as a new edition in 2004, accompanied with an introduction by Robert Anton Wilson. Wilson believed that Parsons was "the one single individual who contributed the most to rocket science",[206] describing him as being "very strange, very brilliant, very funny, [and] very tormented",[207] and considering it noteworthy that the day of Parsons' birth was the predicted beginning of the apocalypse advocated by Charles Taze Russell, the founder of the Jehovah's Witness movement.[208]

A second biography of Parsons was published in 2005 through Weidenfeld & Nicolson with the title *Strange Angel: The Otherworldly Life of Rocket Scientist John Whiteside Parsons*; it was authored by George Pendle, who described Parsons as "the Che Guevara of occultism" and noted that although Parsons "would not live to see his dream of space travel come true, he was essential to making it a reality."[209][111] Pendle considered that the cultural stigma attached to Parsons' occultism was the primary cause of his low public profile, noting that "Like many scientific mavericks, Parsons was eventually discarded by the establishment once he had served his purpose." It was this unorthodox mindset, creatively facilitated by his science fiction fandom and "willingness to believe in magic's efficacy", Pendle argued, "that allowed him to break scientific barriers previously thought to be indestructible" — commenting that Parsons "saw both space and magic as ways of exploring these new frontiers — one breaking free from Earth literally and metaphysically."[210][211]

L. Ron Hubbard's role in Parsons' Agape Lodge — and the ensuing yacht scam — was explored in Russell Miller's 1987 Hubbard biography *Bare-faced Messiah*. Parsons' involvement in the Agape Lodge would also be discussed by Martin P. Starr in his history of the American Thelemite movement, *The Unknown God: W.T. Smith and the Thelemites*, published by Teitan Press in 2003.[212] Parsons' occult partnership with Hubbard was also mentioned in Alex Gibney's 2015 documentary film *Going Clear: Scientology and the Prison of Belief*, produced by HBO.[213]

Before his death, Parsons appeared in science fiction writer Anthony Boucher's murder-mystery novel *Rocket to the Morgue* (1942) under the guise of mad scientist character Hugo Chantrelle.[214] Another fictional character based on Parsons was Courtney James, a wealthy socialite who features in L. Sprague de Camp's 1956 short time travel story *A Gun for Dinosaur*.[215] *Pasadena Babalon*, a stage play about Parsons written by George D. Morgan and directed by Brian Brophy, premiered at Caltech as a production by its theater Arts Group in 2010, the same year Cellar Door Publishing released Richard Carbonneau and Robin Simon Ng's graphic novel, *The Marvel: A Biography of Jack Parsons*.[216][217] In 2012 the Science Channel broadcast a documentary dramatization titled *Magical Jet Propulsion* in an episode of its *Dark Matters: Twisted But True* television series — in which Parsons was portrayed by English actor Adam Howden — while independent record label Drag City released *Parsons' Blues*, an instrumental tribute single by experimental rock act Six Organs of Admittance.[218][219] In 2014 AMC Networks announced plans for a serial television dramatization of Parsons' life titled *Strange Angel*, produced by Ridley Scott and David Zucker, and written by Mark Heyman.[220]

23.5 See also

- Chaos magic

- JATO Rocket Car

- New Age

- Occult science

- Scientology and the occult

- UFO religion

23.6 Patents

- U.S. Patent 2,484,355

- U.S. Patent 2,563,265

- U.S. Patent 2,573,471

- U.S. Patent 2,693,077

- U.S. Patent 2,771,739

- U.S. Patent 2,774,214

- U.S. Patent 2,783,138

23.7   Notes

[1] Parsons' name was never formally changed. Although legal documents referred to him as John, the obituary at his funeral used his birth name, and his death certificate refers to him as "Marvel aka John". (Carter 2004, pp. 2, 182, 199).

23.8   References

23.8.1   Footnotes

[1] Huntley, J.D. (1999). "The History of Solid-Propellant Rocketry: What We Do and Do Not Know" (PDF). Armstrong Flight Research Center/Pennsylvania State University. p. 3. CiteSeerX: 10.1.1.8.3448.

[2] Carter 2004, p. 1; Pendle 2005, p. 26.

[3] Pendle 2005, p. 1.

[4] Carter 2004, pp. 1–2; Pendle 2005, pp. 26–27.

[5] Pendle 2005, pp. 103–105.

[6] Carter 2004, p. 2.

[7] Carter 2004, pp. 2–3; Pendle 2005, p. 28.

[8] Pendle 2005, pp. 33–40.

[9] Pendle 2005, pp. 42–43.

[10] Carter 2004, pp. 4–5; Pendle 2005, pp. 44–47.

[11] Keane, Phillip (August 2, 2013). "Jack Parsons and the Occult Roots of JPL". *spacesafetymagazine.com*. International Association for the Advancement of Space Safety. Retrieved March 6, 2014.

[12] Eng, Christina (February 20, 2005). "It took a rocket scientist / Research pioneer also delved into the occult". *sfgate.com*. Hearst Corporation. Retrieved May 12, 2014.

[13] Carter 2004, p. 4; Pendle 2005, p. 46.

[14] Pendle 2005, pp. 47, 182.

[15] Carter 2004, p. 5; Pendle 2005, pp. 56–57.

[16] Carter 2004, p. 6; Pendle 2005, pp. 57–59.

[17] Carter 2004, p. 6; Pendle 2005, pp. 59–60.

[18] Carter 2004, p. 6; Pendle 2005, pp. 60–61.

[19] Pendle 2005, pp. 54–55.

[20] "JPL 101" (PDF). *jpl.nasa.gov*. Jet Propulsion Laboratory/California Institute of Technology. 2002. Retrieved January 18, 2015.

[21] Carter 2004, p. 7; Pendle 2005, p. 61.

[22] Carter 2004, p. 6; Pendle 2005, p. 61.

[23] Pendle 2005, pp. 62–64.

[24] Carter 2004, p. 209: *John Parsons in dark vest, Ed Forman bending over in white shirt; Frank Malina is probably the individual bending over in the light-colored vest.*

[25] Carter 2004, p. 15.

[26] Conway, Erik M. (2007). "From Rockets to Spacecraft: Making JPL a Place for Planetary Science" (PDF). *calteches.library.caltech.edu*. California Institute of Technology. Retrieved March 22, 2014.

[27] Terrall, Mary (December 14, 1978). "Interview With Frank J. Malina". *oralhistories.library.caltech.edu*. California Institute of Technology. Archived from the original (PDF) on 8 July 2008. Retrieved May 17, 2014.

[28] Carter 2004, p. 8–9; Pendle 2005, pp. 74–76.

[29] Pendle, George (January 2, 2015). "The Last of the Magicians". *motherboard.vice.com*. Vice Media. Retrieved January 5, 2015.

[30] Carter 2004, p. 10; Pendle 2005, pp. 77–83.

[31] Malina, Frank J. (November 1968). "The Rocket Pioneers" (PDF). *calteches.library.caltech.edu*. California Institute of Technology. pp. 8–13.

[32] Landis, Geoffrey (2005). "The Three Rocketeers". *americanscientist.org*. Sigma Xi. Retrieved March 22, 2014.

[33] Carter 2004, p. 22–24; Pendle 2005, pp. 90–93, 118–120.

[34] Carter 2004, p. 7; Pendle 2005, pp. 84–89.

[35] Carter 2004, p. 7; Pendle 2005, p. 89.

[36] Pendle 2005, pp. 105–106.

[37] Carter 2004, p. 12; Pendle 2005, pp. 96–98.

[38] Carter 2004, p. 12; Pendle 2005, p. 99.

[39] Carter 2004, p. 72; Pendle 2005, pp. 196–199.

[40] "The Spark of a New Era". *jpl.nasa.gov*. NASA/Jet Propulsion Laboratory. October 25, 2006. Retrieved February 21, 2014.

[41] Carter 2004, p. 16.

[42] Carter 2004, p. 15–16; Pendle 2005, pp. 98–103.

[43] Carter 2004, p. 17; Pendle 2005, p. 103.

[44] "Early History > First Rocket Test". *jpl.nasa.gov*. NASA/Jet Propulsion Laboratory. Retrieved April 5, 2014.

[45] "GALCIT History (1921–1940)". California Institute of Technology. Retrieved May 7, 2014.

[46] Carter 2004, p. 17; Pendle 2005, pp. 106–107.

[47] Carter 2004, pp. 17–18; Pendle 2005, pp. 108–111.

[48] Carter 2004, pp. 26–28; Pendle 2005, pp. 114–116.

[49] Harnisch, Larry (May 7, 2008). "Jack Parsons, RIP". *latimesblogs.latimes.com*. Tribune Publishing. Retrieved March 29, 2014.

[50] Pendle 2005, pp. 112, 314.

[51] Westwick 2007, p. 1.

[52] Rasmussen, Cecilia (March 19, 2000). "Life as Satanist Propelled Rocketeer". *articles.latimes.com*. Tribune Publishing. Retrieved March 24, 2014.

[53] Carter 2004, pp. 57–60; Pendle 2005, pp. 126–127.

[54] Pendle 2005, pp. 120–123.

[55] Pendle 2005, p. 130.

[56] Starr 2003, pp. 257–258; Carter 2004, p. 33–36; Pendle 2005, pp. 133–136.

[57] Pendle 2005, p. 152.

[58] Starr 2003, p. 266; Carter 2004, p. 41; Pendle 2005, pp. 169–172; Kaczynski 2010, p. 513.

[59] Starr 2003, p. 263; Carter 2004, p. 56; Pendle 2005, p. 172.

[60] Starr 2003, p. 263.

[61] Carter 2004, p. 56.

[62] Pendle 2005, p. 172.

[63] Pendle 2005, p. 173.

[64] Carter 2004, pp. 30–32; Pendle 2005, pp. 156–158.

[65] Carter 2004, pp. 32–33, 48; Pendle 2005, pp. 158–166.

[66] Pendle 2005, pp. 158–166.

[67] Pendle 2005, p. 48.

[68] Pendle 2005, pp. 166–167.

[69] Carter 2004, pp. 70–71; Pendle 2005, pp. 186–187.

[70] Andrews, Crispin (October 13, 2014). "Geek spirit: The man who kick-started the US rocket programme". *eandt.theiet.org/ magazine/.* Institution of Engineering and Technology. Retrieved October 19, 2014.

[71] Carter 2004, pp. 65–66; Pendle 2005, pp. 177–184.

[72] Pendle 2005, pp. 184–185.

[73] US patent 2573471, Malina, Frank J. and Parsons, John W., "Reaction motor operable by liquid propellants and method of operating it", issued 1951-10-30 Retrieved November 10, 2014.

[74] Carter 2004, pp. 70–75; Pendle 2005, pp. 189–191.

[75] "Company History". *rocket.com.* Aerojet Rocketdyne. Retrieved April 30, 2014.

[76] US patent 2563265, Parsons, John W., "Rocket motor with solid propellant and propellant charge therefor", issued 1951-08-07 Retrieved November 10, 2014.

[77] Carter 2004, pp. 73–76; Pendle 2005, pp. 191–192.

[78] Carter 2004, p. 76; Pendle 2005, pp. 223–226.

[79] Pendle 2005, pp. 198, 203.

[80] Pendle 2005, pp. 228–230.

[81] Starr 2003, p. 274; Carter 2004, pp. 93–94; Pendle 2005, pp. 203–205; Kaczynski 2010, p. 537.

[82] Starr 2003, p. 274; Pendle 2005, pp. 203–205.

[83] Starr 2003, pp. 271–273, 276; Carter 2004, pp. 83–84; Pendle 2005, pp. 207–210; Kaczynski 2010, p. 521.

[84] Carter 2004, p. 84; Pendle 2005, pp. 209–210; Miller 2014, p. 117.

[85] Pendle 2005, p. 218.

[86] Pendle 2005, pp. 212–213.

[87] Starr 2003, pp. 283–285; Carter 2004, pp. 87–88; Pendle 2005, pp. 214–215; Kaczynski 2010, p. 525.

[88] Pendle 2005, p. 216.

[89] Pendle 2005, p. 215.

[90] Starr 2003, pp. 278, 280–282; Pendle 2005, pp. 216–217, 220; Kaczynski 2010, pp. 524–525.

[91] Parsons 2008, pp. 217–219.

[92] Starr 2003, p. 289; Carter 2004, p. 88; Pendle 2005, p. 221.

[93] Starr 2003, pp. 290–291; Carter 2004, pp. 92–93; Pendle 2005, pp. 221–222.

[94] Starr 2003, pp. 294–298; Carter 2004, pp. 90–91; Pendle 2005, pp. 221–222.

[95] Starr 2003, pp. 299–300; Pendle 2005, pp. 222–223.

[96] Bullock, William B. (February 1953). "JATO — The Magic Bottle" (PDF). Flying **52** (2): 25, 44. ISSN 0015-4806.

[97] Carter 2004, pp. 93.

[98] Carter 2004, pp. 96–97; Pendle 2005, pp. 231–233.

[99] Carter 2004, p. 100; Pendle 2005, pp. 239–240.

[100] Pendle 2005, pp. 241.

[101] Carter 2004, p. 101; Pendle 2005, p. 242.

[102] Carter 2004, p. 325.

[103] Pendle 2005, pp. 248–249.

[104] Pendle 2005, pp. 243–246.

[105] Carter 2004, p. 86.

[106] Carter 2004, pp. 101–102; Pendle 2005, pp. 252–255.

[107] Carter 2004, p. 102; Pendle 2005, p. 256; Kaczynski 2010, pp. 537–538.

[108] Pendle 2005, pp. 257–262.

[109] Pendle 2005, pp. 303.

[110] Carter 2004, pp. 107–108, 116–117, 119–128; Pendle 2005, pp. 259–260.

[111] Metzger 2008, pp. 196–200.

[112] Hobbs, Scott (June 15, 2012). "Rocket Man". *The Huffington Post*. Retrieved March 30, 2014.

[113] Carter 2004, p. 135.

[114] Carter 2004, pp. 130–132; Pendle 2005, pp. 263–264; Kansa 2011, pp. 29, 35–37.

[115] Urban 2006, p. 136–137.

[116] Carter 2004, pp. 132–148, 150; Pendle 2005, pp. 264–265; Kaczynski 2010, p. 538; Miller 2014, pp. 121–125.

[117] Carter 2004, p. 150; Pendle 2005, pp. 266–267.

[118] Carter 2004, pp. 155–157; Pendle 2005, pp. 267–269, 272–273; Kaczynski 2010, pp. 538–539; Miller 2014, pp. 127–130.

[119] Pendle 2005, pp. 273–274.

[120] Carter 2004, p. 158; Pendle 2005, p. 270; Kaczynski 2010, p. 555.

[121] Carter 2004, pp. 158–159; Pendle 2005, p. 275.

[122] Pendle 2005, p. 275.

[123] Kansa 2011, pp. 48–49.

[124] Carter 2004, p. 158; Pendle 2005, p. 277; Kansa 2011, p. 39.

[125] Carter 2004, p. 159; Pendle 2005, pp. 277–278.

[126] Pendle 2005, pp. 277, 279.

[127] Carter 2004, p. 159; Pendle 2005, pp. 281–284; Kansa 2011, pp. 46–47.

[128] Carter 2004, pp. 161, 166; Pendle 2005, p. 284.

[129] Pendle 2005, p. 283; Kansa 2011, pp. 48, 51–52.

[130] Carter 2004, p. 160–169; Pendle 2005, p. 284–285.

[131] Carter 2004, p. 160–169, 189; Pendle 2005, p. 284–285.

[132] Carter 2004, p. 171; Pendle 2005, p. 288; Kansa 2011, pp. 51–53.

[133] Pendle 2005, p. 288.

[134] Carter 2004, p. 161; Pendle 2005, pp. 286–287.

[135] Carter 2004, pp. 169–170; Pendle 2005, pp. 286–287.

[136] Carter 2004, pp. 170–172; Pendle 2005, pp. 291–293, 296; Kansa 2011, pp. 54–55.

[137] Anderson, Brian (October 29, 2012). "The Hell Portal Where NASA's Rocket King Divined Cosmic Rockets With L. Ron". *vice.com*. Vice Media. Retrieved March 31, 2014.

[138] Carter 2004, p. 172; Pendle 2005, p. 296; Kansa 2011, pp. 63–64.

[139] Carter 2004, p. 177; Pendle 2005, pp. 294, 297; Kansa 2011, p. 57.

[140] Doherty, Brian (May 2005). "The Magical Father of American Rocketry". *reason.com*. Reason Foundation. Retrieved April 20, 2014.

[141] Carter 2004, p. 219.

[142] Carter 2004, p. 169; Pendle 2005, p. 293; Kansa 2011, p. 57.

[143] Pendle 2005, pp. 294–295; Kansa 2011, pp. 57–63.

[144] Carter 2004, p. 99; Pendle 2005, p. 295.

[145] Nelson, Steffie (October 8, 2014). "Cameron, Witch of the Art World". *lareviewofbooks.org*. Tribune Publishing. Retrieved November 14, 2014.

[146] Carter 2004, p. 179; Pendle 2005, pp. 296–297; Kansa 2011, p. 64.

[147] Pendle 2005, p. 299; Kansa 2011, p. 65.

[148] Carter 2004, pp. 177–178; Pendle 2005, pp. 1–6; Kansa 2011, pp. 65–66.

[149] Carter 2004, pp. 178–179; Pendle 2005, pp. 6–7; Kansa 2011, p. 66.

[150] Carter 2004, pp. 179–181; Pendle 2005, p. 8.

[151] Pendle 2005, p. 301.

[152] Carter 2004, p. 181; Pendle 2005, pp. 11–12.

[153] Pendle 2005, p. 9; Pendle 2005, p. 311.

[154] Starr 2003, p. 327; Pendle 2005, pp. 13, 301.

[155] Carter 2004, p. 185; Kansa 2011, pp. 77–79.

[156] Carter 2004, p. 184.

[157] Carter 2004, p. xxv.

[158] Carter 2004, pp. 182, 185–187; Pendle 2005, pp. 7–10.

[159] Pendle 2005, pp. 300–303.

[160] Kansa 2011, pp. 74–79.

[161] Starr 2003, p. 327; Pendle 2005, p. 300.

[162] Pendle 2005, p. 176.

[163] Pendle 2005, p. 319.

[164] Carter 2004, p. 88.

[165] Pendle 2005, p. 238.

[166] Carter 2004, p. 83.

[167] Pendle 2005, p. 87.

[168] Pendle 2005, p. 226.

[169] Pendle 2005, p. 242.

[170] Pendle 2005, p. 296.

[171] Carter 2004, p. 159.

[172] Pendle 2005, p. 18.

[173] Beta 2008, pp. x–xi.

[174] Pendle 2005, p. 171.

[175] Pendle 2005, p. 146–147.

[176] Carter 2004, pp. 106–107.

[177] Parsons 2008, p. 67.

[178] Parsons 2008, pp. 69–71.

[179] Carter 2004, p. 158–163.

[180] Beta 2008, p. xi.

[181] Beta 2008, p. ix.

[182] Pendle 2005, pp. 90–93.

[183] Pendle 2005, p. 122.

[184] Parsons 2008, p. 11.

[185] Pendle 2005, p. 293.

[186] Pendle 2005, p. 290.

[187] Parsons 2008, p. 4.

[188] Parsons 2008, p. 9.

[189] Parsons 2008, p. 13.

[190] Cashill 2007, pp. 43–46.

[191] "Hugh Urban". *comparativestudies.osu.edu*. Ohio State University. Retrieved January 1, 2015.

[192] Wilson 2004, pp. vii–x.

[193] Pendle 2005, p. 304.

[194] Carter 2004, p. 188.

[195] Pendle 2005, p. 190.

[196] Mather, Annalee (October 17, 2014). "Look back at Anger: Film maker Kenneth Anger's work on display". *independent.co.uk*. Independent Print Limited. Retrieved October 19, 2014.

[197] "Early History > JPL Joins NASA". *jpl.nasa.gov*. NASA/Jet Propulsion Laboratory. Retrieved January 17, 2014.

[198] Carter 2004, p. 195.

[199] Pendle 2005, p. 306.

[200] Carter 2004, p. 192; Pendle 2005, p. 307.

[201] Covault, Craig (November 2, 2009). "Father of the Chinese space program dies". *spaceflightnow.com* (Spaceflight Now Inc.). Retrieved June 24, 2015.

[202] Carter 2004, p. 193.

[203] Meth, Clifford (October 1998). "ALAN MOORE talks to Cliff - pt 2". *cliffordmeth.com*. Retrieved June 24, 2015.

[204] "The Cameron-Parsons Foundation, Inc.". The Cameron-Parsons Foundation, Inc. Archived from the original on January 10, 2014. Retrieved January 10, 2014.

[205] Carter 2004, p. 196.

[206] Wilson 2004, p. xi.

[207] Wilson 2004, p. vii.

[208] Wilson 2004, p. ix.

[209] Pendle 2005, pp. 201, 304.

[210] Pendle 2005, pp. 1-20.

[211] Solon, Olivia (April 23, 2014). "Occultist Father of Rocketry 'Written Out' of NASA's history". *wired.co.uk*. Condé Nast. Retrieved May 8, 2014.

[212] Starr 2003.

[213] Collins, Sean T. (March 29, 2015). "Suppressive Persons: 'Going Clear,' Scientology, and the Appeal of Absolutism". *observer.com*. The New York Observer. Retrieved June 19, 2015.

[214] Carter 2004, p. 73; Pendle 2005, p. 230.

[215] Pendle 2005, p. 305.

[216] "Caltech Theater Arts Premiers "Pasadena Babalon" This Month". *caltech.edu*. California Institute of Technology. February 16, 2010. Retrieved May 9, 2014. Audio clip

[217] Carbonneau & Simon 2010.

[218] "Dark Matters: Twisted But True: Season 2, Episode 13: Magical Jet Propulsion, Missing Link Mystery, Typhoid Mary". *imdb.com*. Amazon.com. December 26, 2014. Retrieved January 2, 2015.

[219] "Six Organs Of Admittance – *Parsons' Blues*". *discogs.com*. Zink Media, Inc. Retrieved March 5, 2014.

[220] Ruderman, Dan (October 28, 2014). "Ridley Scott to produce miniseries on rocket scientist, occultist Jack Parsons". *boingboing.net*. Boing Boing. Retrieved November 6, 2014.

23.8.2 Bibliography

Beta, Hymenaeus (2008). "Foreword" to *Three Essays on Freedom* (J.W. Parsons). York Beach, Maine: Teitan Press. ISBN 978-0-933429-11-6.

Carbonneau, Richard; Simon, Robin (2010). *The Marvel: A Biography of Jack Parsons*. Portland, Oregon: Cellar Door. ISBN 978-0-9766831-4-8.

Cashill, Jack (2007). *What's the Matter with California?: Cultural Rumbles from the Golden State and Why the Rest of Us Should Be Shaking*. New York City, New York: Simon & Schuster. ISBN 978-1-4165-5424-0.

Carter, John (2004). *Sex and Rockets: The Occult World of Jack Parsons* (new ed.). Port Townsend, Washington: Feral House. ISBN 978-0-922915-97-2.

Kaczynski, Richard (2010). *Perdurabo: The Life of Aleister Crowley* (second ed.). Berkeley, California: North Atlantic Books. ISBN 978-0-312-25243-4.

Kansa, Spencer (2011). *Wormwood Star: The Magickal Life of Marjorie Cameron*. Oxford: Mandrake of Oxford. ISBN 978-1-906958-08-4.

Metzger, Richard (2008). *Book of Lies: The Disinformation Guide to Magick and the Occult* (second ed.). Newburyport, Massachusetts: Red Wheel/Weiser/Conari. ISBN 978-1-934708-34-7.

Miller, Russell (2014). *Bare-faced Messiah: The True Story of L. Ron Hubbard* (third ed.). London, England: Silvertail Books. ISBN 978-1-909269-14-9.

Parsons, John Whiteside (2008). *Three Essays on Freedom*. York Beach, Maine: Teitan Press. ISBN 978-0-933429-11-6.

Pendle, George (2005). *Strange Angel: The Otherworldly Life of Rocket Scientist John Whiteside Parsons*. London: Weidenfeld & Nicolson. ISBN 978-0-7538-2065-0.

Starr, Martin P. (2003). *The Unknown God: W.T. Smith and the Thelemites*. Bollingbrook, Illinois: Teitan Press. ISBN 0-933429-07-X.

Urban, Hugh B. (2006). *Magia Sexualis: Sex, Magic, and Liberation in Modern Western Esotericism*. Oakland, California: University of California Press. ISBN 978-0-520-93288-3.

Westwick, Peter J. (2007). *Into the Black: JPL and the American Space Program, 1976–2004*. New Haven, Connecticut: Yale University Press. ISBN 978-0-300-13458-2.

Wilson, Robert Anton (2004). "Introduction" to *Sex and Rockets: The Occult World of Jack Parsons* (John Carter) (new ed.). Port Townsend, Washington: Feral House. ISBN 978-0-922915-97-2.

23.9 External links

- Jack Parsons at NNDB

- Biography at The Cameron-Parsons Foundation, Inc.

- Biography at *Encyclopedia Astronautica*

- Biography at Rotten.com

- Correspondence between Jack Parsons and Marjorie Cameron, 1949–50 at xenu.ca

- *Jack Parsons: Sorcerous Scientist* by Douglas Chapman (1990)

- Marvel Whiteside Parsons at Ancestry.com

- *The Rocketmen*, NASA video on the JPL's early history

- Kaos Magazine 14, contains a review of Carter's biography of Parsons from page 168

Frontispiece

Aleister Crowley (pictured in 1912), founder of Thelema, was Parsons' spiritual mentor.

Grady McMurtry was recruited to the OTO by Parsons.

The GALCIT JATO engineering team during the solid propellant tests in January 1940. Parsons is visible cropped out on the extreme left alongside Clark Blanchard Millikan, Martin Summerfield, Theodore von Kármán, Frank Malina and pilot, Captain Homer Boushey.

Take-off on August 12, 1941 of America's first "rocket-assisted" fixed-wing aircraft, an Ercoupe fitted with a GALCIT developed solid propellant JATO booster.

GALCIT Project Number 1 during the JATO experiments (date as above). From left to right: Fred S. Miller, Jack Parsons, Ed Forman, Frank Malina, Captain Homer Boushey, Private Kobe (first initial unknown), and Corporal R. Hamilton.

Solid-fuel JATO unit manufactured by Aerojet at the National Air and Space Museum.

The JPL Arroyo Seco site in February 1942.

Parsons standing above a JATO canister at JPL June 1943.

Parsons worked on developing the SM-64 Navaho missile (pictured launching in 1957).

FEDERAL BUREAU OF INVESTIGATION

CASE ORIGINATED AT	LOS ANGELES			FILE NO. 6-5131
REPORT MADE AT	DATE WHEN MADE	PERIOD FOR WHICH MADE	REPORT MADE BY	
LOS ANGELES	11/2/50	9/25-29;10/2-5, 9/50	████████	rsl
JOHN WHITESIDE PARSONS, aka Jack Parsons	CONFIDENTIAL		CHARACTER OF CASE ESPIONAGE - IS	

SYNOPSIS OF FACTS:

Subject, on September 15, 1950 removed certain documents pertaining to jet propulsion motors and rocket propellants without authority from Hughes Aircraft Company, Culver City, California, his place of employment. On September 16, 1950, he left same at the residence of ████████ ████████, California, who was to make typewritten copies of them. Above documents procurred from ████████ on September 25, 1950 by ████████ Security officer, Hughes Aircraft Company and writer, and placed in custody MAJOR E. J. KRENZ, U. S. Air Force, Hughes Aircraft Company, pending determination security classification. Subject voluntarily came to the Los Angeles office September 27, 1950 and in signed statement admitted removing documents without authority stating he desired to extract certain information from them as aid in computing cost proposal on jet propulsion motors. He planned to submit this with employment application through American Technion Society for employment in the country of Israel. Subject

ALL INFORMATION CONTAIN HEREIN IS UNCLASSIFIED EXCEPT WHERE SHOWN OTHERWISE

65-1595??

NOV 8 1950

CONFIDENTIAL

COPY IN FILE

(OVER)

November 1950 FBI synopsis of espionage allegations against Parsons.

Dark Angel, *a painting by Marjorie Cameron portraying Parsons as the "Angel of Death".*[141]

The modern logo of the Jet Propulsion Laboratory.

Parsons is credited for inventions used in rocket technology such as the Space Shuttle.

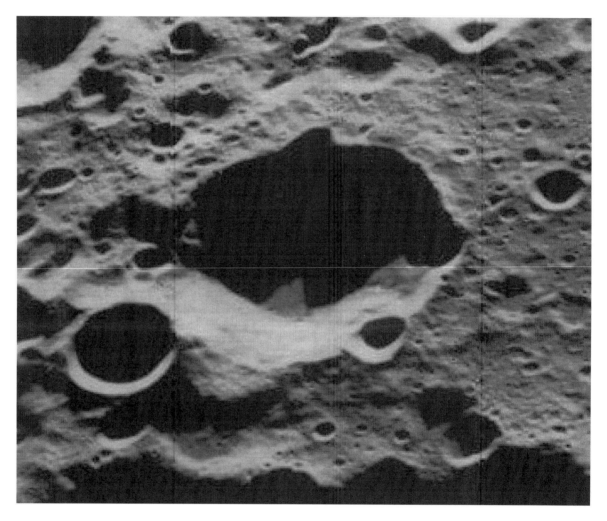

The Parsons Moon crater.

Chapter 24

Theodor Reuss

Albert Karl Theodor Reuss (June 28, 1855 – October 28, 1923) was an Anglo-German tantric occultist, freemason, police spy, journalist, singer, and head of Ordo Templi Orientis.

24.1 Early years

Reuss was the son of an innkeeper at Augsburg. He was a professional singer in his youth, and was introduced to Ludwig II of Bavaria, in 1873. He took part in the first performance of Wagner's *Parsifal* at Bayreuth in 1882. Reuss later became a newspaper correspondent, and travelled frequently as such to England, where he became a Mason in 1876. He also spent some time there as a journalist and as a music-hall singer under the stage name "Charles Theodore."

In 1876, Reuss married Delphina Garbois from Dublin, and moved to Munich in 1878. Their marriage was annulled, due to bigamy (Hergemöller, 1998). They had a son, Albert Franz Theodor Reuss (1879–1958), a self-educated zoologist who lived in Berlin (Krecsák and Bohle 2008).

24.2 Police spy

In 1885, in England, Reuss joined the Socialist League. He had been quite involved as a librarian and labour secretary. On May 7, 1886 he was expelled as a police spy in the pay of the Prussian Secret Police. This took place in a sectarian atmosphere, with tensions between anarcho-communist Josef Peukert and the Bakuninist Victor Dave where such accusations were often made without substance. However, this accusation came from the Belgian Social Democrats, and was raised here by Henry Charles. Peukert and the Gruppe Autonomie published a rebuttal of these allegations which appeared in the *Anarchist*, which also accused Dave of being a spy. However, in February 1887 Reuss used the unwitting Peukert to track down Johann Neve in Belgium, who was then arrested by the German police. This was major coup for the police as Neve had been smuggling arms and propaganda into Germany. He died shortly after in a prison in Munich, perhaps murdered. (This incident is touched upon in John Henry Mackay's *Die Anarchisten*.)

24.3 Founds Ordo Templi Orientis

In 1880, in Munich, he participated in an attempt to revive Adam Weishaupt's Bavarian Order of Illuminati. While in England, he became friends with William Wynn Westcott, the Supreme Magus of the Societas Rosicruciana in Anglia and one of the founders of the Hermetic Order of the Golden Dawn. Westcott provided Reuss with a charter dated July 26, 1901 for the Swedenborgian Rite of Masonry and a letter of authorization dated February 24, 1902 to found a High Council in Germania of the Societas Rosicruciana in Anglia. Gérard Encausse provided him with a charter dated June 24, 1901 designating him Special Inspector for the Martinist Order in Germany. In 1888, in Berlin, he joined with Leopold

Engel of Dresden, Max Rahn and August Weinholz in another effort to revive the Illuminati Order. In 1895, he began to discuss the formation of Ordo Templi Orientis with Carl Kellner.

The discussions between Reuss and Kellner did not lead to any positive results at the time, allegedly because Kellner disapproved of Reuss's connections with Engel. According to Reuss, upon his final separation with Engel in June 1902, Kellner contacted him and the two agreed to proceed with the establishment of the Oriental Templar Order by seeking authorizations to work the various rites of high-grade Masonry.

The French occultist and physician Gérard Encausse (perhaps better known by his pen-name Papus) was one such contact. Although not a member of a regular Masonic order, he had founded two occult fraternities: the Martinist group, l'Ordre des Supérieurs Inconnus and the Rosicrucian Kabbalistic Order of the Rose-Croix. In addition, he was a member of the Hermetic Order of the Golden Dawn, and a Bishop in a neo-Gnostic church, l'Église Gnostique de France. Encausse provided Reuss with a charter dated June 24, 1901 designating him Special Inspector for the Martinist order in Germany. He also assisted Reuss in the formation of the O.T.O. Gnostic Catholic Church by proclaiming the E.G.C. a "child" of l'Église Gnostique de France, which linked the E.G.C. to French neo-gnosticism.

Meanwhile, Westcott assisted Reuss in contacting the English Masonic scholar, John Yarker (1833–1913). Along with his associates Franz Hartmann and Henry Klein, he activated the Masonic Rites of Memphis and Mizraim and a branch of the Scottish Rite in Germany with charters from Yarker. Reuss received letters-patent as a Sovereign Grand Inspector General 33° of the Cernau Scottish Rite from Yarker dated September 24, 1902. On the same date, Yarker appears to have issued a warrant to Reuss, Franz Hartmann and Henry Klein to operate a Sovereign Sanctuary 33°–95° of the Scottish, Memphis and Mizraim rites. The original document is not extant, but a transcript of this warrant was published in Reuss's newsletter, The Oriflamme in 1911, which commenced publication in 1902. Yarker issued a charter confirming Reuss's authority to operate said rites on July 1, 1904; and Reuss published a transcript of an additional confirming charter dated June 24, 1905. Reuss and Kellner together prepared a brief manifesto for their Order in 1903, which was published the next year in *The Oriflamme*.

When Carl Kellner died in 1905, the leadership of the Academia Masonica of O.T.O. fell upon Reuss's shoulders, and he incorporated all his other organizations under its banner, developing the three degrees of the Academia Masonica, available to Masons only, into a coherent, self-contained initiatory system, open to both men and women. He promulgated a constitution for this new, enlarged O.T.O. on June 21, 1906 in London (his place of residence since January 1906) and the next month proclaimed himself Outer Head of the Order (O.H.O.). That same year he published *Lingham-Yoni*, which was a German translation of Hargrave Jennings's work *Phallism*, and issued a warrant to Rudolf Steiner (1861–1925, who was at the time the Secretary General of the German branch of the Theosophical Society), making him Deputy Grand Master of a subordinate O.T.O./Memphis/Mizraim Chapter and Grand Council called "Mystica Aeterna" in Berlin. Steiner went on to found the Anthroposophical Society in 1912, and ended his association with Reuss in 1914.

On June 24, 1908, Reuss attended Encausse's "International Masonic and Spiritualist Conference" in Paris. At this conference, Reuss raised Encausse to the X° of the O.T.O.'s Ecclesia Gnostica Catholica and gave him a patent to establish a "Supreme Grand Council General of the Unified Rites of Ancient and Primitive Masonry for the Grand Orient of France and its Dependencies at Paris. " He possibly received in return some position of authority in the Église Catholique Gnostique. Reuss also appointed Dr. Arnold Krumm-Heller (Huiracocha, 1879–1949) as his official representative for Latin America.

24.4 Meets Aleister Crowley

While living in London, Reuss became acquainted with Aleister Crowley. In 1910, he made Crowley a VII° of O.T.O. (based on Crowley's previously held 33° in the Scottish Rite), and in 1912, he conferred upon him the IX° and appointed him National Grand Master General X° for the O.T.O. in the United Kingdom of Great Britain and Ireland by charter dated June 1, 1912. Crowley's appointment included authority over an English language rite of the lower (Masonic) degrees of O.T.O. which was given the name Mysteria Mystica Maxima, or M∴M∴M∴. In 1913, Crowley issued a Constitution for the M∴M∴M∴ and the Manifesto of the M∴M∴M∴, which he subsequently redrafted and issued as Liber LII (52), the *Manifesto of the O.T.O.* In 1913, Crowley wrote Liber XV, the Gnostic Mass for Reuss's Gnostic Catholic Church. Crowley also dedicated his Mystery Play *The Ship* (1913) and a collection of poetry, *The Giant's Thumb* (1915) to Reuss. In 1913 he became Grand Master of the Rite of Memphis-Misraïm, a masonic group which previously included the revolutionaries Louis Blanc and Giuseppe Garibaldi amongst its ranks.

In 1914, at the outset of World War I, Reuss left England and returned to Germany. He worked briefly for the Red Cross in Berlin, then, in 1916, moved to Basle, Switzerland. While there, he established an "Anational Grand Lodge and Mystic Temple" of O.T.O. and the Hermetic Brotherhood of Light at Monte Verità, a utopian commune near Ascona founded in 1900 by Henri Oedenkoven and Ida Hofmann, which functioned as a center for the Progressive Underground. On January 22, 1917, Reuss published a manifesto for this Anational Grand Lodge, which was called "Verità Mystica." On the same date, he published a *Revised O.T.O. Constitution of 1917* (based in a large part on Crowley's 1913 Constitution of the M∴M∴M∴), with a "Synopsis of Degrees" and an abridgment of "The Message of the Master Therion" appended. Reuss held an "Anational Congress for Organising the Reconstruction of Society on Practical Cooperative Lines" at Monte Verità August 15–25, 1917. This Congress included readings of Crowley's poetry (on August 22) and a recitation of Crowley's Gnostic Mass (on August 24). On October 24, 1917, Reuss Chartered an O.T.O. Lodge, "Libertas et Fraternitas" in Zürich. This Lodge later placed itself under the Masonic jurisdiction of the Swiss Grand Lodge Alpina.

In 1918, Reuss published his German translation of Crowley's Gnostic Mass. In a note at the end of his translation of Liber XV, he referred to himself as, simultaneously, the Sovereign Patriarch and Primate of the Gnostic Catholic Church, and Gnostic Legate to Switzerland of the Église Gnostique Universelle, acknowledging Jean Bricaud (1881–1934) as Sovereign Patriarch of that church. The issuance of this document can be viewed as the birth of the Thelemic E.G.C. as an independent organization under the umbrella of O.T.O., with Reuss as its first Patriarch.

Reuss was clearly impressed with Thelema. Crowley's Gnostic Mass, which Reuss translated into German and had recited at his Anational Congress at Monte Verità, is an explicitly Thelemic ritual. In an undated letter to Crowley (received in 1917), Reuss reported exitedly that he had read *The Message of the Master Therion* to a gathering at Monte Verità, and that he was translating The Book of the Law into German. He added, "Let this news encourage you! We live in your Work!!!"

24.5   After the First World War

Reuss left Monte Verità some time before November 1918. On May 10, 1919, Reuss issued a "Gauge of Amity" document to Matthew McBlain Thomson, founder of the ill-fated "American Masonic Federation." On September 18, 1919, Reuss was reconsecrated by Bricaud, thus receiving the "Antioch Succession," and re-appointed as "Gnostic Legate" to Switzerland for Bricaud's Église Gnostique Universelle. In 1920, Oedenkoven and Hofmann abandoned Monte Verità in 1920 to establish a second colony in Brazil, and Reuss published a document titled *The Program of Construction and the Guiding Principles of the Gnostic Neo-Christians: O.T.O.*

On July 17, 1920, he attended the Congress of the "World Federation of Universal Freemasonry" in Zürich, which lasted several days. Reuss, with Bricaud's support, advocated the adoption of the religion of Crowley's Gnostic Mass as the "official religion for all members of the World Federation of Universal Freemasonry in possession of the 18° of the Scottish Rite." Reuss's efforts in this regard were a failure, and he left the Congress after the first day. On May 10, 1921, Reuss issued X° Charters to Charles Stansfeld Jones and Heinrich Tränker to serve as Grand Masters for the U.S.A. and Germany, respectively. On July 30, 1921, Reuss issued another "Gauge of Amity" document, this time to H. Spencer Lewis, founder of A.M.O.R.C., the San Jose, California based Rosicrucian organization. Reuss returned to Germany in September 1921, settling in Munich.

24.6   Death and succession

There is some reason to believe that Reuss suffered a stroke in the spring of 1920, but this is not entirely certain. Crowley wrote to W.T. Smith in March 1943: "the late O.H.O., after his first stroke of paralysis, got into a panic about the work being carried on... He hastily issued honorary diplomas of the Seventh Degree to various people, some of whom had no right to anything at all and some of whom were only cheap crooks." Shortly after appointing him his Viceroy for Australia, Crowley appears to have corresponded with his friend Frank (Allan) Bennett and discussed with him his doubts about Reuss's continuing ability to effectively govern the Order.

It would appear that Reuss discovered the correspondence; he wrote Crowley an angry, defensive response on November

9, 1921, in which he appeared to distance himself and O.T.O. from Thelema, which, as shown above, he had previously embraced. Crowley replied to Reuss's letter on November 23, 1921, and stated in his letter, "It is my will to be O.H.O. and Frater Superior of the Order and avail myself of your abdication—to proclaim myself as such." He signed the letter "Baphomet O.H.O." Reuss's response is not extant, but Crowley recounts in his *Confessions* that Reuss "resigned the office [of O.H.O.] in 1922 in my favour."

However, it does not appear that Crowley waited for Reuss's response to assume his duties. In a diary entry for November 27, 1921, Crowley wrote: "I have proclaimed myself O.H.O. Frater Superior of the Order of Oriental Templars." Reuss died on October 28, 1923. In a letter to Heinrich Tränker dated February 14, 1925, Crowley stated the following: "Reuss was very uncertain in temper, and in many ways unreliable. In his last years he seems to have completely lost his grip, even accusing *The Book of the Law* of communistic tendencies, than which no statement could be more absurd. Yet it seems that he must have been to some extent correctly led, on account of his having made the appointments of yourself and Frater Achad (Charles Stansfeld Jones), and designating me in his last letter as his successor." In a letter to Charles Stansfeld Jones dated Sun in Capricorn, Anno XX (Dec. 1924 - Jan. 1925), Crowley said, "in the O.H.O.'s last letter to me he invited me to become his successor as O.H.O. and Frater Superior." Reuss's letter designating Crowley his successor as O.H.O. has not been found, but no credible documentation has surfaced which would indicate that Reuss ever designated any alternative successor.

24.7 Bibliography

Reuss's writings include:

- *The Matrimonial Question from an Anarchistic Point of View* (1887);
- *Die Mysterien der Illuminaten* (1894);
- *Geschichte des Illuminaten-Ordens* (1896);
- *Was muss man von der Freimauerei wissen?* (1901);
- *Was ist Okkultismus und wie erlangt man occulte Kräfte?* (1903);
- *Was muss man von Richard Wagner und seinen Ton-dramen wissen?* (1903);
- *Lingam-Yoni; oder die Mysterien des Geschlechts-Kultus* (1906);
- *Allgemeine Satzungen des Ordens der Orientalischem Templer O.T.O.* (1906);
- *Parsifal und das Enthüllte Grals-Geheimnis* (1914);
- *Constitution of the Ancient Order of Oriental Templars* (1917);
  - with an Introduction and a Synopsis of the Degrees of O.T.O.
- *Die Gnostische Messe'* (1920);
- *Das Aufbau-Programm und die Leitsätze der Gnostischen Neo-Christen* (1920);
- and numerous articles published in his periodical Oriflamme (1902–1914).

24.8 References

- Free Encyclopedia of Thelema. Theodor Reuss. Retrieved May 24, 2005.
- Sabazius X. Theodor Reuss. Retrieved Oct. 6, 2004. Released under the GNU FDL at .

- Hergemöller, B.-U.; *Mann für Mann: biographisches Lexikon zur Geschichte von Freundesliebe und mannmännlicher Sexualität im deutschen Sprachraum.* Hamburg: MännerschwarmSkript-Verlag 1998. 911 pp.

- Howe, Ellic; "Theodor Reuss: Irregular Freemasonry in Germany, 1900-23" in *Ars Quatuor Coronati*, Feb. 1978 online edition

- König, Peter-Robert; *Das OTO-Phänomenon, A.R.W.*, München 1994

- Krecsák, L. & Bohle, D. (2008) "The eccentric adder man: note on the life and works of Albert Franz Theodor Reuss (1879–1958)". *The Herpetological Bulletin*, 103: 1–10.

- Merlin Peregrinus (Theodor Reuss); *I.N.R.I., O.T.O., Ecclesiae Gnosticae Catholicae, Canon Missae, Die Gnostische Messe* [1918], privately published by the Oriflamme 1920, translated by Marcus M. Jungkurth

- Möller, Helmut and Ellic Howe; *Merlin Peregrinus, vom Untergrund des Abendlandes*, Königshausen & Neumann, Würzburg 1986

- Reuss, Theodor; *I.N.R.I. Constitution of the Ancient Order of Oriental Templars, O.T.O., Ordo Templi Orientis, with an Introduction and a Synopsis of the Degrees of the O.T.O.*, 1917

- Reuss, Theodor; *Ordo Templi Orientis — Hermetic Brotherhood of Light. Anational Grand Lodge & Mystic Temple: "Verità Mystica", or Ascona.* Manifesto, Ascona, Switzerland 1917

- Reuss, Theodor; *I.N.R.I. The Programme of Construction and the Guiding Principles of the Gnostic Neo-Christians, O.T.O.*, 1920

- Reuss, Theodor; *Introduction to Lingham-Yoni (Phallism, by Hargrave Jennings)*, Verlag Wilsson, Berlin 1906

- Shepard, Leslie (ed.); *Encyclopedia of Occultism and Parapsychology*, 2nd ed., Gale Research Co., Detroit MI 1984

- Symonds, John & Grant, Kenneth, eds.; *The Magical Record of the Beast 666*, Duckworth, London 1972

24.9   External links

- Quotations related to Theodor Reuss at Wikiquote

Theodor Reuss (1855 - 1923)

Chapter 25

Saints of Ecclesia Gnostica Catholica

The **Gnostic Saints of Ecclesia Gnostica Catholica** are a series of historical and mythological figures commemorated within the current of Thelema. They were first listed in Liber XV, the Gnostic Mass, which is the central rite of Ordo Templi Orientis and its ecclesiastical arm, Ecclesia Gnostica Catholica. They are found in the fifth Collect of Liber XV, titled "The Saints".

25.1 Background

In Ecclesia Gnostica Catholica, as in the Catholic and Orthodox churches, a saint is usually officially recognized after his or her death, though Aleister Crowley was certainly alive when he wrote Liber XV and included himself in the list.

All of the Saints listed in the Gnostic Mass are male, and are invoked during the Collect.[1]

25.2 Modern additions

The list of Saints in Liber XV remained static from the original writing in 1913 until relatively recently. However because the original list contains the names of four previous Patriarchs of EGC, Gerard Encausse, Carl Kellner, Theodor Reuss and Aleister Crowley, this has now been taken as a precedent for the addition of the names of succeeding Patriarchs, Karl Germer and Grady McMurtry.

The current Patriarch of EGC, Hymenaeus Beta, has exercised his authority to canonise further Gnostic Saints, and two have been officially added to the original list. William Blake was so recognized in Fall 1997 e.v. based on Crowley's essay "William Blake," which described him as such.[2] Giordano Bruno was added to the list on February 17, 2000 e.v., the 400th anniversary of his martyrdom.[3]

In the Collect, some names are italicised. In ordinary masses only names in italics are commemorated, with the full list reserved for special masses (e.g. rites of baptism, confirmation etc.).

25.3 Full list

The saints are:[4][5]

25.3.1 A

- Amoun

- Andrea (Johann Valentin Andreae)

- Apollonius Tyanæus (Apollonius of Tyana)

- Arthur (King Arthur)

- Elias Ashmole

25.3.2   B

- Francis Bacon, Lord Verulam

- Roger Bacon

- Bardesanes

- Basilides

- William Blake[6]

- Roderic Borgia, Pope Alexander the Sixth

- Giordano Bruno

- Sir Richard Francis Burton

- Jacob Boehme

25.3.3   C

- Carolus Magnus (Charlemagne) and his Paladins

- Catullus

- Aleister Crowley

25.3.4   D

- Johannes Dee (John Dee)

- Dionysus

25.3.5   E

- Doctor Gérard Encausse

25.3.6   F

- Robertus de Fluctibus (Robert Fludd)

- Frederick of Hohenstaufen (Frederick II, Holy Roman Emperor)

- Forlong dux (James George Roche Forlong)[7]

- Ludwig von Fischer[8]

25.3.7   G

- Paul Gauguin

- Karl Johannes Germer

- Johann Wolfgang von Goethe

25.3.8   H

- Heracles (Hercules)

- Hermes

- Hippolytus

- Ulrich von Hutten

25.3.9   J

- Hargrave Jennings

25.3.10   K

- Kamuret (Gahmuret)

- Sir Edward Kelly

- Carl Kellner

- Khem

- Sir Richard Payne Knight

- Krishna

25.3.11   L

- Laotze (Lao-tsu)

- Alphonse Louis Constant (Eliphas Levi)

- Ludovicus, Rex Bavariae (Ludwig II of Bavaria)

25.3.12   M

- Michael Maier

- Manes

- Martialis

- Major Grady Louis McMurtry

- Melchizedek

- Mentu

- Merlin

- Jacobus Burgundus Molensis the Martyr (Jacques de Molay)

- Molinos (Miquel de Molinos)

- Mosheh (Moses)

- Mohammed

25.3.13   N

- Friedrich Nietzsche

25.3.14   O

- Odysseus

- Orpheus

- Osiris

25.3.15   P

- Paladins of Carolus Magnus (Charlemagne)

- Pan

- Paracelsus

- Parzival

- Priapus

- Pythagoras

25.3.16   R

- Rabelais (François Rabelais)

- Doctor Theodore Reuss

- Christian Rosenkreuz

25.3.17   S

- Siddhartha (Gautama Buddha)

- Simon Magus

- Swinburne

25.3.18   T

- Tahuti

- To Mega Therion

25.3.19   V

- Valentinus

- Thomas Vaughan

- Vergillius (Virgil)

25.3.20   W

- Richard Wagner

- Adam Weishaupt

- William of Schyren; may be Guillaume du Bellay[9]

25.4   Notes

[1] The Gnostic Mass: Annotations and Commentary by Helena and Tau Apiryon (2004)

[2] Crowley, Aleister *The Revival of Magick* (1998) Thelema Media ISBN 978-0-9726583-9-3

[3] *Agape: The Official Organ of the U.S. Grand Lodge of Ordo Templi Orientis* Volume IX, Number 1 (2007)

[4] Wasserman, Bishop James (ed.) *Current List of Saints* (2007)

[5] Wasserman, James; Wasserman, Nancy; Crowley, Aleister (2013). *To Perfect This Feast: A Performance Commentary on the Gnostic Mass*. Red Wheel/Weiser. ISBN 9780971887060.

[6] http://www.hermetic.com/sabazius/gmnotes.htm#Blake

[7] http://www.hermetic.com/sabazius/forlong.htm

[8] http://hermetic.com/crowley/libers/lib15-international.html Ctrl+F Ludwig Von Fischer

[9] http://hermetic.com/sabazius/schyren.htm

25.5   References

- Apiryon & Helena *Mystery of Mystery: A Primer of Thelemic Ecclesiastical Gnosticism* (2001) Red Flame ISBN 0-9712376-1-1

- Wasserman, James & Wasserman, Nancy *To Perfect This Feast* (2009) Sekmet Books ISBN 978-0-9718870-3-9

- Liber XV, The Gnostic Mass

Chapter 26

Phyllis Seckler

Phyllis Evalina Seckler (1917–2004), also known as **Soror Meral**, was a ninth degree (IX°) member of the "Sovereign Sanctuary of the Gnosis" of Ordo Templi Orientis, and a student of Jane Wolfe, herself a student of Aleister Crowley.[2] Sr. Meral was Master of 418 Lodge of O.T.O. from its inception in 1979 until her death.[3] She was also founder of the College of Thelema; and co-founder (with Anna-Kria King and James A. Eshelman) of the Temple of Thelema, both of which organizations she also led until her death. Prior to her death, she also warranted the founding of the International College of Thelema (formerly known as the College of Thelema of Northern California) as an autonomous continuation of her work, as well as the Temple of the Silver Star (the initiatory Order within the International College of Thelema.) She was a writer for and editor of *In the Continuum*, the journal of the College of Thelema, for nearly 25 years.[1]

For a brief period in the 1970s, she was married to Grady McMurtry. It was as a result of a 1968 letter from Seckler that McMurtry (Fra. Hymenaeus Alpha) invoked his "emergency powers" to reconstitute Ordo Templi Orientis, which had flagged following the death of Aleister Crowley's successor as Outer Head of the Order, Karl Germer. It was under their combined leadership that O.T.O. was incorporated under California law and began to grow in North America for the first time since Crowley's death.[4]

26.1 Publications

- Seckler (2003). Jerry Cornelius and Marlene Cornelius, ed. *Jane Wolfe: Her Life With Aleister Crowley (Part 1)*. Red Flame #10. ISBN 0-9712376-2-X.

- Seckler (2003). Jerry Cornelius and Marlene Cornelius, ed. *Jane Wolfe: Her Life With Aleister Crowley (Part 2)*. Red Flame #11. ISBN 0-9712376-3-8.

- Seckler (2010). Rorac Johnson, Gregory Peters, and David Shoemaker, ed. *The Thoth Tarot, Astrology & Other Selected Writings*. Teitan Press & College of Thelema of Northern California. ISBN 978-0-933429-27-7.

- Seckler (2012). Rorac Johnson, Gregory Peters, and David Shoemaker, ed. *The Kabbalah, Magick, and Thelema. Selected Writings Volume II*. Teitan Press & College of Thelema of Northern California. ISBN 978-0-933429-28-4.

26.2 References

[1] College of Thelema (4 June 2004). "Religious Leader, Educator Phyllis Seckler Dies at 86". Retrieved 2011-02-01.

[2] Starr, Martin P. (2003). *The Unknown God: W. T. Smith and the Thelemites*. Bolingbrook, Illinois: Teitan Press. ISBN 0-933429-07-X.

[3] "Phyllis Seckler". *Thelemapedia*. 2008. Retrieved 2011-02-01. External link in |work= (help)

[4] Crowley, Aleister; et al. (July 1990) [March 1986]. Hymenaeus Beta, ed. *The Review of Scientific Illuminism: The Official Organ of the O.T.O.* The Equinox #10 **III**. Soror Meral, Research Ed. (Revised ed.). York Beach, Maine: Weiser Books. ISBN 0-87728-719-8.

26.3 External links

- Red Flame memorial page at the Wayback Machine (archived March 29, 2006)

- College of Thelema and Temple of Thelema

- Website of 418 Lodge, O.T.O.

- The International College of Thelema and the Temple of the Silver Star

Chapter 27

Wilfred Talbot Smith

Wilfred Talbot Smith (born **Frank Wenham**; 8 June 1885 – 27 April 1957) was an English occultist and ceremonial magician known as a prominent advocate of the religion of Thelema. Living most of his life in North America, he played a key role in propagating Thelema across the continent.

Born the illegitimate son of a domestic servant and her employer in Tonbridge, Kent, Smith migrated to Canada in 1907, where he went through a variety of jobs and began reading about Western esotericism. Through Charles Stansfeld Jones he was introduced to the writings of Thelema's founder, Aleister Crowley. He subsequently joined Crowley's Thelemite order, the A∴A∴, and the Thelemite wing of the Ordo Templi Orientis (OTO). In 1915, he joined the OTO's British Columbia Lodge No. 1, based in Vancouver, and rose to become one of its senior members.

In 1922 Smith moved to Los Angeles in the United States, where he, Jane Wolfe, and Regina Kahl tried to establish a new Thelemite community. They founded an incorporated Church of Thelema which gave weekly public performances of the Gnostic Mass from their home in Hollywood. Seeking to revive the inactive North American OTO, in 1935 Smith then founded the OTO Agape Lodge, which subsequently relocated to Pasadena. He brought a number of prominent Thelemites into the OTO, including Jack Parsons and Grady Louis McMurtry, but he had a strained relationship with both Crowley and Crowley's North American deputy, Karl Germer, who eventually ousted him from his position as Agape Lodge leader, replacing him with Parsons. Smith retreated to Malibu, where he continued to practice Thelema until his death.

27.1 Early life

27.1.1 Youth: 1885–1914

Smith was born as Frank Wenham in Tonbridge, Kent, on 9 June 1885.[1] He was the illegitimate son of Oswald Cox, a member of a prominent local family who resided at Marl Field House, and one of his domestic servants, Minnie Wenham, whom Frank would never come to know.[2] Considered an embarrassment by the wealthy Cox family, from an early age he was sent away to live with relatives, and aged four sent to a boarding school where he was physically abused by staff before being removed from the institution by his paternal grandmother, who took him for a year in Switzerland.[3] From 1899 to 1901, he studied at Bedales School, where he developed his lifelong hobby of book binding, before becoming the apprentice to a cabinet maker in Kendal until 1906.[4]

With few ties in Britain, he decided to emigrate to Canada, arriving in Nova Scotia in 1907, where he gained work on a farm in Saskatchewan. From 1909 to 1911 he worked at a confectioner's warehouse, and then for a further nine months at a logging camp, before gaining a job as an accounting clerk at the British Columbia Electric Railway in April 1912.[5] He had come to loath Christianity and the Victorian moral systems that he associated with it; instead he began reading about Eastern religion, yoga, and Western esotericism.[6] While at work, he met Charles Stansfeld Jones, a Thelemite who shared Smith's interest in these subjects and who lent him copies of Aleister Crowley's *Book 4* and volume one, number one of *The Equinox*.[7] Intrigued, Smith paid to join Crowley's Britain-based magical order, the A∴A∴, in doing so obtaining more of Crowley's writings. He began performing many of the practices encouraged by the group, including yoga and the keeping of a diary recording his magical endeavours.[8]

Smith entered into a relationship with a woman twenty years his senior, Emily Sophia "Nem" Talbot Smith, although it remains unclear whether they ever married. With Nem and her daughter Katherine, Smith moved into a specially-constructed house designed by the Thelemite architect Howard E. White. Located at 138 13th Street East, North Vancouver, Smith converted the attic into a temple for Thelemic rituals.[9]

27.1.2   OTO British Columbia Lodge No. 1: 1915–1922

Smith also decided to join the Ordo Templi Orientis (OTO), an occult organisation whose British branch, the Mysteria Magica Maxima (MMM), was run by Crowley, who used it to promote Thelema. In January 1915, Smith signed up to the MMM, and in April went through the Minerval degree initiation at the British Columbia Lodge No. 1.[10] In May, he took part in the Lodge's public performance of the Rites of Isis, which it was hoped would attract further members.[11] In a private capacity, he meanwhile continued performing his A∴A∴ practices, and also began experimenting with the entheogenic properties of anhalonium.[12] In October 1915, Crowley visited the Lodge, where he met with Smith.[13] Soon after, Smith would be upgraded to the position of Master Magician within the Lodge, and in March 1916 received the Probationer level in the A∴A∴, adopting as his personal magical motto the Latin words *Nubem Eripiam* ("I will snatch away the cloud").[14]

Smith's relationship with Nem was strained, and he began an affair with his step-daughter, Katherine. In November 1916, the three of them tried to resign from the OTO lodge so as to prevent their problems affecting the group. Their resignations were rejected, and by January 1917 they were once again active within the lodge.[15] Nevertheless, in March the lodge shut down for 13 months, during which time Crowley and Jones scrutinised Smith's diaries to ascertain his magical progress.[16] Katherine became pregnant with Smith's child, who was born in December 1917, and named Noel Talbot-Smith. Jones proclaimed that Noel represented "the Crowned and Conquering Child" prophecised in the main Thelemite holy book, *The Book of the Law*.[17] Jones was soon named OTO Viceroy for Canada, and in April he re-initiated the lodge at Smith's home, with Smith himself being appointed the lodge's Right Worshipful Master.[18] Jones himself claimed that he had undergone a "Great Initiation" and was now an Ipsissimus; his relationship with Crowley broke down, and he subsequently resigned from the OTO, deeply disappointing Smith.[19]

Smith meanwhile continued working towards the A∴A∴ grade of Zelator, while the British Columbia Lodge No. 1 became increasingly moribund following the death of White, a key member, who had succumbed to Spanish Flu aged 33 in November 1918.[20] Jones had rejoined the OTO and relocated to Detroit in the United States. When Smith was fired from his job following a bout of flu in February 1920, he decided to join Jones in Detroit, where there was a small OTO community; there he gained work as a clerk with the Detroit City Gas Company. In his absence, Nem was appointed Right Worshipful Master of the Vancouver lodge.[21] In March 1921, Jones and Smith proceeded to Chicago, but in June Smith returned to North Vancouver to see his family.[22] That year, Jones convinced Smith to join an esoteric organisation known as the Universal Brotherhood (UB). Smith however was unnerved that rather than expressing a Thelemic viewpoint, the UB adhered to Roman Catholicism, and he also considered its literature purposeless, vague, and grandiose; he soon dropped out.[23] Back in Vancouver, Smith aided one his initiates, Frank Page, in founding the British Columbia Lodge No. 3 in Kamloops, creating all the furniture for their temple. Nevertheless, the lodge closed after a year, with Smith's own British Columbia Lodge No. 1 also becoming defunct in February 1922.[24]

27.1.3   Los Angeles: 1922–1935

Unable to find work in Vancouver, Smith headed to Los Angeles in California, United States. On the way he stopped at San Francisco, where he met with Cecil Frederick Russell, a Thelemite who had departed from the Crowleyan orthodoxy to found his own group, the Choronzon Club. Smith however disliked Russell, and later claimed that he had been unnerved when Russell began expressing a sexual interest in children.[25] After settling in Los Angeles, Smith gained a job at the Southern California Gas Company, entered into a relationship with a woman named Ann Barry, and began attending occasional meetings of the United Lodge of Theosophists, an esoteric organisation centred in the city. Jones meanwhile had united Thelema with auto-suggestion to found his own group, the Psychomagian Society (PMS), and he appointed Smith to be its Local Recorder for Los Angeles; out of friendship to Jones, Smith did so, but was uninterested in the PMS' teachings.[26] Through their correspondences, Crowley came to reject the PMS and relations between himself and Jones once again broke down, this time permanently. Smith retained much affection for Jones, whom he saw as his mentor and friend, but nevertheless agreed with Crowley over the PMS and also rejected Jones' ongoing fascination with the UB, which Smith considered incompatible with Thelema; their relationship too came to an end in 1926.[27]

Now based in Los Angeles, Smith applied for US citizenship but was rejected, due to the fact that in his application he had claimed to be married but he was unable to prove with paperwork.[28] Seeking to promote Thelema in the city, he adopted his own student, Oliver Jacobi, whom he mentored in the A∴A∴ system,[29] and in the autumn of 1927, he developed a close friendship with fellow Thelemite and Hollywood actress Jane Wolfe.[30] Although he continued to have sexual relationships with other women, Smith retained his love for Katherine, who came to visit him in Los Angeles, where they were legally married on 24 August 1927 at the Forest Lawn Memorial Park in Glendale, the day before she returned to Montreal.[31] She tried to get Smith to abandon occultism and Thelema and return to her in Canada, but he refused, leading her to file for divorce in May 1930, taking sole custody of their child.[32] Smith continued to have sexual and romantic relationships with other women, and – influenced by Crowley's bisexuality – also experimented with same-sex sexual relations, but felt no attraction to men.[33] From July to September 1929, a married woman named Leota Schneider moved in with Smith, and they had an affair, but she soon returned to her husband, while from July to December 1930, Smith began undertaking sex magic rituals with Wolfe, although their relationship remained platonic.[34] Smith soon met Regina Kahl and her sister Leona "Lee" Watson, whom he initiated into the OTO in early 1931, with Regina also joining the A∴A∴. Smith had sexual relations with both sisters, but while Regina – with whom his activity became sadomasochistic – became romantically attached to him, Lee soon abandoned Thelema.[35]

In 1932, Crowley, now based back in England, fell seriously ill, and believing his death to be imminent, he sent Smith a testament proclaiming that in the event of his death, Smith would become Frater Superior and Outer Head of the Order (OHO) of the OTO; he soon however recovered.[36] In May of that year, Smith and Kahl began renting the large house at 1746 Winona Boulevard in Hollywood, and began to take in lodgers to help pay for it. Kahl and Wolfe began using the attic for Thelemic rituals, and in March 1933 they performed their first public Gnostic Mass in the room, hoping to attract interested persons to Thelema. Crowley was pleased with their progress, and asked them to raise funds so that he could afford to visit.[37] The weekly performances of the Gnostic Mass began to attract increasingly large crowds, with their "Crowley Nights" attracting around 150 guests, among them the film star John Carradine.[38] In April 1934, Smith incorporated the Church of Thelema under US law, although retained the North American OTO as an unincorporated secret society. Crowley however was confused, and believed that Smith had incorporated the OTO, something which angered him; he subsequently complained about Smith in letters to other initiates.[39] After an argument, Crowley and Smith ceased correspondence for a time.[40] Smith also attempted to revive the largely defunct North American OTO, attracting 15 initial initiates, many of whom were dissatisfied members of the Choronzon Club, which was now in decline.[41]

27.2 Later life

27.2.1 The Agape Lodge: 1935–1944

With the OTO now being revived in North America, Smith founded the Agape Lodge No. 1, based at his Hollywood home, and brought in 7 initiates to the Minerval level in September 1935.[42] He advertised the foundation of his group through an advert in *American Astrology* magazine and printed a pamphlet explaining what the OTO was.[42] The Agape Lodge held regular meetings, lectures, and study classes, as well as social events and a weekly Gnostic Mass open to the public.[43] In February 1936 they held a Mass in honour of Wayne Walker, a proponent of New Thought who ran a group known as The Voice of Healing; they had hoped to attract Walker and his supporters to Thelema, but they were put off by the Lodge's sexual openness.[44] Later that year, Smith and Jacobi's employer, the Southern California Gas Company, discovered their involvement in the Lodge, demoting Smith to bookkeeper and firing Jacobi. Angered, Jacobi left the Lodge altogether, while Smith shut down the group's private ritual activities for the next three years.[45] As a result, the public attendance of the Gnostic Mass plummeted.[46]

Activities picked up again when Kahl, who worked as a drama teacher, brought three of her interested students into the group, among them Phyllis Seckler, and other individuals also joined the group, among them Louis T. Culling and Roy Leffingwell. However, the rising number of members caused schisms and arguments, and the Lodge again ceased its private activities from March 1940 to March 1941.[47] They returned to their activities to initiate a couple who had become interested in the OTO through attending the Gnostic Mass, rocket scientist Jack Parsons and his wife Helen. Parsons became enamored with Thelema,[48] although initially expressed both "repulsion and attraction" for Smith.[49] Smith wrote to Crowley, claiming that Parsons was "a really excellent man ... He has an excellent mind and much better intellect than myself ... JP is going to be very valuable".[50] The Parsons would help bring new members into the group; Grady McMurtry and his fiancee Claire Palmer, and Helen's sister Sara Northrup.[51] In February 1939 a young college student who had attended the mass, Ayna Sosoyena, was murdered; although police drew no connection to the Lodge, sensationalist local tabloids connected the two, although were unaware that the Lodge was involved with Crowley or Thelema. A sympathetic local radio reporter allowed Smith to explain the purpose of the Mass to allay fears of the group, but the interview was never aired in an agreement with local press that they would drop the story.[52]

By this point, the Agape Lodge was fully operational once more, although Crowley had remained highly critical of Smith, believing that he was failing to raise sufficient funds for Crowley's personal use. He appointed Karl Germer, a German Thelemite recently arrived in the US, to be his representative on the continent, and instructed Germer to oversee the payment of dues to himself. He also specified that it would now be Germer, and not Smith, who was his chosen successor.[53] Attempting to placate Crowley, in December 1941 Smith stated that all Lodge members now had to contribute 5% of their earnings as an "Emergency Fee" that went to Crowley.[54] Crowley's criticisms nevertheless continued, and Smith suffered a mild heart attack, retiring prematurely from work at the age of 56 before undergoing an operation to remove haemorroids in February 1942.[55]

Smith decided to relocate Agape Lodge to a larger premises, renting the large house at 1003 South Orange Grove Avenue in Pasadena from June 1942 for $100 a month, moving many of the lodge members in to the house, living as a form of commune and raising livestock and vegetables in the grounds.[56] Parsons had begun a relationship with Sara Northrup, while Smith consoled Helen, who would become his partner for the rest of his life; nevertheless the four remained friends.[57] Although they had ceased to publicly perform the Gnostic Mass, membership of the lodge continued to grow.[58] A number of prominent members however left, among them Regina Kahl and Phyllis Seckler.[59] Soon, both the FBI and the Pasadena police department began to investigate the OTO and Agape Lodge, particularly as Germer, now leader of the North American OTO, was German; ultimately, they decided that the group was no threat to national security, describing it as a probable "love cult".[60] Crowley however had remained highly critical of Smith's leadership of the lodge, and ordered Wolfe to send him on a personal magical retreat; she felt conflicted, but eventually conceded to Crowley's demands.[61] Both Crowley and Germer wanted to see Smith ousted permanently, believing that he had become a bad influence on the other lodge members; many of the members, including Jack and Helen Parsons, wrote to them to defend their mentor, but Germer nevertheless ordered him to stand down, with Parsons appointed head of the lodge.[62]

In April Helen gave birth to Smith's son, who was named Kwan Lanval Parsons.[63] In May, Smith and Helen left for a two-room cabin in Rainbow Valley with their baby, where Smith undertook his magical retirement.[64] Back in England, Crowley undertook an astrological analysis of Smith's birth chart, and came to the conclusion that he was the incarnation of a god, greatly altering his estimation of him; Smith however remained sceptical.[65] Refusing to take orders from Germer any more, Smith resigned from the OTO, while Parsons – who remained sympathetic and friendly to Smith during the conflict – ceased lodge activities and resigned as its head. In a letter informing Crowley of this decision, Smith remarked "Would to God you knew your people better."[66] Germer subsequently appointed Max Schneider head of the Agape Lodge, which remained inactive, while Crowley, Germer, and Schneider began spreading lies about Smith, including that he was responsible for raping initiates, claims that were denied by many Lodge members.[67]

27.2.2   Final years: 1944–1957

In September 1944 Smith went on a second magical retirement, during which he performed pranayama and the lesser banishing ritual of the pentagram, invoked Thoth, and recited the Holy Books of Thelema from memory. During the retreat he learned that Kahl, his former lover, had died, which greatly upset him.[68] Returning to his Pasadena home, he was welcomed by Parsons, but Crowley insisted that Smith be shunned by the lodge members, and so he moved back to Hollywood. Increasingly alienated by Crowley's attitude, Parsons resigned from the OTO in August 1946.[69] Now renting a house, Smith sought out various handyman jobs, when he learned that Crowley had died and been succeeded as OHO of the OTO by Germer.[70] He became good friends with the art dealer Baron Ernst von Harringa, who commissioned Smith to construct Asian-style furniture for his gallery.[71] Smith's own health was deteriorating, and in 1948 he suffered from a number of mild heart attacks. He nevertheless continued to believe in Thelema, and hoped to revive the Church of Thelema through performing the Gnostic Mass once more.[72] Following Parsons' death in an explosion – which Smith suspected was a case of suicide – Smith was invited to perform the Gnostic Mass in his memory.[73]

Although they had long disliked each other, Germer recognised that Smith was the only living individual with a good practical knowledge of the OTO degree system, and so put him in contact with Kenneth Grant, who was then trying to revive the OTO in London.[74] Smith and Germer would only meet in person for the first time in June 1956, when the latter was visiting California, and soon after Germer introduced him to young Brazilian Thelemite Marcelo Ramos Motta, who would later grow to despise Smith.[75] Smith purchased a plot of land in Malibu where he built his own house for himself, Helen, and their son, which he named "Hoc Id Est" ("This Is It"). Construction was interrupted in February 1955 when he underwent surgery for an enlarged prostate.[76] This developed into prostate cancer, and mistrusting of conventional medicine, he sought out an alternative treatment at the Hoxsey Clinic in Dallas, Texas, which he visited in December 1956, but they were unable to help him.[77] Smith died as a result of the disease at home on 27 April 1957, subsequently being cremated at the Grandview Memorial Park in Glendale.[78]

27.3 Legacy and influence

The Unknown God was reviewed by Robert Ellwood of the University of Southern California for the peer-reviewed journal *Nova Religio: The Journal of Alternative and Emergent Religions*. Ellwood described it as "the definitive work on American Crowleyanity", noting that it was the product of 15 years of "careful and documented" research. He praised "Starr's lucid style and the inherent fascination of the material, replete with vivid characters, epic rows, and sexual intrigue".[79]

27.4 References

27.4.1 Footnotes

[1] Starr 2003, pp. 2, 4.

[2] Starr 2003, pp. 3–5.

[3] Starr 2003, pp. 5–6.

[4] Starr 2003, p. 6.

[5] Starr 2003, p. 8.

[6] Starr 2003, pp. 8–9.

[7] Starr 2003, pp. 9–11.

[8] Starr 2003, pp. 12–13.

[9] Starr 2003, pp. 14–17.

[10] Starr 2003, pp. 18, 31–32.

[11] Starr 2003, pp. 35–36.

[12] Starr 2003, p. 37.

[13] Starr 2003, pp. 38–40; Churton 2011, p. 199.

[14] Starr 2003, pp. 42, 48.

[15] Starr 2003, pp. 58–64.

[16] Starr 2003, pp. 64–66.

[17] Starr 2003, pp. 68, 82.

[18] Starr 2003, pp. 88.

[19] Starr 2003, pp. 83–84, 90–91.

[20] Starr 2003, pp. 91–92.

[21] Starr 2003, pp. 96, 103–104; Kaczynski 2010, p. 350.

[22] Starr 2003, pp. 107–108.

[23] Starr 2003, pp. 17–120.

[24] Starr 2003, pp. 120–123.

[25] Starr 2003, pp. 125–129.

[26] Starr 2003, pp. 131–138.

[27] Starr 2003, pp. 140–162.

[28] Starr 2003, p. 138.

[29] Starr 2003, p. 168.

[30] Starr 2003, pp. 170–172; Kaczynski 2010, p. 468.

[31] Starr 2003, pp. 169–170.

[32] Starr 2003, pp. 173–175.

[33] Starr 2003, p. 176.

[34] Starr 2003, pp. 176–179.

[35] Starr 2003, pp. 180–186.

[36] Starr 2003, p. 188; Churton 2011, p. 308.

[37] Starr 2003, pp. 189–195; Kaczynski 2010, p. 468.

[38] Starr 2003, pp. 119–200.

[39] Starr 2003, pp. 196–200; Kaczynski 2010, p. 485.

[40] Starr 2003, pp. 200–201.

[41] Starr 2003, pp. 224–226; Kaczynski 2010, pp. 486–487.

[42] Starr 2003, pp. 227.

[43] Starr 2003, p. 237.

[44] Starr 2003, pp. 235–236.

[45] Starr 2003, pp. 239–241.

[46] Starr 2003, p. 246.

[47] Starr 2003, pp. 246–252.

[48] Starr 2003, pp. 252–258.

[49] Pendle 2005, p. 136.

[50] Pendle 2005, p. 172.

[51] Starr 2003, p. 266; Pendle 2005, pp. 169–172.

[52] Starr 2003, pp. 258–262.

[53] Starr 2003, pp. 263–264.

[54] Starr 2003, p. 267.

[55] Starr 2003, pp. 268–270.

[56] Starr 2003, pp. 271–273, 276; Pendle 2005, pp. 207–210.

[57] Starr 2003, p. 274; Carter 2004, pp. 93–94; Pendle 2005, pp. 203–205; Kaczynski 2010, p. 537.

[58] Starr 2003, pp. 276–277.

[59] Starr 2003, p. 279.

[60] Starr 2003, pp. 283–285; Pendle 2005, pp. 214–215.

[61] Starr 2003, pp. 278, 280–282.

[62] Starr 2003, pp. 278, 280–282; Pendle 2005, pp. 216–217, 220.

[63] Starr 2003, p. 289; Carter 2004, p. 88; Pendle 2005, p. 221.

[64] Starr 2003, pp. 290–291; Carter 2004, pp. 92–93; Pendle 2005, pp. 221–222.

[65] Starr 2003, pp. 294–298; Carter 2004, pp. 90–91; Pendle 2005, pp. 221–222.

[66] Starr 2003, pp. 299–300; Pendle 2005, pp. 222–223.

[67] Starr 2003, pp. 301–302.

[68] Starr 2003, pp. 307–310.

[69] Starr 2003, pp. 311–314.

[70] Starr 2003, pp. 315–315.

[71] Starr 2003, pp. 322–323.

[72] Starr 2003, pp. 319–320.

[73] Starr 2003, p. 327.

[74] Starr 2003, p. 324.

[75] Starr 2003, pp. 333–336, 339.

[76] Starr 2003, p. 332.

[77] Starr 2003, p. 338.

[78] Starr 2003, p. 340.

[79] Ellwood & 2006 125–126.

27.4.2 Bibliography

Carter, John (2004). *Sex and Rockets: The Occult World of Jack Parsons* (new edition). Port Townsend: Feral House. ISBN 978-0-922915-97-2.

Churton, Tobias (2011). *Aleister Crowley: The Biography*. London: Watkins Books. ISBN 978-1-78028-012-7.

Ellwood, Robert. "Review of Martin P. Starr's *The Unknown God*". *Nova Religio: The Journal of Alternative and Emergent Religions* **10** (1) (University of California Press). pp. 125–126.

Kaczynski, Richard (2010). *Perdurabo: The Life of Aleister Crowley* (second edition). Berkeley, California: North Atlantic Books. ISBN 978-0-312-25243-4.

Pendle, George (2005). *Strange Angel: The Otherworldly Life of Rocket Scientist John Whiteside Parsons*. Weidenfeld & Nicolson. ISBN 978-0-7538-2065-0.

Starr, Martin P. (2003). *The Unknown God: W.T. Smith and the Thelemites*. Bollingbrook, Illinois: Teitan Press. ISBN 0-933429-07-X.

Frontispiece

Crowley, of whom Smith became a devotee.

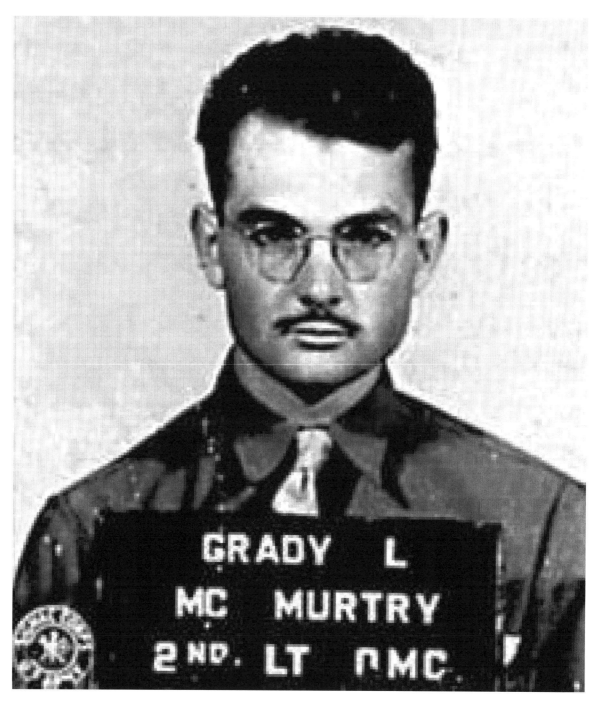

Grady McMurtry was an early Lodge member. He later became head of the OTO.

Chapter 28

James Wasserman

James Wasserman (born 1948)[1] is an American author and occultist. A member of Ordo Templi Orientis since 1976 and a book designer by trade, he has written extensively on spiritual and political liberty.

28.1 Publishing career

Wasserman began working in 1973 at Weiser Books, then the world's largest bookstore and publishing company to specialize in esoteric literature. While working at Weiser, he met and befriended legendary filmmakers and occultists Harry Smith and Alejandro Jodorowsky.[2] Wasserman worked with Brazilian occultist Marcelo Ramos Motta to publish the *Commentaries of AL* in 1975, for which he wrote the introduction. Additionally, he supervised the 1976 Weiser publication of The Book of the Law, the first popular edition to append the holograph manuscript to the typeset text.[3][4] In 1977, Wasserman arranged to professionally re-photograph Frieda Harris' Tarot paintings for use in an improved second edition of Aleister Crowley's Thoth Tarot deck, and also wrote the instruction booklet.[5]

Wasserman left Weiser in 1977 to found Studio 31, where he produced the *Simon Necronomicon*, a volume purporting to be the mythological *Necronomicon* made famous by Howard Philips Lovecraft.[6] In 2008, it was reissued in a high-quality 31st anniversary edition by Ibis Press. In 1994, Wasserman assembled a team of scholars, photographers, and editorial staff to produce a full-color version of *The Egyptian Book of the Dead* featuring the Papyrus of Ani as discussed in In the Center of the Fire[7] His edition of the Book of the Dead was described as offering "much of value in presentation, layout and commentary"[8] by John Baines, professor of Egyptology at the University of Oxford.

28.2 Ordo Templi Orientis

A member of O.T.O. since 1976, Wasserman founded one of its oldest lodges, Tahuti Lodge, in New York City in 1979.[9] He has played a key role within the Order in publishing the literary corpus of Aleister Crowley. In 1983, he worked with two other members of O.T.O. to produce *The Holy Books of Thelema*,[5][10][11] a collection of Crowley's Class A (inspired) writings. In 1986, his essay "An Introduction to the History of the O.T.O." appeared in *The Equinox III, No. 10*. In 2009, he and his wife Nancy published *To Perfect This Feast*,[12] a performance commentary on the Gnostic Mass. Wasserman is described by Dan Burstein as "a founder of the modern Ordo Templi Orientis" in his guide to Dan Brown's novel *Angels & Demons*.[13] In 2012, Wasserman wrote an extensive account of his own experiences in the development of the modern O.T.O.[14]

28.3 Public appearances

Wasserman has appeared on several television and radio shows.[15] In 2009, he discussed his book *Secrets of Masonic Washington* at the National Press Club in Washington, D.C.[16] In 2012, his performance of Liber Israfel was broadcast on The Discovery Channel in a program entitled Secrets of Secret Societies.

28.4 Works

28.4.1 As writer

- "Introduction" in Motta, Marcelo (1975). *The Commentaries of AL*. New York, NY: Samuel Weiser. pp. ix-xi. ISBN 0-87728-287-0.

- *Instructions for Aleister Crowley's Thoth Tarot Deck*. New York, NY: Samuel Weiser. 1978. ISBN 0-87728-444-X.

- "An Introduction to the History of the O.T.O." in Crowley, Aleister (1986). *The Equinox III, Vol. 3, No. 10*. Samuel Weiser. p. 87. ISBN 0-87728-719-8.

- *The Templars and the Assassins: The Militia of Heaven*. Destiny Books, 2001. ISBN 978-0-89281-859-4

- *The Slaves Shall Serve: Meditations on Liberty*. Sekmet Books. 2004.

- *The Mystery Traditions: Secret Symbols & Sacred Art* (a revised and expanded edition of *Art & Symbols of the Occult*, 1993). Destiny Books, 2005. ISBN 978-1-59477-088-3

- *An Illustrated History of the Knights Templar*. Destiny Books, 2006. ISBN 978-1-59477-117-0

- *The Secrets of Masonic Washington: A Guidebook to Signs, Symbols, and Ceremonies at the Origin of America's Capital*. Destiny Books, 2008. ISBN 978-1-59477-266-5

- Wasserman, James; Nancy Wasserman (2010). *To Perfect This Feast: The Gnostic Mass* (Revised second ed.). Sekmet Books. ISBN 978-0-9718870-3-9.

- *The Temple of Solomon: From Ancient Israel to Secret Societies*. Inner Traditions, 2011. ISBN 978-1-59477-220-7

- *In the Center of the Fire: A Memoir of the Occult 1966-1989*. Ibis Press, 2012. ISBN 978-0-89254-201-7

28.4.2 As editor

- Crowley, Aleister (2006). *Aleister Crowley and the Practice of the Magical Diary*. Weiser Books. ISBN 978-1-57863-372-2.

- Birch, Una (2007). *Secret Societies: Illuminati, Freemasons, and the French Revolution*. Nicolas Hays. ISBN 978-0-89254-132-4.

- Stanley, Thomas (2010). *Pythagoras: His Life and Teaching*. Ibis Press. ISBN 978-0-89254-160-7.(with co-editor Daniel Gunther)

- *The Weiser Concise Guide Series*(5 titles) |publisher=Redwheel/Weiser

28.4.3 As publisher

- Eva Von Dassow, ed. (1994). *The Egyptian Book of the Dead*. San Francisco: Chronicle Books. ISBN 978-0-8118-6489-3.

- Simon, ed. (2008). *The Necronomicon*. Lake Worth, Florida: Ibis Press. ISBN 978-0-89254-146-1.

28.4.4   Screenplay

- *Divine Warriors: The Birth of Heresy*. With Keith Stump and Harvey Rochman, 2007.

28.5   See also

- William Breeze

- Lon Milo DuQuette

- Richard Kaczynski

- Rodney Orpheus

- Lionel Snell

28.6   References

[1] "James Wasserman Biography". *Jameswassermanbooks.com*. James Wasserman Books. Retrieved 2011-07-19.

[2] Igliori, Paola (1996). *American Magus: Harry Smith*. New York, NY: Inandout Press. p. 275. ISBN 0-9625119-9-4.

[3] Crowley, Aleister (1976). *The Book of the Law*. New York, NY: Samuel Weiser. ISBN 0-87728-334-6.

[4] Wasserman, James (2012). *In the Center of the Fire: A Memoir of the Occult 1966-1989*. Lake Worth, FL: Ibis Press. p. 111. ISBN 978-0-89254-201-7.

[5] Louise, Rita. "James Wasserman - Secrets of Masonic Washington". *Justenergyradio.com*. Body, Mind & SoulHealer. Retrieved November 22, 2011.

[6] Simon, ed. (1977). *The Necronomicon*. New York, NY: Schlangekraft/Barnes Graphic.

[7] Wasserman, James (2012). *In the Center of the Fire: A Memoir of the Occult 1966-1989*. Lake Worth, FL: Ibis Press. pp. 145–147. ISBN 978-0-89254-201-7.

[8] Baines, John (1995-04-21). "The Egyptian Book of the Dead". *Times Higher Education* (London). Retrieved 2011-07-19.

[9] "Tahuti Lodge O.T.O., serving the New York City Metropolitan Area". *Tahutilodge.org*. Tahuti Lodge, Ordo Templi Orientis. 2009. Retrieved November 22, 2011.

[10] Crowley, Aleister (1983). *The Holy Books of Thelema*. York Beach, Maine: Samuel Weiser. ISBN 0-87728-579-9.

[11] Wasserman, James (2012). *In the Center of the Fire: A Memoir of the Occult 1966-1989*. Lake Worth, FL: Ibis Press. p. 187. ISBN 978-0-89254-201-7.

[12] Wasserman, James & Nancy (2010). *To Perfect This Feast: A Commentary on Liber XV* (2nd ed.). Sekmet Books. p. 3. ISBN 978-0-9718870-3-9.

[13] Burstein, Dan (2004). *Secrets of Angels and Demons*. New York, NY: CDS Books. p. 140. ISBN 1-59315-140-3.

[14] Wasserman, James (2012). *In the Center of the Fire: A Memoir of the Occult 1966-1989*. Lake Worth, FL: Ibis Press. p. 3. ISBN 978-0-89254-201-7.

[15] James Wasserman Media Page

[16] James Wasserman at the National Press Club 2009 Part 1 on YouTube

28.7 External links

- Official website

- Studio 31, Inc.

- Intrinsic Books - Publishing, Intellectual Property Management, Marketing

- The Egyptian Book of the Dead - Wasserman

- Wasserman podcasts at *Thelema Now!*

- Radio interviews at Hieronomus & Company, 21st Century Radio

- A Treasure of Antiquity Reborn: Recreating the Papyrus of Ani

- at In the Center of the Fire website

- at GnosticMass.org website

Chapter 29

Jane Wolfe

Jane Wolfe (March 21, 1875 — March 29, 1958) was an American silent film character actress and Thelemite.

29.1 Early life

Of Pennsylvania Dutch stock, Wolfe was born in the tiny Pennsylvania borough of St. Petersburg in Clarion County. As a young girl she went to New York City to pursue a career in the theatre but soon became involved with acting in the fledgling motion picture industry.

29.2 Career

She made her film debut in 1910 at the age of 35 with Kalem Studios in *A Lad from Old Ireland* under the direction of Sidney Olcott.

In 1911, Wolfe was part of the Kalem Company's crew in New York City who relocated to the company's new production facilities in Los Angeles. She went on to become one of the leading character actors of the decade, appearing in more than one hundred films including an important secondary role in the 1917 Mary Pickford film, *Rebecca of Sunnybrook Farm*.

29.3 Association with Aleister Crowley

In 1918, Jane Wolfe began corresponding with the English author and occultist Aleister Crowley, and two years later she gave up her career in Hollywood to join Crowley at his "Abbey of Thelema" at Cefalù, Sicily, living there from 1920 until it closed in 1923. There she kept records about her magic practice, which were later published by the College of Thelema of Northern California as *The Cefalu Diaries*.[1]

Wolfe is considered an important female figure in magick as, in addition to her friendship and work with Crowley, she took part in the founding of the Agape Lodge of the Ordo Templi Orientis in southern California as well as being its lodge master.

29.4 Later years

After not appearing on screen for 17 years, in 1937 Jane Wolfe had a small role in a B-movie Western named *Under Strange Flags*.[2]

Jane Wolfe, the "Red Flame", at the Abbey of Thelema in Cefalù, Italy

29.5 Ouija

Wolfe used the Ouija board and credited some of her greatest spiritual communications to the use of this implement.[3]

29.6   Death

Jane Wolfe died in the Southern California city of Glendale eight days after her 83rd birthday.

29.7   Partial filmography

- *The Roses Of A Virgin (1910 film)*
- *The Wild Goose Chase* (1915)
- *Blackbirds* (1915)
- *On Record* (1917)
- *Castles for Two* (1917)
- *Rebecca of Sunnybrook Farm* (1917)
- *Mile-a-Minute Kendall* (1918)
- *The Cruise of the Make-Believes* (1918)
- *The Poor Boob* (1919)
- *The Grim Game* (1919)
- *The Six Best Cellars* (1920)
- *Why Change Your Wife?* (1920)
- *Thou Art the Man* (1920)
- *The Round-Up* (1920)
- *Behold My Wife!* (1920)
- *Under Strange Flags (1937)*

29.8   References

[1] *Jane Wolfe: The Cefalu Diaries 1920 – 1923.* College of Thelema of Northern California, 2008.

[2] IMDB: http://www.imdb.com/title/tt0029710/

[3] Cornelius, J. Edward (2005). *Aleister Crowley and the Ouija Board.* ISBN 1-932595-10-4

29.9   External links

- Jane Wolfe at the Internet Movie Database
- Jane Wolfe at the AFI Catalog of Feature Films
- Jane Wolfe at the TCM Movie Database
- Jane Wolfe at AllMovie
- Book *Jane Wolfe: Her Life with Aleister Crowley*

29.10 Text and image sources, contributors, and licenses

29.10.1 Text

- **Ordo Templi Orientis** *Source:* https://en.wikipedia.org/wiki/Ordo_Templi_Orientis?oldid=686430853 *Contributors:* The Cunctator, Dan~enwiki, The Anome, Olivier, Tobin Richard, Michael Hardy, Pit~enwiki, Nixdorf, Docu, Andres, Daniel Quinlan, Maximus Rex, Fibonacci, Khranus, Optim, JorgeGG, Fredrik, Jmabel, Lupo, Gil Dawson, Ferkelparade, Everyking, Eequor, Bacchiad, Old Nol, Pm356, Jossi, Sam Hocevar, Trilobite, Ashami, MunirS, Guanabot, Rubicon, Djordjes, Jarsyl, Ben Standeven, Jpgordon, Cmdrjameson, Giraffedata, Hooperbloob, Hanuman Das, Greba, Apoc2400, Flata, Denial, Anlala, Bsadowski1, Scriberius, LOL, Isomeme, Sburke, The-Watermammal, Tabletop, Bbatsell, SeventyThree, Search4Lancer, Rjwilmsi, PinchasC, Philosophygeek, DickClarkMises, Cavalorn, FlaBot, Somecallmetim, Kmanheim, Valermos, NotJackhorkheimer, Silivrenion, DVdm, Kellymac, YurikBot, Wavelength, NTBot~enwiki, 999~enwiki, Pigman, Takwish, Wgungfu, Lusanaherandraton, Lexicon, MSJapan, Morgan Leigh, Scope creep, Wishdiak, BorgQueen, Dr U, Willbyr, Harthacnut, KnightRider~enwiki, SmackBot, KnowledgeOfSelf, Xaosflux, Ppntori, WeniWidiWiki, Allengreenfield, Frap, Blueboar, King Vegita, JonasRH, Fuzzypeg, Pharaoh480, ALR, SashatoBot, Rory096, Imacomp, Vanished user 9i39j3, Aroundthewayboy, Skeptismo118, Meco, Midnightblueowl, Hu12, David Legrand, JoeBot, CapitalR, Tawkerbot2, ScottW, CmdrObot, Estéban, Dave Null, Ekajati, Kantiandream, Idolater718, Synergy, Frater5, Raistlin Majere, Clyde2003, BetacommandBot, Thijs!bot, Qevlhma, Astynax, Frater Xyzzy, Widefox, Dereckson, Mousescribe, Solis93, Captainbarrett, Username22, TLF93, Lkleinjans, Antmusic, StefanPapp, Mermaid from the Baltic Sea, Thiebes, Sororyzbl, Crimsongecko, Crakkpot, Kasanax, Zara1709, Psykhosis, Funandtrvl, MensKeperRa, DYBoulet, Chaos5023, Tunnels of Set, Aesopos, BackMaun, IPSOS, John Carter, Sintaku, Khabs, Pralaya, DivaNtrainin, SieBot, Prometheus93, Motuleños, Alabaster Crow, Starofisis, Emnx, Hierophant777, Stealthepiscopalian, Photouploaded, SuperHamster, Rich Uncle Skeleton, CounterVandalismBot, Mo99, 718 Bot, -Midorihana-, JDPhD, Frater-sphinx, Hrumachis418, Will in China, Addbot, ColDickPeters, Lightbot, Luckas-bot, Yobot, Flagsofscarlet, AnomieBOT, Rubinbot, Piano non troppo, RayvnEQ, Ulric1313, LilHelpa, Xqbot, Khephra93, J04n, Omnipaedista, Mvaldemar, Ankhefenkhons, Kobnach, Vihorn, Rodneyorpheus, Aleister Wilson, An'el Haqq, Skyerise, MastiBot, Ex Orient Lux, Thetrucharirman, RjwilmsiBot, EmausBot, Theseus1776, Osisotonewzealand, RaqiwasSushi, ClueBot NG, Central418, PT67Tunggul, Helpful Pixie Bot, Jeraphine Gryphon, BG19bot, Parzivalamfortas, Swiftsr, Ananghi, ArcanumHermetica, Dara Allarah, Jayaguru-Shishya, FraterPalamedes, JackTheVicar, Hatesville77 and Anonymous: 189

- **William Breeze** *Source:* https://en.wikipedia.org/wiki/William_Breeze?oldid=663360381 *Contributors:* Dan~enwiki, Charles Matthews, Ashley Y, Jossi, D6, Rich Farmbrough, Jpgordon, DCEdwards1966, Gene Nygaard, Deloyola~enwiki, NotJackhorkheimer, 999~enwiki, Splash, MSJapan, GeoffCapp, White Mouse~enwiki, SmackBot, Bluebot, GoodDay, Axem Titanium, Zero sharp, JayHenry, Dave Null, Idolater718, JamesAM, Headbomb, RobotG, AlexOvShaolin, Johnpacklambert, Crakkpot, John Carter, Alabaster Crow, Oculi, Jax 0677, Good Olfactory, Lightbot, Yobot, Flagsofscarlet, AnomieBOT, Rodneyorpheus, Aleister Wilson, DrilBot, Jonesey95, Skyerise, Autumnalmonk, Theseus1776, Crose78, CactusBot, Lashuto, Helpful Pixie Bot, Smcg8374, BattyBot, Jayaguru-Shishya and Anonymous: 35

- **Marjorie Cameron** *Source:* https://en.wikipedia.org/wiki/Marjorie_Cameron?oldid=673099045 *Contributors:* Emperor, Woohookitty, Crisco 1492, Infamous30, SmackBot, Sticky Parkin, Ser Amantio di Nicolao, Gobonobo, Midnightblueowl, Norm mit, Kencf0618, GiantSnowman, Cydebot, JustAGal, Modernist, Waacstats, Johnpacklambert, GrahamHardy, Deconstructhis, Flyer22 Reborn, Pirfle, Dthomsen8, Genesee.gbh, CactusWriter, Yobot, AnomieBOT, Cantons-de-l'Est, Omnipaedista, Erik9bot, FrescoBot, Rodneyorpheus, Aleister Wilson, RjwilmsiBot, Manytexts, Scotthobbs, DPL bot, Mogism, VIAFbot, Visionvictoria, CensoredScribe, StaceyEOB, Filedelinkerbot, KasparBot and Anonymous: 23

- **William C. Conway** *Source:* https://en.wikipedia.org/wiki/William_C._Conway?oldid=690095171 *Contributors:* Bkonrad, Robert Weemeyer, Petersam, BD2412, RussBot, Pigman, SmackBot, Iridescent, Cydebot, Fayenatic london, ARTEST4ECHO, Waacstats, Enaidmawr, Aboutmovies, IPSOS, Jdaloner, UbiTerrarum, Rich Uncle Skeleton, Ninja247, SilvonenBot, Good Olfactory, Rich jj, Download, Lightbot, AnomieBOT, Skyerise, Full-date unlinking bot, RjwilmsiBot, EmausBot, Helpful Pixie Bot, Khazar2, Broter, AsteriskStarSplat and Anonymous: 2

- **Aleister Crowley** *Source:* https://en.wikipedia.org/wiki/Aleister_Crowley?oldid=689504585 *Contributors:* AxelBoldt, Eloquence, Dan~enwiki, Mav, Bryan Derksen, Ed Poor, Eclecticology, Fubar Obfusco, Ortolan88, William Avery, Ben-Zin~enwiki, DW, Tzartzam, ChrisSteinbach, Olivier, Edward, Michael Hardy, Paul Barlow, Kwertii, Modster, Bewildebeast, Nixdorf, Shyamal, Wapcaplet, Cyde, Tgeorgescu, Skysmith, Paul A, Pcb21, Tregoweth, Ihcoyc, Emperor, Pseudo daoist, Jdforrester, Julesd, Nikai, Andres, Jacquerie27, RL Barrett, Rbraunwa, Dysprosia, Daniel Quinlan, Andrewman327, WhisperToMe, Tpbradbury, Jakenelson, Fibonacci, Omegatron, Gaidheal, Khranus, Stormie, Optim, Carbuncle, Palefire, Dimadick, Bearcat, Ray Radlein, RedWolf, Moncrief, Sam Spade, Phatsphere, Babbage, Bertie, Auric, Blainster, UtherSRG, JackofOz, ElBenevolente, Comrade~enwiki, Oobopshark, Mattflaschen, Dina, Alan Liefting, Snobot, Martinwguy, Centrx, CorpDan, Gtrmp, Luis Dantas, Tom harrison, Lupin, Bradeos Graphon, Alterego, Everyking, Supergee, Emuzesto~enwiki, Curps, Guanaco, Mboverload, Siroxo, Eequor, Sexyfoxboy, Infinitysnake, Bacchiad, DougEngland, Jariku, Old Nol, Gadfium, Woggly, Alexf, Sonjaaa, Quadell, Antandrus, Piotrus, Quarl, Elembis, Murple, DragonflySixtyseven, Bodnotbod, Satori, Kuralyov, F13nd, DenisMoskowitz, Karl-Henner, Salvadors, Gary D, Pitchka, Marcus2, Klemen Kocjancic, Trilobite, Subsume, Lobosolo, Ashami, D6, Freakofnurture, Pyrop, Discospinster, Rich Farmbrough, Guanabot, NrDg, YUL89YYZ, Bishonen, Crowley, User2004, MeltBanana, Auto movil, Pavel Vozenilek, Gonzalo Diethelm, SpookyMulder, Bender235, ESkog, Violetriga, Pietzsche, Huntster, Kwamikagami, Kross, Art LaPella, Triona, Jpgordon, Bill Thayer, JRM, Fugazi32, Bobo192, Smalljim, Cje~enwiki, Cmdrjameson, .:Ajvol:., Brim, Foobaz, Ziggurat, Compulsion, Giraffedata, Cavrdg, Rajah, TheProject, Solar, DCEdwards1966, Pacula, DannyMuse, Linuxlad, Jumbuck, Macai, Hanuman Das, Alansohn, Eraserhead~enwiki, Jared81, Arthena, Punarbhava, Lectonar, Hoary, Theri, Laurencetimms, DreamGuy, Ross Burgess, Oneliner, Mdriftmeyer, Leoadec, Stygian23, Kusma, Pauli133, Arthur Warrington Thomas, Versageek, Djsasso, Nightstallion, Blaxthos, Throbblefoot, Dismas, Zorblek, Sk4p, Mullet, Angr, Richard Arthur Norton (1958-), Woohookitty, FeanorStar7, Scriberius, Ataru, S36e175, Benbest, Broquaint, Pol098, GeorgeOrr, Pogue, Trevor Andersen, Jleon, GregorB, Philodox-ohki, FluffyPanda, Daniel Lawrence, Matthew Platts, Palica, Rgbea, Marudubshinki, KrisW6, Graham87, Sparkit, Cuchullain, BD2412, Wizardswand, Kbdank71, RxS, SouthernComfort, Sjö, Rjwilmsi, Wahoofive, Koavf, Gryffindor, Vary, SpNeo, Vegaswikian, Dewrad, Ligulem, ElKevbo, Fish and karate, Somecallmetim, Nivix, Aloneyouaregeek, Mitsukai, Born2cycle, The Dogandpony, Wingsandsword, NotJackhorkheimer, SpectrumDT, Gareth E Kegg, Theshibboleth, Amchow78, Spencerk, Mongreilf, Hatch68, Visor, Zef, DVdm, Bgwhite, Geg, YurikBot, Kinneyboy90, 999~enwiki, JarrahTree, RussBot, KamuiShirou, Ericorbit, Pigman, Kooshmeister, Scott5834, Al Hallaj, Gaius Cornelius, Megastar, Rsrikanth05, Naukhel, Complainer, Aboverepine, Justin Eiler, VinceBowdren, PhilipC, Moe Epsilon, Formeruser-82, Tony1, Mooveeguy, Morgan Leigh, Bota47, GeoffCapp, Scope creep, Djdaedalus, Igiffin, Cmskog, Tuckerresearch, Slunky,

FF2010, Womble, KingKane, SFGiants, Chase me ladies, I'm the Cavalry, Fang Aili, Rms125a@hotmail.com, BorgQueen, Fram, Scoutersig, Arundhati bakshi, NickJones, Curpsbot-unicodify, Sepand, Pfistermeister, Mjroots, NeilN, Tom Morris, AlfredL, Ross Lawhead, NetRolller 3D, Harthacnut, Telewis, Pearce.duncan, Attilios, SmackBot, OthelloMT, Zazaban, Slashme, Hydrogen Iodide, Melchoir, McGeddon, CRKingston, Rokfaith, Blue520, Bomac, Allixpeeke, Setanta747 (locked), Bwithh, Wandjina, Horawiki~enwiki, Gjs238, Ian Rose, Marktreut, Gilliam, Portillo, Hmains, Spacelord~enwiki, Theavalonian, Chris the speller, Autarch, DStoykov, AntelopeInSearchOfTruth, Metarob, Sadads, Dustimagic, Jeff5102, ASigIAm213, Can't sleep, clown will eat me, Skoglund, DéRahier, Writtenright, OrphanBot, Snowmanradio, Liberaljoe, Krsont, Pax85, King Vegita, Soosed, Feazey, X-Flare-x, Nakon, Mcorco2, Dreadstar, RandomP, Fuzzypeg, Jklin, DMacks, Hobbs von Wackamole, Smerus, Rhkramer, J.smith, Leon..., Ohconfucius, Snowgrouse, Clown in black and yellow, Eliyak, Arnoutf, Ser Amantio di Nicolao, Valfontis, Srikeit, JzG, Soap, John, Gobonobo, Five-, Edwy, Merchbow, Mary Read, ManiF, Runningfridgesrule, A. Parrot, XWayfarer, JValenc1, Renwick, MCWicoff, Mr Stephen, Meco, Midnightblueowl, E-Kartoffel, Ryulong, Sharnak, Dr.K., Novangelis, MTSbot~enwiki, Caiaffa, Vince In Milan, Sethian, AndyBoyd, Hu12, Quaeler, Patrick Schwemmer, Iridescent, JustInLillich, Laddiebuck, JoeBot, Skapur, Onefinalstep, Catherineyronwode, Paul Knight, Deporodh, IvanLanin, Cls14, CapitalR, Courcelles, Nuttyskin, Secos5, Tawkerbot2, Lokiloki, Kendroche, J Milburn, CmdrObot, Gowron, Smiloid, ShelfSkewed, Hopsyturvy, Avillia, Bb1230, Jagle, Chicheley, John S Moore, Ekajati, Cydebot, Death metal, Kovzhun, DrunkenSmurf, Gogo Dodo, Bellerophon5685, Red Director, Bazarov, Xxanthippe, Jeremy68, TEPutnam, Sloth monkey, Synergy, Frater5, Tawkerbot4, Taschenrechner~enwiki, Chris Henniker, MikeOso, Karuna8, Ward3001, Boboroshi, Mtpaley, Carsonc, Algabal, PamD, Raschd, Malleus Fatuorum, Jon C., Thijs!bot, Epbr123, Barticus88, Biruitorul, D4g0thur, Fourchette, AgentAJD, Daniel, Bear475, Rrose Selavy, HappyInGeneral, Mibelz, Memty Bot, N5iln, CynicalMe, Missvain, Bobblehead, Neil916, Second Quantization, Lotans, Nick Number, Phobe, Ted Newsom, Noclevername, DennisRandall, Rulerboyz, Sidasta, AntiVandalBot, Frater Xyzzy, Widefox, Akradecki, Emeraldcityserendipity, Augusta2, Bookworm857158367, Julia Rossi, Marquess, Dragon Emperor, Canadian-Bacon, Lesterjames, Deflective, Kprateek88, Dsp13, Nthep, Shaftman1, Sophie means wisdom, Andonic, Necrogolem, NSR77, TAnthony, PhilKnight, Adroito, Msalt, Repku, Bencherlite, Andreas Toth, Magioladitis, Captainbarrett, 75pickup, SyG, Xn4, TheTank264, SHCarter, ***Ria777, Usien6, Zenomax, Brusegadi, Zelator, JackLondon77, Upholder, Lordbutterfly, Justanother, Systemlover, St.Jimmy666, Memotype, DerHexer, Edward321, Coffeepusher, Truthordare, Pax:Vobiscum, Mr Vain, Jonomacdrones, B9 hummingbird hovering, FisherQueen, Alien666, MartinBot, Mermaid from the Baltic Sea, GoldenMeadows, Naohiro19, Thiebes, Rettetast, Keith D, Bruin69, Kostisl, CommonsDelinker, Cathar maiden, EdBever, J.delanoy, Millenium kid 1, Amyeis, Herbythyme, SteveLamacq43, Polenth, Beveridge.r, Johnnybriggs, Ramblingwithoutadestination, Cpiral, Thedeadlypython, Stuffentein, Mgmax~enwiki, Amoghasiddhi, NewEnglandYankee, Al B. Free, Kasanax, STBotD, FrankEldonDixon, Choronzonclub, The Behnam, Squids and Chips, Coachs, CardinalDan, Idioma-bot, Aurashafa, ACSE, Deor, VolkovBot, Hovaness, Chaos5023, Aeqea, Tunnels of Set, Indubitably, Jmrowland, Embobee, Philip Trueman, TXiKiBoT, BackMaun, Godo Larner, Technopat, Cath reen, Richard Gillard, Veronica max, Barbieyou, Aymatth2, IPSOS, Qxz, Secrowl, Voorlandt, Steven J. Anderson, John Carter, Khabs, Eldaran~enwiki, Ra-Hoor-Khu, S t hathliss, Mannafredo, Lashtal.com, Sumafi, K d f m, MRaphael68, Malick78, Hyper7, Unholy One, Tam Patton, The Devil's Advocate, Dick Shane, Bitbut, Jarhurst, Daveh4h, Vodak, SieBot, RHodnett, Hiram816, TJRC, Aristarco de Samotracia, ClarkSavageJr, Motuleños, Alabaster Crow, Transcendentalist, ProfessorWilhelmSmerthy, Vincentjennings, Chelseyrl, Yintan, Crash Underride, Jessemilby, EternityExplosion~enwiki, KingRantheMan, Phil Bridger, Granf, Bagatelle, Filiusvita, Lightmouse, Hemlock850, Moletrouser, Nancy, Dogbeast, Dravecky, Maelgwnbot, CharlesGillingham, TheTaternumber13, Hadit93, 9eyedeel, Anchor Link Bot, Dabomb87, Ryukaiel, Wonchop, Randy Kryn, Rabbelrauser, ImageRemovalBot, Invertzoo, SpiderMum, ClueBot, ParlerVousWiki, IPAddressConflict, Momosgarage, StevethePaladin, Jaydoubleyew, Agnostic Gnostic, The Thing That Should Not Be, All Hallow's Wraith, Stealthepiscopalian, Zderjoos, Thepeeblesman666, Boing! said Zebedee, Iconoclast.horizon, CounterVandalismBot, Intlmusique, Kinlaso, Septemberfourth476, Nmate, Excirial, Nymf, Jusdafax, Zddoodah, Lartoven, Simon D M, Sun Creator, Kiiss Marks, Romanov55, Arjayay, Jotterbot, Brianboulton, Gaz wit da gatz~enwiki, Basil45, Redthoreau, Mebadatbball, Thehelpfulone, Cjarbo2, Aitias, Mapadin, Brandoid, JDPhD, Jlamrhein, Canihaveacookie, Stupod, Indopug, Bluegoatrampant, DumZiBoT, Agentxyz, Frater-sphinx, Leninliker, XLinkBot, Fastily, RogDel, Pichpich, Lucas Malor~enwiki, Detroitgoth, Wikigonish, Sjouker, Will in China, Tthheeppaarrttyy, NHJG, Dubmill, Good Olfactory, ColtM4, Deantuhka, Hollyprobert, Bookbrad, Cxz111, Grayfell, Willking1979, Some jerk on the Internet, Jojhutton, Fyrael, ZhaneXeditor, Sashafresh, DougsTech, Metagraph, Sadiemonster, PositiveSpin, AkhtaBot, SiegfreidZ, CanadianLinuxUser, In Tyler We Trusted, Teagleton Steves, Rosewater Alchemist, LaaknorBot, FerrousTigrus, Gtk123, Digitalpear, D.c.camero, Michael772292, YasOcratic, Chzz, AnnaFrance, Favonian, LemmeyBOT, Teflon Dog, Aacugna, Qwrk, Tassedethe, Ehrenkater, Tide rolls, Kzazar, Gail, Barnt001, BlackMarlin, Contributor777, Ochib, Ben Ben, Legobot, Luckas-bot, Yobot, Granpuff, JJARichardson, Ptbotgourou, Hansihippi, Avatar723, KamikazeBot, SwisterTwister, DropShadow, Eduen, Flagsofscarlet, Dickdock, Eric-Wester, Mission Fleg, AnomieBOT, Pabs77, AnthonyBurgess, Dwayne, Taam, Mintrick, Piano non troppo, Blindmanoregon, RayvnEQ, Ian Rons, Jeff Muscato, Materialscientist, Dendlai, Paranormal Skeptic, Citation bot, QaBobAllah, Wrelwser43, Ruby2010, ArthurBot, Watery Tart, Xqbot, TheAMmollusc, The Elves Of Dunsimore, JimVC3, NikVandiver, Chilas123, Termininja, 4twenty42o, Wicked lemm, MyDerniereDanse, Ragityman, Anonymous from the 21st century, J04n, Firedrum71, Omnipaedista, RibotBOT, XTech102, Mvaldemar, Beechka, Slarty2, Abacchus1974, Piquant00, Laughingmemeboy, Auréola, RoundDisc, Sqgl, Sissssou, Smallman12q, Ankhefenkhons, Marlen Vargas, Shadowjams, Eugene-elgato, Volatile.memory, WebCiteBOT, Thehelpfulbot, Green Cardamom, MarkkuP, FrescoBot, Artimaean, Ryryrules100, MLKLewis, Rodneyorpheus, Seanbond5, Gekke11, Aleister Wilson, Enver62, DivineAlpha, Stephen Morley, HamburgerRadio, Nonexyst, Citation bot 1, Chenopodiaceous, Kenzey818, Warbuff 4, Tyrenon, Eameece, Sarandioti, Skyerise, Moonraker, 5tgoodyer, B-Machine, Dallas1991, Dr.Szląchedzki, Kgrad, Lightlowemon, Trappist the monk, Jondalf, Stifyn, Badasa, Lotje, Changeay, MissAli555, Thesniperremix, A Star Is Here, GreyDaWolf, Reaper Eternal, Reach Out to the Truth, Bigrz15, RjwilmsiBot, Bossanoven, Felixiscool, Hajatvrc, Salvio giuliano, DASHBot, 4rock4roll, Whywhenwhohow, EmausBot, And we drown, Man without qualities, Immunize, Gfoley4, Torsrthidesen, GoingBatty, DaltonGD, Jwloohou, GoatGod, TurkishSultan, Aquidneck, Solarra, Khatai, Camocon, ArchangelIdiotis, The Blade of the Northern Lights, ZéroBot, SVG, Fæ, Traxs7, Liadmalone, Akerans, Empty Buffer, AmericanHeraldist, Krispaige78, Access Denied, Matthew weiner, Jarikrun, AManWithNoPlan, Wikignome0530, Taterdono, Larryyr, MelissaYvonne, Toshio Yamaguchi, L Kensington, Theplastik, Donner60, Morgan TG, MALLUS, Orange Suede Sofa, Bill william compton, ClamDip, Will Beback Auto, ClueBot NG, Penforge, FourLights, Ronald418, BarrelProof, Jørdan, *half-moon* bubba, Widr, Andrew Thomas 2, Lisatree, St.HocusPocus, RafikiSykes, Helpful Pixie Bot, Stn-wiki, Nirame, HMSSolent, Wuweiguru, Titodutta, Jeraphine Gryphon, BG19bot, Smcg8374, Parzivalamfortas, Marcocapelle, Gaulish~enwiki, Toccata quarta, Codylmoore1314, Addaline, The Traditionalist, Okeyes (WMF), Glacialfox, 9711CA, TBrandley, H. 217.83, Henry McClean, Killuminati666999, Fylbecatulous, Fiddlersmouth, AnonNep, The Illusive Man, ChrisGualtieri, Synthgod, Pobtron, EuroCarGT, Jebediah M, Alois Kruise, Semarkham, Reverend Mick man34, Zgoutreach, Mogism, Dnaspark99, Jackninja5, Periglio, Everything Is Numbers, VIAFbot, Sophg6, MaybeMaybeMaybe, LordAnon of Essex, Shariqchhapra, Globuel, Dara Allarah, Aufels, Diana Wyndham, Los358, Homechallenge55, FrankRadioSpecial, CensoredScribe, Berengaria, Eric Corbett, NottNott,

GustavoCarneiro, Frater AA, StraightOuttaBrisbane, Jack C2, Falconettifalconetti, Agroupaccount, Xenxax, Eşşeğinziki, Londonstudent13, Halfman halfthing, Frater UI, Mystical13, Posen607, Patrick jason, Peter238, Morgenstern91, Grzegorz Thelemski, Niga756, TorqueGreg, Bljenkins, ClaraJones1986, 360noscopelsr, HinataFan928, Sir NIJOLOT of Treshholdington, Feoffer, KasparBot, Symmetricbomb, Cszek, Vast Ego Humility, TGIFFTW!, Cisjazcorn, Emilym15, Mscottdunder, You better look out below!, RaymondLull and Anonymous: 1342

- **Lon Milo DuQuette** *Source:* https://en.wikipedia.org/wiki/Lon_Milo_DuQuette?oldid=689799949 *Contributors:* Fubar Obfusco, Cool Hand Luke, Jfdwolff, Jossi, D6, Cnwb, Elwikipedista~enwiki, Cmdrjameson, Hanuman Das, Stemonitis, Rjwilmsi, Koavf, NotJackhorkheimer, Sherool, 999~enwiki, Hiyya54, Pburka, Pigman, Morgan Leigh, Jkelly, Sepand, SmackBot, Timeshifter, Pasha Abd, Bluebot, Ser Amantio di Nicolao, Meco, Catherineyronwode, Tawkerbot2, Vaughanwj, Dave Null, DanielRigal, AndrewHowse, Cydebot, Twobeans, Frater5, Motionrotarytoad, Lon Milo Duquette, Epbr123, Waacstats, Aboutmovies, IPSOS, John Carter, Tsumaru, Treehugger18a, Fratrep, ImageRemovalBot, EAEB, Niceguyedc, Alexbot, Good Olfactory, Addbot, Lightbot, Yobot, Flagsofscarlet, AnomieBOT, J04n, Sam wines, Rodneyorpheus, Aleister Wilson, Skyerise, EpsilonOmega, RjwilmsiBot, Helpful Pixie Bot, Jeraphine Gryphon, Miszatomic, Alanmcorcoran, Khazar2, VIAFbot, Magnolia677, Liberlotus, KasparBot, Magicalegypt and Anonymous: 44

- **Ecclesia Gnostica Catholica** *Source:* https://en.wikipedia.org/wiki/Ecclesia_Gnostica_Catholica?oldid=674661269 *Contributors:* Dan~enwiki, Fibonacci, Mboverload, Ashami, Dbachmann, PhilHibbs, Circeus, Hanuman Das, Gpvos, Anlala, Mel Etitis, Isomeme, Marudubshinki, BD2412, Rjwilmsi, FlaBot, 999~enwiki, RussBot, Pigman, SmackBot, Rune X2, Betacommand, Msalvoni, CapitalR, Idolater718, Synergy, Frater5, Thiebes, Crakkpot, Tunnels of Set, IPSOS, John Carter, Mort pp~enwiki, Stealthepiscopalian, Will in China, Addbot, PaterMcFly, OlEnglish, Baronflopsy, Omnipaedista, Rodneyorpheus, Aleister Wilson, Full-date unlinking bot, Theseus1776, H3llBot, Music Sorter, Ben Ammi, Odysseus1479, Helpful Pixie Bot, Drift chambers, BattyBot, Jayaguru-Shishya, Monkbot and Anonymous: 17

- **Gérard Encausse** *Source:* https://en.wikipedia.org/wiki/G%C3%A9rard_Encausse?oldid=675479034 *Contributors:* Deb, AlexR, Ihcoyc, Charles Matthews, Wetman, Bearcat, Humus sapiens, Jfdwolff, Spooky, Ganymead, Ashami, Vague Rant, Bender235, Alai, TShilo12, Vitruvius~enwiki, Velvetsmog, Rjwilmsi, Pyb, Gadig, FlaBot, Eldamorie, YurikBot, 999~enwiki, Gaius Cornelius, Leutha, ExRat, Kewp, Mrbluesky, That Guy, From That Show!, SmackBot, Unyoyega, Betacommand, Siorse, Fuzzypeg, Ser Amantio di Nicolao, Kaarel, Catherineyronwode, Smiloid, Cydebot, Travelbird, Boboroshi, Raistlin Majere, Bookworm857158367, Manderion, Waacstats, CommonsDelinker, Johnpacklambert, Tgeairn, Ian.thomson, Hashomer, VolkovBot, TXiKiBoT, Buddhipriya, SieBot, Monegasque, Randy Kryn, Salon Essahj, Lx 121, Wednesday Next, Q Valda, Addbot, Madagascar periwinkle, Lightbot, Filip em, Luckas-bot, RevelationDirect, Omnipaedista, Rodneyorpheus, SuperJew, AQUIMISMO, AmenMaatRa13, DixonDBot, Ohjay, RjwilmsiBot, WikitanvirBot, Tiedoxi, ZéroBot, Migel Sances Huares, Manytexts, The Traditionalist, Rí Lughaid, Lex.lb, MarshalRight, VIAFbot, SayPeanuts, KasparBot and Anonymous: 19

- **Gerald Gardner (Wiccan)** *Source:* https://en.wikipedia.org/wiki/Gerald_Gardner_(Wiccan)?oldid=687087741 *Contributors:* Dan~enwiki, Winelight, Paul Barlow, SGBailey, Skysmith, RickK, HarryHenryGebel, Dimadick, Ashley Y, Sheridan, Wereon, Alba, Xanzzibar, Eequor, Phe, Scott MacLean, Necrothesp, Gary D, Shadowlink1014, Klemen Kocjancic, D6, Dbachmann, Bender235, CanisRufus, El C, Huntster, Giraffedata, ProbablyX, Hanuman Das, Titanium Dragon, Arthur Warrington Thomas, Chamaeleon, Galaxiaad, Megan1967, ^demon, Yst, BD2412, Canderson7, FlaBot, Vidkun, Sus scrofa, YurikBot, Wavelength, 999~enwiki, RussBot, Pigman, Bhoeble, NawlinWiki, Aaron Brenneman, Romarin, Kyle Barbour, AdelaMae, Morgan Leigh, Jkelly, SmackBot, Zazaban, Septegram, Canonblack, Gilliam, Hmains, Bluebot, John Halloran, Thumperward, MalafayaBot, Bazonka, Aaron Solomon Adelman, Chèvredansante, Bluebear, Nakon, Fuzzypeg, Ser Amantio di Nicolao, John, Heimstern, Hoodinski, MrArt, Midnightblueowl, RodCrosby, Dl2000, Catherineyronwode, J Milburn, JForget, CmdrObot, Penbat, Cydebot, Jpb1301, Jayen466, Chris Henniker, Barticus88, Escarbot, Ilion2, DenCA, Julia Rossi, WikiLambo, Fayenatic london, Alphachimpbot, JAnDbot, Zeb edee, Kim Dent-Brown, Waacstats, Silentaria, Vishvax, NatureA16, R'n'B, CommonsDelinker, BillWSmithJr, Penguinwithin, Clerks, Jevansen, Typometer, Hehkuviini, Ffetcher, Richard Gillard, IPSOS, SieBot, StAnselm, JohnManuel, GrimThunderbrew, Fratrep, Maelgwnbot, GrouchoPython, Canglesea, EmanWilm, ImageRemovalBot, ClueBot, Rodhullandemu, The White Duke, Stealthepiscopalian, DragonflyDC, Niceguyedc, DragonBot, Sun Creator, Arjayay, 0XQ, SoxBot, Ah0000000ga, XLinkBot, Pichpich, Bilsonius, Dmcm2008, Good Olfactory, Addbot, Ronhjones, BabelStone, Kitana-Galatea, Lightbot, Zorrobot, Luckas-bot, Yobot, Bunnyhop11, PMLawrence, Rogerb67, AnomieBOT, Piano non troppo, Ulric1313, Materialscientist, Citation bot, Eumolpo, LilHelpa, Tuesdaily, Jsmith1000, Almabot, Globe Collector, FrescoBot, Olijven, Rodneyorpheus, Aleister Wilson, PigFlu Oink, Xxglennxx, SuperJew, DrilBot, WoodeWpecker, Moonraker, Gerald c gardner, HazManianDevil, Full-date unlinking bot, Crusoe8181, Moscow Connection, RjwilmsiBot, Wkp123, Camocon, Chryed, SporkBot, Δ, Targaryen, Crown Prince, ClueBot NG, Helpful Pixie Bot, SueTwo, Jeraphine Gryphon, Marcocapelle, Lieutenant of Melkor, Muffin Wizard, Oremorziurgnivri, Witch1b4, ChrisGualtieri, Myxomatosis57, Khazar2, Schwert von Feuer, Victitze, Sowlos, Regularshow123, PinkAmpersand, Gerald Ryder, Leandrogfcdutra, Mactownes, DavidLeighEllis, Eric Corbett, Wdanusha, WiccaUruguay, Sunblade1500, 7Sidz, Slenderdan, Lagoset, WHRex, KasparBot and Anonymous: 108

- **Karl Germer** *Source:* https://en.wikipedia.org/wiki/Karl_Germer?oldid=668082218 *Contributors:* Jpgordon, Hanuman Das, Rjwilmsi, FlaBot, CalJW, SmackBot, Meco, Sethian, Amalas, Frater5, Thijs!bot, Darklilac, Waacstats, John Carter, VVVBot, ImageRemovalBot, Stealthepiscopalian, Dthomsen8, Good Olfactory, Addbot, Lightbot, Yobot, Citation bot, Mvaldemar, Rodneyorpheus, Aleister Wilson, Full-date unlinking bot, Phellodendron, RjwilmsiBot, John of Reading, SporkBot, Odysseus1479, Helpful Pixie Bot, The Traditionalist, Mogism, OccultZone, CaptainStegge, KasparBot and Anonymous: 2

- **Kenneth Grant** *Source:* https://en.wikipedia.org/wiki/Kenneth_Grant?oldid=682694841 *Contributors:* Fubar Obfusco, Ijon, Rbraunwa, Fibonacci, Bearcat, RedWolf, Old Nol, Antandrus, Ashami, Discospinster, Guettarda, Cmdrjameson, Knucmo2, Hanuman Das, Hoary, Denial, Alhazred93, Firsfron, Riumplus, Rjwilmsi, Henchperson, Eubot, CalJW, NotJackhorkheimer, 999~enwiki, RussBot, Bhoeble, Theli 93, BorgQueen, Paolo sammut, Sepand, SmackBot, Master Forcide, Quidam65, Betacommand, Theavalonian, Happydog, Ser Amantio di Nicolao, Midnightblueowl, Catherineyronwode, Panpiper, CmdrObot, Cybergrunt, Estéban, Bobjones2, Cydebot, Lugnuts, Synergy, Raistlin Majere, Pjvpjv, Frater Xyzzy, ***Ria777***, Waacstats, Revdrbrown, Garethb2, Patstuart, B9 hummingbird hovering, Thiebes, Keith D, Cer1056, Squids and Chips, TXiKiBoT, IPSOS, John Carter, JukoFF, Lord Liber, SpiderMum, Stealthepiscopalian, Briantgrove, Niceguyedc, El bot de la dieta, Will in China, GregoryEsteven, Good Olfactory, Addbot, Tassedethe, Lightbot, Yobot, Amirobot, AnomieBOT, RayvnEQ, Materialscientist, Spidern, GrouchoBot, Rodneyorpheus, Aleister Wilson, Skyerise, Jauhienij, RjwilmsiBot, Crown Prince, MrGraphis, Lord Roem, Helpful Pixie Bot, Jeraphine Gryphon, Khazar2, VIAFbot, Blackmetalskinhead, Taivorist, KasparBot and Anonymous: 53

- **Lady Frieda Harris** *Source:* https://en.wikipedia.org/wiki/Lady_Frieda_Harris?oldid=660384341 *Contributors:* Charles Matthews, Lupin, Jossi, Ashami, Noisy, Bobo192, Jmdavid, Hanuman Das, Danaman5, Logophile, Youngamerican, Rjwilmsi, Scott Mingus, Mikalra, 999~enwiki, DanMS, DWC LR, Sepand, SmackBot, Midway, Hmains, Robth, Blueboar, Hgilbert, Drinibot, Cydebot, Frater5, JamesAM, Kbthompson, Arch dude, Magioladitis, Waacstats, CommonsDelinker, Nedrutland, Billinghurst, Annlanding, MystBot, Good Olfactory, Addbot, Redheylin, Lightbot, Yobot, AnomieBOT, Ulric1313, RevelationDirect, FrescoBot, Rodneyorpheus, Aleister Wilson, RjwilmsiBot, H3llBot, The Traditionalist, Hmainsbot1, VIAFbot, OccultZone, Xenxax, KasparBot and Anonymous: 13

- **L. Ron Hubbard** *Source:* https://en.wikipedia.org/wiki/L._Ron_Hubbard?oldid=690315069 *Contributors:* Matthew Woodcraft, Brion VIBBER, Bryan Derksen, Shsilver, XJaM, Fubar Obfusco, William Avery, Zoe, Modemac, Olivier, Frecklefoot, Edward, Michael Hardy, Liftarn, Gabbe, Tannin, Zeno Gantner, Shoaler, Minesweeper, Tregoweth, CesarB, Mkweise, Ahoerstemeier, Docu, JWSchmidt, Bueller 007, Julesd, Rossami, Vzbs34, Susurrus, Scott, Andres, Jiang, John K, Mulad, JCarriker, Fuzheado, Andrewman327, WhisperToMe, Wik, Zoicon5, Timc, Hyacinth, Tempshill, Bloodshedder, AnonMoos, Pakaran, Carlossuarez46, Huangdi, Dimadick, Vardion, ChrisO~enwiki, Moriori, Chris 73, RedWolf, Altenmann, Kowey, Yelyos, Mirv, Mikedash, Wjhonson, Pingveno, Rfc1394, Academic Challenger, Rholton, LGagnon, Sunray, Hadal, Spider Jerusalem, JackofOz, Anthony, Cyrius, Mattflaschen, Jooler, Carnildo, BTfromLA, David Gerard, Johnjosephbachir, Christopher Parham, Crimson30, Andries, Elf, Haeleth, Nunh-huh, Halda, Muldrake, Peruvianllama, Everyking, No Guru, Alison, Gamaliel, Kadzuwo~enwiki, Iceberg3k, Deus Ex, Chowbok, Gadfium, Auximines, CryptoDerk, Vanished user svinet8j3ogifm98wjfgoi3tjosfg, Slowking Man, Formeruser-81, Antandrus, OverlordQ, Elembis, Carolus~enwiki, Jossi, Noirum, Dunks58, Phil Sandifer, Imlepid, DragonflySixtyseven, Sharavanabhava, Tothebarricades.tk, Marc Mongenet, Cglassey, Gscshoyru, Gary D, Aidan W, Neutrality, Ropers, Mschlindwein, Ukexpat, Dcandeto, Marine 69-71, Jh51681, Adashiel, Ginger ale, Davidstrauss, Mike Rosoft, D6, Jayjg, Freakofnurture, DanielCD, GaidinBDJ, Spiko-carpediem~enwiki, Hayford Peirce, Discospinster, Solitude, Rich Farmbrough, Pmsyyz, YUL89YYZ, User2004, Nuview, Mjpieters, Quiensabe, Antaeus Feldspar, Byrial, Bender235, ESkog, Kbh3rd, Kaisershatner, Elwikipedista~enwiki, Konstantin~enwiki, CanisRufus, Karmafist, Nickythebishop, Easyer, Shanes, Dennis Brown, Cacophony, Phiwum, Mairi, Rimshot, Causa sui, Bobo192, Circeus, J44xm, Smalljim, Func, John Vandenberg, Shenme, Cmdrjameson, Foobaz, Bill Conn, Kjkolb, LostLeviathan, Sam Korn, Amcl, Chicago god, A2Kafir, Jumbuck, Storm Rider, Alansohn, Gary, Qwe, Polarscribe, Jamyskis, Borisblue, Visviva, Inky, Andrewpmk, Minority Report, Riana, Ashley Pomeroy, Yamla, Jamiemichelle, Derumi, Goldom, SlimVirgin, Apoc2400, Fawcett5, Elchupachipmunk, Malo, Caesura, Benna, Krappie, Wtmitchell, Schapel, Velella, Bbsrock, Fourthords, Yuckfoo, RJII, Harej, Tony Sidaway, CloudNine, Anlala, GabrielF, Bookandcoffee, Tchaika, RyanGerbil10, Oleg Alexandrov, Tariqabjotu, Preost, Mwalcoff, Kelly Martin, OwenX, Woohookitty, Mindmatrix, Pinball22, Lancelottjones, Sburke, Thivierr, Swiftblade21, Mazca, Mpj17, Bratsche, Queerudite, ~Ria777~, Pogue, Mangojuice, Steinbach, GregorB, SCEhardt, Ignus, Zzyzx11, Brendanconway, Wayward, Prashanthns, Gimboid13, Exult, Mandarax, Graham87, Deltabeignet, Magister Mathematicae, BD2412, FreplySpang, Raymond Hill, OMouse, Jclemens, Kane5187, Rjwilmsi, Mayumashu, Fahrenheit451, Coemgenus, Patrick Cowsill, Nightscream, Koavf, TitaniumDreads, Vary, Ikh, Bill37212, PinchasC, Shakaka36, MZMcBride, Alvonruff, Vegaswikian, Crazynas, HappyCamper, ElKevbo, Durin, Afterwriting, The wub, Truthtell, Reinis, Nandesuka, Dar-Ape, Yamamoto Ichiro, Staples, Leithp, Drrngrvy, FlaBot, Da Stressor, Naraht, SchuminWeb, Ahasuerus, RobertG, Ground Zero, Oliver Chettle, Jak123, OgabDT, Nihiltres, JdforresterBot, Crazycomputers, SouthernNights, Nivix, AI, RexNL, Gurch, Valermos, TheDJ, Exelban, Fresheneesz, TeaDrinker, Wingsandsword, D.brodale, Alphachimp, Cpcheung, Gareth E Kegg, Sherool, Sundevilesq, Design, Bgwhite, Cactus.man, NSR, Gwernol, Former user 6, The Rambling Man, Wavelength, Crotalus horridus, Freerick, Kinneyboy90, Sceptre, Musicpvm, SpuriousQ, Chaser, RyokoMocha, Hydrargyrum, Akamad, Sneak, Gaius Cornelius, ValentinKostadinov, CambridgeBayWeather, Pseudomonas, Wikimachine, NawlinWiki, Razzledazzle, Wiki alf, BigCow, Cquan, Irishguy, Robdurbar, Brandon, Abb3w, PhilipC, Wolbo, Raven4x4x, RL0919, Jcurious, Froth, Vivaldi, MSJapan, EEMIV, Kyle Barbour, Samir, Pablomartinez, DeadEyeArrow, Psy guy, Nescio, Sebleblanc, Maunus, Bronks, Black Falcon, Alpha 4615, Wknight94, HistoricalPisces, AjaxSmack, Deeday-UK, Mholland, BazookaJoe, FF2010, Tilman, BenBildstein, Lt-wiki-bot, Thnidu, Nikkimaria, Chase me ladies, I'm the Cavalry, Jwissick, Arthur Rubin, Pb30, Chanheigeorge, Th1rt3en, Dr U, Red Jay, GinaDana, T. Anthony, Garion96, Extension, Katieh5584, Kungfuadam, Jasongetsdown, Rehevkor, Exit2DOS2000, FyzixFighter, Nick-D, Groyolo, DVD R W, CIreland, Kf4bdy, Entheta, Swpmre, Narkstraws, Grojasp, SmackBot, Looper5920, Nahald, Narf88, Ashenai, Hux, Tarret, Slashme, InverseHypercube, KnowledgeOfSelf, Olorin28, Chazz88, Bjelleklang, C.Fred, Thunderboltz, BPK2, Delldot, Sarysa, Frymaster, Lexo, HalfShadow, Yamaguchi☒☒, Aksi great, Gilliam, Truff, Ohnoitsjamie, DividedByNegativeZero, Hmains, Skizzik, ERcheck, Marc Kupper, Schmiteye, Chris the speller, Kurykh, Parmesan, Josh215, SlimJim, Cadmium, Kisholi, Achmelvic, Martyhol, JDCMAN, Jprg1966, MartinPoulter, Oli Filth, Rothery, SchfiftyThree, Stevage, Mego2005, Wikipediatrix, DoctorW, Ctbolt, Sparsefarce, Colonies Chris, Firetrap9254, Rlevse, SaintShade, Sct72, XSG, Lynchical, Lenin and McCarthy, Veggies, Muboshgu, Can't sleep, clown will eat me, Allemannster, Shalom Yechiel, Abyssal, Jwillbur, Big Cowboy Kev, OrphanBot, Racklever, The Fading Light, Addshore, Flubbit, Bolivian Unicyclist, Terryeo, Edivorce, Celarnor, Steven X, Jmlk17, Krich, Flyguy649, BesselDekker, Cybercobra, Sc00t, Nakon, Savidan, Fullstop, AndroidCat, VegaDark, Whipsandchains, FedLawyer, Daniel.o.jenkins, Austinfidel, Lcarscad, BullRangifer, Xiamcitizen, The Thing, GODSyemino, Wizardman, Lciaccio, Jitterro, Where, Johnor, CountZ, Michael IFA, Ck lostsword, Wikipedical, FelisLeo, Kukini, TTE, Drunken Pirate, Ifrit, Tesseran, Nchoe123, Thor Dockweiler, Ohconfucius, Will Beback, Evets70, Birdman1, Synthe, Judesalmon, Rory096, Nahald, Narf88, Ashenai, Hux, Tarret, Slashme, Ser Amantio di Nicolao, Rootbeerinacan, Rayonne, Srikeit, Zahid Abdassabur, Atomic23112, Kuru, John, DavidCooke, Scientizzle, Dryzen, Iglew, CPMcE, JohnCub, Bo99, Edwy, Mary Read, Sjlewis, Scetoaux, Mr. Lefty, IronGargoyle, MarkSutton, TWHansen, Pazuzu1990, STL Dilettante, Major Bonkers, Meco, SandyGeorgia, Midnightblueowl, Anonymous anonymous, Really Spooky, Ryulong, Dr.K., Citicat, MarkThomas, Johnny 0, ShakingSpirit, Amitch, Fasach Nua, BranStark, Bluefret, OnBeyondZebrax, Iridescent, JMK, Basicdesign, Makgraf, Westfall, Dave420, R~enwiki, Zero sharp, Tony Fox, HongQiGong, California guy, Dp462090, Majora4, Courcelles, GiantSnowman, Túrelio, CommunistHamster, WakiMiko, Tawkerbot2, RookZERO, Seasniffer, Dlohcierekim, Daniel5127, Cesar Tort, Zeke pbuh, JForget, Ollie, Denaar, TORR, CmdrObot, Wikiwarlock, D L Curtis, IFight, BeenAroundAWhile, Kushal one, THF, Johnalexwood, Tim Long, ShelfSkewed, BluToof, Boomdoggidogg, Lazulilasher, ONUnicorn, Karozoa, Tim1988, MobberleyKirsty, Akira1984, Chicheley, Jpierreg, Ispy1981, Stevenup7002, Moofoo, JohnJT-Smith, TheNagChampa6969, Cydebot, F montpelier, Hydraton31, JackWilliams, Peripitus, Sloeyjoey, Mike65535, Treybien, Mike Christie, Henrymrx, Cutepsychokitty, Insley, Gallup, Gogo Dodo, Bellerophon5685, Anonymi, Anthonyhcole, JFreeman, Ivant, Llort, Matt d84, Jayen466, Malcolm McPlopVtick, B, Krator, Bigjake, Tawkerbot4, UISKuwait, MatthewAJYD, DumbBOT, Olberon, SolarianKnight, Crell, Akcarver, The Mad Bomber, Chris Henniker, SuperGerbil, Paranoid123, Viridae, Kozuch, Omicronpersei8, Daniel Olsen, Algabal, Kingstowngalway, FrancoGG, Rjm656s, Thijs!bot, Epbr123, Unicyclopedia, Ultimus, CSvBibra, O, 271828182, Fredinator, Kablammo, Ucanlookitup, Keraunos, Steve Dufour, Aspectacle, Smee, Simeon H, John254, Tapir Terrific, Neil916, Woody, Patrician Vetinari, Elhector, Metatronscube6, Chavando, Nycdi, Mkamel26, Josephkuzma, Natalie Erin, Afabbro, Omaunder, Porqin, Ju66l3r, KrakatoaKatie, AntiVandalBot, The Obento Musubi, Konman72, Yonatan, Luna Santin, SickBoy, Seaphoto, Opelio, Bigtimepeace, Shirt58, EarthPerson, Casalda, Quintote, Robjessel, Nick8030, Dr who1975, Jj137, Ringdo, Tjmayerinsf, Fayenatic london, Arghlookamonkey, Tybalt1212, 0mel, JivaGoswami, Hamjamt, Bjenks, Arx Fortis, Myanw, Zagsa, MurunB, Canadian-Bacon, Golgofrinchian, MikeLynch, Fluffbrain, JAnDbot, Deflective, Husond,

Nathano235, MER-C, CosineKitty, Matthew Fennell, Instinct, Boguslinks, Niro87, Laureapuella, Bahar, Ribonucleic, Indian Overlord Xenu, Symode09, InterLNK, GoodDamon, Y2kcrazyjoker4, Psicorps, Thejax, Samthedragon, Zengar Zombolt, Magioladitis, Dsv1, Connormah, WolfmanSF, 75pickup, Parsecboy, Bongwarrior, VoABot II, Nickpheas, BenRain, Camhusmj38, MastCell, JNW, Jay Gatsby, Mbc362, Cadsuane Melaidhrin, The Enlightened, ***Ria777, Mwanzi, Prestonmcconkie, Matts30, Avicennasis, Sam Medany, BrianGV, Vitiation, Indon, JohnnyChicago, Zelator, PIrish, Cgingold, Originalname37, Sarita2380, Lethonomia, 28421u2232nfenfcenc, Allstarecho, Justanother, Elmorell, Mr. POV Vandal-Sockpuppet esquire, Fhb3, TehBrandon, Glen, DerHexer, JaGa, JIMBO WALES TOTALLY FUCKING HATES SCIENTOLOGISTS, Grunge6910, Grantsky, Coffeepusher, Johnbrownsbody, Skylights76, Bobbycgifford, Pax:Vobiscum, Jeejeee, Patstuart, Thongthoru, Quietpopcorn, BabyDweezil, Hdt83, MartinBot, Bassplayer05, Arjun01, Misou, Middlenamefrank, Foraminifera, Nachtman434, HOT L Baltimore, Lahaun, R'n'B, CommonsDelinker, Abridgetoofar, PrestonH, Tgeairn, RockMFR, Woodwardiocom, ScienoSitter, DrKay, Trusilver, Rrrobocccop, JamesR, Jdlund, Karanacs, Eliz81, Dictionar, Fubarmeister1, Senser1080, Ian.thomson, Ownage2214, Paulhorner, MartinSFSA, Bernandoo, Makoshack, GKJ~enwiki, Acalamari, Sphdjl, Dictionari, Skullketon, Fluffiliscious, JPDele2, File13, Katalaveno, Lollerskat3r, Plooft, Whatrusmokin68, Joe1141, AHSSCHOOLS, Ryan Postlethwaite, Chriseay, IliveinsalemOR, Stopsigndown, JayJasper, Floaterfluss, Plasticup, D.W. Aley, Matthardingu, DadaNeem, Tinned Elk, MKoltnow, TheScotch, Toon05, Slightlyright, Tascha96, Kibbles&fritz, Heyitspeter, Blood Fire Death, 5ft element, Son of steven, RWAtkinson, Jamesward22, Angular, Tesneddon, Nake-Blade, BrettAllen, TimonofAthens, Chankachankaboo, Tighelander, Dorftrottel, GOTMILK555, Useight, WLRoss, Jefferson Anderson, Beckyvolley, JulesVerne, Squids and Chips, Mokgen, RJASE1, Grrrilla, Fainites, Egghead06, Lights, X!, Jrugordon, 28bytes, Hammersoft, VolkovBot, JGHowes, AmesG, Totalstorage, TallNapoleon, Jmrowland, Rtrace, Alexandria, AlnoktaBOT, Majoreditor, Hjorten, Davidwr, Gtg207u, Dominics Fire, Barneca, The WikiWhippet, Philip Trueman, Photonikonman, Anynobody, Poison the Well, Mercurywoodrose, GimmeBot, Knverma, Jacob Lundberg, Ann Stouter, Z.E.R.O., Malakaville, Drestros power, BlueLint, Qxz, James.Spudeman, Rito Revolto, John Carter, Lradrama, Yilloslime, Bobbyj84, Fuckjohnnydepp, Zenswashbuckler, Ellav1187, Mardhil, LeaveSleaves, JamesReau, Wassermann~enwiki, McM.bot, Cremepuff222, S. M. Sullivan, Frater SD, Jessecorti, Robert1947, Liberal Classic, Rumiton, CSI LA, Wykypydya, Kaiketsu, Shutterbug, Chillowack, DSCramon, Dick Kimball, Plazak, RandomXYZb, Nickmiehl, Thecassowary, Y, Carinemily, Buddemeyer, P.s., Rackoflamb, Insanity Incarnate, Brianga, Zeldazackman, Truthanado, Laval, Closenplay, Rbenton, Fatassboblbbicus, NHRHS2010, Scientology-Wants-All-YOUR-MONEY, Mcrman90, Chris.lt18, Stephencolbertrox, GirasoleDE, Spoonfoon, Vasuba, Tyrnell, StAnselm, Pablo587, Stan En, Anyep, Fridago, Tresiden, Plopper, Aka1986, Tiddly Tom, Mccreedy, Scarian, WereSpielChequers, Jimboroni, Bennerz, CurranH, Vanished User 8a9b4725f8376, VolcanoXeni, Archangel 32, Tiptoety, Radon210, Exert, Arbor to SJ, Momo san, Trinen, Hagrath, Redmarkviolinist, SayNoToCults, Su-Jada, Oxymoron83, Leocomix, Android Mouse Bot 3, Lightmouse, Gitmo911, Tombomp, GrimThunderbrew, Camille32, Kmorrisk, Ahangar-e-Gaz, Starranger00, AMbot, OKBot, Kumioko (renamed), Dillard421, Jwoz 1, Maelgwnbot, Thebeatlesrule44, Jahilia, AlexCatlin, Realm of Shadows, Stevolution, Anyeverybody, Lateralis91, Altzinn, Jcdonelson, Ken123BOT, Dabomb87, Superbeecat, Pinkadelica, Hordaland, Lloydpick, Richard David Ramsey, Randy Kryn, God of Slaughter, Steveasdf, Rikkaa, Invertzoo, Faithlessthewonderboy, RegentsPark, Loren.wilton, ClueBot, Sykos1s, Artichoker, Megaman89, All Hallow's Wraith, 4077MASH, Meisterkoch, Mattgirling, SoylentGreenIsPeople91, Hypatea, Focktart74, Dean Wormer, RODERICKMOLASAR, John Sturges Jr, XBuffxSabres48x, Moskaudancer, Lord Holy Ono, Meekywiki, Tigerboy1966, Suddenrage, Drmies, Wooboo~enwiki, VQuakr, TheOldJacobite, Uncle Milty, Foofbun, Xenubox, Ted Smoove, P. S. Burton, Piledhigheranddeeper, Trivialist, Cirt, Privatemusings, Rockfang, Wikifrankk123, SamuelTheGhost, Geodyde, Masterpiece2000, Jeanenawhitney, SteveRamone, Excirial, Okysaka, Timhenderson, Butt2face, Panyd, Darkglass, Youngblues83, John Nevard, Thisisjeffsmail, Wildniggor, Zaharous, FLAGTO, Coinmanj, Biznacho, NuclearWarfare, Millionsandbillions, Razorflame, Dekisugi, El Nastro, Espang10, Whassits, Sleepless168, BOTarate, Thehelpfulone, Derflipper, Another Believer, ALL HAIL MEGATRON!, Danevansno1fan, Newport Backbay, Peregrine005, Ggreenspoon, Thingg, Hiring.bookstore, DanielW4444, JDPhD, Mikeyblueyes1988, Johnuniq, Editor2020, Classicrockfan42, DumZiBoT, Karppinen, Acis1, AgnosticPreachersKid, Pichpich, Habhab38, Truthtalker, Zechs83, Jbmweb1, Laser brain, Davethom, PopzTartz, Spider Pig, Spider Pig, does whatever a Spider Pig does, HellGuard99, Gaura79, WillOakland, Richard-of-Earth, Jprw, Doc9871, Maxj96, Incunut7, Womansworld, PhilSchabus, Colliric, Mr. Tacopants, Bobobobobobob321, Dancinmad, V5HVC074, TFBCT1, Algebran, BOBLO1356, Samueljfisher1955, Joshua Ryan Dellinger, Bob the biro, Addbot, Some jerk on the Internet, DOI bot, Ave Caesar, Tcncv, Ryman94, Metagraph, SunDragon34, MartinezMD, Startstop123, Trainrobber1974, CanadianLinuxUser, CactusWriter, MasteRic9, This is Paul, Skyezx, Bfair2mychurch, Coltey, Concernedindividual22103, Ginosbot, Jotuns, Jastudios, Elsuperbeanerman, Sogeki, GabeCorbin, Teaandbeer101, Tide rolls, Teles, Mathiasshaw, LumpyGravyFlava, MassiveSplat, LordTeringal, Bakerofclams, Vegaswikian1, Anon-russian, Legobot, Luckas-bot, Yobot, WikiDan61, JJARichardson, Legobot II, DisillusionedBitterAndKnackered, Murchadah, Mmxx, Tao2911, Armchair info guy, AnomieBOT, Krelnik, Jim1138, Paranormal Skeptic, Citation bot, ArthurBot, LovesMacs, Cliftonian, LilHelpa, Gymnophoria, Spidern, Drilnoth, Nasnema, Sellyme, Tyrol5, Shirik, Mixmoney, RibotBOT, Mvaldemar, Smallman12q, Islander99, Chaheel Riens, A.R.Isom, Cybninja, Tktru, George2001hi, FrescoBot, HJ Mitchell, Endofskull, Cannolis, Afg22948, Citation bot 1, EarwigBot, Pinethicket, Elockid, Alyeska2112, Skyerise, Jamesinderbyshire, Beao, Jujutacular, Walkabout12, Blades95, Jauhienij, White Shadows, FoxBot, Mercy11, Scythre, Taikohediyoshi, Fama Clamosa, Livingrm, Vrenator, MrX, Jeremystalked, Kitfoxxe, Canuckian89, Chronulator, Tbhotch, ArchArk~enwiki, Mean as custard, RjwilmsiBot, Bossanoven, Noommos, Balph Eubank, Slon02, EmausBot, And we drown, Mikerodeman, Ajraddatz, Osiriscorleone, Lieswell, RA0808, Jim Michael, Wikipelli, Tasbian, 15turnsm, ZéroBot, John Cline, Stellabystarlight, EmersonWhite, Fæ, A2soup, Eggilicious, MithrandirAgain, Érico, AvicAWB, Access Denied, H3llBot, Burbridge92, Wayne Slam, Ocaasi, Rcsprinter123, Intelligentsock, Alex0408, Julierbutler, RaqiwasSushi, L Kensington, Bryman27, Oldschoolrider, Warren A. Paexed, Carmichael, Ego White Tray, Sugar-Baby-Love, Themanwiththemagichat, Digitalshiner, Echobase99, 1qaz0okm13, Tolesi, Anonymous1239, Forever Dusk, ResidentAnthropologist, CharlieEchoTango, ClueBot NG, Fluttershy~enwiki, Mrsbrinker326, Aaron Booth, Prioryman, Peter James, Tanbircdq, Intromcs, Satellizer, Baseball Watcher, NestleNW911, Millermk, Cntras, Gekk00, Helatrobus, Bob House 884, Donkeyshmex1, Saywhatnow, Helpful Pixie Bot, Frogglish, Calabe1992, Wbm1058, Lowercase sigmabot, Qbgeekjtw, Pvgreenzebra, Sww1rb, Thunderchunqy, Nathan2055, Metricopolus, BizarreLoveTriangle, Mark Arsten, Pushp vashisht, Dkspartan1, AvalidContribution, F0shizil, Flaskit, Flaskit1, MrBill3, Mafres, Wilhelm666666, Achowat, Anbu121, Fylbecatulous, Guarosipper, Avalon636, Bundleofjoy, Systems Theorist, Sfarney, Axioanimus, Ruready12, Luke 19 Verse 27, ChrisGualtieri, Myxomatosis57, John from Idegon, LokeÞórr, SD5bot, Khazar2, Ducknish, The User 567, Futurist110, Co$lol12341, CarolinaDove, Linkubus06, Webclient101, Lightning230, TwoTwoHello, Lugia2453, VIAFbot, Klebble, Glegbowl Clegwhello, Knevbol Bnebwevvo, Rednello Plezbello, Pezbello Credwello, Mknjbhvgcf, Mr Marrmite, East Wello, Sock Puppet 2013, Keefta, Redvsblue42, Ilacin, Poooooooopascoopa, Poooooooopascoopa, Red-eyed demon, Poooooooooopascoopa, Percy the Plopper, Kurfk, Hemmersuft, Klevbo Pedwezzle, Ploofglug, Bahooka, Pietro13, Inanygivenhole, Spaceboyjosh, SNUGGUMS, Archlinux, Literally Satan, DustBowlTroubadour, MagicatthemovieS, Agroupaccount, LordFixit, SkateTier, Stomachinknots, DrSocPsych, At252wikie, Feoffer, KasparBot, Benjetson and Anonymous: 1262

- **Christopher Hyatt** *Source:* https://en.wikipedia.org/wiki/Christopher_Hyatt?oldid=678171584 *Contributors:* David Gerard, Smalljim, BenM, Hanuman Das, Woohookitty, Niffweed17, Rjwilmsi, TheRingess, FlaBot, Moocha, Korg, 999~enwiki, Anders.Warga, Danharms, SmackBot, Frasor, Betacommand, Chris the speller, Berney, Roman Spinner, Meco, Lucian Gregory, CmdrObot, Patternhunter, ST47, Synergy, TheJC, Raistlin Majere, Zappernapper, Alphachimpbot, Mobiusframe, Magioladitis, Waacstats, Aboutmovies, Chaosagent68, Fleela, TheWikiWiki, Altzinn, SpiderMum, Stealthepiscopalian, TheRedPenOfDoom, Thehelpfulone, DumZiBoT, RogDel, Good Olfactory, Kbdankbot, Addbot, Lightbot, Yobot, Gongshow, Eduen, AnomieBOT, Citation bot, J04n, Rodneyorpheus, Aleister Wilson, Skyerise, BigDwiki, Trappist the monk, RjwilmsiBot, CragJensen, Helpful Pixie Bot, AdventurousSquirrel, Hmainsbot1, Monkbot, New Falcon Publications, AnthonyBaldwin, KasparBot and Anonymous: 19

- **Richard Kaczynski** *Source:* https://en.wikipedia.org/wiki/Richard_Kaczynski?oldid=685662226 *Contributors:* Eep², Xezbeth, MBisanz, Stesmo, Hanuman Das, Calton, Gene Nygaard, 999~enwiki, Pigman, CorbieVreccan, SmackBot, BostonMA, Ser Amantio di Nicolao, Ekajati, Waacstats, Rosencomet, Timmy12, Thiebes, Johnpacklambert, MaxReg, Varnent, IPSOS, John Carter, Thehelpfulone, Dthomsen8, Will in China, Good Olfactory, MuZemike, Yobot, Aldebaran66, AnomieBOT, Rodneyorpheus, Aleister Wilson, Skyerise, RjwilmsiBot, Polisher of Cobwebs, CactusBot, Helpful Pixie Bot, VIAFbot, Pola.mola, Kennethaw88, KasparBot and Anonymous: 1

- **Carl Kellner (mystic)** *Source:* https://en.wikipedia.org/wiki/Carl_Kellner_(mystic)?oldid=682376201 *Contributors:* Babbage, Lupo, Ashami, Rich Farmbrough, Hanuman Das, Woohookitty, Rjwilmsi, FlaBot, YurikBot, 999~enwiki, RussBot, Pigman, MSJapan, SmackBot, Jprg1966, Imacomp, DabMachine, Catherineyronwode, Drinibot, Dave Null, Liberal Freemason, Cydebot, Synergy, Bookworm857158367, IPSOS, John Carter, Alabaster Crow, Monegasque, Ottawahitech, JDPhD, Dthomsen8, Addbot, Lightbot, Yobot, GrouchoBot, Omnipaedista, Rodneyorpheus, Aleister Wilson, Kwiki, Peterrivington, RjwilmsiBot, The Traditionalist, BattyBot, VIAFbot, Baby Hayes, KasparBot and Anonymous: 4

- **Liber OZ** *Source:* https://en.wikipedia.org/wiki/Liber_OZ?oldid=684004932 *Contributors:* Ukexpat, Bgwhite, GeoffCapp, Colonies Chris, Alaibot, Jgbell, SpiderMum, Harbard the Ancient, Random Fixer Of Things, Good Olfactory, Addbot, Sikovin, Yobot, Rodneyorpheus, Aleister Wilson, Helpful Pixie Bot, Futuri, BattyBot, Registered somethin and Anonymous: 5

- **Liber XV, The Gnostic Mass** *Source:* https://en.wikipedia.org/wiki/Liber_XV%2C_The_Gnostic_Mass?oldid=672189870 *Contributors:* Fibonacci, Ashami, Andy Smith, Alai, 999~enwiki, Pigman, Asarelah, GeoffCapp, SmackBot, Colonies Chris, JoeBot, CapitalR, Synergy, Psuliin, John254, Pixiebat, R'n'B, Tgeairn, Adavidb, AntiSpamBot, IPSOS, John Carter, Alabaster Crow, SpiderMum, Valtyr, Good Olfactory, Addbot, Lightbot, Yobot, AnomieBOT, LilHelpa, Tahuti418, Rodneyorpheus, Aleister Wilson, Skyerise, Mk5384, Theseus1776, Ben Ammi, Manytexts, Helpful Pixie Bot, SofiaCantor, PhnomPencil, Drift chambers, BattyBot, Jayaguru-Shishya, One-one-one-fool and Anonymous: 23

- **Grady Louis McMurtry** *Source:* https://en.wikipedia.org/wiki/Grady_Louis_McMurtry?oldid=686234746 *Contributors:* Pseudo daoist, HarryHenryGebel, Altenmann, Ashami, Pyrop, Jpgordon, Hanuman Das, Anlala, Mandarax, Rjwilmsi, Somecallmetim, 999~enwiki, Bachrach44, GeoffCapp, SmackBot, Huon, Ser Amantio di Nicolao, CapitalR, Cydebot, Frater5, JustAGal, Captainbarrett, TLF93, Waacstats, Mercurywoodrose, Steven J. Anderson, John Carter, Kumioko (renamed), Cyfal, ImageRemovalBot, Stealthepiscopalian, Good Olfactory, Tassedethe, Lightbot, Xqbot, Mvaldemar, Moxy, Rodneyorpheus, Aleister Wilson, RjwilmsiBot, Theseus1776, Gmcmurtry, The Traditionalist, Gerald Edward Cornelius, Barrettdylanbrown and Anonymous: 21

- **Noname Jane** *Source:* https://en.wikipedia.org/wiki/Noname_Jane?oldid=685996697 *Contributors:* WhisperToMe, Topbanana, Naufana, Mboverload, Golbez, Phil1988, CALR, Brianhe, Kross, Haham hanuka, Rebroad, Grenavitar, Gene Nygaard, K3rb, Nightstallion, Dismas, Joe Beaudoin Jr., Starwed, Dysepsion, BD2412, Tabercil, Rjwilmsi, Koavf, FlaBot, Draven5, YurikBot, RobbieNomi, 999~enwiki, RussBot, CambridgeBayWeather, A314268, Jaxl, ONEder Boy, BOT-Superzerocool, Asarelah, NickD, Zzuuzz, Closedmouth, Dark Tichondrias, Scoutersig, Garion96, EdgarAllanToe, SmackBot, BenBurch, Kurykh, Udansk, CSWarren, Nakon, Pinworm, Jcurtis, AnonEMouse, Dubthach, Ale jrb, Iafd staff, DeadLeafEcho, Irishninja1980, Cydebot, Wikien2009, Argus fin, Bigtakeshi, Epbr123, Philippe, Armpitso, .anacondabot, Wildhartlivie, Hullaballoo Wolfowitz, Waacstats, GrammarNSpellChecker, Lord Love a Duck, Jy90274, Joie de Vivre, LethalSRX, LabFox, IPSOS, AjitPD, Bluedenim, RalphHogaboom, HTurtle, RozzWilliams, OKBot, Kumioko (renamed), Videmus Omnia, JohnnyMrNinja, Organicmiser, Mfregeau, Badger Drink, MikeVitale, Photouploaded, Morbidthoughts, Nymf, PixelBot, Takeshiito, Groval, Scalhotrod, XLinkBot, King Willan Bot~enwiki, MystBot, Good Olfactory, Bazj, Addbot, JBsupreme, Kelly, BecauseWhy?, Whistling42, Yobot, Guy1890, AnomieBOT, Ufoalien, Materialscientist, Julle, J04n, Youngtee99, Rodneyorpheus, Skyerise, 12er, RjwilmsiBot, EmausBot, Erpert, SporkBot, DASHBot~tAV, ATX-NL, Kaltenmeyer, Qetuth, BattyBot, Winkelvi, Rebecca1990, Hanswar32, Casbufo, ID man12 ID and Anonymous: 60

- **Sara Northrup Hollister** *Source:* https://en.wikipedia.org/wiki/Sara_Northrup_Hollister?oldid=689710389 *Contributors:* Shsilver, Gabbe, Huangdi, Bearcat, ChrisO~enwiki, Moriori, Antaeus Feldspar, Bender235, Bustter, Jeodesic, Gargaj, Philip Cross, Koavf, MZMcBride, Design, Bgwhite, Gadget850, Caerwine, Garion96, SmackBot, Groon, Stifle, Chris the speller, Sadads, AndroidCat, Wizardman, Ser Amantio di Nicolao, Tony Fox, Fvasconcellos, CmdrObot, Cydebot, Steve Dufour, Smee, TangentCube, Waacstats, Misou, CommonsDelinker, WKCole, S. M. Sullivan, GlassFET, Laval, Alex Middleton, ImageRemovalBot, P. S. Burton, Cirt, Mallamace, Karppinen, Yobot, Estudiarme, Ulric1313, Ruby2010, Jezhotwells, Skyerise, RjwilmsiBot, CrimsonBot, Prioryman, Calliopesdaughter, Helpful Pixie Bot, BattyBot, SD5bot, Knevbol Bnebwevvo, Thomas Kreitmayer, Feoffer, StressOverStrain, Dalek Supreme X and Anonymous: 13

- **Rodney Orpheus** *Source:* https://en.wikipedia.org/wiki/Rodney_Orpheus?oldid=670207884 *Contributors:* Timrollpickering, Bender235, Woohookitty, SmackBot, JD, Colonies Chris, Ohconfucius, Mark999, Neelix, Cydebot, Doug Weller, Fayenatic london, Michig, Waacstats, Sjones23, Billinghurst, Phil Bridger, Beeblebrox, ClueBot, Lame Name, SchreiberBike, Subversive.sound, Yobot, AnomieBOT, Erik9bot, Rodneyorpheus, Aleister Wilson, Citation bot 1, Skyerise, Alphaspagbol, RjwilmsiBot, TribalLover121, Theseus1776, Beetlehive, Helpful Pixie Bot, BattyBot, VIAFbot, Monkbot, YL EP, KasparBot and Anonymous: 8

- **Jack Parsons (rocket engineer)** *Source:* https://en.wikipedia.org/wiki/Jack_Parsons_(rocket_engineer)?oldid=689527975 *Contributors:* Mav, Shsilver, Fubar Obfusco, Maury Markowitz, Stevertigo, Skysmith, Ihcoyc, Ronabop, Emperor, Andrewa, Maxomai, Dysprosia, Gestumblindi, Phil Boswell, Pigsonthewing, ChrisO~enwiki, Cljohnston108, Ray Radlein, Auric, Orangemike, Everyking, Gamaliel, DO'Neil, Iceberg3k, Gary D, Ukexpat, RevRagnarok, Ashami, D6, Discospinster, Brianhe, NeuronExMachina, User2004, Antaeus Feldspar, Bender235, GabrielAPetrie, Jpgordon, Cavrdg, JesseHogan, Philip Cross, Labyrinth13, Woohookitty, Etacar11, DESiegel, Graham87, Rjwilmsi, Koavf, Vegaswikian, Paul Hope, Ground Zero, Mark Sublette, Korg, Bgwhite, 999~enwiki, RussBot, Pigman, Hawkeye7, Jpbowen, Be3n, RUL3R, Ospalh, Morgan Leigh, GeoffCapp, Caerwine, Crisco 1492, 2over0, Geoffrey.landis, Sepand, JDspeeder1, SmackBot, Pmw2cc, Ssbohio,

Groon, Ian Rose, Dwain, Chris the speller, SlimJim, John Reaves, Mike hayes, OrphanBot, Rainbowpickett, AndroidCat, Vertigo Acid, Will Beback, Ser Amantio di Nicolao, Gobonobo, NYCJosh, Runningfridgesrule, Mr Stephen, Meco, Midnightblueowl, E-Kartoffel, Fluppy, Liddell, Hu12, Norm mit, ISD, Amakuru, GiantSnowman, Unidyne, ZICO, BullyTheLittleStuffedBull, Penbat, Cydebot, Boboroshi, Thijs!bot, Eggsyntax, Bethpage89, RobotG, Widefox, LDGE, Tillman, Vivelequebeclibre, Xeno, Rothgate, Magioladitis, Waacstats, Nyttend, SlamDiego, Luminousball, Uncle uncle uncle, Skeptic2, Gypsydoctor, KD Tries Again, BrettAllen, Georgemorgan, Squids and Chips, Hirolovesswords, Sdsds, Suprah, IPSOS, Secrowl, AZJustice, Flagman7, Andy Dingley, Jpeeling, The News Hound, AlleborgoBot, Dariusk, Deconstructhis, 1947project, BotMultichill, Leocomix, JohnSawyer, Adam Cuerden, Anyeverybody, Randy Kryn, ClueBot, Gene93k, The Thing That Should Not Be, All Hallow's Wraith, Franamax, Drmies, Niceguyedc, Cirt, Excirial, Jack-A-Roe, Chaosdruid, Dank, JDPhD, XLinkBot, Laser brain, WillOakland, Good Olfactory, Addbot, Baffle gab1978, TriniMuñoz, OlEnglish, Legobot, Yobot, JJARichardson, Victoriaearle, AnomieBOT, Allknowingallseeing, RobertEves92, Citation bot, Ruby2010, Adam9389, Rodneyorpheus, Aleister Wilson, Citation bot 1, Scribemole, Hillarin, Skyerise, ZodKneelsFirst, Barras, Cnwilliams, RjwilmsiBot, Chuck Baggett, SporkBot, 93rdMaster, Manytexts, Rememberway, TheConduqtor, BarrelProof, Reify-tech, Alyzabeth, Helpful Pixie Bot, Wbm1058, BG19bot, Mark Arsten, Dayahead, BattyBot, Bloomm02, Khazar2, Mogism, VIAFbot, Jamesx12345, Ruby Murray, Jamesmcmahon0, Deverestackpole, StraightOuttaBrisbane, AfadsBad, Antikhristos, Filedelinkerbot, TheMagikCow, FACBot, KasparBot, Trusty librarian and Anonymous: 129

- **Theodor Reuss** *Source:* https://en.wikipedia.org/wiki/Theodor_Reuss?oldid=688498665 *Contributors:* Warofdreams, Lupo, Pitchka, Ashami, Hanuman Das, Scriberius, Isomeme, Sburke, NoPuzzleStranger, Wikix, Rjwilmsi, Koavf, Scott Mingus, 999~enwiki, Leutha, GeoffCapp, Allens, Meegs, SmackBot, Colonies Chris, Ser Amantio di Nicolao, Imacomp, Meco, Violncello, Quaeler, Catherineyronwode, Cydebot, Synergy, Boboroshi, Thijs!bot, Bookworm857158367, Skomorokh, Waacstats, Sagabot, IPSOS, John Carter, JhsBot, Synthebot, Brenont, Abuldiz, Stealthepiscopalian, Good Olfactory, Addbot, CarsracBot, Lightbot, LilHelpa, Omnipaedista, Scuffy05, Rodneyorpheus, Aleister Wilson, RedBot, Full-date unlinking bot, RjwilmsiBot, The Traditionalist, Khazar2, Urbanastronaut, VIAFbot, Robert4565, Johnsoniensis, KasparBot and Anonymous: 18

- **Saints of Ecclesia Gnostica Catholica** *Source:* https://en.wikipedia.org/wiki/Saints_of_Ecclesia_Gnostica_Catholica?oldid=668791050 *Contributors:* William Avery, JackofOz, Kwamikagami, QuartierLatin1968, Hanuman Das, Vicxanulo, Isomeme, Mandarax, 999~enwiki, RussBot, Lusanaherandraton, SigPig, GeoffCapp, SmackBot, Bluebot, Scwlong, CapitalR, Jbolden1517, AndrewHowse, Khem Caigan, Frater5, Sororyzbl, Aervanath, Ansat, Jefferson Anderson, Deor, John Carter, Komusou, AntonChanning, SpiderMum, Stealthepiscopalian, Skittleydoober, Dusen189, XLinkBot, Melodious Monk, Will in China, Addbot, Yobot, AnomieBOT, Anonymous from the 21st century, FrescoBot, Rodneyorpheus, Aleister Wilson, Theseus1776, Justlettersandnumbers, The Traditionalist, Jayaguru-Shishya and Anonymous: 17

- **Phyllis Seckler** *Source:* https://en.wikipedia.org/wiki/Phyllis_Seckler?oldid=684702500 *Contributors:* Rich Farmbrough, Bender235, Redvers, 999~enwiki, GeoffCapp, Sticky Parkin, Groon, Bluebot, Amalas, Synergy, Blacklake, Waacstats, IPSOS, SchreiberBike, Revealer93, RogDel, Good Olfactory, Cunard, Addbot, Lightbot, Yobot, Citation bot, J04n, Rodneyorpheus, Aleister Wilson, Skyerise, Aiwass888, RjwilmsiBot, Autumnalmonk, Helpful Pixie Bot, Duckduckstop, Monkbot and Anonymous: 8

- **Wilfred Talbot Smith** *Source:* https://en.wikipedia.org/wiki/Wilfred_Talbot_Smith?oldid=624786818 *Contributors:* Racklever, Ohconfucius, Mr Stephen, Midnightblueowl, J Milburn, Drpickem, JJARichardson, Lightlowemon, Mogism, Taylor Trescott, OccultZone and Vieque

- **James Wasserman** *Source:* https://en.wikipedia.org/wiki/James_Wasserman?oldid=660509232 *Contributors:* Deb, Bearcat, Joe Roe, RussBot, Chris the speller, Seide, Jarkeld, Waacstats, Deepseabattles, M.O.X, Chzz, Tassedethe, Yobot, AnomieBOT, Rodneyorpheus, Skyerise, RjwilmsiBot, Alpha Quadrant, Demiurge1000, Helpful Pixie Bot, Tashif, SofiaCantor, Hewhoamareismyself, Stamptrader, Repeatper and Anonymous: 4

- **Jane Wolfe** *Source:* https://en.wikipedia.org/wiki/Jane_Wolfe?oldid=686653686 *Contributors:* Bearcat, Academic Challenger, ErikNY, Sam, Hanuman Das, Arthur Warrington Thomas, Ted Wilkes, Snake666, 999~enwiki, ExRat, BirgitteSB, Anetode, Tony1, GeoffCapp, Pegship, Attilios, SmackBot, Betacommand, Ser Amantio di Nicolao, BrownHairedGirl, Roman Spinner, Amalas, Frater5, Jj137, Waacstats, CommonsDelinker, Johnpacklambert, Koplimek, Crakkpot, Squids and Chips, IPSOS, John Carter, Wedg~enwiki, Monegasque, Deanlaw, Good Olfactory, Yobot, Aleister Wilson, Skyerise, RjwilmsiBot, Autumnalmonk, Stomper 33, Vladislav0, Manytexts, Ca93 and Anonymous: 5

29.10.2 Images

- **File:Aleister_Crowley'{}s_May_Morn.jpg** *Source:* https://upload.wikimedia.org/wikipedia/en/3/34/Aleister_Crowley%27s_May_Morn.jpg *License:* PD-US *Contributors:* ? *Original artist:* ?

- **File:Aleister_Crowley,_Golden_Dawn.jpg** *Source:* https://upload.wikimedia.org/wikipedia/en/e/ec/Aleister_Crowley%2C_Golden_Dawn.jpg *License:* PD-US *Contributors:*
Used in publicity material for The Rites of Eleusis in 1910 (see deletion discussion). Photograph originally uploaded to Commons by Commons user Dnaspark99 as Commons:File:Aleister Crowley, Golden Dawn.jpg, but now deleted. *Original artist:*
Unknown

- **File:Aleister_Crowley,_Magus.png** *Source:* https://upload.wikimedia.org/wikipedia/en/a/a7/Aleister_Crowley%2C_Magus.png *License:* PD-US *Contributors:*
Book 4, Part 2 (1912). See deletion discussion. Originally uploaded to Commons by Commons user Dnaspark99 as Commons:File:Aleister Crowley, Magus.png, but now deleted. *Original artist:*
Unknown

- **File:Aleister_Crowley,_wickedest_man_in_the_world.jpg** *Source:* https://upload.wikimedia.org/wikipedia/en/7/7e/Aleister_Crowley.jpg *License:* PD-US *Contributors:*
Originally published in *The Equinox* volume 1, issue 10 (1913) (see deletion discussion). This version taken from "Book 4, Part 2" by uploader Commons user Dnaspark99. Originally uploaded at Commons as Commons:File:Aleister Crowley, wickedest man in the world.jpg, but now deleted. *Original artist:*
Unknown

- **File:Aleister_Crowley_1902_K2.jpg** *Source:* https://upload.wikimedia.org/wikipedia/commons/4/47/Aleister_Crowley_1902_K2.jpg *License:* Public domain *Contributors:* http://www.letemps.ch/Page/Uuid/3e54419e-16f2-11e2-9647-3f362e417c28/En_1902_Jules_Jacot_Guillarmod_pionnier_au_K2#.UIBKQBJ5MxC *Original artist:* Jules Jacot Guillarmod (24 December 1868 – 5 June 1925)

- **File:Ambox_important.svg** *Source:* https://upload.wikimedia.org/wikipedia/commons/b/b4/Ambox_important.svg *License:* Public domain *Contributors:* Own work, based off of Image:Ambox scales.svg *Original artist:* Dsmurat (talk · contribs)

- **File:Bio-papus-image-1.jpg** *Source:* https://upload.wikimedia.org/wikipedia/commons/b/b3/Bio-papus-image-1.jpg *License:* Public domain *Contributors:* Biographies *Original artist:* Deucaleon

- **File:Bundesarchiv_Bild_137-031735,_Tsingtau,_Teilansicht.jpg** *Source:* https://upload.wikimedia.org/wikipedia/commons/7/7a/Bundesarchiv_Bild_137-031735%2C_Tsingtau%2C_Teilansicht.jpg *License:* CC BY-SA 3.0 de *Contributors:* This image was provided to Wikimedia Commons by the German Federal Archive (Deutsches Bundesarchiv) as part of a cooperation project. The German Federal Archive guarantees an authentic representation only using the originals (negative and/or positive), resp. the digitalization of the originals as provided by the Digital Image Archive. *Original artist:* Unknown

- **File:COLLECTIE_TROPENMUSEUM_Een_Ibu_Dajak_krijger_uit_Long_Nawan_Z._en_O._afdeling_Borneo._TMnr_60034031.jpg** *Source:* https://upload.wikimedia.org/wikipedia/commons/3/36/COLLECTIE_TROPENMUSEUM_Een_Ibu_Dajak_krijger_uit_Long_Nawan_Z._en_O._afdeling_Borneo._TMnr_60034031.jpg *License:* CC BY-SA 3.0 *Contributors:* Tropenmuseum <a href='//commons.wikimedia.org/wiki/Institution:Tropenmuseum' title='Link back to Institution infobox template'><img alt='Link back to Institution infobox template' src='https://upload.wikimedia.org/wikipedia/commons/thumb/7/73/Blue_pencil.svg/15px-Blue_pencil.svg.png' width='15' height='15' srcset='https://upload.wikimedia.org/wikipedia/commons/thumb/7/73/Blue_pencil.svg/23px-Blue_pencil.svg.png 1.5x, https://upload.wikimedia.org/wikipedia/commons/thumb/7/73/Blue_pencil.svg/30px-Blue_pencil.svg.png 2x' data-file-width='600' data-file-height='600' /></a> <a href='//www.wikidata.org/wiki/Q1131589' title='wikidata:Q1131589'><img alt='wikidata:Q1131589' src='https://upload.wikimedia.org/wikipedia/commons/thumb/f/ff/Wikidata-logo.svg/20px-Wikidata-logo.svg.png' width='20' height='11' srcset='https://upload.wikimedia.org/wikipedia/commons/thumb/f/ff/Wikidata-logo.svg/30px-Wikidata-logo.svg.png 1.5x, https://upload.wikimedia.org/wikipedia/commons/thumb/f/ff/Wikidata-logo.svg/40px-Wikidata-logo.svg.png 2x' data-file-width='1050' data-file-height='590' /></a> *Original artist:* Ishikane (Fotograaf/photographer).

- **File:Cartier_Fear_illo_Unknown_July_1940.jpg** *Source:* https://upload.wikimedia.org/wikipedia/commons/5/5d/Cartier_Fear_illo_Unknown_July_1940.jpg *License:* Public domain *Contributors:*

- Immediate source: Nicholls, Peter (1978). *The Encyclopedia of Science Fiction*. London: Granada. ISBN 0-586-05380-8. P. 108. *Original artist:* Edd Cartier. Copyright was either Cartier, or more likely Street & Smith, who published the magazine.

- **File:Church_of_Spiritual_Technology_ranch_Creston.jpg** *Source:* https://upload.wikimedia.org/wikipedia/commons/1/16/Church_of_Spiritual_Technology_ranch_Creston.jpg *License:* CC BY-SA 2.0 *Contributors:* http://www.flickr.com/photos/vision_aerie/5790822/in/photostream/ *Original artist:* Dean Cully

- **File:CityofCorfu.jpg** *Source:* https://upload.wikimedia.org/wikipedia/commons/1/1c/CityofCorfu.jpg *License:* CC BY-SA 3.0 *Contributors:* Own work *Original artist:* Edal Anton Lefterov

- **File:Commons-logo.svg** *Source:* https://upload.wikimedia.org/wikipedia/en/4/4a/Commons-logo.svg *License:* ? *Contributors:* ? *Original artist:* ?

- **File:Crowley_unicursal_hexagram.svg** *Source:* https://upload.wikimedia.org/wikipedia/commons/4/4c/Crowley_unicursal_hexagram.svg *License:* Public domain *Contributors:* Own work *Original artist:* Elembis

- **File:Dark_Angel.png** *Source:* https://upload.wikimedia.org/wikipedia/en/5/54/Dark_Angel.png *License:* Fair use *Contributors:* **Original publication**: Year painted unknown

  Immediate source: http://www.cameron-parsons.org/jackparsons.html# *Original artist:* Marjorie Cameron

- **File:First_JATO_assisted_Flight_-_GPN-2000-001538.jpg** *Source:* https://upload.wikimedia.org/wikipedia/commons/f/fd/First_JATO_assisted_Flight_-_GPN-2000-001538.jpg *License:* Public domain *Contributors:* Great Images in NASA Description *Original artist:* NASA/JPL

- **File:Flag_of_California.svg** *Source:* https://upload.wikimedia.org/wikipedia/commons/0/01/Flag_of_California.svg *License:* Public domain *Contributors:* Own work *Original artist:* Devin Cook

- **File:Flag_of_Germany.svg** *Source:* https://upload.wikimedia.org/wikipedia/en/b/ba/Flag_of_Germany.svg *License:* PD *Contributors:* ? *Original artist:* ?

- **File:Flag_of_the_United_States.svg** *Source:* https://upload.wikimedia.org/wikipedia/en/a/a4/Flag_of_the_United_States.svg *License:* PD *Contributors:* ? *Original artist:* ?

- **File:Folder_Hexagonal_Icon.svg** *Source:* https://upload.wikimedia.org/wikipedia/en/4/48/Folder_Hexagonal_Icon.svg *License:* Cc-by-sa-3.0 *Contributors:* ? *Original artist:* ?

- **File:Gardner_and_Com.jpg** *Source:* https://upload.wikimedia.org/wikipedia/en/8/80/Gardner_and_Com.jpg *License:* Public domain *Contributors:* ? *Original artist:* ?

- **File:GeraldBrosseauGardnerPlaque.jpg** *Source:* https://upload.wikimedia.org/wikipedia/commons/0/07/GeraldBrosseauGardnerPlaque.jpg *License:* CC BY-SA 3.0 *Contributors:* Open Plaques donation *Original artist:* Centre For Pagan Studies

- **File:Gerryarmstrong-2004-07-05.jpg** *Source:* https://upload.wikimedia.org/wikipedia/commons/e/ef/Gerryarmstrong-2004-07-05.jpg *License:* CC-BY-SA-3.0 *Contributors:* Transferred from en.wikipedia to Commons by Cirt using CommonsHelper. *Original artist:* Gerry Armstrong at English Wikipedia

- **File:Grady_Louis_McMurtry_1941.JPG** *Source:* https://upload.wikimedia.org/wikipedia/commons/5/5b/Grady_Louis_McMurtry_1941.JPG *License:* Public domain *Contributors:* http://www.cornelius93.com/Grady-IdentificationCards-WWII.html *Original artist:* United States Department of War

- **File:Hubbard_and_moulton.jpg** *Source:* https://upload.wikimedia.org/wikipedia/commons/d/d3/Hubbard_and_moulton.jpg *License:* Public domain *Contributors:* From the *Oregon Journal*, April 22, 1943: "Ex-Portlander Hunts U-Boats" *Original artist:* Oregon Journal staff
- **File:IRS_building_on_constitution_avenue_in_DC.jpg** *Source:* https://upload.wikimedia.org/wikipedia/commons/8/80/IRS_building_on_constitution_avenue_in_DC.jpg *License:* Public domain *Contributors:* http://www.ustreas.gov/offices/management/curator/exhibitions/openspace/board_8/ezw1.jpg *Original artist:* US Federal Govt employee
- **File:JATO_Flight_Test_Crew_-_GPN-2000-001537.jpg** *Source:* https://upload.wikimedia.org/wikipedia/commons/3/39/JATO_Flight_Test_Crew_-_GPN-2000-001537.jpg *License:* Public domain *Contributors:* Great Images in NASA Description *Original artist:* NASA/JPL
- **File:JATO_unit.jpg** *Source:* https://upload.wikimedia.org/wikipedia/commons/a/a9/JATO_unit.jpg *License:* Public domain *Contributors:* http://airandspace.si.edu/explore-and-learn/multimedia/detail.cfm?id=A19510046000&file=A19510046000cp001.jpg&name=Rocket%20Motor%2C%20Solid%20Fuel%2C%20JATO%2C%208AS-1000%20%28Jet-Assisted-Take-Off%29%20Unit *Original artist:* Smithsonian National Air and Space Museum
- **File:JPL1942.jpg** *Source:* https://upload.wikimedia.org/wikipedia/commons/a/a2/JPL1942.jpg *License:* Public domain *Contributors:* https://archive.org/details/GPN-2003-00059 *Original artist:* George Emerson
- **File:JackParsons3.jpg** *Source:* https://upload.wikimedia.org/wikipedia/commons/f/f5/JackParsons3.jpg *License:* Public domain *Contributors:* Los Angeles Times. This image is published in John Carter's *Sex and Rockets: The Occult World of Jack Parsons* without attribution (2004, p. 187) and appears on the front cover of George Pendle's *Strange Angel: The Otherworldly Life of Rocket Scientist John Whiteside Parsons* (2005) also without a copyright notice, indicating that it is in the public domain. *Original artist:* Anonymous
- **File:Jack_Parsons.jpg** *Source:* https://upload.wikimedia.org/wikipedia/commons/0/09/Jack_Parsons.jpg *License:* Public domain *Contributors:* John Carter's 1999 book, *Sex and Rockets: The Occult World of Jack Parsons*, attributes this photograph to the Jet Propulsion Laboratory archive. It is used in NASA/JPL multimedia. *Original artist:* NASA/JPL
- **File:Jack_Parsons_FBI.jpg** *Source:* https://upload.wikimedia.org/wikipedia/commons/5/5a/Jack_Parsons_FBI.jpg *License:* Public domain *Contributors:* http://kernelmag.dailydot.com/features/report/8557/jack-parsons-rocket-pioneer-and-occult-genius/ *Original artist:* Federal Bureau of Investigation
- **File:Jane_Wolfe_Cefalù.jpg** *Source:* https://upload.wikimedia.org/wikipedia/en/3/3f/Jane_Wolfe_Cefal%C3%B9.jpg *License:* PD-US *Contributors:*
Digital reproduction or scan of original photo.
Under US laws mechanical reproduction of a work does not create an additional copyright to that of the original.
Original artist: ?
- **File:Jet_Propulsion_Laboratory_logo.svg** *Source:* https://upload.wikimedia.org/wikipedia/commons/c/c6/Jet_Propulsion_Laboratory_logo.svg *License:* Public domain *Contributors:* Transferred from en.wikipedia *Original artist:* Original uploader was King of Hearts at en.wikipedia
- **File:Kanchenjunga_India.jpg** *Source:* https://upload.wikimedia.org/wikipedia/commons/3/37/Kanchenjunga_India.jpg *License:* CC BY-SA 2.0 *Contributors:* originally posted to **Flickr** as Kangchenjunga, Indian Himalaya *Original artist:* Aaron Ostrovsky
- **File:Kellner.jpg** *Source:* https://upload.wikimedia.org/wikipedia/commons/5/5f/Kellner.jpg *License:* Public domain *Contributors:* oto-usa.org *Original artist:* Unknown
- **File:Ketchikan_AK.jpg** *Source:* https://upload.wikimedia.org/wikipedia/commons/1/1c/Ketchikan_AK.jpg *License:* CC BY-SA 2.5 *Contributors:* Transferred from en.wikipedia *Original artist:* Original uploader was MLBbrad at en.wikipedia
- **File:Kris_display.jpg** *Source:* https://upload.wikimedia.org/wikipedia/commons/b/bb/Kris_display.jpg *License:* CC BY-SA 2.0 *Contributors:* ? *Original artist:* ?
- **File:L._Ron_Hubbard.jpg** *Source:* https://upload.wikimedia.org/wikipedia/commons/a/aa/L._Ron_Hubbard.jpg *License:* Public domain *Contributors:* From the *Oregon Journal*, April 22, 1943: "Ex-Portlander Hunts U-Boats" via Hubbard_and_moulton.jpg *Original artist:* Hubbard_and_moult Oregon Journal staff
- **File:L._Ron_Hubbard_House_-_Dupont_Circle.JPG** *Source:* https://upload.wikimedia.org/wikipedia/commons/8/8d/L._Ron_Hubbard_House_-_Dupont_Circle.JPG *License:* CC BY-SA 3.0 *Contributors:* Transferred from en.wikipedia; transferred to Commons by User:Leoboudv using CommonsHelper. *Original artist:* AgnosticPreachersKid
- **File:L._Ron_Hubbard_Signature.svg** *Source:* https://upload.wikimedia.org/wikipedia/commons/f/f2/L._Ron_Hubbard_Signature.svg *License:* Public domain *Contributors:* File:L. Ron Hubbard signature.gif *Original artist:* L. Ron Hubbard
- **File:L._Ron_Hubbard_conducting_Dianetics_seminar_in_Los_Angeles_in_1950.jpg** *Source:* https://upload.wikimedia.org/wikipedia/commons/6/65/L._Ron_Hubbard_conducting_Dianetics_seminar_in_Los_Angeles_in_1950.jpg *License:* Public domain *Contributors:*
- Los Angeles Times photographic archive, Digital collections — UCLA Library. *Original artist:* Uncredited photographer for Los Angeles Daily News
- **File:L._Ron_Hubbard_in_1950.jpg** *Source:* https://upload.wikimedia.org/wikipedia/commons/f/f1/L._Ron_Hubbard_in_1950.jpg *License:* Public domain *Contributors:*
http://unitproj.library.ucla.edu/dlib/lat/display.cfm?ms=uclalat_1387_b155_52178-1&searchType=subject&subjectID=222501
Original artist: Uncredited photographer for Los Angeles Daily News
- **File:L_Ron_and_Sara_Hubbard_June_1946.jpg** *Source:* https://upload.wikimedia.org/wikipedia/commons/7/78/L_Ron_and_Sara_Hubbard_June_1946.jpg *License:* Public domain *Contributors:* https://news.google.com/newspapers?nid=71XFh8zZwT8C&dat=19460630&printsec=frontpage&hl=en *Original artist:* Miami Daily News
- **File:Latimers.jpg** *Source:* https://upload.wikimedia.org/wikipedia/commons/c/c1/Latimers.jpg *License:* Public domain *Contributors:* photo taken by Kim Dent-Brown, originally uploaded on english Wikipedia: http://en.wikipedia.org/wiki/Image:Latimers.jpg *Original artist:* Kim Dent-Brown

- **File:Luquillo,_Puerto_Rico.JPG** *Source:* https://upload.wikimedia.org/wikipedia/commons/0/0b/Luquillo%2C_Puerto_Rico.JPG *License:* CC BY-SA 3.0 *Contributors:* Self-made during trip to w:en:Culebra, Puerto Rico *Original artist:* Mtmelendez

- **File:MastersOfSleep.jpg** *Source:* https://upload.wikimedia.org/wikipedia/commons/f/fa/MastersOfSleep.jpg *License:* Public domain *Contributors:* http://www.collectorshowcase.fr/fantastic_adv__page_9.htm (specific image link http://www.collectorshowcase.fr/images2/fantadv_5010.jpg) *Original artist:* Fantistic Adventures / Robert Gibson Jones

- **File:Navaho_launch.jpg** *Source:* https://upload.wikimedia.org/wikipedia/commons/5/56/Navaho_launch.jpg *License:* Public domain *Contributors:* http://nix.nasa.gov/info?id=MSFC-9142273 *Original artist:* NASA

- **File:Nuvola_apps_aktion.png** *Source:* https://upload.wikimedia.org/wikipedia/commons/2/26/Nuvola_apps_aktion.png *License:* LGPL *Contributors:* http://icon-king.com *Original artist:* David Vignoni / ICON KING

- **File:Nuvola_apps_edu_science.svg** *Source:* https://upload.wikimedia.org/wikipedia/commons/5/59/Nuvola_apps_edu_science.svg *License:* LGPL *Contributors:* http://ftp.gnome.org/pub/GNOME/sources/gnome-themes-extras/0.9/gnome-themes-extras-0.9.0.tar.gz *Original artist:* David Vignoni / ICON KING

- **File:Nuvola_apps_kalzium.svg** *Source:* https://upload.wikimedia.org/wikipedia/commons/8/8b/Nuvola_apps_kalzium.svg *License:* LGPL *Contributors:* Own work *Original artist:* David Vignoni, SVG version by Bobarino

- **File:Nuvola_apps_kcmsystem.svg** *Source:* https://upload.wikimedia.org/wikipedia/commons/7/7a/Nuvola_apps_kcmsystem.svg *License:* LGPL *Contributors:* Own work based on Image:Nuvola apps kcmsystem.png by Alphax originally from [1] *Original artist:* MesserWoland

- **File:OTOlogo.png** *Source:* https://upload.wikimedia.org/wikipedia/en/d/d3/OTOlogo.png *License:* Fair use *Contributors:*
The logo may be obtained from Ordo Templi Orientis.
Original artist: ?

- **File:Office-book.svg** *Source:* https://upload.wikimedia.org/wikipedia/commons/a/a8/Office-book.svg *License:* Public domain *Contributors:* This and myself. *Original artist:* Chris Down/Tango project

- **File:P1-RocketBoys.jpg** *Source:* https://upload.wikimedia.org/wikipedia/commons/5/5f/P1-RocketBoys.jpg *License:* Public domain *Contributors:* http://solarsystem.nasa.gov/multimedia/display.cfm?IM_ID=6383 *Original artist:* NASA/JPL

- **File:P_vip.svg** *Source:* https://upload.wikimedia.org/wikipedia/en/6/69/P_vip.svg *License:* PD *Contributors:* ? *Original artist:* ?

- **File:Parsons_crater_5053_med.jpg** *Source:* https://upload.wikimedia.org/wikipedia/en/b/b6/Parsons_crater_5053_med.jpg *License:* CC0 *Contributors:*
Reprocessed Lunar Orbiter 5 image rotated and cropped in GIMP.
The original image is in the public domain because it is a work of the U.S. Government (NASA).
Immediate source: Lunar and Planetary Institute, Lunar Orbiter Photo Gallery
Lunar Orbiter 5, image 053, med [1] *Original artist:* James Stuby based on NASA image

- **File:Pentacle_2.svg** *Source:* https://upload.wikimedia.org/wikipedia/commons/9/97/Pentacle_2.svg *License:* Public domain *Contributors:* No machine-readable source provided. Own work assumed (based on copyright claims). *Original artist:* No machine-readable author provided. Nyo~commonswiki assumed (based on copyright claims).

- **File:Phoenix-L._Ron_Hubbart_House-1945.JPG** *Source:* https://upload.wikimedia.org/wikipedia/en/7/79/Phoenix-L._Ron_Hubbart_House-1945.JPG *License:* CC-BY-SA-3.0 *Contributors:*
I (Tony the Marine (talk)) created this work entirely by myself. *Original artist:*
Tony the Marine (talk)

- **File:Phoenix-L._Ron_Hubbart_House-Buick_Super_8.JPG** *Source:* https://upload.wikimedia.org/wikipedia/en/b/b9/Phoenix-L._Ron_Hubbart_House-Buick_Super_8.JPG *License:* CC-BY-SA-3.0 *Contributors:*
I (Tony the Marine (talk)) created this work entirely by myself. *Original artist:*
Tony the Marine (talk)

- **File:Portal-puzzle.svg** *Source:* https://upload.wikimedia.org/wikipedia/en/f/fd/Portal-puzzle.svg *License:* Public domain *Contributors:* ? *Original artist:* ?

- **File:Professor'{}s_Gate_-_GWU.JPG** *Source:* https://upload.wikimedia.org/wikipedia/commons/a/a0/Professor%27s_Gate_-_GWU.JPG *License:* CC BY-SA 3.0 *Contributors:* Own work *Original artist:* AgnosticPreachersKid

- **File:QAHS_1909.jpg** *Source:* https://upload.wikimedia.org/wikipedia/en/5/51/QAHS_1909.jpg *License:* PD-US *Contributors:* ? *Original artist:* ?

- **File:Question_book-new.svg** *Source:* https://upload.wikimedia.org/wikipedia/en/9/99/Question_book-new.svg *License:* Cc-by-sa-3.0 *Contributors:*
Created from scratch in Adobe Illustrator. Based on Image:Question book.png created by User:Equazcion *Original artist:*
Tkgd2007

- **File:Rocket-motor-test-browse.jpg** *Source:* https://upload.wikimedia.org/wikipedia/commons/7/77/Rocket-motor-test-browse.jpg *License:* Public domain *Contributors:* http://www.jpl.nasa.gov/news/features.cfm?feature=1217 *Original artist:* NASA/JPL

- **File:RocketSunIcon.svg** *Source:* https://upload.wikimedia.org/wikipedia/commons/d/d6/RocketSunIcon.svg *License:* Copyrighted free use *Contributors:* Self made, based on File:Spaceship and the Sun.jpg *Original artist:* Me

- **File:Sara_Hubbard_custody_hearing_24_Apr_1951.jpg** *Source:* https://upload.wikimedia.org/wikipedia/commons/1/1e/Sara_Hubbard_custody_hearing_24_Apr_1951.jpg *License:* Public domain *Contributors:* http://digitallibrary.usc.edu/cdm/compoundobject/collection/p15799coll44/id/2624/rec/1 *Original artist:* Los Angeles Examiner

- **File:Sara_Hubbard_denunciation_p1.gif** *Source:* https://upload.wikimedia.org/wikipedia/commons/9/9d/Sara_Hubbard_denunciation_p1.gif *License:* Public domain *Contributors:* Federal Bureau of Investigation *Original artist:* L. Ron Hubbard
- **File:Sara_Northrup_Hubbard_declaration.png** *Source:* https://upload.wikimedia.org/wikipedia/commons/c/c1/Sara_Northrup_Hubbard_declaration.png *License:* Public domain *Contributors:* Federal Bureau of Investigation *Original artist:* Sara Northrup Hubbard
- **File:Scientology_e_meter_blue.jpg** *Source:* https://upload.wikimedia.org/wikipedia/commons/c/c3/Scientology_e_meter_blue.jpg *License:* CC-BY-SA-3.0 *Contributors:* ? *Original artist:* ?
- **File:Space_Shuttle_Columbia_launching.jpg** *Source:* https://upload.wikimedia.org/wikipedia/commons/4/41/Space_Shuttle_Columbia_launching.jpg *License:* Public domain *Contributors:* Great Images in NASA (image link) *Original artist:* NASA
- **File:Speaker_Icon.svg** *Source:* https://upload.wikimedia.org/wikipedia/commons/2/21/Speaker_Icon.svg *License:* Public domain *Contributors:* No machine-readable source provided. Own work assumed (based on copyright claims). *Original artist:* No machine-readable author provided. Mobius assumed (based on copyright claims).
- **File:Symbol_book_class2.svg** *Source:* https://upload.wikimedia.org/wikipedia/commons/8/89/Symbol_book_class2.svg *License:* CC BY-SA 2.5 *Contributors:* Mad by Lokal_Profil by combining: *Original artist:* Lokal_Profil
- **File:Templeofrosycross.png** *Source:* https://upload.wikimedia.org/wikipedia/commons/a/a5/Templeofrosycross.png *License:* Public domain *Contributors:* T. Schweighart, Speculum sophicum Rhodostauroticum (1604) *Original artist:* T. Schweighart
- **File:Text_document_with_red_question_mark.svg** *Source:* https://upload.wikimedia.org/wikipedia/commons/a/a4/Text_document_with_red_question_mark.svg *License:* Public domain *Contributors:* Created by bdesham with Inkscape; based upon Text-x-generic.svg from the Tango project. *Original artist:* Benjamin D. Esham (bdesham)
- **File:The_Witches'{}_Cottage.JPG** *Source:* https://upload.wikimedia.org/wikipedia/en/3/3f/The_Witches%27_Cottage.JPG *License:* Fair use *Contributors:*

  The Rebirth of Witchcraft by Doreen Valiente

  Original artist: ?
- **File:Thelema_Abbey_2.jpg** *Source:* https://upload.wikimedia.org/wikipedia/commons/d/de/Thelema_Abbey_2.jpg *License:* CC BY-SA 2.0 *Contributors:* http://www.inventati.org/amprodias/thelema/photo.htm *Original artist:* Frater Kybernetes
- **File:Theodor_Reuss.png** *Source:* https://upload.wikimedia.org/wikipedia/commons/4/4d/Theodor_Reuss.png *License:* Public domain *Contributors:* ? *Original artist:* ?
- **File:Uss_pc-815_1.jpg** *Source:* https://upload.wikimedia.org/wikipedia/commons/8/8e/Uss_pc-815_1.jpg *License:* Public domain *Contributors:* United States National Archives *Original artist:* United States Navy.
- **File:Von_Karman_and_JATO_Team_-_GPN-2000-001652.jpg** *Source:* https://upload.wikimedia.org/wikipedia/commons/4/45/Von_Karman_and_JATO_Team_-_GPN-2000-001652.jpg *License:* Public domain *Contributors:* Great Images in NASA: Home - info - pic *Original artist:* NACA / JPL
- **File:W.T._Smith.jpg** *Source:* https://upload.wikimedia.org/wikipedia/en/1/15/W.T._Smith.jpg *License:* Fair use *Contributors:*

  Published in Martin P. Starr, *The Unknown God* (Teitan Press, 2003). The book does not specify the source of the image.

  Original artist: ?
- **File:Wernher_von_Braun_1960.jpg** *Source:* https://upload.wikimedia.org/wikipedia/commons/5/56/Wernher_von_Braun_1960.jpg *License:* Public domain *Contributors:* http://archive.org/details/MSFC-9131095 higher resolution *Original artist:* NASA/Marshall Space Flight Center
- **File:Wikidata-logo.svg** *Source:* https://upload.wikimedia.org/wikipedia/commons/f/ff/Wikidata-logo.svg *License:* Public domain *Contributors:* Own work *Original artist:* User:Planemad
- **File:Wikiquote-logo.svg** *Source:* https://upload.wikimedia.org/wikipedia/commons/f/fa/Wikiquote-logo.svg *License:* Public domain *Contributors:* ? *Original artist:* ?
- **File:Wikisource-logo.svg** *Source:* https://upload.wikimedia.org/wikipedia/commons/4/4c/Wikisource-logo.svg *License:* CC BY-SA 3.0 *Contributors:* Rei-artur *Original artist:* Nicholas Moreau
- **File:Witches_Hut_2006_side_view.JPG** *Source:* https://upload.wikimedia.org/wikipedia/commons/0/07/Witches_Hut_2006_side_view.JPG *License:* CC BY-SA 3.0 *Contributors:* Own work *Original artist:* Sunblade1500

29.10.3 Content license

- Creative Commons Attribution-Share Alike 3.0

29991388R00159

Made in the USA
Middletown, DE
09 March 2016